BOOKS BY MARCUS CUNLIFFE

The Literature of the United States

George Washington: Man and Monument

The Nation Takes Shape, 1789–1837

The Presidency

Soldiers and Civilians:
The Martial Spirit in America, 1775–1865

SOLDIERS AND CIVILIANS

The Martial Spirit in America

1775–1865

MARCUS CUNLIFFE

SOLDIERS
&
CIVILIANS

The Martial Spirit in America

1775 – 1865

LITTLE, BROWN AND COMPANY

BOSTON · TORONTO

Library of Congress Catalog Card No. 68–22898

First Edition

All of the illustrations in this book are reproduced by courtesy of the Anne S. K. Brown Military Collection, Brown University Library, with the exception of the following:

Illustrations on pages 53 and 396, courtesy of the New York State Historical Association.

Illustrations on pages 71 and 91 are contemporary drawings, courtesy of the Library of Congress.

Illustration on page 251, originally published in Harper's Weekly, *September, 24, 1859.*

Illustrations on page 394, courtesy of the U. S. Military Academy, West Point.

Published simultaneously in Canada
by Little, Brown & Company (Canada) Limited

Printed in the United States of America

For Toni, Shay and Jason

CONTENTS

1

PROLOGUE: FIRST BULL RUN AND ITS MEANINGS

Two armies are two bodies which meet and endeavor to frighten each other.
— Napoleon

It looked a wrong place to be a battlefield.
— Stephen Crane

The serious bloodshed of the Civil War began in northeastern Virginia, between Centreville and Manassas, on a broiling Sunday. The date was July 21, 1861. Irvin McDowell's Union army of some thirty thousand men collided with an equivalent Confederate force led by P. G. T. Beauregard and Joseph E. Johnston. By nightfall — though not even the commanders were able to make any useful estimate — about four hundred men were dead and over a thousand wounded, on each side; and another thousand or so Union troops were prisoners. The battlefield was horribly strewn with dead and dying men and horses, and with smashed or discarded equipment — rifles, knapsacks, water bottles, blankets, wheelless wagons and broken limbers.

The name of the muddy little river that meandered through the midst of this turmoil passed into history: Bull Run. Hundreds of men who had been equally unknown to the world at large began their movement into history: S. P. Heintzelman, William T. Sherman, Ambrose Burnside, Oliver Otis Howard, James Longstreet, Jubal Early, Edmund Kirby Smith, "Jeb" Stuart, Thomas J. Jackson (who acquired his nickname "Stonewall" on this day). Others who were present remained obscure until some later circumstance brought them celebrity. One on the Northern side was the future novelist and carpetbagger Albion Tourgee, a university student who had enlisted in a New York regiment and was badly wounded in the spine. A Confederate colonel, William C. Falkner, in command of the 2nd Mississippi, achieved no particular glory but would serve as an equivocal example of Civil War heroism and absurdity for his great-grandson, the novelist William Faulkner.[1]

First Bull Run (or Manassas — it goes by either name) was in these respects a beginning, a novel departure for the men involved in it and in the eyes of military historians. According to the textbooks, this opening battle introduced new aspects of warfare. It marked, we are told, the beginning of "modern" war, in which armies were made up not of professional soldiers but of civilians. It was the beginning of the first war in which newspaper correspondents played a prominent part. There were five or six correspondents with Beauregard's army and a couple of dozen with McDowell. One of these, W. H. Russell of *The Times* of London, was known thereafter in America as "Bull Run" Russell because of his unflattering and somewhat supercilious account of the Union retreat. Bull Run was the first American battle in which messages were passed by "wigwagging" or signaling. E. P. Alexander, on the Confederate side, used this means to warn Nathan Evans's brigade that their flank was being turned by the Union's curving advance across Sudley Ford. Though McDowell was less enterprising, his resources included a rather wayward observation balloon, which Russell saw swaying above the trees like a church tower in an earthquake.[2]

The most significant innovation of all, for military commentators, was the strategic employment of the Manassas Railroad. Joseph E. Johnston was able to bring several thousand men from the Shenandoah Valley. The trains carried them conveniently near the battle, reasonably fresh and at the vital moment.

For those who fought, Bull Run was of course a grimly novel experience. Most of the men in command of regiments or brigades had seen action in the Mexican War, though Sherman had not. A few were soldiers of fortune, like Chatham Roberdeau Wheat, a Southerner who had filibustered in Central America and been with Garibaldi in Italy, or like the 39th New York's Colonel George Utassy. But for the vast majority it was an initiation. Some had had years of peacetime training, whether rigorously at West Point or a little farcically in militia units. The reality exceeded their wildest imagining.

In the dreams of the two armies, war was a medley of gallant attitudes and sentiments culled from what they had read in magazines. It was largely European in tone, though with a special American flavor. The dream which principally afflicted the senior officers was of Napoleon and his grand army. At this moment it was particularly cherished by Pierre Gustave Toutant Beauregard, with his French ancestry. In his imagination, and in that of subsequent commanders on both sides, Napoleon Bonaparte became telescoped with the current example of Napoleon III,

4

whose nation led the Old World in military prowess. The American generals, or at least those of flamboyant temperament, composed grandiose messages; they tucked their hands into their tunics like Bonaparte, and grew little "imperial" beards in imitation of Napoleon III.

Some units, North and South, sought to borrow the French military magic by dressing and drilling in the baggy, semi-Oriental costumes of French Zouaves. It was the costume of the 7th Louisiana in Jubal Early's brigade; Wheat's battalion of Louisiana Tigers had a company in this garb; and there was a whole battalion of New York Zouaves, recruited from the city's firemen.

Americans had read too of the exploits of other European armies. The 2nd Ohio were among the soldiers at Bull Run who wore "havelocks" — caps with a cloth to protect the neck, named after the British general who had introduced the style in the Indian Mutiny a few years before. The polyglot militia of the Northern cities drew upon a variety of military associations. The 39th New York, known as the Garibaldi Guard, wore the feathered headgear of Italian *bersaglieri* (though their colonel was a Hungarian and their surgeon a German). The 69th New York

THE SEVENTY-NINTH REGIMENT (HIGHLANDERS) NEW YORK STATE MILITIA.

COL. MICHAEL CORCORAN, AT THE BATTLE OF BULL RUN, VA. JULY 21ST 1861.
The desperate and bloody charge of the 'Gallant Sixty Ninth', on the Rebel Batteries.

attested its Irish sympathies with shamrock-blazoned banners. Indeed, the Irish-born colonel of the 69th, Michael Corcoran, had recently been the center of a furious row, when he had refused to parade his militia regiment in honor of the visiting Prince of Wales. He was threatened with a court-martial and the process was still dragging on when the Civil War broke out. The New York 79th was Scottish. As a prewar militia regiment it had secured the same number as the line regiment in the British regular army known as the 79th Cameron Highlanders. In peacetime its officers had kilts, and the men usually wore tartan trews. These were put aside for the approaching battle, though one officer persisted in wearing his kilt in the preliminary advance until he could no longer endure the ridicule of non-Scottish soldiers. The New York 79th had even managed to provide itself with a colonel named Cameron (who happened to be the brother of Lincoln's Secretary of War, Simon Cameron).

There were native touches to the variegated picture. The "cadet gray" of West Point was so admired that gray seemed an admirably workmanlike and yet gentlemanly hue to Jefferson Davis — himself a West Pointer — and to his colleagues who selected it for the official uniform of the Confederate States Army. Though by no means all Confederate units had been supplied with gray uniforms by July 1861, the same might be said of Union blue. The 2nd Wisconsin and the 8th New York were among the units in McDowell's army dressed in cadet gray. Several of the senior Confederate officers were still wearing the regular blue uniforms of the U. S. Army. The majority of men were more bizarrely unorthodox. Wheat's Louisiana Tigers looked outlandish enough in their scarlet skullcaps: the effect was heightened by the slogans with which the caps were decorated — TIGER BY NATURE, TIGER ON THE LEAP, TIGER IN SEARCH OF A BLACK REPUBLICAN were among the belligerently cheerful mottoes. John B. Gordon, a Georgia lawyer, was elected captain of a volunteer company calling itself the Raccoon Roughs. The company was finally incorporated in the 6th Alabama. Gordon's men refused to wear the gray caps of the other companies, but insisted on clinging to coonskin headgear. All the field officers, obeying a whim of their colonel, wore "double-breasted frock coats made of green broadcloth, with the brass buttons of the United States army."[3]

Whatever their dress — and some men were still in ordinary civilian clothing — the two armies were, inevitably, gesturing at war. Beauregard, announcing to his troops that the Northern "invaders" had taken "Beauty and Booty" as their cry, was harking back to the British invasion of his native Louisiana at the end of 1814, when the same accusation was leveled in the same words. (The accusation, more plainly put, was that McDowell's men, like the British, were bent on rape and theft.) Many of the soldiers at Bull Run had not expected to fight at all but merely to make a demonstration of patriotic ardor. The natural garb of patriotism was martial: it was a matter of processions, music, speeches, cheering, presentations of inscribed swords, dedications of silk banners embroidered by committees of the "fair sex," romantic farewells and swift reunions. That was why, among the Union's ninety-day regiments, the 4th Pennsylvania and the 8th

New York Artillery felt no undue shame when they marched away from Bull Run on the very morning of the battle. They had *performed* their duty, as they interpreted the verb: they had made a show and now their time was up. Even the ninety-day regiments such as the New York 69th and 79th which stayed and fought were only held to service for a few more days. Then they too were being cheered up Broadway, instant heroes and instant veterans.

This is not to say that men were reluctant to enlist for longer periods but that they did not yet know what was expected of them. They postured because they knew of no other way of behaving. Even in retreat their gestures seemed extravagant. A journalist noted that fleeing Union troops flung their rifles from them "as if they were venomous serpents." In a sense, the novelty of the occasion was immemorial. The same conflicting and hectic emotions would surge up among the youth of Europe in the summer of 1914. *Nach Paris!* or *À Berlin!* were boasts as wildly and pathetically misguided as the *Forward to Richmond!* of 1861. The American youths, on both sides, were caught up by emotions at once superficial and profound. They were escaping from ordinariness, seeking other selves, impelled by vanity and by nobility. So, enlisting, they cheered and sang and even perhaps wept a little. Once in uniform, they added to the effect of ferocity by sticking pistols and bowie knives into their belts and by cultivating moustaches. They crowded into photographers' parlors in their panoply, scowling at the camera as they tensed themselves in front of the incongruously genteel backcloth and the potted plants. And strangely, in this interlude of warlike preparation while they mustered and drilled, they were enveloped in tenderness. Love's promise was omnipresent. They felt it in the enthusiasm of the crowds that lined the streets at their passing, in the eyes of girls who had once seemed unapproachably demure, in the cakes and Bibles and keepsakes that came their way as gifts.

On the eve of Bull Run, the emotion among the Union and Confederate camps was more sweetly intense than ever before, though mixed now with sharper, rawer reactions. Each side regarded the other with contempt, yet with an almost superstitious awe. The Yankees would be chased away; but then, there were a terrible lot of them, very well armed and with some good men in command . . . The Rebs were a bunch of slaveholders and poor whites; but then, they seemed confoundedly sure of themselves, and their cavalry and their masked batteries were things to beware of . . . Still, each army felt irresistibly big to the men within it. While the flow of civilian visitors was a nuisance to poor harried McDowell (Beauregard had wisely declared the battle zone closed to civilians, except for those unlucky enough to live in it), the Union soldiers were flattered and intrigued to see congressmen, journalists and well-wishers moving among the tents. There were even some ladies, charming in bonnet and parasol. Their presence was reassuring: the battle would be a picnic, a play with a happy end.

As darkness fell the scene was a confirmation of romantic literature. Campfires made snug caves of light. The air was delicious with the odors of coffee and frying bacon. The moon came up mellowly full. Henry Raymond of the *New York Times,* attached to McDowell's headquarters, heard in the distance a regimental band playing a serenade from Donizetti's *Don Pasquale.* Nearer him in the warm midsummer night a chorus sang "The Star-Spangled Banner."

Profaner notes were struck. A party of Philadelphians, permitted to tour the camp, were shocked by the shouts, the card-playing and whiskey-drinking of raucous soldiers who seemed under no discipline. These no doubt saw themselves as desperadoes rather than as crusaders or Byronic heroes. They were raising themselves to the necessary pitch — whatever that might be. After all, there was no point in trying to go to sleep: the leading brigades of McDowell's advance would move out long before dawn.

Here and there, again immemorially, men were struck with secret dread. Most of those who foresaw their own death were probably wrong, at any rate among the regiments that were to play little part in the battle. Some premonitions, however, proved true. John Slocum, colonel of the 2nd Rhode Island, told his brigadier Ambrose Burnside that he knew he would be mortally

9

wounded. Hit twice, Slocum did in fact die a day or two later. A Confederate brigadier, Francis S. Bartow, also told a friend before the battle that he knew he would die; the prophecy was borne out. As usual, stories of miraculous preservation circulated afterward. Southern newspapers, when Bull Run was over, carried an item about Lieutenant Willie P. Mangum of the 6th North Carolina, son and namesake of Senator Mangum, who owed his life "to a copy of the Bible presented him by his sister. . . . It was struck by a ball . . . , but the book changed the direction of the bullet, and it glanced off." Alas, the miracle was incomplete: young Mangum proved to be fatally wounded in spite of the first reports.[4]

No wonder that Bull Run was a confused battle. As the unfortunate McDowell explained after Bull Run — buttonholing any who would listen to him in his scapegoat shame — his entire army was green: regulars, volunteers and militia alike. None of them had had the opportunity to maneuver large numbers of troops. Neither army was more than a scratch collection of units, hastily and arbitrarily allotted to brigades and divisions. Neither had anything like a proper staff organization. McDowell's plan of

BATTLE OF BULL RUN, V⁴ July 21ˢᵗ 1861.
Gallant charge of the Zouaves and defeat of the rebel Black Horse Cavalry.

attack was good, but he was guessing at the lie of the land. There were no satisfactory maps, his reconnaissance was inadequate. Several commanders showed skill and initiative. But the battle was soon out of hand, dictating its own crazy development, until the Confederate lines were facing west instead of north. Battalions were thrown piecemeal into what the correspondent for the *Charleston Mercury* called the "boiling crater of dust and smoke" around the Henry House. At battalion level, events were without shape. Everyone and no one gave orders. The generals' aides, who galloped to and fro with messages, were a miscellany. They included eager young officers just out of West Point, like Emory Upton and Alfred Mordecai; sons and nephews of commanding officers; civilians anxious to lend a hand, like Governor Sprague, who was accompanying his Rhode Island regiments in Burnside's brigade. Sherman took as one of his aides an incompetent Wisconsin regimental commander, as a way of removing him from a position where he could have done harm.

In the 27th New York Volunteers, the captain of one company was too winded in the advance to keep up — not surprisingly, since he was sixty years of age. The next in command had been elected lieutenant, said a sarcastic companion, because he had led "a company of Wide Awakes, armed with torches, in the Presidential campaign of 1860, so of course he knew all about war." This officer too dropped out. Elsewhere on the regimental front another lieutenant "with the whites of his eyes showing like saucers manfully stood his post and fired his revolver in the air." The lieutenant colonel, a brave and also pious man, was handicapped by a severe stutter. Riding along the line he shouted, "Ne-ne-never mind a f-f-few shells, boys, G-G-G-God Almighty is m-m-merciful," and "G-g-g-give it to 'em, b-b-boys, God l-l-loves a cheerful g-g-giver."

Since neither army had a single, distinct dress, soldiers augmented the confusion by firing on their own side. The most serious mischance occurred at the height of the battle when McDowell's artillery chief, Colonel William F. Barry, mistook the 33rd Virginia for a Union column and allowed them to approach within easy rifle shot of Griffin's battery, which had been dominating the field. The Virginians poured in a shattering volley and the whole balance of the battle shifted. But the confusion affected both sides. At one moment the Louisiana Tigers were fired on by South Carolina troops — and fired back. Many of Beauregard's men were convinced that the cunning enemy had carried Confederate flags into battle as a ruse. The *Richmond Dispatch* spoke of "great confusion and slaughter among our own men," caused by "the similarity of uniform and the mean advantages . . . taken by our unscrupulous foes." The truth was simpler and more chaotic.

Bull Run was a zone between dream and nightmare, a black comedy of errors. Parched by the heat, the acrid smoke and the soaring clouds of dust, men broke formation to search for water. Others, including Kirby Smith's brigade in the midst of a charge, were seduced from duty by blackberry bushes. Sherman with an amazed pity watched a Negro, frantic with fear, caught in no-man's-land between fusillades. At the headquarters of the Confederate brigadier R. S. Ewell, a young girl suddenly rode up to tell him what she had seen of the other side. Ewell, never known for placidity, was preoccupied with the scene before him. Finally he burst out, in an angry parody of the little sentences to be found in school primers: "Look there, look there, miss! Don't you see those men with blue clothes on, in the edge of the woods? Look at those men loading those big guns. They are going to fire, and fire quick, and fire right here. You'll get killed. You'll be a *dead damsel* in less than a minute. *Get away from here! Get away!*"

The girl, apparently immune to his excitement, continued calmly to proffer her unwanted information.[5]

One of the unreal aspects of the battle was that it was fought on a Sunday. This perturbed the devout West Pointer Oliver Otis Howard, in command of a brigade of New Englanders. He recollected men saying at the outset, "It is Sunday! The attacking party on the Sabbath is sure of defeat!" He commented: "Whether this be the superstition or the religion of a people, wise men will respect it." Perhaps in retrospect, seeking to account for the panic which abruptly gripped the Union army, Howard exaggerated. Some of the soldiers marching to the battle, he also

12

remembered, sang "John Brown's Body"; and John Brown, no less devout, had believed in doing the Lord's work — namely, killing slaveholders — on the Lord's day. One wonders whether Stonewall Jackson, another devout soldier, squared his conscience at Bull Run by reflecting that the other side were the attackers. Perhaps; for some months later he answered his wife, who had questioned his fighting at Kernstown: "You appear much concerned at my attacking *on Sunday*. I was greatly concerned, too; but I felt it my duty. . . . [It was] very distasteful to my feelings, and I hope and pray to our Heavenly Father that I may never be circumstanced as on that day."

There was certainly a Sunday mood behind the lines. McDowell's much-publicized advance drew spectators from as far afield as Concord, Massachusetts; and Centreville was an easy weekend outing on the turnpike from Washington. Several senators and representatives had come along. One of them, Alfred Ely of New York, was actually taken prisoner in the rout; and the civilian carriages undoubtedly added to the shameful confusion of the battle's closing stages. A poem in the *Boston Herald*, which went on for several more stanzas, typified the Union's belated indignation at discovering the incongruity of slaughter and social excursions:

Have you heard of the story, so lacking in glory,
    About the civilians who went to the fight?
With everything handy, from sandwich to brandy,
    To fill their broad stomachs, and make them all tight.

There were bulls from our State Street, and cattle from Wall
        Street,
    And members of Congress to see the great fun;
Newspaper reporters (some regular snorters),
    On a beautiful Sunday went to Bull Run.

Provided with passes as far as Manassas,
    The portly civilians rode jolly along;
Till the sound of the battle, the roar and the rattle
    Of cannon and musket drowned laughter and song.[6]

13

On top of these sources of bewilderment came the fact that this was the beginning of a *civil* war. The officers drawn from the enclave of the old regular army all knew or knew of one another. Close acquaintance did not necessarily make them friends. It did mean that in this first battle they might happen to have more enemies on their own side than in the ranks of the supposed enemy.* Of the Union artillery officers Charles Griffin had long disliked Barry, and he blamed Barry more than the 33rd Virginia for destroying his battery. Good friends, and families, were split apart. Jeb Stuart's father-in-law, Colonel Philip St. George Cooke of Virginia, had remained with the Union, and might for all Stuart knew be facing him across Bull Run. Young Alfred Mordecai, the son of a distinguished serving officer, went with the Union; his father, a North Carolinian, resigned from the army rather than take arms against the South. Sherman, until recently the head of a military school in Louisiana, had numbered among his pupils two sons and a nephew of Beauregard. The Confederate brigadier Nathan Evans, a West Point graduate of the class of 1848, came upon a dying Union captain among the prisoners and recognized him as Otis Hammond Tillinghast, an old companion who had graduated from the Military Academy a year ahead of him. Of the cadets of the class of 1861, Virginia-born Thomas Lafayette Rosser was serving as a lieutenant in the Confederate artillery. In the Federal army was his friend and classmate George Armstrong Custer.

The allegiances of some officers were distressingly ambiguous. Evans's Academy classmate Walter H. Stevens was a New Yorker who through working on forts and harbors along the Gulf Coast had married into a Louisiana family. For this reason he was with Beauregard at Bull Run instead of with McDowell. One of McDowell's cavalry officers in the battle, Frank Crawford Armstrong, resigned his commission less than a month later to become a Confederate cavalryman.

At this stage the war was far from being a war about slavery. The Southerners in general were more clear than their opponents

---

* Bull Run initiated new enmities. Years and years after, Beauregard was still disputing his share of the credit with Joseph E. Johnston, and McDowell his share of the blame with his division commander Daniel Tyler.

as to what the conflict was about. They were fighting for states rights. Indeed, the cause was enshrined in the very name of one of the Confederate officers, States Rights Gist of South Carolina, who took over the command of Bee's brigade when his chief was fatally wounded. It was embodied too in the figure of Edmund Ruffin, the white-haired old South Carolina extremist who had fired the first round against Fort Sumter and who now contrived to appear at Bull Run as a volunteer with the Palmetto Guard. He even repeated his Sumter performance by persuading Kemper's battery to let him send a round after the fleeing Federals.

But radicalism had at least token representation in the Union ranks. O. O. Howard had been an abolitionist since his cadet days. Edward A. Wild, equally zealous, was a Massachusetts doctor who threw up his medical practice to lead an infantry company at Bull Run. William Birney, a captain in the 1st New Jersey, was the son of the abolitionist James G. Birney. Among

15

the congressmen roaming the battlefield — he was chased away by Sherman when he introduced himself and offered the loan of field glasses — was Owen Lovejoy of Illinois. Lovejoy, a fanatical Republican, was the brother of Elijah Lovejoy, the abolitionist martyr murdered by a mob back in 1837. For Owen Lovejoy, Bull Run was a gigantic vengeance; he had sworn on his brother's corpse to follow the antislavery cause wherever it might lead.[7]

First Bull Run then may be thought of as a beginning, a strange new contest in which the combatants were painfully groping for rules to follow. In later battles of the Civil War some of the greenness would disappear; some rules would be discerned.

Yet in many respects it was a culmination rather than a new departure. Bull Run epitomized the variegated confusions of a century and more of American warfare. Even the novelties which have intrigued military historians need qualification. There were photographers and correspondents at the Crimean War of 1854–1856: that was where "Bull Run" Russell made his reputation. Alexander's signaling did not make a great amount of difference, then or later. He was still a fallible human being, who alarmed his superiors by reporting the approach of Union reinforcements, when the distant dust cloud he saw was actually raised by columns arriving from Johnston's army. And the mobility afforded by the railroads of Virginia was less than astonishing. Though the distance on the Manassas Railroad from Piedmont — where Johnston's men entrained — to Manassas Junction was only thirty-four miles, some of the Valley Confederates were in the cars for forty-eight hours. The president of the railroad, promising to carry all of Johnston's men to Manassas before dawn on July 20, had delivered hardly a third by that time. Four regiments never arrived until July 22, when the battle was over. Johnston's cavalry and artillery, which marched by road, were present for the battle in good time. Reinforcements coming by train from Richmond were also slow to arrive. Wade Hampton's Legion, after a thirty-hour train journey, joined Beauregard after the battle had started. If McDowell had attacked a day earlier, which he could have done, historians might have drawn quite opposite conclusions as to the utility of travel by rail.[8]

These are incidentals. The main point is that the Civil War displayed the entire range of American military attitudes, which formed its complex heritage. The same chaos, the same extravagant optimism, the same improvising energy, the same erratic gallantry had been apparent ever since colonial days. It is tempting to argue that nothing was changed in essentials. Every major war fought by the Americans, for example, had been in some degree a civil war. This was certainly true of the Revolutionary War. Eminent soldiers then changed sides (notably Benedict Arnold, a descendant of whom fought as a Union artillery officer at Manassas), or were suspected of hesitating in their allegiance (notably Charles Lee). Brothers, such as the Starks of Vermont, were in opposite camps. It was true of the War of 1812, when large areas of the country denounced their government and threatened secession. President Madison's war message of June 1812 was debated in Congress for more than two weeks. The majority in favor of declaring war was only 19 to 13 in the Senate, and only 79 to 49 in the House of Representatives. Though there was less discussion over the Mexican War, the nation was divided, both sectionally and politically, in its estimates of President Polk's policy. "It is our own President who began this war," declared one Whig congressman. Another associated himself with the Mexicans in welcoming the Americans "with empty hands to bloody graves."

If the Civil War was overwhelmingly civilian in style, so were America's previous wars. In none had the regular army been a stable, numerically significant force. It was in keeping with American experience that at Bull Run the Union's regular contingent consisted merely of a battalion of infantry, a battalion of marines, some artillery batteries and a few squadrons of cavalry. The bulk of the two armies was made up, as in earlier conflicts, of regiments either created from nothing or fashioned out of the militia system. In either case the basic unit was the company of not more than a hundred men. In 1776, in 1812, in 1846 and again in 1861, the generals took the field at the head not of armies but of agglomerations, each particle striving to be a law unto itself.

There was the same exuberant, almost recklessly sacrificial

17

response that had been displayed in the past. The adventurous part of the country flocked to the colors. The rich and the ambitious, sometimes in whole families, offered themselves up, as individuals or at the head of units they had raised. Wade Hampton, reputedly the largest landowner in the South, recruited and equipped a mixed legion of cavalry, artillery and infantry, and led its infantry companies to Bull Run, where he was wounded. James Wadsworth of Genesee, an equally powerful New Yorker who was to be killed in 1864 while commanding a Union division in the Wilderness Campaign, recruited a regiment from his district in the spring of 1861, and served modestly at Bull Run as a volunteer aide. Another Union volunteer in the battle was a sixty-three-year-old Kentucky congressman, William P. Thomasson, a veteran of the War of 1812, who attached himself to the 71st New York. Or there were the "fighting McCooks" of Ohio, three of whom were at Bull Run. Alexander McCook, a West Pointer, was colonel of the 1st Ohio. His father, Daniel McCook, a warrior of the same age as old Thomasson, was present as a volunteer nurse. Alexander's brother Charles, a boy of eighteen, was in the ranks of the 1st Ohio. During the retreat he saw his father toiling with the wounded at a field hospital and stopped behind to help. In the pandemonium they were surrounded by wildly excited Confederate cavalry, who called on the boy to surrender. He refused — and was shot dead before his father's eyes.[9]

Similarly, it was in tradition that Bull Run should be a politically contrived affair. Politics, and civilian demands, had shaped every American war. Bull Run would never have been fought if congressmen and other impatient citizens had not badgered the Union government into ordering an advance. Political leaders were already beginning to secure senior positions. Nathaniel Banks and B. F. Butler, two Massachusetts politicos, already held major generals' commissions, though neither was at Bull Run. McDowell had one congressman, Robert C. Schenck of Ohio, in command of a brigade. The colonel of the 1st Minnesota, Willis A. Gorman, was a former governor of his state. A humbler part was played by John A. Logan, Democratic congressman from Illinois, who rushed from Washington to Bull Run to attach himself as a private to a Michigan regiment. Borrowing a rifle from a wounded soldier, he fought in a congressman's uniform — broadcloth suit and high silk hat. Political generals were less conspicuous in the Confederate army, but several of Beauregard's field officers had served in Congress and in state legislatures. The Confederate President, Jefferson Davis, turned up at Manassas and showed a disposition to act as commander in chief in a more than formal way.

Bull Run marked one other aspect of American military evolution. Though the regular army as such held little prominence, its West Point officer cadre, already coming to the fore in the Mexican War, was now apparently supreme. McDowell, Beauregard and Johnston were all West Pointers. In the Union Army at Bull Run the two division commanders, Daniel Tyler and David Hunter, were Academy graduates; and nine of the eleven brigades were led by men who had been to West Point (of the two exceptions one was Schenck and the other was Louis Blenker, a German with considerable military experience). Of the twelve Confederate brigades involved in the battle, all but two were commanded by West Pointers (the exceptions were Francis Bartow, killed in action, and Milledge Bonham, a veteran of the Seminole and Mexican wars).

The old mutual antipathy between regular and volunteer was again evident. Griffin's battery, driving forward at top speed to a new position, cut disdainfully through a volunteer regiment, the 71st New York. The chronicler of that regiment blames the final panic of the day on Griffin's gunners, when they came back at a reckless gallop to replenish their ammunition, "scattering the ranks of the regiments in every direction. The Volunteers . . . could only understand the movement in one way. Those flying carriages and those madly excited men were rushing to the rear, and their action was therefore construed into a wild retreat."[10]

First Bull Run then is to be seen as an epitome of previous American tendencies. How can we make sense of it and of the heritage which this book investigates?

There have been three principal types of explanation: the professional, the antiprofessional and the antimilitarist.

The professional view, of military affairs in general and of

19

particular episodes such as Bull Run, was given its earliest full statement by the West Pointer Emory Upton.* It has been restated since his day with growing confidence and force and has become almost the standard approach, though in the period covered by this book it was a minority viewpoint. According to Upton and his followers, in 1861 as before and since, the United States paid a heavy price for ignorance and complacence. The regular army was grossly neglected. In every war since 1775, the small band of regulars had borne the brunt and saved the day. Yet politicians pandered to popular sentiment and to foolish state pride by insisting upon the imaginary excellence of the amateur soldier. The Confederacy could have been crushed at the outset, on that heartbreaking day at Bull Run, if only the regular army had been maintained at a reasonable strength, and if only the militia had been organized federally as a genuine force instead of being a temporary rabble. Failing this, McDowell suffered exactly as George Washington had done from being given a raw army of recruits whose enlistments were up before they were ready for action. The Uptonian critic was fond of quoting a dictum of Washington's: "To place any dependence upon militia is assuredly resting upon a broken staff."

The antiprofessional opinion, that of amateur soldiers like John A. Logan and Benjamin F. Butler, is quite opposite. What struck Upton about Bull Run was the magnificent courage of Griffin's and Ricketts's regular artillery, the steadiness of Sykes's battalion of regular infantry in withdrawal, and — conversely — the raggedness and nervousness of the nonregular contingents. The New York Fire Zouaves, for example, had boasted of their own bravado but then ran away at the crucial moment, spreading wild rumors of being charged by some mysteriously invincible body known as the "Black Horse Cavalry." To Logan — also, it must be remembered, present at the battle — quite different lessons were to

---

* His *Military Policy of the United States* was left in manuscript, unfinished, at his death in 1881 and was not published until 1904. Upton's opinions were, however, well known to post–Civil War army officers. Writers who accepted his premises, including Frederic L. Huidekoper and the Harvard historian Richard M. Johnston, are admirably analyzed in Russell F. Weigley, *Towards an American Army: Military Thought from Washington to Marshall* (New York, 1962), which is also good on Upton.

be drawn. The regular battalion of marines had disintegrated as swiftly as any of the volunteers. The most disgraceful display by any field officer was that of Dixon S. Miles, a regular colonel in command of a division, who became steadily more drunk and incapable as the battle wore on. Burnside, another regular, pulled his brigade back without permission, and later in the day was seen by a newspaper correspondent galloping away from his men with the unlikely excuse that he must arrange for their rations. If Upton had a distinguished Civil War career, so did Logan. When Logan later wrote *The Volunteer Soldier of America* (1887), he was still convinced that the nation's faith in its civilian soldiers was well founded. Professional armies were undemocratic, un-American, and almost unnecessary: caste-ridden, cliquish, hidebound. Regular soldiers might perform valiantly, but no better than the enthusiastic amateurs. The typical West Pointer was a less inspiring leader than the vigorous civilian as typified by Logan — or by Wade Hampton.

As for politicians, they had nothing to be ashamed of. Logan could take pride in his own contribution. Representative Lovejoy may have annoyed Sherman: he won the praise of young Emory Upton, whose horse had been badly hit. Upton saw another horse by a small house "where the wounded were being carried." Its owner proved to be Owen Lovejoy. "He was . . . taking care of the wounded, and had exposed his life freely. I told him I was an aide and my horse had been shot, and asked for his. He gave him to me immediately." When the 4th Pennsylvania marched ingloriously away, their politician-colonel John Hartranft stayed behind with McDowell to fight. Before the war ended he was a divisional commander. The correspondent of the *New York World* saw two Illinois congressmen, Elihu Washburne and William Kellogg, trying to halt the panic rush back to Centreville. Washburne had his coat off and was wielding a bayonet. Senator Benjamin F. Wade of Ohio, armed with an old squirrel gun, was also doing his best to stem the tide.[11]

Bull Run proved nothing, except that the Union must summon more men to the colors and that the South had evidently been conspiring to wage war — with an alarming degree of active or passive assistance from West Pointers, whose professionalism did not inhibit them from betraying their country when their loyalty was tested.[12]

The third, antimilitarist sentiment, drowned out in the martial clamor of 1861 but often expressed before and since,[13] is that the United States had no business to engage in war. In its extreme form this took shape as the "peace movement" which flourished from about 1815 to about 1860. It was well exemplified in a notorious oration made in 1845 by Charles Sumner of Massachusetts, when he asked, "Can there be in our age any peace that is not honorable, any war that is not dishonorable?" According to the pacifists, the United States ought to be a shining light for other nations. Americans were — with certain ruffianly exceptions — a fortunate, virtuous people. They did not need warships, fortifications, soldiers: or if at all, only on a minimal scale and for brief emergencies. There were sinful, underlying passions that impelled men to strut in uniform and plunge into bloodshed. The true United States however was a peace-loving nation whose swords should be beaten into plowshares; and who was more at home with such a metaphor than the "Learned Blacksmith," Elihu Burritt the pacifist leader?

In less didactic form, there was the pervasively antimilitarist feeling of men like Abraham Lincoln, who regarded his short period of service in the Black Hawk War as mainly a farce, who burlesqued the militia musters of his youth, and who when challenged to a duel by a political opponent and given the choice of weapons was said to have suggested cow dung at five paces. This attitude, which Lincoln shared with millions of his countrymen, was irreverent, unromantic, unheroic. War was horrible: warlike flourishes in peacetime were grotesque.

Three principal ways of reacting to American military experience: professional, antiprofessional, antimilitarist. Each has been fairly prominent. But neither in sum nor separately do they provide an adequate guide. In sum, obviously, they are incompatible, though this very incompatibility is interesting. Separately, each is partisan, incomplete, and sometimes tedious.

Their limitations will be examined in subsequent chapters. It is enough to note here that the three lines are less distinct than might appear. What for instance is the distinction between regulars and volunteers when the latter are trained? The marines at Bull Run had been recruited less than a month beforehand. They were even less accustomed to army life than the ninety-day militia of whom Upton wrote with laconic contempt. True, Upton praises *well-trained* volunteers; but professional bias prevented him from ever quite admitting that in the American context regulars and volunteers might become virtually indistinguishable. Wrestling with this difficulty after the Civil War, he sought to resolve it by asserting that "volunteers can become veterans but not regulars." Presumably the difference resides in the fact that regulars are led by professional officers. But the regular officers at Bull Run showed themselves unequipped for their task; and special pleaders like Upton weakened their case — as Logan overstated his — by refusing to concede that some regulars could be incompetent and that their training might not have fitted them for wartime commands.[14]

Nor were the regular officers as sharply professional as Upton implied. Though West Point gave them a thorough indoctrination, it was in important respects also a civilian institution — a college for budding engineers and for those generally in search of a respectable free education. Its graduates acted defensively, seeking to prove their worth in civilian ways and in many cases maintaining close contact with the world outside the army. Only three years before Bull Run, Beauregard, the Little Napoleon of the Confederacy, tried to have himself elected mayor of New Orleans while still a serving officer.

His action is a curiosity to be explained later. Yet America's military history is full of these curiosities. There is for instance the remarkable lecture tour of Mrs. Myra Gaines and her husband, General Edmund P. Gaines, one of the nation's senior soldiers, during the 1840's. She addressed audiences in various cities on "The Horrors of War." On the same platforms, jabbing with his sword at a map, her uniformed spouse preceded her with a lecture on his pet subject of railroad construction in relation to military preparedness. Or there was Charles Sumner, widely known for his antiwar speeches and writings. A few years earlier young Sumner had yearned to enter as a cadet at West Point. Only with reluctance did he yield to his father's determination that he should go to Harvard instead. Theodore Parker of Massachusetts, no less active in the peace movement, much admired Sumner's famous Boston antiwar address of 1845. Ten years later he spoke otherwise. In face of the slavery crisis, Parker's view that war was "an utter violation of Christianity" was changed to accommodate the prospect of a *just* war. He was after all the grandson of a Revolutionary veteran; two muskets from Lexington hung on the wall above his desk. Writing to a friend about the Italian struggle for unification, he now said that while he still hated war, "yet we see its necessity": "All the great charters of humanity have been *writ in blood,* and must continue to be for some countries. I should let the Italians fight for their liberty till the twenty-eight million were only fourteen million."[15]

Circumstances altered cases. The American man of peace was on occasion capable of the most pugnacious sentiments. Sometimes, of course, he might be the victim of circumstance. The unmartial Abraham Lincoln found himself at the head of an immense war machine for which little in his background or temperament provided any guidance. Yet even the benevolent Lincoln carried in his memory reminders that however ardently men might seek peace, the threat of violence was never entirely absent. His grandfather had been killed by Indians "while labouring to open a farm in the forest." Undramatic though his few weeks of Black Hawk soldiering had been, one gruesome vignette lodged so vividly in his imagination that a quarter of a century later he described it with an extraordinary freshness. He and some comrades stumbled upon the corpses of five Americans who had been killed a few hours before: "The red light of the morning sun was streaming upon them as they lay heads towards us on the ground. And every man had a round, red spot on the top of his head about as big as a collar where the redskins had taken his scalp. It was frightful, but it was grotesque; and the red sunlight seemed to paint everything all over."[16]

PROLOGUE: FIRST BULL RUN AND ITS MEANING

Lincoln's duel with his Illinois political opponent, General Shields, was averted. But the cow-dung anecdote is apocryphal: the weapons agreed upon — cavalry broadswords — were less amusing. And no matter how unmilitary Lincoln may have been, the national destiny committed him, like that other man of peace Woodrow Wilson, to a presidency overshadowed by war.

To stress the ambiguities is not to say that they present an insoluble mystery. "Warlike but unmilitary": some such phrase has often been used to explain the situation. Or we are often told that while the nation as a whole is unmilitary the South is an exception. Such formulas may carry a good deal of truth, though the idea of a "militant" South can stand revision. At any rate America's mixed military heritage is not easy to define with precision. Other factors deserve to be weighed. Thus even before the Revolution, Americans were fond of bestowing military titles on one another. They have favored military heroes as Presidents. They liked to hear of martial exploits, especially American ones, in their books and periodicals. In the half-century before the Civil War numbers of their children were sent to military schools. Much of the American style was in some sense "military."

But how much and in what sense? There are dangers in venturing an assessment. There is the danger, for instance, of reading back into the past professional military inclinations which more properly pertain to the twentieth century. There is the subtler risk of exaggerating the significance of material simply because it is *there,* bulkily lodged in libraries. Information on the militia carries this danger. It exists in quantity and appears central enough. Almost every annual presidential message from George Washington to James K. Polk dwells upon the militia system. Yet most of the discussion is peripheral, dull, inert. It is tempting, though not altogether correct, to suppose that this is one of the justifiably neglected areas of American history: some dry bones are best left undisturbed.

A similar emptiness characterizes the related minutiae of the volunteer movement. All those companies with their fantastic finery, their stillborn endeavors, their tangled and usually ephem-

25

eral lineages, their obscure connections with fire companies, political stunts or ethnic groupings — what do they signify militarily? Emerson confessed his difficulty in trying to read Machiavelli's history. "The Florentine factions," he says, "are as tiresome as the history of the Philadelphia fire-companies."[17] *Mutatis mutandis,* we might feel that the histories of, say, the Salem Light Infantry or New York's Seventh Regiment or Philadelphia's First City Troop are as stultifying as the bygone squabbles of Italian city-states. In fact they are worse, seen in isolation; for the American companies, unlike the Italian gangs, had not much to do with real power or violence.

There is a further danger, inherent in the fact that most of America's "military" phenomena are also, and perhaps primarily, aspects of other things. None, not even the United States Military Academy, can be deemed purely "military." We must beware of forcing comparisons between disparate things which may be military (or antimilitary) in only incidental ways. Lincoln once ridiculed some specious political promises by saying they reminded him of the pantaloons offered for sale by a Yankee peddler as "large enough for any man, small enough for any boy." Unless we take care, there is a serious risk of exaggerating and misinterpreting the diffuse aspects of the military spirit in America.

I would not have persevered in the attempt if I did not believe it was worthwhile despite the difficulties. I have assumed that a nation's military attitudes may throw unfamiliar light upon its social order and its values. A second assumption is that the enquiry needs to be wide in scope. An investigation restricted to the regular army, or even to the regulars plus the militia and volunteers, would be tidier but would miss important nuances.

The chapters that follow are therefore deliberately miscellaneous and discursive. If they seem to labor the obvious, to suggest implausible relationships, and to leave terminology vague, the reader is asked to share my view that something of value will emerge. He is asked also to regard the pictorial matter as not merely decorative. It is meant to re-create a national style, or set of styles, that we have tended to forget about.

PROLOGUE: FIRST BULL RUN AND ITS MEANING

The first part of the book deals with contradictions. It expands the iconography of Bull Run. Here was a nation with an antipathy to regular soldiers which yet kept in being a quite severely professional army.* America's articles of faith included an undying devotion to the militia; yet the militia was allowed to lapse into disrepair, and to die altogether in some states. Here was a nation both peace-loving and violent, indifferent to military activity and yet given to many forms of military enthusiasm. In the first part these seeming contradictions are set against one another.

In the second part they are taken further. Not all the contradictions are resolved. Indeed, it is argued that in the United States even more than in other countries men have followed incompatible styles, usually without being unduly perplexed. It is suggested that the situation is richly, fascinatingly confused, and that major elements in American thought and activity may be discerned by considering the sum of associations conjured up by such objects as a gun, a drum, a trumpet, a flag, a song.

---

* And navy. But in order to delimit the inquiry, only incidental references are made to naval affairs. I do not think the omission gravely weakens the argument.

2
THE CONFUSED HERITAGE AND ITS CONTINUANCE

In free states . . . no man should take up arms, but with a view to defend his country and its laws: he puts not off the citizen when he enters the camp; but it is because he is a citizen, and would wish to continue so, that he makes himself for a while a soldier.

— Blackstone's *Commentaries*, Chapter 13

It is a very improbable supposition, that any people can long remain free, with a strong military power in the heart of their country: Unless that military power is under the direction of the people, and even then it is dangerous.

— Samuel Adams, 1768

On peut militariser un civil, mais on ne peut pas civiliser un militaire.

— Talleyrand

We are warlike enough, but not military. In this we are singularly like the English, and unlike other nations. We have political ideas, but no mould of military ideas.

— Elihu Root, address at the dedication of the Army War College, 1908

THE BRITISH INFLUENCE

The origins of the American military ethos are to be sought two centuries and more before Bull Run, in England. The experiences of seventeenth- and eighteenth-century England were, to a sometimes surprising degree, recapitulated in the New World; and the cautionary tales they embodied made a profound impression upon the colonies. In the quarrels between Charles I and Parliament which led to the English Civil War the control of the nation's armed forces was a hotly contested issue. It was the issue of the purse versus the sword. The King commanded whatever troops might be raised: Parliament voted the money necessary to raise them. His opponents in the House of Commons, apart from thinking Charles rash and extravagant, could cite hoary precedents of what might happen when the ruler of a country also had a praetorian guard obedient to his wishes.[1]

So when he sought to make war on France and Spain, Parliament refused to sanction the expenditure. Charles responded by trying to levy taxes without parliamentary sanction. The Petition of Right (1628) followed. Among other things it grumbled at the billeting of soldiers in people's homes, "against the laws and customs of this realm." There was a sharper quarrel in 1641 over the command of an army raised for a campaign in Ireland. Charles would not give way. In the following year the Civil War broke out. He lost, and in 1649 he was beheaded.

For eleven years England was a republic. But again conflicts arose, and again military affairs were at the center of the trouble. The victorious Parliamentary party had forged a powerful army which soon began to force the pace. Cromwell's regiments asserted their own will, impelling Parliament to execute the King, coercing it in other ways, and finally — in 1653 — bringing the Long Parliament to a contemptuous close by bundling the members out of Westminster. For five years Oliver Cromwell ruled England as Lord Protector. For one year he even experimented at governing the country through twelve major generals, each allotted a district which he held in check by garrisoning. When Cromwell died in 1658 there was an interlude of near anarchy. Parliament and the Cromwellian army were bitterly at odds. If the civilians had grievances, so did the soldiers: their pay was long in arrears.

At the restoration of the Stuarts in 1660, both Charles II and Parliament would for different reasons have liked to be rid of the Cromwellian legacy of the New Model Army. But some troops were needed to keep order. A compromise was reached. First, a small regular force was to be maintained: this was the actual foundation of the British standing army. Second, there was to be a nationwide militia, composed of civilians who could — as in earlier days — be summoned in time of need. The militia, however, was to be under civil law, and to be organized *locally* by the lord lieutenant of each county. It was thus decentralized and divorced from royal control. For these reasons it was often referred to as England's "constitutional" army.

These were tentative compromises. They worked badly in the quarter-century of Charles II's reign, and collapsed altogether when his brother the Duke of York succeeded him as James II. After less than four years of rule James fled the country; and presently William of Orange reigned in his stead, as William III. Though most of James's troubles arose from his determination to restore at least a measure of Roman Catholicism, they focused upon military issues. He was an experienced and competent soldier-administrator. He had grounds for arguing that England needed a larger army, and that the militia was almost useless. Since Parliament did not trust him, it placed the worst interpretation upon his arguments. He was accused of seeking to establish a regular army in order to coerce his subjects; and indeed he did attempt something of the sort when he concentrated fifteen thousand men — the bulk of his army — at Hounslow, outside London. In vain: James's soldiers would not support him. So many deserted that he could not deal with William's landing.

What was now to be done, with William and Mary on the throne and James in exile? In the days of the Commonwealth interregnum the army had in effect run the country, with dire results. The army had failed to back James. It was thus a bad master and a bad servant, dangerous in either case. The ideal solution was to dispense with it altogether. But that was not immediately possible, in view of the risk of a Jacobite invasion led by James. As Britain's power and ambition grew in the eighteenth century, the hope receded still further.

At least the army's power, like that of the monarchy, could be circumscribed. The regiments of the regular army must be brought under civil control. *Cedant arma togae:* let arms yield to the law, in Cicero's phrase (a phrase all the more relevant when men recalled that Cicero, involved in Roman faction, finally had his head cut off by a posse of soldiers).*

Civil control must be Parliamentary control, though it was constitutionally convenient and even desirable to retain the King as commander in chief. Hence the assertion in the Declaration of Right (1689; reenacted in the Bill of Rights) that "the raising or keeping a standing army within the kingdom in time of peace, unless it be with the consent of Parliament, is against the Law." The temporary maintenance of an army to safeguard England in the 1690's was approved, but controlled by a simple and basic device. The army's survival depended on a vote of funds by Parliament, within the so-called Mutiny Act. Gradually this became an annual procedure. Each year the military establishment came under scrutiny, and often under fire. Macaulay remarks in his *History of England* that before the Revolution of 1688–1689, "our ancestors had known a standing army only as an instrument of lawless power." Politicians, "agreeing in scarcely any thing else, were disposed to agree in aversion to the red coats."

There was a furious and prolonged debate over the future of

* Two hundred years after James II, and nearly two thousand after Cicero, *Cedant arma togae* was to end up as the state motto of Wyoming.

the standing army at the end of 1697, following several years of war upon the Continent. The pamphleteers who recommended the "immediate and entire disbanding of the army," says Macaulay, had an easy task. "On their side were claptraps and historical commonplaces without number, the authority of a crowd of illustrious names, all the prejudices, all the traditions, of both the parties in the state." They ransacked history from ancient Greece to the dire days of Cromwellian England, insisting that "no country could be secure which was cursed with a standing army." At most the King might be allowed a few body-guards. Otherwise, "the defence of the realm ought to be confided to the sailors and the militia."[2]

Macaulay's eloquent account makes it clear that he considers the pamphleteers to have been wrong. Nor was the army disbanded. Little by little, apprehension eased, and the extreme tension between Crown and Parliament. But the army, at least in peacetime, continued to be unpopular and subject to continual controversy. Writers of the time were called upon to supply ammunition. Daniel Defoe produced an *Argument Showing, that a Standing Army, with Consent of Parliament, Is Not Inconsistent with a Free Government*. Dean Swift was of the opposite persuasion. In his pamphlet *Of Public Absurdities in England*, Swift described a "standing army in England, whether in time of Peace or War," as a "direct absurdity": "For, it is no part of our business to be a warlike nation, otherwise than by our fleets. In foreign wars we have no concern, further than in conjunction with allies, whom we may either assist by sea, or by foreign troops paid with our money."

Whether the English looked back upon their own century of strife, or compared their vigor and prosperity with that of other countries, they found a ready explanation. A pamphleteer of 1724, in *A Discourse upon the Present Number of Forces in Great-Britain and Ireland*, insisted that "no Kingdom in Europe has been enslav'd, but by an Army," and that "Slavery is no where continued without one." Men had forgotten these truths: how else could they "without Indignation, hear such absurd Propositions advanc'd, as That a Standing Army is necessary for the Preservation of our Constitution, and that Eighteen or Twenty Thousand Soldiers are no more than sufficient for the Defence of it?"

Geography seemed to sustain the opinion of such constitutionalists that the nation's protection depended upon the navy and the militia. The numerous wars that Britain fought during the eighteenth century were conducted overseas. The presence of the army was rarely apparent to most of the population. A good proportion of the regiments serving at home were stationed in Ireland and Scotland, and confined there in barracks. Soldiers were kept away from elections and assizes, for fear that they might cow the voter or juror. Not until the mid-nineteeth century were soldiers permitted to enter the House of Commons, unless they were members or had been summoned as witnesses.

Those stationed in England became still more unpopular because of the practice of billeting. Whenever the army was increased, which became necessary during several national emergencies, the new battalions had to be quartered in inns and private houses. The obvious remedy would have been to build barracks. But as General Wade observed — referring to the troubles of 1739–1740 — "the people of this kingdom have been taught to associate the idea of Barracks and Slavery so closely together, that, like darkness and the devil, though there be no manner of connection . . . , yet they cannot . . . think of the one without thinking . . . of the other." As a professional soldier Wade regretted the situation he described. Wherever the redcoats were lodged they were objects of suspicion. The rationale for this public prejudice was restated later in the century, with as much force as ever, by the jurist Blackstone. Blackstone, whose *Commentaries* was almost as widely read by lawyers in America as in Britain, asserted that soldiers should "live intermixed with the people; no separate camp, no barracks, no inland fortresses, should be allowed."[3]

Life in this army was congenial enough for the officers, most of whom did not take their duties too seriously. It was another matter for the enlisted men, who had to be recruited among the poor, the unemployed and the unlucky. At times of emergency the only way of rapidly augmenting the army was to hire foreign mercenaries. Dutch contingents had to be shipped to England during the Jacobite rising of 1715, again in 1719 and yet again for the second Jacobite rebellion of 1745. Hessians had also to be brought in for the "Forty-Five," and more Hessians together with some Hanoverians at the outbreak of the Seven Years' War in 1756. Though their employment was unavoidable, their presence was distinctly unwelcome — though in the case of the Hanoverians there was a link through the monarchy, since England's kings in the eighteenth century were also Electors of Hanover.[4]

In the second half of the century there was some improvement in British naval and military efficiency. The militia was revived under the elder Pitt, who did so much to prepare the ground for the triumphs of the Seven Years' War. New regular units were raised, including some of the Scottish Highland regiments which were to be among the finest in the British army. On the eve of the American Revolutionary War, however, the dominant attitude toward the standing army was of grudging acceptance. If the legislature had ceased to regard the army as a threat to the public safety, it was still disposed to view regular soldiery as a chief source of executive extravagance. Popular resentment focused on billeting and other military practices — such as the unscrupulousness of recruiting parties in wheedling innocent country boys into "taking the king's shilling."

Recurrent national crises produced hectic but temporary waves of panic and belligerence. Inns were named after successful generals and admirals. The names stuck but the emotion ebbed as rapidly as it had risen. In 1746, gratitude and relief impelled the poet John Collins to ask:

> How sleep the brave who sink to rest
> By all their country's wishes bless'd?

A few years later, the average citizen's attitude was probably summed up in the declaration of another poet, the Quaker John Scott:

> I hate that drum's discordant sound,
> Parading round, and round, and round.

The navy and the militia were praised as being more "constitutional." Sailors, it was urged, would never be the instruments of tyranny. "Hearts of oak," in the words of the patriotic ditties of the period, they were contrasted with the minions of Continental armies and navies.

> *To glory we call you, as freemen, not slaves,*
> *For who are so free as the sons of the waves?*

Despite such sentiment, the navy seemed horribly expensive to members of Parliament. To the public it was associated also with that negation of freedom, the press-gang, and with the ferocious discipline depicted in such novels as Tobias Smollett's *Adventures of Roderick Random* (1748). As for the militia, its value was mainly rhetorical and incidental. The historian Edward Gibbon, looking back on his militia experience in the Hampshire Grenadiers, thought it had perhaps helped him in the writing of *The Decline and Fall of the Roman Empire*. Perhaps; but this was a dubious compliment to the prowess of England's citizen-soldiers. Those with genuine ardor, or with social pretensions, began to associate increasingly in volunteer companies, which weakened as well as strengthened the militia idea.[5]

COLONIAL AND REVOLUTIONARY LESSONS

These attitudes pervaded the American colonies as well as the mother country. They were both modified and sharpened by the special circumstances of colonial life. At home ordinary Englishmen had no need for firearms, or were discouraged from owning them. Across the Atlantic, weapons were considered essential, for protection against the Indians and for shooting game. Militia units, especially in frontier districts, had a vital function.[6]

On the other hand, Britain's larger strategic ambitions had little relevance for the colonists. Their view was local; they would respond to an immediate menace, but as British commanders exasperatedly discovered, they were most unwilling to contribute men, money or supplies to expeditions outside their own colonies. It is significant that American historians have assigned a different name to a major war. What the British refer to as the Seven Years' War is known in the United States as the French and Indian War — which for the colonists started earlier than in Europe. In this war's major campaigns the bulk of the troops consisted of British regulars. When the home government raised an "American" rifle regiment, the 60th, they had difficulty in filling it up to strength. The colonists saw little point in enlisting in a regular unit, with pay and conditions inferior to those of provincial troops, and the risk of being sent to some far-off theater of the war. Some colonial officers with military aspirations — young George Washington among them — would have liked to be given commissions as regulars. This mark of favor eluded them. Colonial officers were not held in high esteem; until Pitt amended matters in 1756, officers like Washington in provincial (non-regular) regiments were outranked by holders of regular commissions. Braddock's defeat at the Monongahela in 1755, and the failure of Abercromby's attack on Fort Ticonderoga three years later, suggested to the colonists that regulars were not only supercilious but also ineffectual, in American conditions.

Such resentments and criticisms should not be exaggerated. On the whole the campaigns of 1755–1763 made a gratifying record for colonists as well as native Englishmen. Nevertheless by the end of the war Americans had reinforced their traditional distrust of standing armies.

In the disputes that culminated in the Revolutionary War, old British sentiments became Americanized and were turned against their originators. The British had seen themselves as the freeborn, the tamers of tyrants, the champions of government by consent, upholding their faith against the despots and slaves of Continental Europe. A London broadsheet of 1659, *The Army Mastered, or Great Brittain's Joy*, congratulated Parliament on having conquered "those (till now) untameable Lyons of the Army, that had . . . transformed the peoples freedom and liberties into their proper food and prey, which to eat up and devour, these most inhumane Monsters have boasted to be the glory and crown of all their victories." With less reason and rather less unanimity, but with powerful effect, the colonists were able to castigate the redcoats in similar language. The language, indeed, worked for them, since it formed the heritage of Whig and Tory alike. The ten thousand British soldiers who garrisoned the colonies after the peace of 1763 were disliked and distrusted. Benjamin Franklin uttered a standard argument — developed by Samuel Adams too — when he maintained in 1770 that the keeping of a standing army in America without the consent of the colonial assemblies was "not agreeable to the Constitution." Not until 1765 was the Mutiny Act amended to apply to the colonies. It could not solve the problems stirred up by the presence of the redcoats. It could not for example prevent soldiers from deserting in quantity, or sympathetic colonists from assisting them to do so. It could not produce a formula that would reconcile American householders to paying for the upkeep of soldiers in peacetime, let alone agreeing to have soldiers billeted on them. When the British commander in chief in America, General Gage, visited Boston late in the autumn of 1769, he found his soldiers shivering in tents on the Common because no billets were being offered. The Boston "massacre" of March 1770, when a party of redcoats fired on a mob, was spoken of as an outrage comparable to the worst excesses of Cromwell's troops in Ireland. One of its most ominous features, according to American radicals, was that the officer in charge of the party had given the order to fire on his own initiative, without seeking the permission of a magistrate. His conduct appeared of a piece with the larger activities of General Gage, who was accused by the first Continental Congress in 1774 of having been granted authority over all "the civil governments in America."[7]

This gathering of aggrieved colonists protested too at the maintenance of a standing army "without the consent" of colonial legislatures. Two years afterward Thomas Jefferson was drafting the Declaration of Independence. Well might he concede that he was not concerned "to find out new principles, or new arguments, never before thought of." In the military as in the other clauses which follow the preamble to the Declaration, Jefferson did indeed draw upon "the harmonizing sentiments of the day, whether expressed in conversation, in letters, printed essays, or in the elementary books of public right, as Aristotle, Cicero, Locke, Sidney, etc."

The charges against George III in the Declaration come straight out of the common discourse of British libertarianism:

He has kept among us, in times of peace, Standing Armies without the Consent of our legislatures.

He has affected to render the Military independent of and superior to the Civil Power.

Though Britain's recourse to the hiring of thirty thousand foreign troops was on an unprecedented scale, and aimed directly at the colonies, this too was not in itself a novel procedure; nor was Jefferson's form of indictment novel:

He is at this time transporting large armies of foreign mercenaries to complete the works of death, desolation and tyranny . . .

In short, the colonists as Englishmen drew upon the deep-seated antimilitary prejudices of the mother country; as colonists they had additional reasons for prejudice; and as affronted Americans, in the years between 1763 and 1775, they developed still more reasons for regarding regular soldiers, whether British or Hessian, as "mercenaries" officered by idlers and dandies.

It followed that in fighting the Revolutionary War, the Continental Congress and the majority of Americans were sometimes more concerned with the danger of military overlordship than the danger of military inefficiency. From a combination of doctrine and habit they were reluctant to create their own version of a standing army. The semiregular units of the Continental line were greatly outnumbered by the shifting mass of short-service militiamen. In the debates of 1778 over ratification of the new nation's Articles of Confederation, some states were at pains to insist on the illegality of peacetime armies, unless with legislative consent. Connecticut proposed an unsuccessful amendment which would have prevented the United States from maintaining an army in time of peace, even with consent.[8]

Possibly the Americans were affected by the anxieties newly expressed in England, on the danger that the army raised to fight across the Atlantic might, on returning home, "totally subvert the remains of freedom," in the words of the Duke of Richmond. At any rate there was acute suspicion of the hereditary, aristocratic aspects of the Society of the Cincinnati, the association of French and American officers established in 1783. The discontents of Washington's Continentals, and especially of his officers, led to mutinies and mutterings in 1781–1783. There may not have been much basis for the mysterious suggestion made to Washington by one of his officers in 1781 that he might become king of the United States. But there was thought to be *some* basis. Americans could not help speculating whether some less scrupulous leader than General Washington might not have been seduced by the suggestion. Noah Webster feared a military *coup d'état* in 1785. Two years later Mrs. Mercy Warren, the sister of the Massachusetts patriot James Otis, claimed: "Many of the younger Class, particularly the students of Law and the youth of fortune and pleasure, are crying out for a monarchy and a standing army to support it. . . . These joined by a whole class of Cincinnati who are panting for a nobility. . . ."[9]

Aedanus Burke, a South Carolina congressman who had been one of the fiercest critics of the Society of the Cincinnati, was among those who distrusted Alexander Hamilton. Hamilton had held an army commission and been close to Washington. Was he hankering for something sinister, in the way of a military aristocracy? Though he disavowed this in a letter to Washington in March 1783, Hamilton — by then a member of the Continental Congress — admitted that he thought "the discontents of the

41

army might be turned to a good account." Namely, their unrest might stimulate the individual states to work together to provide for the nation's debts. States-righters like Burke were ready to put the worst construction on anything that Hamilton and his cronies did or said. In 1790 Burke pounced on a slighting reference which Hamilton had made to the wartime difficulties of General Nathanael Greene, "aided, or rather embarrassed by small fugitive bodies of volunteer militia, *the mimicry of soldiership*." What made the aspersion even worse, to Burke, was that it referred to the militia of South Carolina. Hamilton explained that he had not intended to condemn the militia as such, or the warriors of South Carolina.[10]

This was only a small incident, yet typical of the touchiness of Americans, acutely alert to the risks of military subversion and determined to avoid them. In common with Burke, they could also convince themselves that the American militia was a match for any enemy. The United States had gained victory over professional armies. Liberally minded officers among their French allies spoke flatteringly of the resourceful American fighting man, contrasting him with the "mere machine" produced by European methods. Amateur generals — Washington, Greene, Knox and the rest — had triumphed over Howe and Clinton, Burgoyne and Cornwallis. And on the whole the professionally trained officers on the American side — Charles Lee, Horatio Gates, Thomas Conway — seemed to have blotted their copybooks.

Geography and American patriotism were seen as an unbeatable combination. With the return of peace, a standing army — except for a handful of storekeepers and artillerists — was thus both undesirable and unnecessary. In the mid-1780's America's professional soldiery, administered by Secretary of War Henry Knox, numbered less than seven hundred men. The alarm over Shays's "rebellion" of disgruntled Massachusetts farmers, and the threat to the federal arsenal at Springfield, led Congress to authorize an increase to just over two thousand men. But such a move looked too much like coercion; it was stated that the extra troops were intended for frontier defense, against the Indians. Few of them were in fact raised; Shays's ragged band was dispersed instead by

Massachusetts militia. Through a sad irony, a good many of Shays's followers were ex-Continentals.[11]

THE PATTERN IS SET

Shays's Rebellion was one of the events which led to the Philadelphia convention of 1787, from which emerged the instrument of government designed to replace the Articles of Confederation. The new Constitution summed up some of the lessons America had learned from long and from recent experience. In its military aspects, what might be called the Anglo-American tradition was enshrined in the firm establishment of civil control and in the division of authority between legislature and executive. Adopting the style of England's Mutiny Act, the Constitution provided that Congress should make no appropriation for military purposes "for a longer term than two years." No such restriction hedged the maintenance of a navy. Again, this reflected the traditional view that — as Thomas Jefferson told James Monroe in 1786 — "a naval force can never endanger our liberties, nor occasion bloodshed; a land force would do both."[12]

The declaration of war was left to Congress, and general authority over the employment of the militia. The Executive, in the shape of the President, was like the English king to be commander in chief of the army and navy, and of the militia "when called into the actual Service of the United States." The

President was also, in effect, empowered to award regular commissions. Individual states were prohibited from keeping "Troops, or Ships of War, in time of peace," unless with the consent of Congress.

In retrospect these arrangements appear to have struck an admirable balance between complex and competing claims. They did not, however, satisfy every delegate to the Philadelphia convention, nor everyone present at the subsequent state ratifying conventions. For the 1787 Constitution, in the eyes of critics, was silent or evasive on important features. It was all very well to deprive the states of their right to run their own armies and navies: why did the federal government not apply some similar, self-denying ordinance? Instead, the Constitution entitled Congress "to raise and support armies." No fewer than ten states were concerned enough to debate the military features of the Constitution. Five states — New Hampshire, Virginia, New York, North Carolina and Rhode Island — asked for amendments to lessen the danger of military despotism.

New Hampshire proposed that there should be no standing army in time of peace. In Virginia, Patrick Henry declared that "Congress, by the power of taxation, by that of raising an army, and by their control over the militia, have the sword in one hand and the purse in the other. Shall we be safe without either?" Henry feared the worst. The New York ratifying convention proposed in July 1788 that peacetime military appropriations should require a two-thirds majority in Congress. They wanted the control of the militia to rest, at least temporarily, with the states. And voicing a view which had apparently been expressed at Philadelphia, they argued that the President should not "take the actual command in the field of an army, without the previous desire of Congress." North Carolina, in addition to a clause on the billeting of soldiers, listed other principles which ought to be made explicit in the Constitution:

That the people have the right to keep and bear arms; that a well-regulated militia composed of the body of the people, trained to arms, is the proper, natural and safe defence of a free state. That standing armies in time of peace are dangerous to Liberty, and therefore ought to be avoided, as far as circumstances and protection of the community will admit; and that in all cases, the military should be under strict subordination to, and governed by the civil power.[13]

In the Bill of Rights which was attached a couple of years later to the Constitution as its first set of amendments, some of these complaints were met (Articles II and III):

A well regulated Militia, being necessary to the security of a free State, the right of the people to keep and bear Arms, shall not be infringed.

No Soldier shall, in time of peace, be quartered in any house, without the consent of the Owner, nor in time of war, but in a manner to be prescribed by law.

These changed nothing. The military provisions agreed upon at Philadelphia remained intact. Alexander Hamilton put the case for them in three of the essays that he contributed to *The Federalist Papers* of 1787–1788. It was a brilliantly persuasive performance, cool and genial for the most part — though now and then Hamilton slipped into the rather disingenuous "parade of imaginary horribles," which accounts for his effect on men like Aedanus Burke. He did not urge a large standing army: he simply demonstrated that an army of some sort was unavoidable. Though these essays are less celebrated and have been far less influential than, say, James Madison's *Federalist* number 10, they cover almost every dilemma in American military policy for the next century and more.

In *The Federalist* number 24 Hamilton imagines the bewilderment of an inquiring stranger who seeks an explanation for the antagonism to a peacetime standing army. This "stranger to our politics" might naturally suppose that the proposed Constitution either enjoined that standing armies *should* be maintained in peace, or else entrusted military power to the executive branch. But neither was true. The stranger then assumes that preceding constitutions must have sanctioned such dangerous expedients. Again, not so. Only two of the state constitutions, those of

Pennsylvania and North Carolina, "interdict" peacetime armies. The rest either say nothing or merely stipulate that the consent of the legislature is necessary. As for the Articles of Confederation, these restrain the states but impose no bar to a *federal* army.

Pausing to indulge in a little sarcasm, Hamilton abandons his hypothetical stranger and goes on to assert that restraints on the legislature, the very voice of the people, are both improper and foolish. "The true merits of the question," he says, are "perplexed and entangled by expedients . . . unfriendly to an impartial and right determination."

Finally Hamilton emphasizes the weakness of the western and southern frontiers, and their vulnerability to Britain and Spain. Western garrisons will continue to be necessary, if only against "the ravages and depredations of the Indians." They must be furnished either by the militia, or by "permanent corps in the pay of the government." But the militia could not be used for such a scheme, which would be "as burdensome and injurious to the public as ruinous to private citizens." Therefore a permanent corps must be employed. This amounts to a peacetime standing army: "a small one, indeed, but none the less real for being small." Moreover, if the Americans were to be "a commercial people" they must create a navy. A navy needed dockyards and arsenals; and at least in the early stages, before the fleet was large enough to give coastal protection, fortifications and "moderate garrisons" were likewise necessary.

In the next number, *Federalist* number 25, Hamilton explains why national defense should not be entrusted to the state governments. The burden, he insists, would be unequal. Jealousies between one state and another would be disastrous when they began to compete in military establishments. "As far as an army may be considered as a dangerous weapon," he contends, "it had better be in those hands of which the people are most likely to be jealous" — namely the federal government — "than in those of which they are least likely to be jealous" — namely the state governments.

As for the kind of force to be maintained, it is in Hamilton's view impossible to conduct a successful war against a professional army except with a similar army:

The American militia, in the course of the late war, have, by their valor on numerous occasions, erected eternal monuments to their fame; but the bravest of them feel and know that the liberty of their country could not have been established by their efforts alone. . . . War, like most other things, is a science to be acquired and perfected by diligence, by perseverance, by time, and by practice.

In *Federalist* number 26 Hamilton retraces some of his steps in order to emphasize the essential and beneficial role of the federal legislature. In particular he is anxious to point out why legislatures should not needlessly limit their own military jurisdiction. The origin of the American prejudice against a peacetime soldiery "must be traced to those habits of thinking which we derive from the nation from whom the inhabitants of these States have in general sprung." In the English Bill of Rights the prime concern was to curb the executive (the Crown), not the legislature (Parliament). From the English crises of the seventeenth century the people of America "derived an hereditary impression of danger to liberty, from standing armies in time of peace." The events of the American Revolution "in some instances raised the warmth of our zeal beyond the degree which consisted with the due temperature of the body politic." This "injudicious excess" led Americans to extend to "the representatives of the people in their popular assemblies" the hostility formerly directed at the monarchy. It was impossible otherwise to explain why some of the state constitutions declared that "standing armies ought not to be kept up, in time of peace, WITHOUT THE CONSENT OF THE LEGISLATURE." This was a superfluous if not absurd declaration — "that a matter should not be done without the consent of a body, which alone had the power of doing it." Worse still, even in the two states of Pennsylvania and North Carolina, which went further, their constitutions did not say that standing armies "shall not be kept up," but that "they *ought not* to be kept up": "This ambiguity of terms appears to have been the result of a conflict between jealousy and conviction; between the desire of excluding such establishments at all events, and the persuasion that an absolute exclusion would be unwise and unsafe."

Hamilton compares such provisions, which by aiming too high achieve nothing, with the system of two-year appropriations proposed in the new Constitution. These recurrent debates, he accurately prophesied, "will always be a favorable topic for declamation." Controversy would become automatic. In such an atmosphere military dictatorship was unthinkable.

Hamilton had more to say on military affairs, especially about the militia, in the next three *Federalist* essays, number 27 through number 29. Taken together, and allowing for an element of special pleading, his views — to reiterate — epitomize a great deal of subsequent argument. He was correct in asserting that, like it or not, the United States could not dispense with regular forces; that an inefficient militia would be an extravagance without much military value; and neither the nation nor the states had anything to fear from the existence of a regular army, still less of a semi-federalized militia.

But, then and later, these arguments reached only a limited public. Many of those who did read them were not converted. They did not trust any marked extension of federal authority; and they did not trust Alexander Hamilton. His low opinion of the militia and his additional comments on the value of an army for suppressing disorder made him suspect. Several members of the first Congress under the newly ratified Constitution, including Senator Maclay of Pennsylvania, continued to believe that their liberties were threatened. Maclay, commenting in his diary in March 1790 on a bill to fix America's military establishment (a bill which, when passed a month later, increased the army from 700 to a grand total of 1,216), said it seemed to be "laying the foundation of a standing army." In his view there were three reasons for military force: enforcing the law, quelling insurrection, repelling invasion. All three, he claimed, were entrusted by the Constitution to the militia. If the United States were unfortunate enough to be involved in a war, then and only then should an army be raised. And it should go and fight in the enemy's country, "as the most effective mode of keeping the calamity at a distance and enforcing an adversary to terms." So Maclay opposed the bill. The initial error, he thought, had been in appointing a Secretary of War (Henry Knox, who had served in the same office under the Articles of Confederation) "when we were at peace, and now we must find troops lest his office should run out of employment."[14]

Later in the 1790's the same suspicions were expressed by Republicans who objected to the "provisional" army raised by President John Adams in anticipation of war with France. A letter from a Connecticut citizen printed in the *New London Bee* in May 1799 declared that young farmers would never volunteer "under Prussian military discipline, or devote their valor to promote the views of ambition or to oppose their country and prosperity with a standing army." Though they would eagerly repel invaders, they would never consume their youths "in arms and vice, in order to glitter in regimentals, . . . and lounge in idleness." Still worse, how could they be expected to serve under the effective head of the provisional army, General Alexander Hamilton, who only two years before had had to confess that he was an adulterer? Standing armies were idle, and indolence led to dissipation.

A year afterward Charles Holt, the editor of the *Bee,* was put on trial on a charge of sedition. The district attorney, who could not but concede the truth of the statements on Hamilton's misconduct, built and won his case on a proposition which illustrates the bizarre confusion of American thought in this agitated period. Holt, he asserted, had published a malicious falsehood in stigmatizing as a "standing" army a force which was merely "provisional." In so doing he had sought to undermine popular confidence in the government. The argument was also used in this month of April 1800 by Judge Samuel Chase in another trial of a Republican radical editor, Thomas Cooper. Chase explained to the jury that it was criminal to impute to the President the intention of maintaining a standing army. There could not be a standing army in the United States, he said, since Congress determined the life of the army by voting (or withholding) supplies at two-year intervals. Therefore all armies in the United States were provisional, not permanent.

Such sophistries were ridiculed by Republican sympathizers. One defiant editor pointed out that under a similar parliamentary device, England had an unmistakable standing army. Another, commenting on Holt's trial, said that editors would have to consult a special dictionary if they were to avoid prosecution. "It would require . . . a connoisseur in legal terms," he contended, "to tell why the word *standing* was more seditious and libellous than the word *provisional*." He suggested that the word "provisional" was appropriate, at least in the sense that it applied to "men who did nothing but eat provisions"; whereas during the Revolutionary War "the army was properly called a standing army because they had to stand and face their enemies."[15]

The Republican editors were justified in their taunts at the Federalist courts. These were bad decisions, under the aegis of harsh legislation which was soon repealed when the Republicans came into power with the new administration of Thomas Jefferson. Nevertheless they revealed the uncertainty and the complexity of military policy. Neither the Articles of Confederation nor the Constitution provided clear guidance. In the 1780's and 1790's no one could be sure just what was meant by the term "standing army." The little force maintained under the Articles started out with one regiment of 700 men, raised from the militia and enlisted for only twelve months. It could hardly have been more "provisional." Subsequently the enlistment was extended to three years. This seemed somewhat less provisional; yet could one speak of an "army" when it contained a single regiment? How much did the ranks have to be increased to form a genuine standing army?

A desire to avoid embarrassments of terminology, and perhaps to economize on officers, led Secretary Henry Knox to propose that an augmented force, raised for Indian warfare, should be known not as an army but as a "legion." In fact from 1792 to 1796 the various arms of service under Major General Anthony Wayne were officially styled the Legion of the United States, a name which had possibly originated with General Steuben in 1781.[16] Though it ceased to be formally applied to the regular army after 1796, it was a designation with an attractively classical and republican tinge, soon to be given more splendid associations by Napoleon Bonaparte. As late as 1861 it was the name chosen by Wade Hampton of South Carolina, to describe the little private army of mixed units that he recruited for the Confederacy.

Otherwise the idea of a "legion" rather than a regular army lapsed. Long-standing prejudices could not be overcome by modifications in vocabulary. The awkward questions remained. As late as 1799 an executive head, Secretary of the Treasury Oliver Wolcott, could tell another Federalist that peacetime soldiers, being condemned to inactivity, tended to become morally corrupt.[17] When the war scare died down, President Adams was able to disband the provisional army in 1800. Paradoxically, this happy outcome underlined one of the chief reasons why Americans were reluctant to accept a peacetime soldiery. They could not convince themselves that they were in any real danger from an external enemy. They had absorbed old English assumptions. Most of them might have felt that Dean Swift's view — "it is no part of our business to be a warlike nation, otherwise than by our fleets" — applied also to the United States. The English had survived a succession of invasion threats, from the Armada of 1588 to Napoleon's concentration at Boulogne. If foreign invaders could not cross twenty miles of English Channel, how could they cross three thousand miles of the Atlantic? True, the British had done so in the Revolutionary War; but the British war effort had failed. With the turn of the century, as America's population and strength increased and as Europe's hold on the New World weakened, the risk diminished. If the United States should get into a war with a European power, there would surely be ample time in which to prepare an army. The few ships of the American navy had accomplished miracles in the Revolutionary War, and again in Jefferson's operations of 1801–1807 against the Barbary pirates of North Africa. It could be said that Jefferson only embarked on the enterprise because he disliked the Barbary powers of Tripoli, Tunis and Morocco even more than he disliked the idea of an American navy.[18] No matter: his attitude was understandable, and the result successful.

The second major complication was over the status of the militia. The vexed history of the militia will be traced in Chapter 6. Basically, the problem was to create a sizable and efficient militia without making it too much like a standing army, and without demanding more of the time and energy of American males than they were prepared to give. There was the further difficulty of mediating between the wish of the federal government to unify militia organization, training and equipment, and the determination of the states to retain control and patronage of the militia in their own hands. In the 1780's Washington, Knox, Steuben and others all put forward ambitious and ingenious schemes for an active militia. They envisaged an armed force which, in peace or war, would consist predominantly of militia units, with close rapport between the militia and the small nucleus of the permanent army. Their plans were not carried out. What survived were slogans and comfortable assurances, mingled with prejudices and some perfectly sensible attitudes. Their fellow Americans opted for a minimum of efficiency and compulsion, and a maximum of patriotic rhetoric blended with various shades of antimilitarism.[19]

So the young United States evolved. In the words used by Secretary of War Elihu Root a hundred years later, his nation like the English had "political ideas, but no mould of military ideas." Out of acquired libertarian beliefs and real or fancied Revolutionary lessons, out of state pride and suspicion of centralized authority, out of actual isolation and emotional isolationism, out of a commendable desire for economy and a less commendable parsimony, out of peaceable inclination and self-centered individualism, Americans established a set of vaguely defined rules. They were rules of thumb rather than neat propositions. There was to be a tiny standing army, and a relatively less tiny regular navy. There was to be a militia in which every male American was supposed to serve but none were to be given any rigorous training. In time of need an army would be improvised in various ways: by augmenting the regulars, by embodying militia and by raising volunteer regiments. A military academy — recommended by Washington and by a number of other military figures of the Revolutionary era — came into being at West Point in 1802; but its functions remained for some years indeterminate.

The War of 1812, with its initial setbacks and its continued humiliations and frustrations, might have forced the young nation to clarify its military policy. Instead, Andrew Jackson's sensational victory at the Battle of New Orleans in January 1815 set the seal on everything that patriots liked to believe about themselves. The invading British force was led by Lord Pakenham, the brother-in-law of the great Duke of Wellington, and made up of seasoned regiments which had fought against Napoleon's armies in Spain. Their assault on Jackson's hastily gathered and outnumbered force was a disaster. Pakenham was killed, and some two thousand of his men killed or wounded. Jackson's casualties were a mere handful. The disproportion was almost unbelievable. Some American contemporaries noted that much of the work of destruction had been done by Jackson's artillery, firing at close range into the dense, immobile ranks of Pakenham's army; and some historians have followed this explanation. Within a few years of the battle, however, Americans were firmly convinced that the slaughter had been produced by the backwoodsmen in Jackson's force: men who were the antithesis of Pakenham's professionals. It was Lexington, Concord and Bunker Hill all over again, but with a far more decisive and indeed miraculous outcome. Jackson the amateur, the frontier democrat, had worsted

CORRECT VIEW of the BATTLE *Near the City of* NEW ORLEANS, *on the* *8th January 1815, Under the Command of* Gen! And **v** Jackson, *Over* 10,000 *British Troops, in* *3 of their most distinguished Generals were killed &* *several wounded and upwards of* 3,000 *of their choicest* *Soldiers were killed, wounded.* *and made Prisoners, &c*

Pakenham the expert and aristocrat. The Kentucky rifleman had routed the British musketeer. Spontaneity had triumphed over premeditation. Thus it had been; thus would it always be: "I came, I saw, I conquered, says the *American Husbandman,* fresh from his plough. . . . The God of Battles and of Righteousness took part with the defenders of their country and the foe was scattered as chaff before the wind."[20]

When the emergency was over, the indomitable hunters and farmers would go back to their forests and plains and resume their useful tasks. What more cheering and wholesome proof could there be of America's immunity from the military necessities of Europe? Those who, like President Madison, had drawn somewhat different conclusions from the previous course of the fighting were not disposed to press very hard for fundamental reforms of the military system. The return of peace, and the weight of public sentiment, made the task pointless. John C. Calhoun, Secretary of War under President Monroe, recommended to Congress in 1818 that there should be no reduction of the army below the peacetime establishment of 10,000 which had been authorized at the end of the War of 1812. By 1820 the retrenchment idea was uppermost in congressmen's minds. They decided upon a reduction to 6,000 men: eleven regiments. With this as his frame of reference, Calhoun elaborated a scheme for an "expansible" army. The staff and cadres would be maintained on the peacetime establishment. In wartime the nucleus of 6,000 (6,316 in Calhoun's actual plan) could be doubled or trebled (to a figure of 19,035 in Calhoun's calculation) by a simple filling-out process.

His scheme was not adopted, but the assumptions which governed it gained almost universal acceptance. The army would be diminutive, capable of limited expansion, and highly professional. The militia would as before constitute the main mass, but — in Calhoun's eyes — a mass of unskilled auxiliaries. The nation's first line of defense would consist of the navy's score of 74-gun line-of-battle ships and 44-gun frigates, backed up by coastal batteries.[21]

Thus was the pattern set. Military commentators have poured scorn on it as shortsighted, inefficient and ultimately wasteful. No doubt it was all of these things, and potentially hazardous. But it was the expression of one large element in the nation's thinking: the element which drew a contrast between plain, go-ahead republicanism and corrupt, dynastic, panoplied European society. If Americans needed reassurance that theirs was the saner policy, they could draw it from a study of such a work as *The Extraordinary Black Book* (1831), an English volume listing the innumerable pensions and sinecures enjoyed by generals and admirals in company with bishops and other privileged groups. English radicals like Richard Cobden stressed the good sense as well as the frugality of American policy. In the early 1830's, he pointed out, the officers alone in the British army and navy outnumbered the entire strength of the American army and navy. In the British army list of 1835 more than two thousand field officers, of the rank of major and above, were enumerated. The British service estimates for 1833 amounted to over eleven million pounds. The American figures for 1832, including internal improvements, fortifications, arsenals and armories, were the equivalent of less than two million. Britain was spending more than six times as much on military affairs as the United States — "a country, be it repeated, whose population, trade, and registered tonnage, are more than the half of our own — a country, too, whose public debt is cancelled, whilst ours amounts to nearly eight hundred millions." These remarks appear in a pamphlet on whose title page Cobden printed the — for him — crucial words from Washington's Farewell Address: "The great rule of conduct for us, in regard to foreign nations, is, in extending our commercial relations, to have with them as little political connection as possible."[22]

Cobden and his fellow reformers were sure that America was right. Peaceful competition in international trade was their moral equivalent of war. In the volumes of statistics which appeared in increasing quantity and which embodied the nineteenth century's vision of progress, the credit side was expressed in numbers of spindles and looms and bales, in ship tonnage and railroad mileage, and in population increase. The armed forces, in such computations of utility, figured on the debit side, as equipment and manpower locked up unproductively, almost as if they were being reckoned as monasteries. They are not even mentioned in George Tucker's *Progress of the United States in Population and Wealth in Fifty Years* (1843), a compilation by a professor from the University of Virginia. In a similarly optimistic book called *The Half Century* (1851), its clerical author refers to the army only under the head of "Educational Changes," with a brief description of West Point which ends: "The money expended there, annually, would sustain six hundred normal schools, which would furnish annually 30,000 accomplished school teachers. Which will benefit our country most, to furnish it annually with 30,000 good school teachers, or sixty men well skilled in the art of war?"[23]

From this bustling milieu of commerce and progress, with its inherent antimilitarism, it was not a great step to argue that armies and navies should not simply be diminished: they should be dispensed with altogether. Until that ultimate step, the good man of trade could make common cause with the good Christian. Time and life were precious: wars squandered both.

THE PEACE MOVEMENT

Pacifist sentiment in the United States represented the extremest statement of antimilitarism. The Quakers, dominant in

Pennsylvania until the mid-eighteenth century, had refused to raise a militia in their colony or to serve under arms. During the Revolution several colonies recognized the right of men with conscientious scruples to be exempt from military service, usually with the proviso that they should "pay an equivalent." Conscientious objection was protected in a number of the state constitutions drawn up at this period.[24] The Philadelphia physician Benjamin Rush, who had been surgeon general of the Continental Army, argued in 1793 that if the young nation needed to establish a war department it stood in still greater need of a peace office. Though he wrote in an ironical vein his proposal was basically serious. The Secretary of Peace (anticipating responsibilities which the federal government in fact assumed many decades later) was to preside over a system of free schools in which the sanctity of human life would be expounded as a central doctrine. In addition, he would work toward the repeal of all laws that encouraged war, and the abolition of military titles and uniforms. As for the War Department, signs should be placed over its various doors which read "an office for butchering the human species," "a widow- and orphan-making office," and so on; and

In the lobby of this office let there be painted the representations of all the common military instruments of death; also human skulls, broken bones, unveined and putrefying dead bodies, hospitals crowded with sick and wounded soldiers, villages on fire, mothers in besieged towns, eating the flesh of their children, ships sinking in the ocean, rivers dyed with blood, and extensive plains without tree or fence, or any other object but the ruins of deserted farm houses. Above all this group of woful figures, let the following words be inserted in red characters, to represent human blood: — "NATIONAL GLORY."[25]

The prolonged bloodbath of the revolutionary and Napoleonic wars in Europe sickened men of good will. They shuddered at Goya's *Disasters of War* or at the fearful story of Napoleon's invasion of Russia, from which only 100,000 of his army of 600,000 were ever reassembled. Nor was there any need for such horrors to be repeated. The world was becoming more rational and more virtuous, despite appearances to the contrary. Human worth was more esteemed, death (whether of little children or of young men in battle) less and less taken for granted. The change in sentiment can be studied from the inscriptions in old cemeteries. The sense of loss, of protest struggling with resignation, becomes more and more apparent with each decade of the nineteenth century. Readers who might once have been impressed mainly by the stoic courage expressed in a play like Corneille's *Horace* were now touched by the *human* response of Corneille's heroine:

> *Quand je songe à leur mort, quoi que je me propose,*
> *Je songe par quel bras, et non pour quelle cause,*
> *Et ne vois les vainqueurs en leur illustre rang*
> *Que pour considérer aux dépens de quel sang.* *

Liberals everywhere looked to the United States for a lead. The Englishmen who established the London Peace Society in 1816 were delighted to learn that a similar body had already been founded in New York in 1815, and that a Massachusetts Peace Society had come into being at almost exactly the same moment as the London movement.

The New York group was launched by a Connecticut-born businessman, David Low Dodge, who spread the word by enclosing peace tracts in boxes of merchandise. Within a few years peace societies were reported in Ohio; Raleigh, North Carolina; Augusta, Georgia; Rhode Island, Vermont, Maine, Connecticut and Philadelphia. The most active however was the Massachusetts Peace Society. Its founder, the Reverend Noah Worcester, had served in the Revolutionary War but then had begun to doubt whether military service was compatible with Christian benevolence. In 1814 he published his *Solemn Review of the Custom of War,* an able little book which recommended the formation of local peace societies and, on a grander scale, of a sort of league of nations. The *Solemn Review,* while never widely

---

* When I think of their death, no matter what I tell myself, I think by whose arm, and not for what cause, and only picture the conquerors in their illustrious rank to ask myself, at the expense of whose blood?

popular, had a sober originality that led to its being reprinted several times over the next thirty years. Worcester was joined in his efforts by such distinguished Bostonians as the president of Harvard, Josiah Quincy, and the Reverend William Ellery Channing. They issued a periodical, *Friend of Peace*. They appealed to the clergy to take their rightful place at the head of the crusade. They took comfort from the assurance of Quincy that "Revolutions go not backward! Neither does the moral and intellectual progress of the multitude. Light is shining where once there was darkness." They made elaborate calculations of the extent of warfare. According to their figures mankind had been afflicted with 286 major wars, and altogether 3,346,000,000 lives had been "sacrificed to the idol of war."[26]

The drawback of their activity, as they knew, was that it reached only a few like-minded people. They were greatly heartened by the emergence of a new leader, William Ladd. He was not a minister or a college professor but a man who had had a varied, vigorous and successful career as ship's captain, merchant and farmer. Throwing his energies into the movement, he proceeded to organize it on a nationwide basis as the American Peace Society (1828). Under his driving force and his cheerful inspiration a wider range of Americans was drawn in. Colleges were stimulated to offer prizes for essays on the theme of "A Congress of Nations for the Prevention of War." Ladd assembled a selection of these papers, with a brilliant essay of his own, in a volume published in 1840.

Close contact was maintained with English pacifists. Channing, James Russell Lowell and Ralph Waldo Emerson were among the men of letters who broadened the appeal of the movement. "War," said Emerson in a lecture of 1838, "is on its last legs; and a universal peace is as sure as the prevalence of civilization over barbarism, of liberal governments over feudal forms. The question for us is only, *How soon?*" It became linked with most of the other reform movements of the time — abolitionism, temperance, women's rights. Thomas C. Upham, a philosophy professor at Bowdoin College, expressed this sense of total, and religious, involvement, in his *Manual of Peace* (1836):

Every great moral and religious principle is a pillar in the millennial temple. The principle of total abstinence from all intoxicating liquors is one pillar . . . : the doctrine that all slave-holding is a sin is another pillar . . . : the doctrine of the absolute inviolability of human life is another; . . . and thus principle after principle will be established, column after column will be erected, till the spiritual house of the Lord shall be established in the tops of the mountains.

An eloquent new voice was that of the remarkable Elihu Burritt, a self-taught blacksmith who burst upon the circle of reformers with a vehement lecture on international peace which he delivered in Boston in 1843. In the next ten years he campaigned tirelessly. He traveled in Europe, fascinating British sympathizers. He badgered public men. In the face of every sort of discouragement he managed with others to organize four international peace conferences in Europe.[27]

Disputes over America's Mexican policy brought support to the peace advocates from a number of Northerners who were alarmed not merely by the threat of war but by the prospect of the spread of slavery into newly conquered provinces. The young lawyer-orator Charles Sumner electrified a Boston audience when in 1845, invited to deliver a Fourth of July oration, he held forth not on the expected theme of American virtue and valor, but on the idea that "stripped of all delusive apology . . . , War falls from glory into barbarous guilt, taking its place among bloody transgressions, while its flaming honors are turned into shame." What use, he asked, were the nation's army and navy, its fortifications, its militia? The army was too small to have any real function. Most of its sixty posts were pointless: thus, why should there be artillery detachments in "the quiet town of New London, in Connecticut" and in "that pleasant resort of fashion, Newport"? The navy was likewise too small to perform its pretended duties, and absurdly expensive. One of the peace advocates, Samuel E. Coues, claimed that "the annual profits of the whole mercantile marine of the country do not equal the annual expenditure of our Navy," which was supposed to be protecting it. The free cities of Bremen and Hamburg managed to carry on an extensive commerce overseas with not a single warship to back them up.

America's ponderous coastal fortifications had locked enormous sums "in the odious mortmain of their everlasting masonry," and to no purpose except perhaps to "invite the attack they might be inadequate to defeat." The militia, worthless even as a domestic police, was a charade of warlike pomp. Its grotesque uniforms catered to the same primitive taste for finery which "fantastically bedecks the dusky feather-cinctured chief of the soft regions warmed by the tropical sun." The ideas of Sumner and of more moderate liberals such as Francis Wayland, the author of widely read texts in political economy and moral philosophy, were too much in the air to be ignored. Henry W. Halleck felt obliged to devote a long introductory section in his *Elements of Military Art and Science* (1846) to a refutation of Wayland and Sumner.

When the Mexican War broke out the testimony of the peace advocates was intensified. James Russell Lowell made his spokesman Hosea Biglow declare:

> *Ez fer war, I call it murder —*
> *There you have it plain and flat;*
> *I don't want to go no furder*
> *Than my Testyment fer that.*

The American Peace Society offered a prize of five hundred dollars "for the best Review of the Mexican War on the principles of Christianity, and an enlightened statesmanship." It was won by a New Hampshire clergyman, Abiel Abbot Livermore, who gave a comprehensive summons of arguments against carnage in general and this carnage in particular. Among the other deplorable features of the war, he noted that many of its battles "were fought wholly or partly on the Sabbath. . . . When men commit themselves to this murderous business, they generally shut out God, and the thought of his laws, and their accountableness to him, from their mind, and know no religion, no Sabbath, no mercy."[28]

Much of this writing is repetitive, as in antislavery or other reform propaganda. One finds the same quotations from Kant and Hume and Milton, the same proofs (for instance, of the fallaciousness of the maxim "in time of peace, prepare for war"), and the same examples of what could be done constructively with the money spent on armaments ("for the annual sum lavished on a single ship of the line," as Sumner put it, "*four* institutions like Harvard University could be supported"), the same praise for peace-loving men (Numa Pompilius, the Quakers, the Moravians, the Shakers) and peace-loving societies such as Switzerland, San Marino and "the Loochoo Islands, situated in the neighborhood of the Chinese Sea." Indeed the Chinese themselves were sometimes held by Jeffersonian Americans to provide an object lesson for the United States. Here was a large, stable, civilized nation, whose rulers were philosophers and whose people were farmers, which lived by having as little as possible to do with the world outside: "It is well understood that the Chinese are almost entirely destitute of military resources and power; nor do they appear to have any military aptitudes. . . . But what nation stands more secure?"[29]

Some of the contentions of the peace advocates were open to more than one interpretation. Some of their views were eccentric. The movement revealed the characteristic weakness of reform organizations, in becoming divided within itself between the moderates, who believed that in special circumstances men might be right to defend themselves by force, and the "ultras," who would admit no such circumstance. Men like William Lloyd Garrison, who founded the New England Non-Resistance Society in 1838, insisted that they were citizens of the world. The slogans of nationalism — "my country, right or wrong" — could not command allegiance when they clashed with Christian duty. Such extreme declarations alienated sympathizers; and the movement as a whole disintegrated in the face of the growing sectional crisis of the 1850's. When war was impending, in Europe as in America, the slogans of peace seemed to fade into irrelevance — at least for the public men who, like Horace Greeley, had formerly associated themselves with the cause. Even in the United States it had after all not proved possible to abolish the regular army and navy, let alone abolish war itself. Men who had once asserted hopefully that it takes two to make a quarrel were now resignedly conscious that it may take two to preserve a peace.[30]

3

THE MARTIAL SPIRIT

A universal and perpetual peace, it is to be feared, is in the catalogue of events which will never exist but in the imaginations of visionary philosophers, or in the breasts of benevolent enthusiasts.

— James Madison, *National Gazette*, 2 February 1792

Have republics in practice been less addicted to war than monarchies?

— Alexander Hamilton, *The Federalist*, No. 6

Our country not only puts in her claim for her military prowess, but also for her naval feats of skill and bravery, from the early days of our existence.

— Samuel Lorenzo Knapp, *Lectures on American Literature*, 1829

I doubt whether there has ever been a strenuous pacifist who has not been fascinated by war and violence.

— H. Stuart Hughes, *History as Art and as Science*, 1964

DEATH OF GENERAL PIKE.

WAR AND PATRIOTISM

The failure of the peace movement was, however, more deeply rooted. It was not just the collapse of one more bizarre minor program of social reform. Though there were only a few thousand active participants, millions of Americans were antimilitarist enough to respond to at least some part of the peace message. But only in part. It was a message for Sundays; and two other days of the week were named for the god of war — Wotan, Thor — who also had a message. Nor of course was the Christian God an entire worshipper of peace. *Blessed are the meek* might be the lesson of Christ; it was not the word of God the Father, the God of wrath as He appeared in the Old Testament.

War had been a recurrent, almost endemic element in American history. For several generations of colonial settlers, fighting and bloodshed were inescapable. The French, the Spanish and the Indians were real enemies, as a hundred American communities could testify.[1] King William's War ran on intermittently from 1689 to 1697. Five years later began the sporadic combat of Queen Anne's War, which continued until 1713. There was war again with the Spanish from 1739 to 1743, with the French from 1744 to 1748, and with the French again from 1754 to 1763. Indian tribes like the Abenakis, the Tuscaroras and the Yemasees — now long vanished — were very present realities to the frontier settlements of New England or the Carolinas. Detroit, Pittsburgh, Vincennes, Pensacola, St. Augustine are only a handful of the places whose early history was bound up with war. By the end of the Revolutionary War nearly every town of any size in the colonies had been attacked or occupied, or both, by the British. The nation's capital was raided and burned in 1814. The Revolutionary War, the War of 1812, the Mexican War and a score of campaigns against the Indians kept alive the traditions of belligerence. American statesmen retained family reminders of the heritage. Lincoln's grandfather was murdered by Indians; so was the grandmother of John C. Calhoun. Henry Clay and Daniel Webster both had sons killed in the Mexican War. Service in the Revolutionary War was an important formative influence upon the young men who were to furnish the nation's leaders. Thus in Washington's bold assault on the Hessians at Trenton, in December 1776, were Lieutenant James Monroe, not yet eighteen years old, in the lead with a company of Virginia troops; and with the artillery, Captain Alexander Hamilton, who was not much older. Even those who did not serve were stirred by the martial atmosphere. John Adams, excited by the military activities he saw in Philadelphia in May 1775, when he was a Massachusetts delegate to the Continental Congress, burst out, "Oh, that I were a soldier, I will be. I am reading military books. Everybody must, will, and shall be a soldier." The notion of enlisting occurred to him several times during the long struggle. He consoled himself with the thought that he was helping the war in his own way. As American minister to France, in March 1780, he noted: "My business is peace, but I think of nothing but war. While our enemies think of nothing else, we ought not to think more of peace than to be ready to treat of it, as soon as it shall be put into the hearts of our foes to be willing for it. Americans must be soldiers, they must war by land and sea; they have no other security."[2]

There was nothing unique in such a record. The peace advocates had to look far afield to cull a few exotic examples of societies which eschewed war. As Sumner and his associates noted with dismay, world literature from Homer to modern times was steeped in martial sentiment. The growing child, said Sumner, "is fed like Achilles, not on honey and milk only, but on bears' marrow and lions' hearts. He draws the nutriment of his soul from a literature whose beautiful fields are moistened by

"Washington at Princeton [January 1777]. Fall of Gen' Hugh Mercer." By M. M. Sanford. Oil on canvas, 35″ x 54″. American amateur painters delighted in rendering battle scenes, even — as in this case — sixty or seventy years after the event.

human blood." Some reformers, including the Grimké sisters of South Carolina, wished to drop Latin and Greek from school curricula, on the ground that these literatures were imbued with a warlike spirit. Upham felt this would accomplish nothing, since the works of modern as well as ancient historians were full of "covert and open approvals and panegyrics of those who have secured great worldly objects by . . . violence and bloodshed. Nor is this evil limited to history. We meet with it in poetry, in statuary, in architecture, in painting; wherever we turn our eyes, we behold it." All nations cherished stories of their battle heroes. Their emblems were, Sumner pointed out, "beasts and birds of prey — lions, leopards, eagles." He regretted that the United States had followed the old mode in choosing the eagle — "carnivorous, ravenous, plundering, destroying, fighting" — instead of some gentler creature for the national escutcheon. He scolded his own state of Massachusetts for including on its seal "a raised arm holding a drawn sabre in a threatening attitude — . . . precisely the emblem once borne on the flag of [piratical] Algiers."[3]

Did this "bellicose anachronism" mean that America was no different from other nations? Had there been no advance since the barbarous dark ages? Sumner, Upham, Livermore and the rest may seem to have had quite unreal expectations for their country. Yet they touched on a real problem, and an embarrassing one for those who wished to believe that the United States was the first truly enlightened nation.

The problem was that warfare was a basic ingredient of American patriotism. From the expeditions of colonial times were derived proofs of native spirit and British ineptitude. The lessons of the Revolutionary War were of a loftier, more memorable dimension. America's national origin, and the first expressions of national character, were largely military in form. They were reinforced by the more gratifying military and naval episodes of the War of 1812. "The Star-Spangled Banner" is a good example of this formative martial impulse: here was a nation fashioned on the battlefield no less than in the council chamber — brought into existence through violence, among the thud of guns and in the rockets' red glare. "The Star-Spangled Banner" is both anthem and battle cry. What other way was there for peoples to secure independence? Was this not a new kind of patriotism, unlike the older nationalisms in being heroically liberal? Were peace-loving Americans, having fought for their own liberty, to condemn the inevitable bloodshed of similar struggles waged in Latin America, in Greece and Poland and Italy? Peace advocates could not agree upon acceptable answers. Thomas Upham, the Bowdoin professor, was in a lonely minority when he asserted that the American Revolution ought to have been initiated gradually and nonviolently, by continuing the policies of protest which had impelled the British to repeal the Stamp Act. America would then eventually have "taken a stand among nations, without that vast amount of crime and misery which attended the [Revolutionary] war."

He was on surer ground, though, in noting that national glory had become "a complex conception, embracing the various elements and capabilities of War": "And as such it is revolved, mused upon, and cherished, till it becomes a sort of personification, a species of animated existence, floating in the air, and radiant with celestial hues, and beckoning the beholders onward and upward to the transcendent heights." He was not greatly exaggerating when he maintained that history was still being written as "a mere series of battles. . . . Military matters are predominant, and everything else is thrown into the background."[4] And this was as true of the United States as it was of European nations. A recent survey has shown that about a third of the space in American history textbooks published before the Civil War was "devoted to military events, fully three times as much as appears in most modern textbooks."[5] The adult appetite for martial literature was no less copiously fed. One need not accept the contention of the peace advocates that this appetite was insatiable and fatal, in agreeing with them that it existed and was supplied on a considerable scale. As a young man, Abraham Lincoln pored over Amos Blanchard's *American Military Biography*, published in 1825. Popular writers like Joel T. Headley, Benson J. Lossing, Charles Jacobs Peterson and John Frost churned out book after book on America's military heritage. *Battles of America by Sea and Land, Daring Deeds of American Generals, Battle-Fields of the Republic* and *Thrilling Incidents of the Wars of the United States* were typical titles. Some accounts were fairly crisp, others bombastic. But in general they followed the same mode as contemporary European literature in equating gallantry and patriotism. Here is a sample comment on the death of Zebulon Montgomery Pike (whose father had also been a soldier) in the War of 1812: "He died thinking of his wife and children, and regretting that his career was cut so short. His wife was a woman who shared all his ambitious longings, and would have incited him to glory, if he had been less athirst for it himself. She heard of her loss with the fortitude of a Roman matron, and lived thereafter to cherish his memory, as a sacred deposit."[6]

Herman Melville, in a letter from Lansingburgh, New York, written in May 1846, said: "People here are all in a state of delirium about the Mexican War. A military order pervades all ranks — Militia Colonels wax red in their coat facings — and 'prentice boys are running off to the wars by scores. — Nothing is talked of but the 'Halls of the Montezumas.' "

A. A. Livermore, three years later, counted forty-eight newly published works on the Mexican conflict, with still more announced. In addition, "not less than half a dozen novels of the cheap kind . . . have already taken their plots and incidents from the war with Mexico." Artists were equally enterprising: "every village has its 'views' of battles, and the siege at Vera Cruz, or the charge at Buena Vista." A British soldier, traveling in the United States shortly afterward, concluded that Americans were "passionately fond of military display and the profession of arms." He prophesied that "such an intense passion for soldiering will . . . eventually lead to . . . more ambitious . . . aspirations after national glory and the achievements of arms."[7]

PRESIDENTS, TITLES, SCHOOLS

In common with some American observers, this foreign traveler may have drawn extravagant conclusions. He was not alone, however, in finding some significance in the American fondness for military Presidents. It must be said that of those with military experience who were elected or nominated up to the end of the Civil War — Washington, Monroe, Andrew Jackson, William H. Harrison, Lewis Cass, Zachary Taylor, Winfield Scott, Franklin Pierce, John C. Frémont, George B. McClellan — none was exactly a Napoleon. Most were amateur soldiers. Harrison became a hero through victory over the Indians in his one Tippecanoe encounter. Pierce's reputation rested on even slighter foundations; serving as a brigadier general in Mexico, he hurt himself by falling off his horse in the only battle in which he was closely involved. Zachary Taylor, nicknamed "Old Rough and Ready" by his soldiers on account of his plain speech and his plain clothes, was no doubt genuine when he told a friend in July 1846 that he did not think himself suitable for the presidency. "My opinion has always been against the elevation of a Military Chief to that

General Zachary Taylor, with bloody sword, sits complacently on a mound of skulls — the victims of the Mexican War. This cartoon is as much anti-Whig as anti-war. It nevertheless indicates the distaste felt by some Americans for war as such, and also for "military chieftains." The message is emphasized by depicting Taylor in the uncharacteristic pomp of full-dress uniform.

MAJOR GENL. WM. H. HARRISON.

This colored lithograph was no doubt produced (ca. 1840) in order to promote the Presidential candidacy of William H. Harrison, better known to us as the "log-cabin and hard cider" man. The interesting feature is that it makes no reference to the peaceable pursuits of Harrison. On the contrary: the central pose is almost Napoleonic, and the surrounding vignettes all show scenes of war.

position," he wrote. When the Whigs persisted in nominating him in 1848 they were sufficiently aware of the force of this objection to present him to the electorate as a man of peace who had also said that he looked upon war "at all times and under all circumstances as a national calamity." Neither Taylor nor his 1848 rival, General Cass, nor any of the other nominees would have been chosen if they had been thought to approve of military predominance in the body politic. Soldier-candidates had two valuable assets which could be deemed military only in a remote sense: they were known to the public and yet their political views were vague enough to avoid alienating any particular group.

Nevertheless, heroism in warfare was admired and was believed to constitute an important claim to America's chief office. Campaign posters of soldier-candidates usually portrayed them in uniform — even if like Taylor they actually preferred civilian dress. Though he was an unorthodox, untidy old warrior, Taylor was after all a regular with forty years' service behind him. Traveling up the Mississippi on his way to be inaugurated as President, he might tell one audience in Memphis that he was opposed to war; he told another at Nashville that "we are emphatically a nation of soldiers." Winfield Scott, the Whig candidate in 1852, was a regular with a similar span of service whom no one would have called untidy. "Old Fuss and Feathers" was open to ridicule and was badly beaten by Pierce, but he *was* chosen. McClellan too might appear to have overweening impulses, and he too was beaten — by Lincoln in 1864 — but he too was chosen by a major party. The military candidate was an equivocal figure, both attractive to the electorate and vulnerable to the ancient charge of military despotism. Andrew Jackson's Democratic supporters pooh-poohed the accusation that he was a "Military Chieftain" but raised the same cry against Taylor. "It is to pave the way for future wars," complained Livermore, "to place camp-schooled and battle-trained Presidents in the White House. . . . We want civilians, not swordsmen. . . . If our consciences were . . . awake, we should reject the idea with horror of making a military man the great man of the nation, and enthroning him aloft as our grand representative. . . . We virtually . . . say by such an act, *that* is our highest ideal of what a great and good man is; *that* is the American man." The interesting feature is that on balance during these decades, the politicians and the electorate seemed to find more appeal than menace in candidates who had been warriors.[8]

The American relish for military titles is another phenomenon which puzzled foreign travelers. It would be foolish to pretend that the explanation was narrowly military. Honorific titles (including "Judge" and "Doctor") attested to the need of an open society to invent distinctions. They were a useful adjunct, especially for men in public life, and were distributed wholesale by state governors anxious to reward political followers. "Colonel" House of Texas, Woodrow Wilson's friend and adviser, was the recipient in a later day of such a favor. Back in seventeenth-century Massachusetts, said a military chronicler, "it is remarkable, in the early . . . records, to observe, that those who filled important civil offices are noticed by the appellation of Mr. only, while such as held military commissions were always distinguished by the titles which their rank conferred." The custom was universal in the America of Andrew Jackson. "Colonel" Dick Thompson, a Whig politician from Indiana, acquired the title in 1834 through being appointed an honorary aide by the governor. The *Army & Navy Chronicle,* noting that the custom flourished in several states, mentioned in 1840 a list of "thirty-two gentlemen" of Georgia, "announced as having been appointed aids to the Governor, with the rank of *colonel.*" The abundance of these titles, though not amusing to regular soldiers, provided a stock theme for humorists. Martin Chuzzlewit, in Dickens's novel, discovered that he shared his New York boardinghouse with "four majors . . . , two colonels, one general, and a captain, so that he could not help thinking how strongly officered the American militia must be; and wondering . . . whether the officers commanded each other; or if they did not, where on earth the privates came from." A Texas newspaper said in 1842:

If the little army with which we are preparing to contend with Mexico should perish, . . . and Texas should erect a monument to their memory, . . . giving the fallen heroes their nominal titles, then will future generations suppose the two opposing armies to have out-numbered the countless hosts of Xerxes. . . .

> *Forty generals died like heroes*
> *To break the chains of modern Neroes.*
> *Eighty Colonels lie beneath; —*
> *In freedom's cause they suffer'd death.*
> *One hundred majors shed their blood,*
> *Like water for their country's good.*
> *One thousand Captains led the van. .*
> *And all died fighting — to a man. . . .*[9]

But when all the necessary allowances are made, some military significance remains. Not all military titles were honorary, and not all the holders unversed in military affairs. Who would grudge Daniel Boone or David Crockett their colonelcies? As for "Colonel" Dick Thompson, he had at least served an apprentice-ship in a militia cavalry company. Chapter 7 gives other instances to show that although the currency of military titles was wildly inflated in the United States, it was not altogether baseless. The humorists are not a complete guide to the spirit of the age.

If we hesitate in assessing the significance of military titles, the same uncertainty surrounds the question of military academies. Though many were founded, the majority seemed to have closed down after a few years. In some cases they tried to keep going by decreasing the military portion of the curriculum. In a few instances — La Grange Academy in Alabama is one — the school was converted *into* a military establishment. The fortunes of all private schools, military or otherwise, were shaky. The failure rate for military academies may have been no higher than that of purely civilian institutions. The unexpected fact — unexpected if one is accustomed to think of the United States as essentially unmilitary — is that so many American boys were sent to prepar-atory schools where they wore uniforms and learned to drill and handle firearms. °

° The distinction between preparatory schools and colleges was blurred in nineteenth-century America. Ages of admission and graduation varied widely, and

SOLDIERS AND CIVILIANS

The best-known of such academies are the Virginia Military Institute (V.M.I.) at Lexington, which began its independent existence in 1839, and the Citadel at Charleston, South Carolina, which opened its doors in 1843. Both are still in existence. They were soon established on a sound footing, thanks to a convenient scheme which was copied elsewhere. Each state had one or more arsenals in which militia weapons were housed. The state was obliged to provide a handful of men to guard and maintain this equipment. At V.M.I., the Charleston Citadel and the Arsenal at Columbia, South Carolina, the annual appropriation for weapons storage was allotted to a military school which could take over guard duties. Such schools caused little or no extra expense to individual states. They therefore satisfied the demands of economy, the call for military instruction, the anxieties of parents who felt their sons were out of control, and the need for more educational institutions. Some states offered scholarships for poor boys, who in return undertook to become schoolteachers in their own counties. V.M.I. and the Citadel — the Columbia Arsenal did not prosper — were accordingly imitated by the Georgia Military Institute (1851) and by a number of other Southern military establishments, including Louisiana's Military Academy, which opened in 1860 with William T. Sherman as its first head. Most of them adapted their regulations, their uniforms and their methods of instruction from West Point practice. A good many of their professors, like Sherman in Louisiana and T. J. Jackson at V.M.I., were West Point graduates.[10]

These are Southern examples. But the earliest military school in the country was Alden Partridge's American Literary, Scientific and Military Academy at Norwich, Vermont. Partridge, a former superintendent at West Point, started his own academy in 1819. It and he had checkered careers — though it is worth

within the same class. A further complication is that on the eve of the Civil War a few states, including Tennessee and Alabama, began to introduce military education into their university systems. Some academies were mainly preparatory to college education; others, especially in the South, were academy and college in one. There is no nationwide study of military schools. For the South, see John Hope Franklin, *The Militant South, 1800–1861* (Cambridge, Mass., 1956), 144–170; and Edgar W. Knight, *Documentary History of Education in the South before 1860* (5 vols., Chapel Hill, N.C., 1949–1953), IV, 149–243.

KENTUCKY MILITARY INSTITUTE.

noting that his original foundation is still in being, and still with a military flavor, as Norwich University. For the next thirty-five years, until his death in 1854, Partridge tirelessly drummed home the lessons of his first prospectus: American liberty depended upon proper military training, for "if the great body of American Citizens do not feel that they are something more than merely nominal soldiers, our population will gradually degenerate." At the start his enterprise flourished, first at Norwich, then (1825–1829) at Middletown, Connecticut (where "no doubt he felt that a location by the ocean would bring him many naval . . . students"), then back at Norwich. He invented expedients that were later followed by Southern schools, and even went further than they did, in offering courses of lectures intended mainly for militia officers, and in successfully petitioning Congress to lend him "seven cannon and the necessary ammunition." He persuaded the Vermont and Connecticut authorities to lend him muskets.

He advertised his academy, and delighted the young men and women of New England, by taking his cadets on summer marching tours. A Connecticut man who met Partridge's cadets on one of these tours remembered them admiringly as "a bright bevy of blooming boys, carrying little guns, and dressed in gray jackets, white trousers, and jaunty caps, [who] manoeuvred with the pride and precision of veterans."[11] Among the cadets who attended his school in its heyday were Horatio Seymour, Thomas H. Seymour, and Thomas Bragg, future governors of New York, Connecticut and North Carolina respectively; Gideon Welles, Lincoln's Secretary of the Navy; Orestes Brownson, the erratic New England reformer, whom it is hard to think of in military guise; and George H. Derby, later a West Point graduate who was better known as the humorist "John Phoenix."

The popularity of Partridge's academy declined for various reasons, but it continued to be headed by him until 1843, as Norwich University. He had an interest in many other establishments — indeed in so many that it is a wonder he could remember them all. Thus after 1835 he was principal of the American Classical and Military Lyceum at Germantown, Pennsylvania. It had been founded in 1807 as Mount Airy College and had become a military school in 1826, under the direction of a West Point graduate. Some of Mount Airy's cadets in turn entered West Point: for example, Henry du Pont and George G. Meade. Partridge or his former students (with himself usually to the fore) founded or transformed schools based on the Norwich pattern all over the Union. The list includes New Jersey Institution (Orange, New Jersey, 1828), Jefferson Military College (Washington, Mississippi, ca. 1828), the Literary, Scientific and Military Academy of Fayetteville, North Carolina (1825), an academy of similar name at Oxford, North Carolina (1829), one at Portsmouth, Virginia (1839), successive academies at Bristol and Harrisburg, Pennsylvania (1842 and 1845), another at Pembroke, New Hampshire (1850), Mount Pleasant Military Academy (Sing Sing, New York, 1854), and the Highland Military Academy (Worcester, Massachusetts, 1857).

Alden Partridge was an unlucky man. Whatever he put his

hand to seemed to meet with frustration and eventual failure.
Most of the schools he was directly concerned with burned down,
lost their impetus, or were otherwise unfortunate. The academy
at Portsmouth, Virginia, for instance, opened at the moment
when V.M.I. was emerging as the state's chief military school;
Partridge's could not stand the competition. But his preachments
were influential, and at least some of the establishments with
which he was connected had a long life. The schools at Sing Sing
and Worcester, Massachusetts, were particularly successful. So
was the Collegiate and Commercial Institute of New Haven,
Connecticut — a more martial affair than its name disclosed. Its
proprietor, Major General William H. Russell, was a onetime
pupil of Partridge's, and the school became well known. A guide-
book which praises the soldierly precision of the students refers
to two other military schools in the New Haven area. One of
these, at Hamden, was started by a clergyman in 1843. He
employed two instructors in military tactics and the boys wore
uniforms of "West Point Gray."[12] The academy at Weston, Connecticut, was similar; and so was Hlasko's Academy in Philadelphia, which was active in the 1850's.

Whether or not Partridge was the promoter, whether or not a

WESTON BOARDING SCHOOL,
A COMMERCIAL AND MILITARY INSTITUTE FOR BOYS,
WESTON, CONN.
A. S. Jarvis   Principal

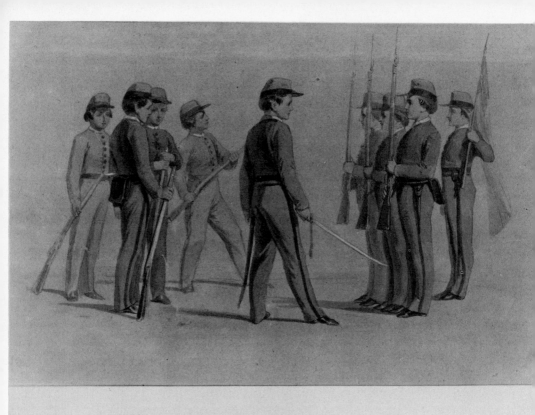

PHILADELPHIA CADETS

school was guaranteed a measure of permanence by receiving state support, the number and variety of military academies show that in this respect as in others America was not entirely unsympathetic to martial practices. The idea took hold that education for boys could well be conducted on lines resembling those of West Point. Military schools tended, not surprisingly, to be founded in periods when war was a recent memory or a future possibility. Hence the patchy nature of their development. But they were generally well received and were discussed approvingly in the press and in periodicals. There were no such schools in England, though the British regular army of the period was six or seven times larger than that of the United States. They are a manifestation of a people that believed in teaching "the young idea how to shoot" — however we choose to interpret the phrase.

Another quasi-military phenomenon, the veterans' organization, did not come into full swing until after the Civil War, with the foundation of the G.A.R. (Grand Army of the Republic). But the idea goes back as early as the Cincinnati (1783). During the Mexican War a group of officers, including Zachary Taylor and Robert E. Lee, founded a hereditary society, the Aztec Club, based on the same principles. A society for regulars and volunteers who had served in the Mexican War, the Scott Legion, was established in Pennsylvania in 1850. After a Rip Van Winklish slumber, the War of 1812 veterans began to come to life in various states — no doubt stirred by the prospect of cheap excursion rates on the railroads, as well as by vague but heady notions of land grants and pensions. "Who but the Soldier and his family," they asked, "should eat the bread from the Soil his own blood has enriched?"[13]

The Revolutionary War laid down a thick stratum of martial-patriotic lore. Each fresh war laid down another. These brightly colored patches were separated by eras of a quieter and therefore less conspicuous hue. The warlike interludes associated with national independence were succeeded by the truculence of Young America. According to Livermore, a supposedly peace-loving nation was thoroughly indoctrinated in war and violence. How? "It is," he answered,

by the wooden sword, and the tin drum of boyhood. It is by the training and the annual muster. It is by the red uniform and the white plume, and the prancing steed. It is by the cannon's thunder, and the gleam of the bayonet. It is by ballads of Robin Hood, and histories of Napoleon, and "Tales of the Crusaders." It is by the presentation of flags by the hands of the fair, and the huzzas for a victory. It is by the example of the father and the consent of the mother. It is by the fear of cowardice, and the laugh of the scorner. It is by the blood of youth, and the pride of manhood, and stories of revolutionary sires. It is by standing armies, and majestic men-of-war. It is by the maxims of self defence, and the cheapness of human life, and the love of excitement. It is by novels of love, and the "Pirate's Own Book." It is by the jars of home, and the squabbles of party, and the controversies of sect. . . . It is by the bubble of glory, and the emulation of schools, and the graspings of money making. By one and all, the heart of the community is educated for war, from the cradle to the coffin.[14]

BRAVADO AND VIOLENCE

Lincoln in his 1838 lecture to the Young Men's Lyceum in Springfield said that America was utterly safe from foreign invasion. But he did not mean that there was no danger. On the contrary, the theme of his talk was that the nation faced a serious *internal* danger from the "increasing disregard for law" which could, he thought, lead in time to the appearance of some exceptional man with the ambitions of "an Alexander, a Caesar, or a Napoleon."

The problem which Lincoln examined was hardly new. Its polar aspects are set out in Crèvecoeur's *Letters from an American Farmer* (1782). The famously idyllic passages in Crèvecoeur depict a society which is rational, modest, tolerant, agrarian. War and bloodshed are alien to this peaceable kingdom of Quakerish farmers. Yet in other, less familiar chapters — especially in the *Sketches* which were omitted from the 1782 edition — Crèvecoeur shows that even in America, the nearest approach to the earthly paradise, men are still capable of savagery. In the Carolinas, Crèvecoeur finds a Negro imprisoned in a cage and left to die of starvation and exposure. Whether he in fact witnessed such a spectacle is immaterial. He introduces it as the image of an injustice so monstrous that it invaded and was liable to destroy the dream of tranquility. What Crèvecoeur *did* witness was still more nightmarish to him. His idyllic America was that of pre-Revolutionary days, under the mild yet powerful influence of

British rule. Suddenly the quiet days were gone. Caught in the midst of anger, accusation, violence, he was unable to commit himself to the colonists' side, and sailed for Europe. The American experiment that Crèvecoeur extolled was that of successfully diminishing social restraint. External, governmental authority had been reduced almost to the vanishing point. With the Revolution, the vital invisible underpinning was removed. The basic sense of order was now in jeopardy. Freedom might prove equivalent to bloody anarchy.

Crèvecoeur's worst fears were not realized. But the succession of wars and alarms produced a civilization in which, as Livermore said, there was probably not "a house in the country, unless it belong to a Quaker or a Non-resistant, without its sword, pistol, musket, or rifle." In the 1830's the nightmare Crèvecoeur had glimpsed seemed to be returning. In Lincoln's words: "Accounts of outrages committed by mobs, form the every-day news of the times. They have pervaded the country, from New England to Louisiana; . . . they are not the creature of climate — neither are they confined to the slaveholding, or the non-slaveholding States. . . . Whatever . . . their cause may be, it is common to the whole country."[15]

Lincoln went on to describe some recent examples. He was not alone in expressing alarm. In October 1834 the *Boston Whig* said: "The history of . . . the past year furnishes examples of outrage and violence altogether unprecedented in the annals of our country." The *New England Magazine* published an article in November 1834 entitled "The March of Anarchy." *Niles' Register* commented (5 September 1835): "During the last and the present week we have cut out and laid aside more than 500 articles, relating to the various *excitements* now acting on the people of the United States, public and private! *Society seems everywhere unhinged.*"

Some of this violence was particularly prevalent in the raw frontier communities of the West and South. All along the frontier there was sporadic trouble between whites and Indians, in which the brutality of the Americans became steadily more disproportionate to the size of the real or imagined offense. The

83

whites too went on the warpath. Regular officers in the Mexican War were horrified by the behavior of American amateur soldiery. One officer wrote that the volunteers stationed in Matamoros "have killed five or six innocent people walking in the streets, for no other object than their own amusement; to-be-sure, they are always drunk, and are in a measure irresponsible. . . . They rob and steal the cattle and corn of the poor farmers, and in fact act more like a body of hostile Indians than of civilized whites. Their own officers have no . . . control over them."[16]

Dueling, a ceremonial form of violence imported from Europe, was fairly common in the early republic. The shooting of Alexander Hamilton by Aaron Burr in 1804 is a celebrated instance. In 1806 a prominent Boston Federalist got into a fight with a political opponent on State Street and shot him dead. Andrew Jackson killed a man in a pistol duel in the same year, outside Nashville, Tennessee. In 1813 he was involved in two comical yet sanguinary encounters with Jesse and Thomas Hart Benton, the latter of whom was to be one of his staunch supporters in the Senate. Members of Congress were frequently at odds. Sam Houston, while a representative from Tennessee, wounded an opponent in a duel. John Randolph of Virginia exchanged shots with Secretary of State Henry Clay in 1826. Representative Jonathan Cilley of Maine, in a duel with rifles at eighty paces, was killed by Representative William Graves of Kentucky in 1838. This incident aroused so much public comment that the custom of dueling virtually ended in the North. It had in any case become rare there by 1830.

Southern and Western politicians — and newspaper editors — continued to flout the law. A South Carolinian badly wounded the young banker August Belmont in a duel in Indiana in 1841. William L. Yancey of Alabama staged a duel in 1845 with a fellow congressman from Kentucky, though they were interrupted before they had done any damage. Some Southerners carried their truculence into Congress. One of the most notorious incidents, in 1856, took place in the Senate chamber, when Representative Preston Brooks caned Charles Sumner into unconsciousness. Six years earlier, also in the Senate, Henry S. Foote of

84

Mississippi had drawn a loaded revolver on Thomas Hart Benton. Not quite all the truculence came from the South. When Benjamin F. Wade of Ohio entered the Senate in 1851 he dared Southerners to fight him, and laid a brace of pistols on his desk to demonstrate that he was in earnest. After the attack on Sumner, Wade joined forces with Senator Zachariah Chandler of Michigan and Senator Simon Cameron of Pennsylvania to challenge any Southern senator who affronted the North.

These were stylized brawls, with much talk of honor and gentlemanliness. But the usual fight in frontier settlements was a savage affair of fists, knives, pistols, shotguns — any weapon that came to hand. Some towns were plagued by murderous bullies like Alexander McClung of Vicksburg, the "Black Knight of the South," who slaughtered seven members of a family with which he was feuding and who eventually committed suicide. One such person set off a train of violence in Natchez, Mississippi, which was among the stories of disorder cited by Lincoln. The occasion, in 1835, was a Fourth of July celebration. A bellicose drunk interfered with a militia parade. The infuriated militiamen tarred and feathered him, recognizing him as one of the gamblers who infested the town. Later a crowd of militia and other citizens began to break up the Natchez gambling houses. One of the crowd was shot. In revenge, five gamblers were hanged.[17]

This was lynch law. Eighteenth-century groups such as the Carolina Regulators had been quick to take the law into their own hands. The term "Lynch's law" came into use in Virginia sometime after the Revolution. By the 1820's it was the name commonly applied throughout the United States to describe the "popular administration of justice." At its worst it was a mere excuse for private vengeance — Bacon had defined revenge as "a kind of wild justice" — or for mob violence. Though at first it was a frontier phenomenon, in which the punishment allotted might be nothing worse than tarring and feathering or being ridden out of town on a fence rail, by degrees lynch law became a feature of some well-settled communities; and the punishment was more and more commonly death. As the Natchez incident shows, the evolution could be rapid, and the victims might be white or

Negro. The only discrimination was in the degree of brutality. Thirty-seven Negroes were summarily executed in Charleston in 1822, when word got out that Denmark Vesey, a free Negro, was planning an insurrection. About a hundred Negroes were shot down in the giant manhunt that followed the Nat Turner slave rising in Southampton County, Virginia, in 1832; and another twenty, including Turner, were executed after trial. There was some excuse for violence on this scale, given the Southern dread of slave insurrections and the fact that Turner's followers slaughtered over fifty whites before the outbreak was crushed. There was no excuse for the episode in St. Louis in 1836 in which — as Lincoln said — a free Negro was "chained to a tree, and actually burned to death." The same appalling treatment was meted out in 1835 to two Negroes near Mobile, Alabama, who were supposed to have murdered a couple of children.

White men escaped burning. But they could not escape lynch justice. Illinois mobs murdered the "abolitionist martyr" Elijah P. Lovejoy in 1837 and the Mormon leader Joseph Smith in 1844. Fanatical abolitionists of the John Brown stamp retaliated in kind: martyrdom and massacre were two sides of the same coin. The boxes of rifles sent to warring abolitionists in "Bleeding Kansas" in the 1850's were nicknamed "Beecher's Bibles" after the abolitionist clergyman Henry Ward Beecher. The devout could cite contrary texts — "They that live by the sword shall perish by the sword" and "I bring you not peace but a sword." Mormon doctrine was peaceful enough, and the Mormons were abominably treated. Yet their own behavior was hardly lamblike. Shortly before his death Joseph Smith persuaded the governor of Illinois to commission him as a militia general, so that he became in effect the head of a private army of three thousand Mormons, the Nauvoo Legion. The Mormons were feared as well as disliked by the other Americans who took the Oregon Trail west with them in 1846. Once in Utah, they committed the "Mountain Meadows Massacre," and the ensuing "Mormon War" of 1857–1858 occupied a sizable contingent of the United States regular army. Military and paramilitary activity were confused in the public mind. A character in William Gilmore Simms's novel *Woodcraft*

(1854), about to lynch someone, explains to the victim with no trace of irony: "The good citizens of a country must always constitute a standing army for the purposes of public justice and public security."

This was certainly the belief of the vigilance committees which sprang up in San Francisco (and then rapidly in other Western communities) in the 1850's. A contemporary wrote that San Francisco "seems to be a doomed city. . . . They have there the scum of the lazar-houses of Europe and Australia. There are regularly-formed gangs of desperadoes, who would as readily burn the city, murder, rob and steal, as eat." When a fire department was established in 1847, its first duty was "to hang seven men for setting a building on fire, and murdering the inmates of another dwelling."[18] A gang variously styling itself as the "Hounds" and as the "Society of Regulators" terrorized the neighborhood. Though it was driven out, disorder continued until the more respectable citizens formed a vigilance committee in 1851. They restored order by fairly drastic means. But after a few years things were worse than ever. There were over a hundred murders in the area during the six months before May 1856, when the San Francisco vigilantes came into being for the second time. Their achievement was remarkable. In the next six months there were only two murders. They enrolled over two thousand men, with extraordinary speed and efficiency, grouped them into companies, selected officers and started to drill. They procured muskets from a supplier who had originally intended the weapons for a filibustering expedition in Central America. They acquired twenty cannon from ships lying in the Bay. The Vigilance Committee set up headquarters in a building protected by sandbags — and so known as "Fort Gunnybags." In it were stores, an armorer's shop and a small hospital. Other equipment they improvised included a barricade on wheels for street fighting. By the time they disbanded, in August 1856, the committee was in control of a force of eight thousand men — as large as some of McDowell's divisions at Bull Run.

A laudable achievement, no doubt; and the same may be said of much of the justice dispensed in frontier mining and farm settlements, in which the aim was to provide a form of law where none existed. The important elements for our purposes are first, the American talent for *ad hoc* organization, and second, the American enthusiasm for what we have called paramilitary organization. In San Francisco the 1856 vigilantes were after all not the only representatives of law and order. A police force already existed. There were several volunteer companies and the skeleton of a state militia system. There were regular troops with artillery in the vicinity, and a warship commanded by David Farragut. A former regular officer, William T. Sherman, now a San Francisco banker, accepted a major general's militia commission to restore law and order where it properly belonged — namely to the authorities, instead of Fort Gunnybags. Sherman was prepared to fight a pitched battle with the vigilantes, and asked Farragut and the regular army commander for naval support and for arms. After Sherman resigned in disgust, the tension between the vigilantes and the "law and order" party continued to grow. Judge Terry of the state Supreme Court fatally wounded a vigilante in an affray. He took refuge in one of the "law and order" strongholds, the arsenal of the San Francisco Blues. The arsenal was at once surrounded by a posse of vigilantes who arrested Terry and took him off to Gunnybags, along with the Blues' collection of arms. Terry was eventually released and the vigilantes disbanded. Posterity has been kind to them and critical of Sherman, Terry and others who sought to interpose official authority between the vigilantes and San Francisco's criminals. In truth Sherman comes out of the story badly; but then, as he said of the vigilantes in his memoirs: "They controlled the press, they wrote their own history . . . but their success has given great stimulus to a dangerous principle, that would at any time justify the mob in seizing all the power of government."[19]

Possibly they provided a stimulus for rival groups in the New Orleans municipal elections of 1858, when Pierre G. T. Beauregard ran as mayor on a coalition ticket against the Know-Nothing party. Beauregard's followers, stigmatizing their opponents as a lawless mob, constituted themselves into a vigilance committee with over a thousand armed men at their back. They appropriated artillery from a state arsenal. The Know-Nothings in turn demanded arms from the city government. For several days a battle seemed imminent. In spite of the vigilantes' activity, and their virtuous condemnation of the Know-Nothings, they lost the election.

Still, the stimulus was hardly needed in American cities, whose growing pains were rendered worse by the lack of adequate police. They had known a generation of rioting, much of it paramilitary in flavor. Nativism, minority sentiment and political faction formed a curious amalgam. The fire companies were a perfect epitome of this. Their members, whether in Boston, New York, Philadelphia or New Orleans, were volunteers. They wore uniforms. They were competitive, high-spirited and reckless. Some were hostile to immigrants, others were made up of Irishmen. They were closely involved in ward politics and were linked with military companies (so that they were ready-made recruits for the Zouave companies of 1860–1861). A short-lived periodical, the *New York Pioneer*, began publication in 1840 with the announcement that it was to be "devoted to the Military and Fire Department." A similar claim was made by the *Eclaireur*, another New York militia periodical which ran in the 1850's.

In New York in the early 1840's, the Black Joke Fire Company (until abolished by the Common Council, after it got into a brawl with other companies) was an offshoot of Tammany Hall, the Democratic machine. One of its leaders, Malachi Fallon, a Tammany politico, was warden of the Tombs prison — when he was not looking after the Ivy-Green Saloon of which he was proprietor — and also found time to command two independent military companies, the Baxter Blues and the Black Joke Volunteers. When the Common Council broke up his little empire, Fallon moved west to a post he must have felt at home in: he became San Francisco's chief of police.

A contemporary, David Dana, claimed that in one American city the aldermen, "who had failed to sustain an efficient [fire] department on account of opposing political sentiments, . . . were engaged in hiring gangs of rowdies to assault the firemen while in the discharge of their duties." He gives an example from the New York chief engineer's report for 1856 ("Engine Company No. 41 was proceeding at great speed to a fire, when they were attacked by these miscreants with clubs, sling-shots, and stones. Several members of the company were knocked down, and one of them was run over by the engine, and maimed for life"). He adds: "It is useless to look to the police . . . for the remedy. They DARE NOT APPLY IT, the political influence of these villains is so great."[20]

It was not always easy to tell whether the New York fire companies were for or against the law. More precisely, they were their own law — their own standing army. Street gangs of obviously criminal propensity also uniformed themselves like private armies. One of the many riots for which the orthodox militia had to be called out took place in 1857 between two gangs known as the "Roach Guards" and the "Dead Rabbits." They clashed on Independence Day in the Bowery; eight men were killed and "clubs, stones, and even pistols were freely used. The 'Dead Rabbits' were beaten and retired, yelling and firing revolvers in the air, and attacking everybody that came in their way. Their uniform was a blue stripe on their pantaloons, while that of the Roach Guards was a red stripe." This account comes from a book by Joel T. Headley, *The Great Riots of New York* (1873). Military and paramilitary seem to have been all one to Headley, whose other popular books included *Napoleon and His Marshals* (1846) and *Washington and His Generals* (1847).

Dana's history of fires is in large part a history of mob violence in the large cities. His tone is odd, for he is bitterly anti-Irish and shows a distinct relish in describing death and destruction. In 1834, when "a party of from fifty to one hundred men, disguised with masks and fantastic dresses and painted faces," smashed and burned a Catholic convent outside Boston, he blandly reports that several fire companies appeared on the scene, but that they made no effort to stop the blaze. Dana's version of a serious Boston riot of 1837 is even more partisan. The riot began when some firemen jostled a crowd of mourners at an Irish funeral procession. More joined in on each side, throwing brickbats and lumps of coal at one another:

The ranks of the Irish were gradually thinned by the arrest of some of their more prominent members, who were carried off to jail amid loud shouts. . . . Finally the Irish gave up the contest just in time to save themselves from the bayonets of the [militia], several companies of which were ordered to the scene. . . .

During the conflict the firemen demolished several tenements, throwing furniture, provisions and children into the street. Feather-beds were ripped open. . . . The east wind wafted the feathers all over the city, causing such a shower as might have been taken, at a little distance, for a snow-storm. A large number of persons were badly injured on both sides, but the Irish suffered most severely. . . . There is not the least doubt that the riot originated in the assault upon the firemen. . . .

Much prejudice and ill blood had, for several years, existed between the fire department and the Irish. . . . It cannot be expected that the members of the fire department will look passively on and see their brethren assaulted, or their "machines" overturned.

Dana's picture of the great Philadelphia riot of 1844 is half-gloating, half-apocalyptic. Again the antagonists were American nativists — by this time politically organized as the Native Amer-

Fighting in Southwark, a Philadelphia suburb, in July 1844, outside the Roman Catholic church of St. Philip Neri. The cannon in the background, manned by sailors, had been brought from a ship at the wharves. The soldiers in the left foreground may represent native militia, or an Irish company known as the Hibernia Greens, at least one member of which was killed. The rioters also had a cannon.

icans — and the Irish. Again fire companies were involved, though now the Irish had their own company to serve as a quasi-military focus. The riot was set off, says Dana, when a meeting of Native Americans was shot at from the Hibernia hose company's headquarters. There was an hour or two of chaos before order was restored. Next day the rioting was resumed. Both sides had plenty of weapons and kept up a running exchange of shots. An Irishman seen with a musket was caught and lynched. The Hibernia building was set on fire. The militia, with cavalry and artillery, paraded about the streets but could not prevent the fire from spreading, since the nativist fire engines stood idly by until many neighboring houses had caught alight. Several Irishmen were shot dead as they escaped from the flames. During the night a Catholic church was destroyed by the mob and the next day, though charged by volunteer cavalry, they burned down another church. Again the fire companies allowed the blaze to spread to adjoining Irish Catholic — or in Dana's word "obnoxious" — property. The rioters burned down a school, a third church, a nunnery and a total of seventy other buildings. Thirteen citizens were killed and more than fifty injured before, on the third day, control was restored with the aid of a detachment of marines and with the imposition of martial law. This was the City of Brotherly Love.[21]

Baltimore's experiences were similar. Paralleling the firemen's "record of good deeds, was a dark record of bloody street fights between rival companies; riots perpetrated in the name of fire companies; murders incidental to these disgraceful scenes; attempting burning of engine houses, and destruction of rival apparatus." Indeed, Baltimore at one time had the nickname "Mob-town." Often, of course, the firemen were participants rather than prime causes. This was true of the riot of 1835 when the mob set fire to the houses of several directors of the failed Bank of Maryland, and of some of the furious election riots of the 1850's. But in the municipal elections of 1856 a fight broke out between the New Market Fire Company and a political gang called the Rip Rap Club, both of them heavily armed, for which a chronicler adopts the vocabulary of a war correspondent: "The battle . . . was bloody and prolonged. The firing is said to have been as regular as by platoons. Many persons were wounded and carried from the ground. The drug stores in the neighborhood were filled with the wounded."[22]

Much the same lurid tale can be told of other cities in other years. There were minor race riots in New York and Philadelphia in 1834. The same year New York suffered the Spring Election riots, whose spirit can be gauged from the subheadings in Headley's *Great Riots:* "A Bloody Fight — Mayor and Officers wounded — Mob triumphant — . . . The Streets blocked by fifteen thousand enraged Whigs — Military called out." In 1834–1835 New York saw riotous attacks made on Dr. Fox, Arthur Tappan and other abolitionists. There was the relatively minor Flour Riot of 1837. There was the savage Astor Place Riot of 1849, which began as a demonstration against the visiting English actor W. C. Macready, a hated rival of the Bowery's favorite American tragedian, Edwin Forrest, and resulted in the death of more than twenty men. There was the complicated feud between the Municipal Police, established in 1853, and the supposedly less corrupt Metropolitan Police, founded in 1857 to replace them. The mayor of New York, Fernando Wood, refused to disband the Municipal force. The two bodies met in a major clash, neither being able to claim total victory. For several weeks afterward the city suffered from two swaggering police gangs, each more concerned to smash the other than to put down crime.[23] George Templeton Strong voiced in his diary the frustrated disgust of civic-minded New Yorkers at these recurrent disorders. He was outraged, for example, by the destruction of the Quarantine Station on Staten Island in 1858. The mob, he says, was led by senior members of the police force and the fire service, who for discreditable reasons hated the hospital and its wards of yellow fever victims. They launched their attack on the hospital one evening when the city's chief dignitaries were being distracted at a banquet. In this combined operation Staten Island was invaded and the hospital surrounded. Fire companies acted as expert arsonists. The whole establishment was burned down. The flames "lighted up the island and bay for miles around. The patients, many delirious and some dying, were carried out and laid on the grass; and there they remained the rest of that night and most of the following day. . . . A boatload of marines and the Eighth Regiment of state militia arrived after it was all over."[24] The list could be multiplied, and capped by the terrible New York Draft Riots of 1863.

Even the militia sometimes had complex attitudes to law and order. As later chapters explain, they were caught up in political and ethnic squabbles. Some units had darkly secret aspirations. In 1844 an Italian company of New York volunteer militia was formed as a cell or "congregation" of the "Young Italy" movement, which dreamed of uniting all Italy under one flag by force of arms. There were other congregations in Boston, Cincinnati and New Orleans. The New York 69th, whose ranks at Bull Run included such revolutionaries as Thomas Francis Meagher, was (according to another revolutionary) "formed as a distinctively Irish Regiment for the express purpose of aiding in the liberation of Ireland. . . . The finest types of young Irish-Americans joined it and drilled assiduously in the ardent hope that by becoming proficient in military tactics they might better be equipped to strike a blow for Ireland." A Phoenix Society seems to have been organized within the 69th, and comprised most of its men. Members of this revolutionary order arrested in Belfast were said to have boasted that "the Sixty-ninth Regiment New York State Militia was coming over to relieve Ireland from the British yoke." A news item in a New York military magazine announced in 1860: "THE PHOENIX BRIGADE — a military organization composed of patriotic Irishmen, having for its object the liberation of Ireland — is recruiting largely in every section of the Union."[25]

This sort of evidence is of course tinged with exaggeration and fantasy. So were the respective views that North and South held of one another during the Civil War. Such views, it becomes clear, grew out of the previous turbulent half-century. Under the heading REIGN OF TERROR IN NEW YORK, the *Richmond Whig* in April 1861 reported the impressions of a Virginia gentleman, after a recent visit:

The scenes which he witnessed in the streets reminded him of the descriptions of the Reign of Terror in Paris. Nothing was wanting but the guillotine to make the two pictures identical. The violent and diabolical temper everywhere conspicuous, showed but too clearly whither all things are tending in the commercial metropolis. . . . The desperadoes of that great city are now in the ascendant.

The report, like those of Dana, is a mixture of horror and gratification. There is an underlying dread of city mobs out of control — an old agrarian bogey reinforced by what newspapers had also been telling of scenes in Europe: governments overturned, assassination attempts, barricades, blood and wine flowing in the gutters. Since the South had no great cities (apart from Baltimore and New Orleans, which were conveniently left out of the reckoning), it could believe itself safe from the contamination. "We have never seen a mob in Richmond," a local chronicler boasted in 1852.[26] In the South, claimed W. J. Grayson of Charleston in the complacent couplets of his *Hireling and Slave* (1854):

> No mobs of factious workmen gather here,
> No strikes we dread, no lawless riots fear;
> Nuns, from their convent driven, at midnight fly,
> Churches, in flames, ask vengeance from the sky,
> Seditious schemes in bloody tumults end,
> Parsons incite, and Senators defend,
> But not where Slaves their easy labours ply,
> Safe from the snare, beneath a Master's eye.

The North, on the other hand, saw the South and Southwest as the violent regions, in contrast to its own more civilized ways. The South was the land of the bowie knife, the swordstick and the slave-lash, the home of the bully and the braggart. It was, in the 1850's, the mustering ground for soldiers of fortune like Chatham Roberdeau Wheat and megalomaniac adventurers like William Walker, the "'Grey-Eyed Man of Destiny," with their ferocious filibustering raids into Nicaragua, Cuba and Mexico. It was the home of the bizarre movement known as the Knights of the Golden Circle, whose promoter, George Washington Lafayette Bickley, dreamed of a vast "Americanized" and "Southernized" empire stretching round the Caribbean in a golden arc. One of the agencies of his operation — which in a characteristically

American way combined clandestine rigmarole and blatant publicity — was a Baltimore newspaper called the *American Cavalier*.[27]

More will be said of Northern and Southern attitudes in Chapter 10. For the moment we may merely observe that though they chose to attribute lawlessness to one another, and claimed superiority, their behavior had much in common. The secret meetings and drillings of the Knights of the Iron Hand, the military wing of Bickley's organization, were not very different in spirit from those of the Phoenix Brigade, or of John Brown's band of followers whom he led against Harpers Ferry. The same feverish sense of fraternity, provocation, partisanship, patriotism, chivalry animated the young men who ran with the fire companies or enrolled in the volunteer militia, or marched with bands in torchlit processions as the "Wide-Awakes" who campaigned for Lincoln in 1860. All were in some degree paramilitary. All had a taste for glory. All in some degree were ambiguous in their relation to authority; the principle of resistance was easier to grasp. Men spoke in codes and parables, not sure whether they were engaged in make-believe or in something more deadly.

How, for example, were contemporaries to interpret the alleged mutiny aboard the U.S. brig-of-war *Somers* in 1842? The affair aroused considerable excitement and alarm. The brig's commander, Alexander Slidell Mackenzie, arrested three men for a plot to seize his ship. They were at once tried, convicted, and hanged at the yardarm. The ringleader was not an ordinary seaman but a junior officer — a midshipman named Philip Spencer. In his seabag were found a dirk and a list of the ship's company under three heads: *certain, probable,* and *to be kept on board "nolens volens."* According to the testimony he was a lazy, sullen youth who had been dismissed from college. He had once told some children that he meant to become a pirate; also in his seabag was a copy of the *Pirate's Own Book* — an item included by Livermore in his analysis of the American appetite for violence. Presumably his reference was to the Spencer case. It was revealed at the court-martial that Spencer, in conversation with members of the crew, had suggested seizing the *Somers* and venturing on a pirate cruise.

THE MARTIAL SPIRIT

The incident was a scandal; it was also a profound puzzle. Spencer was only nineteen, and possibly a little unhinged. He was the son of J. C. Spencer, the Secretary of War, with all the supposed advantages of a good home. Mackenzie was an educated gentleman, the author of a travel book on Spain. The *Somers* was a training ship, organized as such on Mackenzie's initiative. A sort of floating schoolroom, it seemed the most unlikely setting for a mutiny. But then, there were said to be feuds between leading naval families, of which Mackenzie's was one. The young officers who conducted the court-martial were his protégés (among them was a cousin of Herman Melville, who long afterward drew upon the *Somers* affair for his *Billy Budd*). The guilt of at least one of the three hanged sailors seemed in doubt. Was Spencer anything but an overgrown schoolboy, converting his resentments into fantasy? Or, in an age of flogging, slave-running, privateering and actual piracy, was something more sinister involved? A British naval vessel had recently been seized by its crew.

Such were some of the bits of the puzzle. Public opinion divided on the issue. Some, including R. H. Dana and the poet Longfellow, praised Mackenzie for his prompt upholding of discipline. Others viewed him as a snobbish martinet, biased against Spencer because the lad liked to mix with the crew, who had committed judicial murder. A puzzle indeed to a society suspicious of authority and yet afraid of anarchy.

There could hardly have been two gentler men than Ralph Waldo Emerson and Henry David Thoreau of Concord, Massachusetts. By their lights, however, they would have preferred *Discord* as a postal address. Law-abiding citizens were dullards and conformists. Emerson said that "a company of soldiers is an offensive spectacle," but he thrilled to the belligerence of John Brown at Harpers Ferry. Thoreau too hated the spectacle of "a file of soldiers, colonel, captain, corporal, privates, power-monkeys, and all, marching in admirable order . . . to the wars." But the point of the criticism (from his essay on "Civil Disobedience") was that such docility was the result of "an undue respect for law," leading men to act against common sense and conscience. "Our country has become so democratic," lamented

W. T. Sherman in January 1861, "that the mere popular opinion of any town or village rises above the law. . . . The old women and grannies of New England, reasoning from abstract principles, must defy the Constitution. . . . The people of the South . . . must allow their people to favor filibustering expeditions against the solemn treaties of the land, and everywhere from California to Maine any man could do murder, robbery or arson if the people's prejudices lay in that direction."[28]

Even churchmen despite themselves used the language of warfare. In part this was an attempt to steal the enemy's thunder. No one would pretend that "Onward Christian Soldiers" was a battle hymn, or that the Cold Water (temperance) Army and the later Salvation Army were militarist organizations. But the martial drama was contagious. The evangelist Edward Payson Hammond, whose preaching greatly stirred the founder of the Salvation Army, was fond of reciting Tennyson's "Charge of the Light Brigade." Elihu Burritt distributed "Olive Leaf" literature among the peace-minded citizens of America and Europe. The American eagle held an olive branch in one set of its talons. But in the other the national bird clutched the arrows of war. Burritt at least was consistent. His countrymen were less so: an element they had in common with other high civilizations of the century.

4

THE PROFESSIONALS: UNPOPULARITY

Sir, we are, in the European sense of the term, not a military people. We have no business for an army; it hangs as a dead weight upon the nation, officers and all.

    — John Randolph, House of Representatives, 1 February 1828

Our good *republican* people look down on the regular as a pariah. This is the surest possible way to make him one.

    Hints bearing on the United States Army . . . , by a Late Captain
                of Infantry [August v. Kautz], 1858

"A CANCER UPON THE BODY POLITIC"

By the beginning of the nineteenth century, as we have seen, the pattern was set. In the next sixty years American military attitudes did not basically change. A regular army continued to be regarded as a doubtful necessity. The regular soldier was still thought of as an idle and possibly sinister figure, not fully "American."

In part these attitudes, British in origin, continued to mirror or at any rate to resemble British nineteenth-century views. Americans concerned to reduce their army after the War of 1812 would have heartily agreed with a petition presented to Parliament in 1816, only a year after the battle of Waterloo, which protested at the size of the British military establishment — "uncalled for by the internal and external state of the country, repugnant to all the wise principles and maxims of our ancestors, highly dangerous to the liberties of the people, subversive of the constitution, . . . increasing and perpetrating a corrupt and overwhelming influence, poisoning the very sources of national happiness and prosperity." Americans would likewise have agreed with the criticisms of an army officers' club which it was proposed to found in London. Lord Liverpool wrote in 1815 that he considered the club "most ill-advised." It was bound to create a prejudice against the army, "and we shall feel the effects of it even in Parliament, when we consider the question of a peace establishment."

Though the United Service Club was finally launched, its members had to be careful not to offend public sentiment. Like other officers in London, they discovered the advisability of wearing civilian clothes on all possible occasions. A young officer who had just entered the army made the mistake of attending a London theater in full regimentals. He was jostled by the audience. Outside on the street, he was so much whistled and shouted at that he complained to a constable — only to be treated with the utmost contempt:

I'll larn him, that he sha'n't come out of a night with his feathers, and his flipper flappers, and his red coat, to kick up a bobbery with the people. Ve don't vant sodgers in London — thank God! ve can do without 'em. Ve vant no milentary govament here, my lad; and if you come amongst us, vy you must leave off your implements o' war, and behave like a spectacle abitant. The sodgers, I say, ought to be pulled up, for they are a d——d impudent set.[1]

Such scenes had their American counterpart. Ulysses S. Grant, wearing his new uniform in Cincinnati just after his graduation in 1843, was greeted by a grubby barefoot urchin who shouted at him: "Soldier! will you work? No, sir-ee; I'll sell my shirt first!" Richard W. Johnson, on graduating from West Point in 1849, went home on leave to Owensboro, Kentucky. Friends prevailed on him to wear his uniform at a performance given by a traveling circus. Johnson was mistaken for one of the performers. Humiliated by being asked when the show would begin, he went back to his room and changed into civilian clothes. "From that day to this," he said nearly forty years later, "I do not remember to have ever worn uniform when it was not absolutely necessary." At about the same time Randolph B. Marcy, another army officer, halted one day with his men near the Choctaw line in Arkansas. Marcy fell into conversation with a settler who, puzzled by the column, wanted to know what kind of soldiers they were, and described his own experiences in a battle against the Indians. "He then produced a bottle of whisky, and gave me a pressing invitation 'to liquor,' remarking that 'he war not too proud to take a horn with a fellur-soger, even if he war a reg-lar.' "[2]

The difference between these situations was that while British civilians at least recognized an officer, and would have done so in any part of the country, Americans in many areas had no idea what a regular officer looked like. Regular soldiers existed for them only as caricatures — the enlisted men as drunkards and "mercenaries," the officers as haughty "aristocrats." There is a revealingly callous comment on regular soldiers in the otherwise benevolent pages of Mason Weems's *Life of Washington.* Referring to the casualties incurred in defeats by the Indians, before Anthony Wayne's decisive victory at Fallen Timbers in 1794, Weems remarks that "after the first shock, the loss of these poor souls was not much lamented. Tall young fellows, who could easily get their half dollar a day at the healthful and glorious labours of the plough, to go and enlist and rust among the lice and itch of a camp, for *four dollars a month,* were certainly not worth their country's crying about." Weems is always aware of the economic factor. To him, and to most American contemporaries, the folly of passing up the fifteen dollars a month from farming for four dollars a month in the army is proof in itself of a wicked intent, or of such crass stupidity that the enlisted men hardly deserve to live in bountiful America.

By the eve of the Civil War, little had changed. In January 1861, Parmenas T. Turnley (U.S.M.A. 1846)* a major of nearly twenty years' experience, was on furlough in his home district of East Tennessee. The army, he says, was disliked throughout the country, "but more especially among the rural people, who seldom came in contact with army officials":

This feeling was, of course, the fruit of seeds planted by our ancestors, a century previously in their enmity to British troops, and a standing army, and such dislike has been fostered by every demagogue and stump speaker in the land. . . . In fact, to caution the dear people against the military was the chief stock in trade of nine-tenths of the political mountebanks, whose fields of action were far removed from the large cities, and among constituencies not accustomed to see or mingle with the military of our frontiers.

* Here, and subsequently, the parenthesis means the year of graduation from West Point.

A BIVOUACK IN SAFETY OR FLORIDA TROOPS PREVENTING A SURPRISE.

A lithograph by H. R. Robinson, Washington, D.C., ca. 1838–1839. A hostile cartoon, jeering at the effeminate lethargy of regular army officers in the Seminole war. While they snooze, smoke, play cards and chess and primp themselves, the unfortunate American people foot the bill, with no sign that the campaign will ever be concluded.

Turnley believed that Andrew Johnson was one of the Tennessee mountebanks who had denounced the army as "enemies of the people."[3]

A glance at almost any of the congressional debates on military affairs, from Washington's day to Lincoln's, shows that Turnley was not far wrong. Circumstances varied: the arguments remained the same, down to the very phrases. Here, to choose a typical instance, are some sentences from a speech delivered during the Mexican War, by Joshua R. Giddings of Ohio, in the House of Representatives:

I have witnessed the baleful effects of a standing army. It has brought us into this war. Had we been destitute of an army, the President would have been unable to involve us in hostilities with

Mexico. . . . We see the officers of the army on every street of this city, living at their ease, and at the expense of those who toil for their daily bread. These things are inconsistent with republican institutions. Rather than vote for resolutions lauding our military officers for shedding the blood of our fellow men, I would vote to bring back the fifty thousand troops from Mexico and disband them. I would have them return to civil life; I would have each earn his own support, and by his labor contribute something to the general wealth of the nation. The army is a cancer upon the body politic. It is striking its fibres into the vital parts of society, and extending its virus into the veins and arteries of the Government, and if continued must sooner or later dissolve our institutions.

It is hard to assess the precise mixture of motives and antipathies that underlay such speeches. In the case of Mr. Giddings one would have to take note of his total opposition to the Mexican War, and of antislavery, anti-Democratic and anti-Polk emotions. The point is that whatever the closer reasons for a political diatribe, the orator felt he could always add weight to his speech by dragging in an allusion to the "baleful effects of a standing army." This was a tested and tried, universal ingredient, one of the assertions which commanded public assent in Jacksonian America. Giddings was no doubt sincere in opposing the Mexican War. But the logic of his speech is specious. Starting with the proposition that standing armies are "baleful," he blames the Mexican War on the American regular army, merely because the army existed. He then refers to the officers "living at their ease" in Washington, and to the fifty thousand troops in Mexico, as if they were all regulars and all unproductive idlers, whereas the great majority were of course temporary, volunteer soldiers. Every aspiring politician in the United States learned to add the army to his outfit of ready-made invective. Thus young Edwin Stanton, who was later to be Lincoln's Secretary of War, derided professional soldiers on at least one occasion at Kenyon College, Ohio, where he was a student and a prominent member of the debating society.[4]

The most conspicuous hostility to the regular army was displayed in the recurrent attacks upon the United States Military

Academy at West Point, New York. Founded in 1802, the Academy endured fifteen to twenty years of slow and shaky existence. Its cadets were not numerous enough to make any decisive contribution to the War of 1812. The terms of entry, the course of study and the administrative structure were not clear enough to endow it with much authority. Perhaps its very obscurity gave it immunity. By the mid-1820's, under the superintendency of Sylvanus Thayer, its academic reputation stood high. There was fierce competition for places. West Point graduates at the rate of about forty a year were passing into the regular army as commissioned officers.

Criticisms of the Academy began to be voiced in strength with the advent of the Jackson administration. They continued intermittently until the Mexican War. Complaints were registered by individuals, by state legislatures, by members of Congress and by militia conventions. One of the earliest and most influential attacks took the form of a pamphlet published in 1830: *The Military Academy, at West Point, Unmasked,* by "AMERICANUS." "AMERICANUS" was the pseudonym of Alden Partridge, Thayer's predecessor at the Academy. His main charge was that

there is not on the whole globe an establishment more monarchial, corrupt, and corrupting than this, the very organization of which is a palpable violation of the constitution and laws of the country, and its direct tendency to introduce and build up a privileged order of the very worst class — a military aristocracy — in the United States.

Addressing "the people of the United States," Partridge exclaimed:

these young men are to be *gentlemen* soldiers . . . Yes, Fellow Citizens, they are intended for gentlemen soldiers — to sit high in *authority,* and exercise *command,* while you and your sons, who pay $200,000 annually for their education, must approach them cap in hand, and move at their nod. You and your sons are to march in the ranks; to carry the musket and knapsack; to be the *drudges,* yea, the mere *packhorses* of military service. Are you prepared for this? If not, then prostrate this unconstitutional and aristocratical establishment, before the yoke is too firmly fixed on your necks to be shaken off.[5]

Most of the subsequent attacks upon the Academy repeated and enlarged on Partridge's contentions. They provided the substance of resolutions by state legislatures calling for the abolition of West Point from Tennessee (1833), Ohio (1834), Connecticut (1842), Maine (1843) and New Hampshire (1844). Partridge himself memorialized Congress in January 1841, and so did some citizens of Pomfret, Connecticut. Denunciations of the Academy were forwarded to Congress by state militia conventions held at Rome, New York, in 1841, at Albany in the following year, and at New York in 1843. During the 1830's and 1840's there were a number of sharp debates in Congress on the annual appropriations for the Academy. Among its vehement opponents in the House of Representatives were Albert Gallatin Hawes (Kentucky), David Crockett (Tennessee), Francis O. J. Smith (Maine), Abigail Mann (New York), George N. Briggs (Massachusetts), Amasa Dana (New York), Henry P. Williams (Massachusetts), Cave Johnson (Tennessee), George O. Rathbun (New York) and William Sawyer (Ohio). In the Senate, Thomas Hart Benton of Missouri objected to many aspects of the Academy. Some congressmen wished to destroy it altogether, others to transform it into an institution resembling the Virginia Military Institute, or one offering relatively short courses of instruction for enlisted men, militia officers and others. A minority group of the Academy's annual Board of Visitors — civilians drawn from all parts of the Union — registered their disapproval of West Point in 1840. Congress refused to appropriate funds for the Board of Visitors in 1843. Since cadets could not graduate without the presence of the examining board, the authorities had to make do in that year with a board composed of army officers.[6]

Partridge's claim that the Academy was unconstitutional rested on the apparent contradiction between the practice of confining regular commissions to West Point graduates and the implication of the Constitution that offices of honor, trust and emolument should be open to all. It was also argued that, on a strict-construction interpretation, there was no constitutional power to create a national military school. True, George Washington had recommended it, Jefferson had founded it, Madison had enlarged it and Monroe had reformed it. But, said Thomas Hart Benton,

"Washington . . . never recommended such an academy as we have here; he never dreamed of such a thing."

Again, it was said that there was no constitutional sanction for free education at federal expense. This was the view of a select committee of the House, under the chairmanship of Francis Smith of Maine, expressed in 1837: "If schools may be established by Congress to educate men for the army, at the public expense, and without their yielding any current recompense to the government, or binding themselves to its future service, in consideration thereof, may they not, by the most obvious . . . reasoning, be established to educate them . . . for diplomatists, or for the needs of departments, or for clerks and accountants . . . ?" Partridge insisted in his 1841 memorial that if Congress did possess the power to expend public revenue on the education of the poor, which he doubted, then "All the poor in the United States have an equal right to the benefits . . . derived from its exercise, and that, consequently, the institution at West Point is on quite too limited a plan for the accomplishment of the contemplated object." Similar doubts were expressed by individual members of the annual Boards of Visitors — by John Hamm (Ohio), William Smyth (New York) and J. W. Scott (Pennsylvania) in 1834; by John D. Phelan (Alabama) in 1836; and, in addition to the dissenting minority in 1840, by Jesse Beene (Alabama), though he was otherwise in favor of the Academy.

The 1840 minority raised a further constitutional scruple concerning internal improvements. Jacksonian like Jeffersonian Democrats maintained that the federal government was not empowered to promote the building of roads, bridges, railroads and the like. But West Point graduates were engaged by the score, either officially or as civilians, upon such internal improvements. If, the 1840 minority asked, "the United States constitution cannot provide the material for, or conduct the work itself, by what authority can it go a step further, and expend the public treasure in educating men to enable them to exercise the proper skill in expending the funds of private individuals or corporations upon similar objects?"[7]

Doctrinaire Democrats likewise fastened upon the criticism

that West Point, in common with the Bank of the United States, was a "monster" and a monopoly; or in the words of the 1840 minority report, an "eleemosynary school for the education of the aristocracy of political favorites." Partridge in his 1841 memorial called the Academy "a public charity institution for the sons of broken-down politicians, or the support of the cringing syco-phants for office." Selection, it was said, went by political favor: and the lucky few thus privileged went on after graduation to monopolize commissioned rank. Only a few congressmen, for understandable reasons, pressed the first part of this contention. The Kentucky Democrat A. G. Hawes demonstrated this in De-cember 1834, when he introduced a resolution into the House of Representatives to inquire into the expediency of "amending the laws relating to the Military Academy . . . or whether it would not comport with the public interest to abolish the said institu-tion." Another Kentuckian, the Whig Benjamin Hardin, opposed Hawes on the ground that Hawes had presented no specific charge. Hawes quickly silenced Hardin. A relative of that gentle-man, he said, "a gentleman of wealth and standing, had been admitted [to West Point] to receive its advantages, while hun-dreds and thousands of the children of the poor were excluded. . . . The gentleman now had a specific charge to go on."

However, it was easier for congressmen to agree that West Point was generally tinged with "aristocratic" and "un-American" elements. This diffused resentment is apparent, for instance, in a speech in the House made by Sawyer of Ohio in May 1846. He said of the cadets that "after leaving the cool shade of the Hudson with a diploma in their pockets — after having basked for years under the guardian protection and pay of the Government, . . . they enter upon some profession . . . more congenial to their tastes than that of . . . the army."

Part of the criticism was that graduates stayed on in the army, barring entry to other worthy candidates for commissions. Sawyer's, an opposite criticism though sometimes leveled simul-taneously, was that West Pointers promptly left the army for well-paid civilian jobs. This criticism gained considerable weight at the time of the Seminole campaigns, when a large number of

109

army officers resigned. They laid themselves open to a double charge: cowardice in the face of the enemy, and cynical opportunism in having used a free public education to advance their private careers. Defenders of the army found difficulty in refuting both charges. One of the fullest defenses was offered in a report of the House Committee on Military Affairs, under the chairmanship of Hamilton Fish of New York, in May 1844. The cost of living, his committee said, had soared under the "wild spirit of speculation" that pervaded the country in 1835–1836; but army pay remained static. There was also a "demand for works of internal . . . improvement, . . . affording employment to vast numbers of scientific men":

Here, then, we see the expense of living greatly enhanced, the style of living partaking of the magnificence of the imagined acquisition of wealth, and the officers' pay remaining without increase. On the other hand, we see most tempting offers of large salaries, . . . and these same officers possessing all the necessary qualifications to fill the situations thus proffered. Is it, then, a matter of reproach that a man seeks by honest means to improve his condition in life?[8]

This was not a convincing argument to opponents of the Academy. It seemed merely to plead that army officers were no greedier than civilians. The case against them remained. An old law of 1812, passed at a time when it was possible to graduate from West Point in as little as a year (as Sylvanus Thayer had done), bound entering cadets to five years of army service. When the Academy course of study was then fixed at four years, they were obliged only to serve for one further year. As a result of public indignation at the mass resignations of the period, a new act of 1838 obliged cadets to serve for not less than eight years.

Militia conventions were not impressed by such changes of law. They wanted more recognition for the militia. In their eyes every gain for West Point meant a loss in prestige and prospects for America's true defenders, its citizen soldiery. The *New York Military Magazine*, reporting on the Rome, New York, convention of October 1841, asked:

Is it a wonder that our militia evince a spirit of discontent, when they see the public funds wasted upon a bloated, proud and partial institution, instead of being equally distributed for the better improvement and encouragement of our militia? . . .

[The Academy] claims the exclusive privilege of making officers for our army, when in many instances better officers could be found among our militia. And again, if the rule is so far outraged as to grant a commission to a citizen soldier, every exertion is made to crush him, and he meets with opposition from every quarter, until he is compelled to retire from the army in disgust. . . . The Academy sits like an incubus upon [our militia] and they cry aloud for justice and equal rights.[9]

Polk's administration acknowledged the vehemence if not the justice of such polemics by providing that the 1846 Board of Visitors at West Point should include not fewer than six serving militia officers. By then the Mexican War was in progress and the Academy was for the moment saved from the threat to abolish it. Complaints died down in the 1850's. Perhaps Fish's 1844 report satisfied some critics. He was able, for example, to point out that Partridge's oft-repeated figures on the cost of the Academy were greatly exaggerated, and that there were serious drawbacks to the various reforms proposed that stopped short of abolition. But the United States did not as a whole take the Academy to its bosom. With the outbreak of the Civil War, we shall see in Chapter 8, the old condemnations of West Point were revived as heatedly as ever.

ENLISTED MEN: RECRUITMENT

If Congress and the country as a whole did not much like the idea of a standing army, the army did not much like itself either.

The regular, whether officer or enlisted man, tended to be un-happy with his lot. He did not know where he fitted in or what his function was supposed to be. There might be compensations for the officers, or for some officers, but not for the average enlisted man. Literate rankers spoke of themselves as "miserable outcasts" whom no one would trust. "Let us leave the army when we may," two such soldiers wrote dismally in 1836 —

we will be regarded with suspicion . . . ; and if we swerve one step from the arbitrary line marked out by the suffrages of society, our destiny is fixed, and sentence of banishment . . . will be irrevocably pronounced. The respectable portion of the community will not . . . employ us, all will avoid us, a few may pity us, but we will be objects of surprise to none; we will only . . . confirm them in the belief that the army is a school of iniquity.

True, the conditions of service were easier than in European armies. The American regular enlisted for only five years (and for only three between 1833 and 1846), years which in peacetime would be spent within the frontiers of his own country. With luck and ingenuity he could end his term of enlistment at some Western post, so that in effect the army would have provided him with a free trip across the continent. Though discipline was strict, brutality was relatively uncommon. Pay — at five dollars a month until 1833, six dollars until 1854, and ten dollars thereafter — was less than that of a laborer. But there was an extra allowance of fifteen cents a day for soldiers employed on "fatigues," including construction work. In 1854 this was increased to twenty-five cents for duty as laborers and teamsters, and forty cents for mechanics, "at all stations east of the Rocky Mountains," or thirty-five and forty-five cents respectively for stations west of the Rockies. This pay, Albert Sidney Johnston claimed in 1859, "with all the ad-vantages of clothing and food and physicians' bills free, with good care in the hospitals when they are sick, makes it appreci-ated by many as more desirable than the precarious wages of the laborer who may lose all his earnings through the grasping cupidity of the doctors."[10] In the British army, which also de-pended on voluntary recruitment and which paralleled the American service in other ways, life was far harsher. The period of enlistment was twenty-one years, twenty-four in cavalry regiments. The British soldier was likely to spend half his time at disease-ridden stations in India or the West Indies — almost a life sentence in more senses than one. Cooped up in airless barracks, in a thick oppressive uniform, subsisting on a monotonous diet of boiled meat and boiled puddings, a prey to yellow fever and cholera, the British soldier seemed to lead an unenviable existence in comparison with his American counterpart in some healthy Western post like Fort Snelling.

It is also possibly true that the American enlisted man had more interesting companions. Only a handful of educated men — the "gentleman rankers" of Kipling's poem, little black sheep who had lost their way — ended up in British barrack-rooms. The ordinary redcoat was a farm boy, an unskilled laborer, an Irish "navvy," a factory hand out of work: a man often illiterate or nearly so. The American ranks held a wider assortment of skills and temperaments. Edgar Allan Poe rose to a sergeant major's rank before he secured a nomination to West Point. Though it may be hard to imagine him in either position, he is not so wildly untypical as might be supposed. The dragoon regiments raised in the 1830's attracted a dashing, well-educated group of men. Other units too had their quota of unusual characters. One military periodical cites an inquiry made in a company fifty-five strong:

It appeared that nine-tenths enlisted on account of female difficulty; thirteen . . . had changed their names, and forty-three were either drunk, or partially so, at the time of their enlistment. Most of them were men of fine talents and learning, and about one-third had once been in elevated stations in life. Four . . . had been lawyers, three doctors, and two ministers.

Percival Lowe, a New Englander who enlisted in the dragoons in 1849, says that "family trouble, disappointments in love, riots and personal difficulties . . . often caused men to enlist who proved to be the best of soldiers. In my troop there were men isolating themselves from society for all sorts of reasons." They included Wagner, a Kentuckian who had "met with business reverses in Louisville" and "wanted to hide himself from all his friends and have time to think"; a recent Irish immigrant, O'Shea, who found himself "among strangers, without money" and so joined up ("I never knew," Lowe remarks, "a handsomer man or a more perfect gentleman"); and an Englishman named Miller, "who had seen better days, and enlisted in New York because he was absolutely hungry — 'too proud to beg and too honest to steal' — a teacher by profession and master of several languages." Apart from a few scoundrels, Lowe concludes, "we had a remarkably good set of men, some scholars, some good singers and quite a smattering of theatrical talent."

Rodney Glisan, a surgeon who served in the army in the 1850's, offers similar testimony:

Even editors, doctors, and lawyers, occasionally . . . enlist. . . . Many of the rank and file are educated foreigners, who, being poor, enter the service for a livelihood until they can learn the English language. There being such a medley of characters among the private soldiers, their resources for diversions . . . in the way of games, . . . theatrical displays, parties, concerts, debating societies, etc., are almost inexhaustible, even at stations far from . . . civilization.[11]

Some of the legends of titled and wellborn Englishmen in the American ranks may be discounted as romantic exaggeration. Perhaps not much credence should be given to such anecdotes in, say, James Hildreth's *Dragoon Campaigns to the Rocky Mountains* (1836) or in the anonymous *Recollections of the United States Army* (1845). But some "respectably connected" British citizens did don an American uniform, whether as immigrants or as deserters from British regiments stationed in Canada. Glisan mentions a hospital steward who had at one time been an officer in the British navy. An able young Scotsman, Thomas Moonlight, ran away from home and in 1853 enlisted in the 4th U. S. Artillery. Later he farmed in Kansas, and he was appointed by President Cleveland as governor of the Wyoming Territory and minister to Bolivia.[12]

As for recruits from other European countries, there are plenty of examples of men turning to the army for want of a livelihood. It may be remembered that the father of Fiorello La Guardia, New York's mayor, was an Italian musician who came to the United States in 1879 and joined the army as a bandmaster soon after Fiorello's birth in 1882. Other foreigners of talent sought the same refuge in earlier decades. Ange Paldi, a Piedmontese musician, enlisted in the 5th Infantry in 1841. His son, Ange Charles Paldi, was enrolled in the regiment three years afterward as a boy musician. The father was a gifted artist who produced some excellent drawings of the Mexican War. Joseph Heger, a Hessian, served a five-year enlistment from 1855 to 1860 in the 1st Regiment of Mounted Riflemen. A lithographer by trade, he too made valuable sketches of military life.[13]

Not all the foreign recruits were so resourceful. Some pathetic letters reached the Secretary of War, Joel R. Poinsett, in 1839–1840. They were written by John de Hordynsky — "a Pole now in the Army," according to the endorsement — in Latin, presumably the only language Hordynsky felt he and Mr. Poinsett might have in common. Poinsett had allowed him to be released from military service if he could procure a substitute. But he had been posted to Florida ("Campania in Indianos exorata est") where substitutes were hard to come by; might he therefore go to New Orleans in search of one?

Such soldiers cannot have been easy to instruct. We learn of a captain in Florida, at the same period, that "thirty out of sixty of his privates could not understand a word he uttered," because they could not speak English. "They never could comprehend the difference between the command to *charge* their muskets, *charge* the enemy, and *charge* the United States for services rendered." An American who was a medical orderly in the 4th Infantry, during the early 1840's, describes an encounter between a helpless foreign-born soldier and the regiment's irritable surgeon:

One morning at sick call one of the band, a German musician by the name of Riter, reported for medical treatment. The doctor inquired, "What ails you?" "French horn, sir," replied Riter. . . . "D——n you!" shouted the doctor, "I did not want to know what instrument you played, but what is the matter with you." Finally the Dutchman got him to understand he had a pain in his stomach. But when Riter reported next morning and the doctor asked him, "How is your chest?" . . . the Dutchman's report . . . was to the effect that some one had broken into it and stole a shirt and pair of drawers the night before, which was a fact. But the doctor . . . supposed it was an attempted joke on him, and he kicked poor Riter out, crying, "D——n you, get out!"[14]

As Surgeon Glisan noted, this medley of backgrounds, native and foreign-born, sought outlets in histrionic performances. The memoirs and service periodicals of the period are full of allusions to ambitious entertainments organized by the enlisted men. A grandiose speech, written by a private, accompanied the opening of the "Amateur Theatre" at Fort Snelling in 1835. After outlining the influence of the stage upon the history of the world, he went on to predict that "the introduction of the drama into this obscure corner . . . may . . . produce very felicitous results. . . . The amateurs of the 1st Infantry have been the pioneers of the drama in the North-West." Less lofty but equally enterprising activities were reported four years later at Fort Towson, "Choctaw Nation West," where the enlisted men opened their season with an address in rhyming couplets and a repertoire that included *The White Warrior*, "an original play, written by one of the soldiers of C Company." The army at Corpus Christi, Texas, on the eve of the Mexican War, built two temporary theaters.[15]

All this sounds gay and spirited; and, indeed, the army was not a slave camp. Some men discovered within it the adventure, security, simplicity and comradeship that the recruiting posters promised. For the majority however the army was an evasion, a bolthole, a last resort, a confession of failure. The educated men in the ranks were in fact a minority, and unhappy cases for the most part. In the ranks, hiding under assumed names where necessary, the misfits, bad hats, transgressors and broken men could sink out of sight, could sink down toward the mudsill of society. If they remained in the army their chances of rising up again were small, since few enlisted men were considered eligible for commissions. Being in the ranks at all militated against them: they must be men with something to hide, or at best something to forget. In saying that professional men could be found in the ranks, Glisan also said that they enlisted "in a paroxysm of disgust," and that such persons, "being in the wrong element, very often cause disturbances — especially the members of the law — who are famous for breeding misunderstandings among all with whom their lot is cast." His hospital steward, the former British naval officer, had been dismissed for drunkenness, and Glisan was forced to reduce him to the ranks for the same weakness.*

As Sergeant Lowe noted, *there were men isolating themselves . . . for all sorts of reasons.* The recreations they devised had a queer forced gaiety; they had condemned themselves to a kind of good-natured prison. The eloquent address of the private at the inauguration of the Fort Snelling "corps dramatique" is also a frustrated appeal to an uninterested world outside: "The soldier . . . is . . . marked out by his countrymen as a fit object of derision; . . . like Cain, he goes forth a fugitive and a vagabond on the face of the earth. These sentiments . . . react on the mind of the soldier, and he begins to believe he is all the world think[s] of him."

The mudsill. As in Britain, though with a greater variety of despairs, the army filled its ranks with men in trouble, out of work, on their beam ends. Such was the story of James Elderkin, who was starving on the streets of Schenectady one day in 1839, sniffing at the window of a restaurant, when

a kindly old gentleman asked me if I would like a bowl of clam soup. . . . I never eat anything I thought tasted quite so good. While in the restaurant a couple of United States soldiers came in. I asked

* These stories help us to realize the force behind the nineteeth-century temperance movement, which we are otherwise apt to dismiss as naïve and hysterical. It was, rather, a reaction to thousands and thousands of cases — so frequent that every family knew or knew of one — of individuals who had wrecked their lives through drink. The mysterious visitations were not confined to the poor or the shiftless. On the contrary, they seemed often to strike at professional men: doctors, lawyers, even clergymen. For some of these the army provided oblivion, anonymity, a state of suspended animation somewhere between cure and total disaster.

them if they knew of any one that wanted a boy for work, and they in turn asked me how I would like to become a soldier. . . . I thought anything would be preferable to the life of a tramp. . . . I was nineteen years of age . . . ; but the officer told me I would have to claim I was twenty-one . . . or I could not enlist. This, of course, I did.

Elderkin reenlisted five years later, "having no place to call home" and because "times were hard."

His story was repeated in the wanderings of James Larson, a youngster from Wisconsin who left home after quarreling with his family. In 1860 Larson was in Kansas, with no money and no idea what to do next. He happened to see a guard-mounting at Fort Leavenworth. The spectacle was new to him, and the "gay uniforms and proud actions and movements pleased me. . . . Thus, slowly, the wish to become a soldier was already creeping into my mind, although I would not acknowledge it to myself."[16]

Or there are the comparable narratives of immigrant rankers. In 1832 Charles Ashworth, the seventeen-year-old son of an English barrister, disappeared; he was last seen at Liverpool. His parents feared he had died in a cholera epidemic. Some time afterward his saga was pieced together. Ashworth had taken ship to America and headed west. In the fall of 1833 he turned up at Fort Dearborn, clad in a buckskin shirt. An officer reported: "His appearance was most forlorn. . . . He was starved, pale, and sick with the ague and fever. He inquired for employment as a clerk; . . . I told him the impossibility of getting employment among strangers with appearances so much against him." The officer persuaded Ashworth to enlist instead. He was taken into the camp hospital and nursed back to health. Three months later he deserted. The next news of Ashworth was from Honolulu; he had managed to make his way west to the mouth of the Columbia River and get a passage on a ship bound for the Sandwich Islands.

Another restless young Englishman, Henry Hamilton, grew tired in the early 1850's of being a printer's apprentice. He broke his apprenticeship and enlisted in Lord Cardigan's elegant 11th Hussars. But when the regiment proved uncongenial he deserted with a friend, a bandsman named Jim, and sailed for America in an emigrant ship. They could not find work in New York or in Albany. Desperate, they responded to the appeal of a recruiting poster ("Wanted in the U. S. Army a few good-looking, intelligent active young men"). Though Hamilton was reluctant to join up, things turned out well. He soon became a sergeant, and was able to learn "the customs of the country" and save enough money to launch him as a civilian at the end of his five years. Jim was less lucky. He discovered that his brother, who had emigrated the previous year, had gone through exactly the same process, also enlisting in the American army. But the brother had died: Jim came across his grave "in the little cemetery at the back of the garrison." Jim deserted a second time and went back to England.

One more fragment to fill out the collective story of the immigrant soldier: the English traveler Laurence Oliphant, visiting Fort Ripley in the 1850's, talked with a soldier who had a broad Irish brogue:

I asked his history. It was a very common one. He had deserted from our own army, and, unable to get his livelihood by his own independant exertions, had entered that of the United States. Here his knowledge of military duty soon enabled him to attain the rank of sergeant; but, as he assured us in a melancholy tone, he suffered from an infirmity which he was unable to overcome, and which had speedily caused his degradation to the ranks.[17]

Gradually the hard-up immigrant replaced the hard-up American in the ranks of the U. S. Army. It is impossible to say just how high the proportion rose, since "hundreds of foreigners book themselves as born in this country." But even ignoring this factor, figures show that by the outbreak of the Civil War the "typical" American ranker was a European. A sample of enlistment registers gives the *official* proportion of native-born recruits, just after the War of 1812, as around 80 per cent. The figure was maintained until the early 1830's, but by 1840 had dropped to 54 per cent, and by 1850 to 40 per cent. One calculation in 1859, probably on the conservative side, put the number of foreign-born regulars at nine thousand out of a total enlisted strength of

119

sixteen thousand: "The Irish element . . . predominates, and next to it, the Germans. It is estimated that we have over two thousand ex-English soldiers in the army and marine corps, besides a large number of Prussians, French, Austrians, Poles and natives of every other European state."[18]

ENLISTED MEN: DISCONTENTS

As the number of foreign-born increased, the status of enlisted men dropped even lower. Their courage in battle seemingly made little difference. Their loyalty was widely questioned when the Mexicans were able to form a whole battalion, the San Patricio or St. Patrick's, from American army deserters — mainly Irish, as the name implies. Not long after the Mexican War, two young West Point instructors, Dabney H. Maury and George B. McClellan, decided to go to church a few miles from the Academy. It was a cold Christmas Day and they were bundled up in heavy blue cavalrymen's coats. Not recognizable as officers in this dress, they sat down in an empty pew in a side aisle. But the sexton, "evidently indignant that private soldiers should intrude themselves into . . . his congregation, marched us out of our position and back into the pauper pews." And though Albert Sidney Johnston, writing in 1859, stresses the worthiness of the enlisted men, he also takes it for granted that they "cannot be associates for refined persons."

Some of the reasons have been indicated. The soldier was

regarded as a good-for-nothing. The conditions of his life reinforced the opinion. He was shut away in small garrisons whose
military duties — drill, guard and the like — resolved themselves
into meaningless drudgery. There was some Indian fighting to
break the monotony, but many army posts were overrun by the
advancing frontier and no longer served any strictly military
purpose. Inertia kept them in being; this and the practice of using
the army for civilian tasks. Recent accounts have emphasized the
importance of the army in settling and civilizing the frontiers.
Perhaps so; but soldiers at the time do not seem to have taken
pride in their mission. "I enlisted for a soldier," one complaint
ran: "I never was told that I would be called on to make roads,
build bridges, quarry stone, burn brick and lime, carry the hod,
cut wood, hew timber, construct it into rafts and float it to the
garrisons, . . . drive teams, make hay, herd cattle, build stables,
construct barracks, hospitals, etc., etc., etc." The complaint was
echoed by an intelligent officer who suggested withdrawing the
army to "the present actual frontiers." This would permit it to be
concentrated and to be properly trained, instead of destroying
morale by "scattering the army in squads, employing soldiers to
build quarters for other corps to live in, or be abandoned, disorganizing them by putting them at every labor known in civil
life without the pay therefor," and thus breaking down the
soldier's "individual as well as his professional pride."[19]

Drink was the chief solace. It had brought some men into the
army in the first place. Others quickly acquired the habit. As in
the British army, the regulations and their interpretation were an
odd mixture of cynicism and severity. The enlisted man was given
a daily ration of whiskey and in most stations could easily buy
more. When he received a money allowance in lieu of whiskey, as
provided by an act of 1846, he took the money to one of the
hutments outside the fort which purveyed expensive cheap liquor
with an open furtiveness. One Irish soldier at a Western fort, in
search of whiskey, asked an old man in civilian clothes where he
might fill his flask—unaware that he was speaking to General
Zachary Taylor. Taylor advised him to try the women's quarters.
"Away went Jack, and, sure enough, he soon came back with his

flask full; and approaching the general said: 'Here, old man, I got some. For your kindness, take a drink with me.' 'No, no,' replied the general. 'Put it up quick, or some of the officers may see you with it, and . . . put you in the guardhouse.'" Next day to his horror Jack Ryan, lined up for inspection, saw his friend approach and discovered him to be "Old Tonkey" — the soldiers' nickname for Taylor. 'Oh, my god!' said Jack. 'I'm killed; I'm killed.'" To his vast relief, the general showed no sign of recognizing him.[20]

The usual outcome was less agreeable; and indeed Jack Ryan's subsequent history may have been somber. An officer of the 2nd Infantry said in 1829 that of thirty-five men on his company roll, twenty-nine were drunkards. Of the remaining six, "five drank daily and may become intemperate before many years, and one was in ill health." Quarrels broke out easily in the cramped atmosphere of isolated posts. Aware that civilians lived under an easier rule, looking ahead to their own not-so-remote discharge, the noisier enlisted men made no secret of their boredom and exasperation. Court-martial records teem with their mutinous stirrings. Private Bourke of the 3rd Artillery, stationed in Florida in 1837, struck his corporal, shouting: "It won't be such a damned little son of a bitch as you, that will confine me." He declared of his subaltern, "I will be damned if I serve under such a damned Cow Boy. He's not fit to be an Officer, and . . . I'll whip him as soon as I get out of the service." Private Theodore Narcisse of the 8th Infantry, taken up by the guard at Madison Barracks in 1838 for drunken and riotous behavior, told the officer of the day, "Go to hell — I don't care for you — you don't know how to drill." A sergeant testified, perhaps with concealed relish, that Narcisse had said "the American officers were loafers from New York the same as ourselves."[21]

All kinds of remedies for drunkenness and insubordination were proposed by worried inspecting officers: the substitution of coffee for the whiskey ration, higher pay, improved amenities, better chances for promotion, inducements to native-born Americans to enlist, shorter enlistments, the withholding of pay, harsher punishments. Some reforms were made, with little effect. Even the reformers seemed oppressed by futility, as when they some-times in the same document recommended both stricter and more lenient treatment for the errant ranker. The root trouble was that many soldiers did not want to be soldiers. For the more crushed the army was the end of the line; for the more buoyant it was only a way-station.

Nothing therefore could be done about the most prevalent crime of all, desertion. The situation was so serious as to become ludicrous. In some years up to a third of the men enrolled on the books were deserters. Soldiers went off because conditions were intolerable and because conditions were tolerable but better still in civilian life. Senior officers revealed their bewilderment in such letters as this, from General Jacob Brown in 1824: "The comforts which the soldier enjoys from the liberal provision of the govern-ment, . . . and the mildness and regularity which distinguish the administration of the Army, leave no imaginable cause for the prevalence of desertion, but the inadequacy of the punishment annexed to it by law."

Brown was alluding to an act of 1812 which abolished flogging in the U. S. Army (it had hitherto been limited to fifty lashes). But the alternative punishments, for desertion and for other major offences, were no less humiliating and drastic. One soldier was sentenced in 1829 "To have his head shaved, to be branded on the forehead with the letter D [for deserter], and to be drummed out of service." Similar punishments in the same year included:

Hard labor with ball and chain attached to his leg, to wear around his neck an iron yoke of 10 lbs. weight, having two arms extending from the neck 10 inches, to be marked on the hip with the word *deserter* an inch long . . .

To be marked on the right hip with the word *Mutiny* and on the left with the word *Deserter* . . .

To be marked on the right forearm and right hip with the word *"deserter,"* and on the left forearm and left hip with the word *"fraud,"* to wear an iron collar with four projecting arms, to have his head shaved, be drummed out of service with straw halter . . .

To stand on the head of a barrel, with a 24 lb. shot on his back, every alternate two hours for fifteen days from sun rise to sun set . . .

Major General Gaines, as inspecting officer at the time, strongly condemned such brutality. His protest was of no avail. He could not suggest more effective punishments; and even he recommended the restoration of "stripes and lashes" for serious crimes. His argument was that men who committed them were already degraded, and so not affected by the nature of the punishment. He also pointed out the value of summary punishment; the alternative, imprisonment, would place a heavier burden in guard duties upon the culprit's innocent comrades.

Unable to think of another solution, the army brought back flogging in 1833 and kept it until 1861, to deal with the express crime of desertion. Flogging was in fact resorted to, nor were standards relaxed with the passage of the years.* In the 1830's, for instance, a private in the 3rd Artillery, who pleaded guilty to desertion at a Florida court-martial, was sentenced "to forfeit all pay . . . , to receive Fifty lashes with a cat o' nine tails on his bare back, and to be drummed out of service." In 1853 another deserter tried at Fort Monroe, Virginia, received "fifty lashes on his bare back, well laid on." *Well laid on* was a standard phrase in court-martial records, though part or all of the punishment in the case of flogging was occasionally remitted. Also at Fort Monroe, in 1854, there is an example of the other primitive forms of degradation that offended Gaines. Private Lafferty of the 1st Artillery, guilty of desertion, was sentenced "To be indelibly marked on the left hip with the letter 'D' one and a half inches long, to be confined to hard labor with a 24 lb. ball attached to his leg for two months, to forfeit all pay and allowances that are now or may be due him at the expiration of the two months, to have his head shaved and to be drummed out . . ."[22]

The penalties were useless. It was too easy to slip away, and too tempting. By enlisting in the right company of the right regiment, an enterprising soldier could be posted to whatever part of the country best suited his future plans. Or of course he could go off on a sudden impulse. One night he would disappear, and if

---

* Flogging was also customary in the navy (and in the merchant marine) — where morale was equally low — until abolished by Congress in 1850. See Leonard D. White, *The Jacksonians, 1829–1861* (New York, 1954), 246.

fortune favored him the army would never hear of him again. Sudden excitements like the California gold rush were enough to empty whole barrack-rooms. An officer stationed at Fort Vancouver, Oregon Territory, in 1850 wrote to his family to describe "a march of eight hundred miles in pursuit of a large body of deserters who attemped to push through to California by land. . . . We overtook and sent back seventy odd. . . . Thirty odd probably got through to the mines, eight were either killed by the Indians, starved or eaten by the others. We followed them to the Klamath River finding from their trail that they had crossed several days in advance from us and being then but about four days march from the upper 'diggins' we returned."[23]

The ranks of the American army contained men of education and talent, and others who were laborers or scoundrels. A steadily increasing proportion were foreigners. Some men made a home for themselves and reenlisted with cheerful resignation. The majority were never quite able to come to terms with the army or themselves. They were told they were unnecessary, unproductive, un-American. Yet where they worked hard at building roads and the like, the task, while useful, seemed to deny their special vocation. Their existence was at once too military and not military enough. So were their conditions of service: they were alternatively babied and bullied, treated as good Americans and then as bad Americans, as children and as convicts. What saved them from disintegration was the occasional chance to fight – in Florida, in Mexico, against the Indians in the West. "Soldiers in peace," said the English poet John Clare, "are like chimneys in summer." The American rank and file fought well: combat gave them a *raison d'être*. But even here there were aggravations. The regulars had to compete with regiments of exuberant volunteers, temporary soldiers whose heroism was extolled in the newspapers and who were rewarded – with land grants and so on – on the same scale as regulars. The regulars felt they by contrast were taken for granted, and suffered the implied taint of being "mercenaries." The patriotism of the volunteer was stimulated by bounties to enlist. In consequence the regulars might be augmented in wartime but were never filled up to strength. The discrepancy remained, in the War of 1812, in the Mexican War and again in the Civil War, as a clear indication that the United States would have liked to do without regular enlisted men altogether, if it had known how.

OFFICERS' GRIEVANCES

Though the officers of the regular army were better placed than the enlisted men their discontents were basically the same. After the War of 1812 the majority entered the army via West Point. Before long, West Point nominations were mainly in the hands of congressmen and were used as a way of rewarding constituents. The nomination was commonly regarded as a free college education — a privilege, but one that might have few military overtones. It is plain from the reminiscences of regular officers that many came into the army by accident. Suddenly they had the opportunity to take the Academy's entrance examination: would they like to try? Some had to be persuaded by eager parents. Some had mothers who sought to dissuade them. Thomas J. ("Stonewall") Jackson of Virginia got the appointment after a previous nominee from his district had taken a look at West Point and had been so unimpressed that he headed straight home again. George Crook of Ohio (U.S.M.A. 1852) was nominated by Congressman Robert C. Schenck. Schenck, with a nomination to fill, "remembered that old Squire Crook, a fine old Whig farmer, . . . had some boys. . . . I inquired if he had a spare boy he'd like to send off to West Point. After studying awhile he said he didn't know but what he had." The boy himself, Schenck recalled, "didn't seem to have the slightest interest."[24]

Large numbers of cadets — three-quarters of the entry at some periods — failed to meet the Academy's strict standards of scholarship and discipline and were "dropped." Those who managed to hang on were often uncertain of their direction. Andrew Jackson's nephew A. J. Donelson graduated in July 1820. His uncle advised him in May of that year that "if peace continues, have no idea of wasting the prime of your life in the army." Donelson took the hint and resigned in February 1822. Again, Jubal A. Early was a Virginia cadet whose family spoke in their letters of honor and gentlemanliness. But their correspondence displays a conviction that the Academy's value for him was purely academic. "I agree with you entirely," an elder brother told him in 1834, "in your notion of avoiding the army." The young cadet "had better improve every opportunity to prepare for any thing and perhaps you may have a choice of some desirable occupations," such as law or medicine. Another brother said the same. A few months later Early's father wrote: "I am glad you are still firm in your resolution of remaining at West Point or at least graduating there. . . . You will never regret it let your after life be what it may and . . . will still have time enough to study any profession you may choose. . . ." Early did graduate safely from the Academy in 1837 at the end of his four-year course. But cadets at this period were obliged to spend only a total of five years in the army, and he promptly resigned in 1838. Stonewall Jackson, while a cadet, announced: "I intend to remain in the army no longer than I can get rid of it with honor, and means to commence some professional business at home." Neither to these Virginians nor apparently to most Americans did army service rate as a profession on the same level as medicine, the law or the ministry.[25]

The inclination to look upon West Point as a college, with special advantages in technical and scientific training, was heightened by two facts. First, it provided the best instruction of this type in the whole country before the Civil War. The Board of Visitors in 1848 called the Academy "the cheap school of science

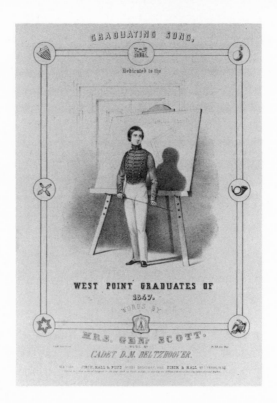

GRADUATING SONG,

Dedicated to the

WEST POINT GRADUATES OF
1847.

WORDS BY

MRS. GEN. SCOTT.

MUSIC BY

CADET D.M. BELTZHOOVER.

of this nation."[26] Second, cadets were graduated in order of merit; and those at the head of the class list had the chance of picking the corps they preferred. The favored branches were the Corps of Engineers, the Topographical Engineers and the Ordnance (the Infantry came lowest, with Cavalry and Artillery in intermediate positions). In other words, the outstanding cadets usually went into technical branches of the service, of "civilian" utility.

The cadet who cherished ideas of military glory soon learned that there was apparently little room for them in the United States. The lesson was dinned into him that he was one of a small and suspect company. Thus, the cadet members of the West Point Dialectic Society were treated in 1839 to an oration by Benjamin F. Butler which incorporates nearly all the antimilitary clichés of the day. One might think it a surprising theme for an address at West Point, especially from a former Secretary of War.* "The

* This B. F. Butler (1795–1858), a New York lawyer-politician, is not to be confused with "Beast" Butler (1818–1893) of the same name and calling.

genius of our political institutions," Butler told his audience, "and the settled convictions of our people, forbid the maintenance among us, of large standing armies . . . , as productive of needless expenditure; injurious to the habits and morals of the people; and dangerous to public liberty." So the Founding Fathers "deemed it wiser to rely, when armies should be wanted, on the militia, and on such regular forces as might then be raised." This decision had become "a fundamental maxim of our national policy."

Butler stressed the peaceful character of American life, the religious objection to war, and the widespread view that war was an evil to which the United States should resort only with great reluctance. Hence it was obvious that "the military profession can never acquire . . . the commanding influence which belongs to it in many other countries. But though likely to be kept within narrow limits, and in constant subordination to the civil power," he went on, almost with a tinge of regret, "it cannot be given up."

He said nothing the cadets had not already heard. There was little new that could be said. No doubt the audience was bored by Butler's tired rhetoric. But such instruction had a powerful cumulative effect. Long before he graduated, the West Pointer knew that he existed somewhat on sufferance. No doubt the American and democratic part of him accepted the proposition that the military ought to be kept in their place — a very small place. But the professional part of him was not cheered by the reiterated information that he was entering a career without much prestige, without much future, and with every kind of negative and positive inducement to turn himself back into a civilian before it was too late. At the period of the most vehement attacks upon West Point the cadet had reason to doubt whether the institution would survive. Edmund Kirby Smith of Florida, who was due to graduate in 1845, reported in the previous year that the commandant expected the downfall of the Academy: he "saw slight hope for commissions and advised against the purchase of uniforms." Cadet U. S. Grant of Illinois, reading of the debates on the Academy in the House of Representatives, expected the same outcome — though he was not particularly depressed, since he did not like the army. Nor for that matter was Kirby Smith wholly wedded to soldiering. Some months later, the Academy having survived, Smith almost missed his commission through defective eyesight. His family had a strong military tradition; his father had been a regular officer, and so were his brother Ephraim (U.S.M.A. 1826) and his brother-in-law Captain Lucien B. Webster (U.S.M.A. 1823). But when Ephraim heard of Edmund's medical difficulties he wrote:

> The army in our country is certainly not a desirable profession. . . . With your talents and education, a few years of industry will . . . place you . . . far in advance of your class-mates, who will lead the enervating and indolent life of subalterns, and I by no means desire that *my* sons should ever wear a sword. I would certainly prefer that they should become honest, industrious mechanics.* So, my dear brother, be not cast down. You can get a better profession than the one I fear you have lost.[27]

Smith and Grant did graduate. What they and their companions were committed to, unless they resigned, was a lifetime of tedium and genteel poverty. True, the more brilliant or fortunate officers, such as Robert E. Lee, George B. McClellan, Pierre G. T. Beauregard, or Montgomery C. Meigs, might be engaged in interesting and important tasks. During the 1820's and 1830's serving officers on detached duty did a great deal of work in planning and supervising the construction of canals and railroads, sometimes on loan to companies like the Baltimore & Ohio. In later decades, in part through sectional and local jealousy of the army's national, centralizing role, officers had fewer opportunities for this work — at least in a military capacity. They tended instead to be involved in the building of fortifications and public structures, or in Western exploration and in geological and mapping surveys. A few privileged officers were sent to Europe on military duty; McClellan was one of three appointed to study the Crimean War. Or a junior officer with the right connections might enjoy himself in one of the Eastern cities as an aide to a general or on staff duty.[28]

* Ephraim was mortally wounded in the Mexican War, at Molino del Rey. One of Ephraim's sons, Joseph Lee Kirby Smith, did "wear a sword": he became a Union brigadier general during the Civil War, and died of wounds received at Corinth.

But for the general run of recent graduates the future was not glittering. Even though many failed to graduate at all — the class of 1852, Philip Sheridan's, "entered one hundred and twenty in numbers and graduated forty-three" — supply often exceeded demand. This was one reason why West Pointers were so angry at the filling of new regiments through civilian appointments. Promotion in the lower grades went by seniority, as in the British army; and as among British regulars, so among Americans there was endless discussion, in service periodicals and in correspondence, of the chances of a rise in grade. A young classmate wrote to Jubal Early in 1838: "I presume I shall remain in the army, and perhaps be a captain, by the time I am sixty, and have grandchildren nearly grown. . . . It seems like a joke, but d———n me if I don't think there is a good deal of truth in it." There was indeed, as a matter of sober calculation. An article in the *Army & Navy Chronicle*, based on actual promotions between 1824 and 1834, estimated that the average second lieutenant, assuming that he was twenty years old on graduation, would be fifty-four before he became the most junior captain in the army, and that it would be virtually impossible for him to reach the rank of major.[29] They would be lean years as well as long years, at any rate in comparison with civilian salaries. Another military statistician computed that it would take nearly thirty years of peacetime service for an officer in the élite Corps of Engineers to attain the rank of major, and a total annual income of $1,500; whereas men in their early twenties with technical qualifications could earn two or three times as much "in the service of railroad companies." A regular captain, who with heavy irony signed himself " 'A YOUNG MAN,' OF TWENTY-TWO YEARS SERVICE," wrote in 1836 from a hotel in New Orleans. His own pay and subsistence amounted to $64 per month:

The "Head Cook," a worthy colored man in this Hotel, receives $75 per month . . . , leaving a balance in favor of the knight of the spit of $11 per month.

The cook had free board and lodging, for which the captain had to pay $3 a day and more:

It requires but little . . . calculation to determine which individual is best rewarded for his services, according to his supposed . . . acquirements; and what the state of the Captain's finances will be at the expiration of the month.[30]

The officer in a Southern or Western frontier post had few opportunities to meet women of what he regarded as a suitable social level. If he eventually married and had children he was still worse off. He must either leave them behind when he was posted to some lonely station, or expect them to share his discomforts. Sooner or later his children would have to be sent away to boarding school. Whatever arrangements were made, expense was entailed and family life disrupted.

Civilians were better off. The comparison with civilian-soldiers was particularly galling for a regular who took his career seriously. Even his "hard earned title" counted for next to nothing:

Let any person try the experiment of calling out "halloo, colonel!" in a loud voice in a large crowd, assembled for any purposes in our cities, and he will be surprised at the number of responses. Hence, military men . . . soon acquire . . . a dread of having their modest titles overshadowed by the higher sounding ones of colonel and general, so common among the militia.

In Tennessee it was stipulated that "the uniform of the generals and generals' staff and field officers of the militia of this State shall be the same as that of officers of the same grade in the United States' army."[31]

The amateur spirit was in the ascendant, and the Jacksonian politician encouraged it. H. M. Rutledge of Tennessee, himself once a regular major, had a son who graduated from West Point in 1837. A year later the son found that "altho' he relished the . . . life, . . . he could not deny that he was likely to remain a lieutenant of Artillery for many years, and if peace should continue, to pass most of his life at some outpost." Rutledge therefore urged the boy to resign his commission when the statutory year was up:

132

> I should have advised the step with reluctance, if I could persuade myself, that there was any possibility of having our Military Establishment placed upon the footing of other nations. But there is no such hope – under our present system of government, composed as Congress is . . ., the interests of the regular Army must be sacrificed to the Volunteers. A species of force, which agrees better with the views of our democratic leaders, than any more efficient means of defending the country.[32]

There is an element of special pleading in these complaints. All groups in society can manage to prove, with figures, that they are badly treated. Promotion moved more rapidly in the late 1830's and in the 1840's, thanks to the large number of resignations and to the opportunities provided by wartime, when the army was considerably augmented. There were also brevet promotions, given out almost lavishly in the Mexican War – so that a subaltern might emerge with the rank of brevet major, as T. J. Jackson did. Frontier life had its attractions. In general it was easy-paced, to suit the indolent, yet allowed the officer with adventurous tastes or a passion for hunting full scope for his enthusiasms.

But for the bulk of officers these advantages were more apparent than real. The flood of resignations was itself a testimony to low morale. Some active service, notably the Seminole campaigns of 1833–1842, was extremely disagreeable. The Seminoles were elusive, the army was split with feuds, the Florida climate dangerously unhealthy. An army surgeon in a letter to a colleague wrote almost dementedly of the futility of campaigns in the "howling wilderness" where "*Ague*, pale and lank, rises from his damp & mouldy hammock and with one hand pale and blue . . . as the lip of death beckons you to his charnel house." He continues: "Dear Doctor forgive all this nonsense but I am crazy with the fever, I have had it three days since I came off that horrible scout. . . . Do write me for I am sick, sick every way."[33] Indian fighting on the Plains might be more romantic, and has certainly generated a copious literature. But the nation's Indian policy did not commend itself to all regulars; Indian removal was a wretched affair to have to supervise.

Those who soldiered on were affronted by the tendency to give direct commissions to civilians, sometimes as a political favor. For the first time since the War of 1812 these began to be granted in quantity by the administrations of Andrew Jackson and his successor Martin Van Buren. In 1833 fifteen civilians were commissioned into the newly raised 1st Dragoons, including the colonel, Henry Dodge of Michigan. In 1836, thirty-three more were commissioned into the new 2nd Dragoons; the list included the regiment's lieutenant colonel, Wharton Rector of Arkansas. In 1837 there were thirty more of these appointments, though two were men commissioned from the ranks of the regular army. The figure for 1838 soared to sixty-three, of whom fifteen went into the Topographical Engineers; six of the total had been promoted from the ranks. In 1839, thirty-three civilians received direct commissions. Thereafter the practice dwindled for a while: two in 1840, only one in 1842. It came to life again in the 1850's, stimulated by the raising of more cavalry. Emory Upton and his West Point classmate Henry du Pont, due to graduate in 1861, complained that the politicians awarded commissions to civilian friends in advance of each Academy graduation, and in the most sought-after units.[34]

Wartime service undoubtedly improved the prospects for promotion. British officers used to drink toasts to "a bloody war and a sickly season" — namely, one that would open up promotion through death in battle and by disease. The motto of Major General William Jenkins Worth in the Mexican War was "a *grade* or a grave." But, though this consideration could hardly be grumbled at, casualties in 1846–1847 were too light to transform the situation. Nor were officers eager to transfer to new regular regiments in search of promotion. They suspected with good cause that the establishment would be reduced once the war was over, leaving them out in the cold.

THE HEROES OF THE WAR OF 1812.

OFFICERS' QUARRELS

As for brevet promotions, these were an empty consolation, since they carried no substantive promotion and no extra pay except in special circumstances. Brevet rank was a device borrowed from the British, who used it to distribute inexpensive rewards to officers on royal birthdays and other official occasions. In the American army brevets provoked extraordinary controversies over rank and precedence. At the senior level they stimulated a debate between Winfield Scott and Edmund Gaines which dragged on from 1822 until Gaines's death in 1849. Scott finally won, though not until he had challenged Gaines to a duel (1824) and engaged in a fantastic pamphlet war, in which Gaines "is pleased to speak of my *productions* and *style* as *hackneyed, crooked, interminable, calumnious, ill-advised,* and *ill-designed* — all of which epithets he has crowded into one sentence of less than three lines," with Scott retaliating in kind:

It has been remarked . . . that General Gaines on the subject of this unfortunate controversy, has the appearance of being deranged; — that the question of rank had become the hallucination of his mind. . . . Then . . . why the severity with which I have treated his aberrations? What! If a madman flies at my throat and attempts my life, shall I not break his hold and chastise him into intellectual sobriety?

The wrangle exasperated President John Quincy Adams. When it came to a head in 1828, with the death of General in Chief Jacob Brown, Adams passed over both men in favor of Alexander Macomb on the ground that Scott and Gaines had quarreled "not only with rancour, but with indecency." Scott was outraged. He did his best thereafter to ignore Macomb — insisting that by virtue of seniority he, Scott, was still Macomb's superior and was under no obligation to obey Macomb's directives.[35]

Scott and Gaines had made their reputations in the War of 1812. They were promoted to colonel and then brigadier general in the regular army on exactly the same dates. Gaines based his claim to subsequent seniority on the fact that his name was printed above Scott's in the army registers. Scott's claim rested on the fact that his *brevet* promotion to major general came three weeks before that of Gaines. Their squabble might seem infantile. One recalls that Scott was always at odds with someone. In 1817–1819 the dispute was with his superior officer, Andrew Jackson, who challenged him to a duel. In the 1830's he fell out again with Gaines and with another old adversary, Brigadier General Thomas S. Jesup, over the conduct of the war against the Seminole and Creek Indians. This, like Scott's previous dispute with Gaines, was aired in public at an unedifying court of inquiry in which Gaines compared Scott to Benedict Arnold. Vast quantities of dirty linen were washed during the Mexican War, with members of the administration and some of Scott's officers accusing him of crimes ranging from military stupidity to financial dishonesty, and Scott replying with his own brand of ponderous, would-be Shakespearean invective.

Finally, in 1855–1856, came the extraordinary exchange of letters between Scott (by then general in chief) and the Secretary of War, Jefferson Davis. The dispute was over pay and rank. Scott was claiming eight years' back pay (over $30,000), since he had been made a *brevet* lieutenant general in 1855, the rank to date from 1847. Davis contended that "the purpose was for

eminent services in the war with Mexico, to confer a complimentary distinction, not to grant a pecuniary reward." Scott took
advice from no fewer than six eminent lawyers and at last carried
his point. The two men detested one another; and it is conceivable that Scott's loyalty to the Union in 1861 was clinched by the
knowledge that his old enemy had become leader of the Southern
Confederacy. They wrote to and at one another in mounting fury,
Davis from Washington and Scott from New York, as far removed
as possible from what he considered the tainted atmosphere of
the capital. Their correspondence, when published as a Senate
document, ran to 254 pages of quibbling and abuse. Its tone may
be gathered from these extracts:

Scott to Davis, 29 September 1855: With all the records of the army
and every compulsory assistance at hand, you have, by a toil of more
than five weeks, on what, to your nature, must have been a "labor of
love," poured out on me, in twenty-seven compacted foolscap pages,
the full measure of your spleen and vengeance. . . .

Scott to Davis, 21 May 1856: I owe you an apology for my long
neglect of your letter dated March 31.
   My silence, under the new provocation, has been the result, first, of
pity, and next, forgetfulness. Compassion is always due to an enraged
imbecile, who lays about him in blows which hurt only himself, or
who . . . seeks to stifle his opponent by dint of naughty words.
Keeping clear of unnecessary invective, I shall at once despatch the
last extraneous matters that you have forced into this discussion.

Davis to Scott, 29 February 1856: Your petulance, characteristic
egotism and recklessness of accusation have imposed on me the task of
unveiling some of your deformities. . . . It is sincerely to be hoped
that those who follow you in the honorable profession in which you
have been eminent, notwithstanding your fame has been clouded by
grovelling vices, will select for their imitation some other model than
one whose military career has been marked by querulousness, insubordination, greed of lucre and want of truth.

Winfield Scott was a difficult customer. When he got his first
commission in 1808 — a captaincy, at the age of twenty-two —
he "immediately ordered a new suit of uniform — sword, sash,

cap — everything complete, and had it carried into the largest room in the house, in the diagonal corners of which he placed two looking glasses. Then he cleared away all the furniture, . . . and strutted back and forth between the mirrors for two hours." His aide, Erasmus D. Keyes (U.S.M.A. 1832) said he had the anecdote from Scott himself. "Old Fuss and Feathers" — his nickname — was "Young Fuss and Feathers" too: huge, handsome and vain, comically fond of dress uniforms, elaborate food, and conversation garnished with literary allusions. According to Keyes, who knew him intimately, Scott's ruling passion was "ambition and its . . . attendant jealousy. In matters of rivalry, he was easily vexed, and when the thing pursued was of great distinction, he seemed to go out of his own skin into that of an angry porcupine with every quill standing fiercely on end."

Yet Scott was not alone in behaving thus. Andrew Jackson, Gaines, Jesup, Jefferson Davis and others with whom he crossed swords were at least as obsessively hot-tempered. Keyes had to listen to endless abuse of Gaines by Scott, who used to describe his rival as an "imbecile commander," a "superannuated old martinet," a soldier "only fit to be a dry nurse in a lying-in hospital" and so on. Scott, proud of his own knowledge of French, ridiculed Gaines's attempts at the language. He pretended that when Gaines tried to say "Je ne sais quoi," he thought his enemy was describing a "Genesee squaw." However, when Keyes met Gaines he had to listen to half an hour of complaints that Scott was puerile, "a vain pretender" and the like. Keyes concluded that Gaines was quite as vain as Scott in his way. Scott was a dinner-table monomaniac: Gaines's conceit took the form of boasting of his "abstemiousness and hardihood, that he never used an umbrella, . . . that he could tire young men in walking, etc., etc."[36]

Some of the reasons for this polemic spirit will be examined in Chapters 8 and 9. Senior officers lived in an atmosphere of constant intrigue. Everything conspired to turn them against politicians, against volunteer soldiers, against one another. There was, for instance, a good deal of latent hostility to West Point graduates within the army. The officers of general rank before the

Civil War had made their names before the Academy was firmly established. Such old "Western" soldiers as Zachary Taylor and Edmund Gaines disapproved of the "European" style inculcated by the Academy. Taylor, "Old Tonkey," "Old Rough and Ready," with his shabby civilian clothes and his readiness to tell an enlisted man where to buy whiskey, was a world away from "Old Fuss and Feathers," who delighted to tell this revealing story about himself:

It was, I think, in the year 1830 . . . when travelling in Ohio, [Scott] stopped at a country store where they sold liquor by the glass. He had on a . . . plain overcoat that concealed his buttons. The landlord having stepped out, [Scott] went behind the counter upon which the glasses stood, . . . and was busy writing a note, when a farmer came in and called out, "Give me a glass of rum toddy." The general straightened up, and turning full upon the man, he exclaimed: "Did you ever know a man six feet four and a quarter inches tall to sell rum toddy?"

Though Scott was not himself a West Pointer he was known to be a staunch supporter of it. He lived there for a number of years during the summer months. Naturally then, as Gaines growled and as President Polk said in almost identical words, Scott's view of warfare was too "scientific and visionary" for their tastes. Straightforward Americans preferred straightforward tactics.[37]

The chief extenuation of Scott and his rivals, however, is that the smallness of the army after the War of 1812 left too little room for them all. Perhaps they got on too fast for their own good in that conflict. Scott, granted a regular captaincy in 1808, was soon suspended for a year for indiscreet comments on superior officers. Even so, in 1812 he became a lieutenant colonel. In 1814 he rose to a regular brigadier general's rank and a brevet major generalcy — this by the age of twenty-eight. He, Gaines, Brown and others were national heroes, the recipients of special medals, swords and ceremonial addresses. Then followed the long anti-climax. By 1821 the army's establishment had been reduced to one major general (Jacob Brown) and two brigadiers (Scott and Gaines, or as the latter would have put it, Gaines and Scott). The seniors felt stuck, stranded, overlooked, still young and with time on their hands. Even scrupulously fair and efficient administrations could not have kept them happy. The administration allotted them different geographical departments, yet in the Black Hawk War of 1832–1833 and again in the Seminole troubles of 1835–1836, sent Scott into Gaines's territory to take charge of operations. No wonder they bickered incessantly, or that it took them scores of pages to express their accumulated grievances.

The results were lamentable for the army as a whole. Junior officers became infected with the arguments of their seniors, and identified with one faction or another. The same was true of the American navy. Junior army officers had their own miniature disputes, which produced an amazing crop of court-martials, courts of inquiry, broken friendships and smoldering resentments. The situation was literally and metaphorically claustrophobic. Some officers were able to pull strings so as to avoid unpleasant duties. Ethan Allen Hitchcock, a well-to-do eccentric with an intellectual bent, fell under this accusation in 1842, at the hands of Scott. Hitchcock's regiment, the 3rd Infantry, was in Florida, while Hitchcock himself was on duty in Washington, where he lived in the same boardinghouse as John C. Spencer, the Secretary of War. Scott protested to Spencer that Hitchcock had been absent "from all *regimental* duty, or *service with troops,* from 1829 except for about 28 months. . . . [He] seems to have lost his military pride and to think the Army would be an excellent place . . . – but for the soldiers." In his reply to Spencer, who appears to have been sympathetic, Hitchcock confessed to "a perfect horror of stagnation, or idleness, of mere existence. Hence the formal duties of a confined garrison life are . . . irksome and despicable. The thought of such a life on a small scale puts me almost into a fever of desperation." Those with wealth and influence, such as Hitchcock, used it to have themselves posted to attractive stations like Newport, Rhode Island, where "Prince" John Magruder (U.S.M.A. 1830) contrived to earn and live up to his nickname. Others secured staff appointments in a profusion which enraged the envious and the reform-minded.[38]

Officers with fewer social or intellectual resources found themselves in little garrisons of two or three companies, sometimes from different regiments. They quarreled over brevet and substantive seniority, over the right to command, over possession of desirable quarters, over leaves of absence. Officers who had enjoyed undisputed sway over some frontier fort acquired a strong sense of their own authority and did not take kindly to being superseded. Except in the Mexican War and on a few other occasions the regiment hardly existed as a larger entity, generating a larger loyalty. To take a few representative cases:

Lieutenant Jefferson Davis (U.S.M.A. 1828), adjutant of the 1st Dragoons in 1833–1834, was put under arrest by his colonel, a circumstance which hastened his decision to resign from the army in 1835.

Lieutenant Braxton Bragg (U.S.M.A. 1837) was on such bad terms with his commanding officer, Colonel Gates of the 3rd Artillery, that he would not speak to him except on official business. There is a story that Gates, trying to be pleasant, offered Bragg a drink and that Bragg, unmollified, answered: "Colonel Gates, if you order me to drink a glass of wine with you, I shall have to do it."

Lieutenant George H. Derby (U.S.M.A. 1846) — "John Phoenix," the humorist — was court-martialed at Sonoma, California, in 1851–1852, over a complicated affair of a stolen horse and an escaped prisoner, when he got on the wrong side of Lieutenant Colonel Joseph Hooker. The case dragged on for months and poor Derby, usually the most cheerful of men, became so despondent that he tried to poison himself.

Lieutenant Thomas J. Jackson, 1st Artillery, a classmate of Derby's, got into a preposterous quarrel over rank and jurisdiction with his senior, Captain French, at Fort Meade, Florida. One trouble was that both were majors in brevet rank. Jackson's complaints included French's habit of opening mail addressed to the "acting assistant quartermaster," an exalted post that Jackson was filling. He also accused French of consorting with a servant girl. Each officer badgered the soldiers at the fort into helping him to compile his laborious dossier of charges. The quarrel was still unsettled when Jackson resigned from the army in 1852 to become a professor at V.M.I.

John P. Hatch (U.S.M.A. 1845) of the Mounted Rifles was threatened with a court-martial in 1859 for insulting his commanding officer, Colonel Loring. Though he apologized and was let off, Loring refused to let him have the period of leave which Hatch had been requesting for the past two years.[39]

The consequences of this puerile yet fundamental discontent were foreseeable. Rankers left the army after one enlistment, or deserted: the officers' remedy was to resign their commissions. The promotion log-jam, the boredom, the lack of esteem, the brooding neurotic mood of army posts were negative factors. The attractions of civilian careers were positive lures. The ninety-eight officers who resigned in the peak year of 1836 were not, as their critics said, recoiling in horror from the prospects of a campaign in Florida, though they were certainly repelled by the dull stalemate of the Seminole campaigns. Nor were they restless youngsters who had not grown accustomed to the army. Half of them had been in the service for more than ten years; only twenty-nine resigned before completing eight years' service. They knew what they were leaving; and many of them were dazzled by civilian prospects.

Some, like Alexander Mitchell of North Carolina (U.S.M.A. 1835) and George B. McClellan of Pennsylvania (U.S.M.A. 1846) busied themselves as engineers, building canals, roads and railroads. Some became educators: D. B. Douglass, former professor of engineering at West Point, and subsequently a civil engineer, became president of Kenyon College, Ohio, in 1840; D. H. Hill of South Carolina (U.S.M.A. 1842) left the army in 1849 for a professorship of mathematics and then (in 1859), the superintendency of North Carolina Military Institute. Isaac F. Quinby of New Jersey (U.S.M.A. 1843) resigned in 1852 (though he returned in 1861 to lead the 13th New York at Bull Run) for a professorship in mathematics and science at the University of Rochester. A number affected by the "holy spirit" — the religious revival that reached West Point in 1825 — resigned to enter the

142

church. Leonidas Polk of Louisiana (U.S.M.A. 1827), who became an Episcopalian bishop, is among the best known of these.

Put starkly, the choice was to stay in the army and rot, or cash in on one's Academy training in some other profession, as Jubal Early did in resigning to enter the law. The gains to the nation, as defenders of the Academy pointed out, were impressive. The effects on the army were unfortunate. When T. J. Jackson resigned in 1852 he was still only a lieutenant, with ten others senior to him in his regiment, and he was convinced that he was being persecuted. Braxton Bragg left the army in 1856 to run a Louisiana plantation. Among others who were to be prominent Confederate soldiers, Abraham Buford (U.S.M.A. 1841) resigned in 1854 to farm in his home state of Kentucky; and Simon Bolivar Buckner (U.S.M.A. 1844), also of Kentucky, in 1855 for a business career in Chicago. Ambrose Burnside (U.S.M.A. 1847) dropped out in 1853, to be a manufacturer of firearms. Joseph Hooker (U.S.M.A. 1837) and William T. Sherman (U.S.M.A. 1840) both resigned in 1853, to try their luck in California. U. S. Grant (U.S.M.A. 1843), who left the army in 1854, had already attempted unsuccessfully to combine soldiering with private ventures in California. Also in 1854, the army lost William S. Rosecrans (U.S.M.A. 1842), who turned to civil engineering in Cincinnati; Gustavus W. Smith (U.S.M.A. 1842), who also became an engineer, and was street commissioner of New York City when the Civil War began; and Henry W. Halleck (U.S.M.A. 1839), to pursue a Western career in law and silver-mining.

Who remained, during the 1850's? A minority of able, well-placed men like Robert E. Lee, of oddities like Hitchcock[40] and George Derby, and of Indian fighters like George Crook (U.S.M.A. 1852) who genuinely enjoyed frontier conditions. The majority might seem to consist of recently commissioned officers who had not yet discovered the drawbacks of military life, or of older men who did not quite know what else to do. John P. Hatch might be taken as typical of these jaded veterans. He wrote to his mother in 1849, about an imminent transfer to California: "If the gold stories are true I shall be rich enough in two or three years to resign. Then I shall come home to live, for I do not wish to be a soldier when I can help it." A year later he was chasing gold-rush deserters. Riches eluded him and he was still glumly planning how to resign when the Civil War broke out.

The army circle embraced a wide range of talents and temperaments. Though some were dullards they were as a whole men of intelligence and integrity. But they felt themselves to be nonentities. Stultified, querulous or apologetic, miscellaneously discontented, not exactly spoiling for a fight and yet aware that only a big one could open their horizons, they were marking time, like Alfred de Vigny, who said of his post-Napoleonic service as an officer in the French army: "We were stifled, immured in the belly of a wooden horse which never opened in any Troy."

5

THE PROFESSIONALS:
CONSOLIDATION

In this age of liberal principles, this mental proximo,
No army will fair freedom's throne attempt to overthrow,
But give the surest guarantee, as politicians know,
Of the solid basis of our rights and Benny Havens, O!
— "Benny Havens, O": traditional West Point song

I recommend to your fostering care, as one of our safest means of national defense, the Military Academy. This institution has already exercised the happiest influence upon the moral and intellectual character of our Army; and such of the graduates as . . . may not pursue the profession of arms will be scarcely less useful as citizens.

— Andrew Jackson, First Annual Message, 1829

WHY REGULARS?

We must now deal with a set of facts which appear to contradict those of the previous chapter. It has been shown that most Americans were either indifferent to or positively hostile toward the regular army. West Point came under sharp and recurrent criticism. Yet the army remained in being. The Academy was not abolished and it was joined in the 1840's by a second, naval academy at Annapolis. Military expenditure, including a considerable budget for the construction of coastal defenses, steadily increased. By European standards these were on a small and grudging scale. The army's spokesmen complained of the nation's ingratitude and of congressional meanness. Military historians have echoed these complaints. They have been less interested to explain why the army remained in being, or how it managed to exercise an influence upon public life.

Part of the explanation is to be found in the complex heritage already outlined. Prowess in arms became an integral feature of patriotic pride. Though their object lessons could be interpreted in very different ways, there is no doubt that the fairly frequent succession of wars and campaigns provided occupation for regular units and a cumulative record of gallantry, fidelity and efficiency. Though the country as a whole might be only half aware of this old yet replenished claim to recognition, men who held national office or were close to the centers of power had a more conscious sense of what was at stake. Among such men existed a real sentiment in favor of a standing army. Few of them held or at any rate upheld this view unequivocally. Some favored regulars in certain circumstances — notably wartime — but not in others. Some continued to believe also in the militia ideal. Some, while privately contemptuous of the militia, or of volunteer regiments, knew that it would be politically disastrous to declare their contempt in public. In covert, qualified ways the argument for an American standing army was maintained – successfully.

If American military thought is reexamined in this light, it can be seen that from George Washington onward there was a continuous if not dominant emphasis on the value of a regular force. One historian suggests that the Revolution bequeathed a dual military legacy: belief in the militia *and* belief in a professional army.[1] By the end of 1776, after a few months in command, Washington was convinced that America must have "a respectable Army." What he meant was an army organized as far as possible on European lines. It must be officered by gentlemen, and they would have to be given genuine inducements to enter the service: adequate pay and status, chances of promotion, and the prospect of *permanent* employment. Wars could not be waged effectively without preparation and precision. Even if Europeans and Americans thought afterward that the Revolution had been won by a spontaneous upsurge of martial spirit, the men who had directed the long struggle knew otherwise. Washington was too hardheaded to dream of an American army entirely composed of regulars. He recognized that he would have to depend largely on scratch units and that he could not hope for more than a nucleus of seasoned Continentals. His aim was to make this nucleus as large as possible, and to enlist its battalions for as long as Congress would allow and Americans would consent to serve. Nor did he intend to fight on unorthodox lines. No doubt he was more flexible than his opponents in his tactics. He was quicker than they to see the advantages of riflemen over musketeers, of inconspicuous clothing and concealment. But the contrast was far from absolute. The British too had their riflemen-skirmishers, clad in green instead of scarlet. By and large, Washington agreed with Howe and Clinton in his conception of warfare. Campaigns, that is, consisted of maneuvering between armies, not bands of guerrillas. The object of the maneuver was to confront the enemy army on a battleground of one's own choosing, and with superior force. Washington had no enthusiasm for dispersing his troops, or for committing them in scattered units. With the primitive weapons and communications of the day it was essential to keep regiments in close order, under the eye of the commander. Mass was what counted.

Washington and such wartime associates as Henry Knox saw no reason to change their opinions afterward. They did not recommend a large regular army; they did endeavor to legislate for an efficient militia. But they did keep alive the idea, and in minuscule form the reality, of a professional army. The inadequacy of the legislation governing the militia strengthened their argument. If the militia were not to constitute a genuine force, all the more need for a little army of professionals who might in emergency save the day.[2]

Professionalism may mean different things, as may terms like "regular army" and "standing army." The old pre-Revolutionary standing armies of Europe were by later standards hardly professional at all. The emphasis on special bodies of knowledge and codes of conduct belongs in origin mainly with the nineteenth century, on both sides of the Atlantic. According to one scholar, Samuel P. Huntington, it was in the United States the particular contribution of Southern officers and theorists.[3] Whether or not this is true, there is plenty of evidence to show that by the 1840's the American regular army had developed professional styles which had little in common with the folklore of amateur soldiering.

Another historian, William H. Riker, detects a marked preference for "regulars as against the militia" from 1790 to 1860. This preference received "repeated legislative and executive endorsement." It led for example to a fluctuating but basically increasing appropriation for federal military expenditure.[4] The point is broadly true. It is important, however, to note that the initiative seems to have been taken by the executive branch of government, at least in proposals to enlarge the army. One reason, of course, is that the existence of a War Department provided an element of professional permanence. The Secretary of War had the President's ear; and certain Secretaries, notably John C. Calhoun, Joel R. Poinsett and Jefferson Davis, were men of considerable quality. A more crucial reason was that in time of crisis the President had to act, and act quickly, to find troops. With the provisional army of 1798 and again with the units raised for the War of 1812, the executive expressed a desire to have a strong force of regulars in addition to whatever might be contributed by militia or by volunteer regiments. On these occasions, and later, Congress tended to prefer volunteer to regular units. The executive's approach is strikingly illustrated in the plan submitted by Secretary of War James Monroe in the fall of 1814. Asked by the Senate Committee on Military Affairs to account for American defeats and to propose remedies, Monroe responded with a scheme to increase the regular army by no less than forty thousand men. This immense enlargement was never carried out: the end of the war made it unnecessary, and in any case recruitment would probably have fallen far short of the total needed. The significant fact is that, despite fierce opposition, Monroe's recommendation did gain congressional approval.[5]

James K. Polk's response to the Mexican War is equally surprising, when we remember the assertion in his first annual message that large standing armies were "contrary to the genius of our free institutions," and that reliance must be "mainly on our citizen soldiers." True, his war message asked for volunteer, not regular, regiments. But here he was acting as his field commander General Taylor had recommended. In the next session, Polk persuaded Congress to let him have ten new *regular* regiments. Once he, like his predecessors, was in office, he began to see the virtues of regular troops. A small regular army was by now conceded to be necessary, although it might be spoken of as a necessary evil. An augmented regular army seemed equally indispensable when the United States faced an emergency. Nor could Polk be said to have contradicted himself. His previous statements could be made to yield an altered interpretation. He was against *large* standing armies: how large? America was to rely *mainly* on amateur soldiers: how much was *mainly?*[6] The new regiments were for the most part disbanded after the Mexican War. In that conflict and again in 1861–1865 the regular contingents were far outnumbered by the volunteers. Yet the principle of professionalism had gained a footing and was not to be dislodged.

PARTRIDGE AND OTHER COMPLAINANTS

In the consolidation of the regulars a central part was played by the Military Academy. Despite the attacks upon it, despite the cynicism and pessimism of some cadets, the Academy survived and flourished. Why? A key figure was Andrew Jackson. If he had conceived a dislike of West Point, if he had become convinced of the parallel argued by some congressmen between the Academy and the Bank of the United States, his antagonism might well have proved decisive. Denied appropriations for a couple of years, the Academy would have withered away. Instead, Jackson praised and supported West Point. In 1823 he described it as "the best school in the world."[7] True, he interfered with its control in minor ways. But neither he nor any other President recommended the abolition of the Academy. Nor did the bulk of congressmen. Hamilton Fish's House report of 1844 was as generous and persuasive a defense of the Academy as any West Pointer could have wished for. West Point nominations became too useful an element in congressional patronage for Fish's colleagues to denounce the institution *en masse*.

A closer look reveals that attacks upon the Academy were more noisy than powerful. And it begins to appear that much of the seemingly widespread criticism emanated from one man, Alden Partridge. He has already been mentioned as an early superintendent of the Academy, and afterward as a champion of other forms of military education. West Point chroniclers have charged him with flouting regulations that did not suit him; graduating cadets when he saw fit, without the stipulated examination; employing an uncle and two nephews at the Academy, not all of whom may have been scrupulously honest; and antagonizing his staff. According to one account Partridge, like Bottom in *A Midsummer Night's Dream*, was "ready to perform all parts, whether of exercising command, filling a professor's chair, supplying the pulpit, drilling a squad or battalion, lecturing on grand tactics or moral philosophy, inspecting mess kitchens or barracks, wrangling with bombardier soldiers, or descending to play police spy upon cadets. He seemed to ignore all division of labor; and, zealous to supervise every detail, completely lost sight of the enlarged functions of his high office."[8]

This particular sketch was intended to form a contrast for a eulogistic portrait of Partridge's successor, Sylvanus Thayer. Though written long after the event, it seems to represent views of Partridge held while he was superintendent. According to the memoirs of Partridge's superior, Joseph G. Swift, the chief engineer officer of the United States, President Madison in February 1816 asked Swift to move Partridge away from West Point, since Secretary of War William H. Crawford did not deem him "the most suitable officer of engineers for duty at the Academy." Crawford found a promising rival in Thayer, who in some respects closely resembled Partridge. They were born in the same year, 1785. Both were New Englanders. Both had attended Dartmouth College, though Partridge did not graduate. Both were bachelors: Thayer never married, and Partridge not until 1832. Both were engineer officers. Both were austere and energetic in personality. But Thayer impressed the authorities as being markedly more efficient. After taking his degree from Dartmouth in 1807 he spent a year at West Point, and was allowed to graduate in 1808. During the next few years he worked on fortifications in the Corps of Engineers, while Partridge was teaching at West Point. Though neither saw combat in the War of 1812, Thayer emerged with the rank of brevet major. Convinced that America must learn from Europe in military affairs, and especially from France, he applied for leave in 1815 to study abroad. His reception was sympathetic; he and another officer were sent to Europe on official duty, to examine French military schools and to assemble a collection of books for the Academy's mediocre library.

Partridge in the meantime had become superintendent at West Point. Thayer on his return from Europe was put in Partridge's place, in 1817. Partridge strenuously objected and it took a court-martial to shift him. He was outraged at what he considered to be thoroughly shabby treatment. He was after all a young and vigorous officer, whose long subsequent career showed him to be anything but somnolent. He was a firm disciplinarian and introduced various routines which are still followed at West Point. He held the superintendency at an early stage in the history of the Academy when opinion as to its future shape was divided. He labored under great difficulties. He was short of staff, and two members in particular — Jared Mansfield and Andrew Ellicott — seem to have been lazy and malevolent. It was never made clear what authority he possessed in relation to Swift, to the staff and to the cadets. Swift appears to have been a moral coward, allowing the President, the Secretary of War, the West Point faculty and Alden Partridge to believe what he thought they wished to believe. At the court-martial, allegations of brutality and incompetence were all disproved. On the face of it the only thing wrong with Partridge was that some people did not like him, or had decided that they preferred Thayer. He was blamed for everything that seemed unsatisfactory at West Point. So he was pushed from office after occupying the superintendency for less than two years.

Partridge's dismissal irked him so much that on resigning from the army he assured General Swift that "the business will not rest . . . until the whole scene of iniquity . . . relative to the affairs of West Point be fully developed. . . . I am near 30 years of age, and should I live to be 70, this subject shall never . . . be abandoned unless justice be done."

He did not rest. His name crops up again and again on petitions and resolutions attacking the Academy. He was a one-man lobbyist against West Point, and he may have shaped the whole discussion of the subject in Congress.[9]

In his own day Partridge was identified by West Point supporters as the principal villain. Speaking of his "AMERICANUS" pamphlet, *West Point Unmasked*, the *North American Review* in 1832 said his allegations were "strongly tinctured with prejudice; . . . and his reflections upon particular individuals are rather too indicative of disappointed ambition and personal resentment." The writer regretted that "his eagerness to gratify any personal feelings should have hurried him so far beyond the

153

limits of prudence and propriety." An editorial in the *Savannah Republican* in 1844 describes Partridge as the *"auctor et princeps* of the first popular sensation against our Military Academy." A Massachusetts educator said, in a laudatory report on West Point written during the Civil War:

More than twenty years ago a memorial was sent to Congress by a graduate who had also been professor and superintendent, asking "that the Military Academy be abolished as a grievance." It throws some light on the origin of his hostility . . . to know that his superintendency of less than two years occasioned more controversy . . . than that of all the others. . . . [From the day of his dismissal] he was an uncompromising and able opponent of the Academy. Probably a large share of the current objections to the institution are due to his influence. . . . This gentleman and his friends labored earnestly, and not without some success, to spread their views.

The report may have been adapted from a recent article in the *American Journal of Education,* whose editor, the knowledgeable Henry Barnard, also maintained that Partridge "more than any one man, and his pupils, and personal friends, . . . were the instigators of the chief attacks on the Academy."[10]

There was much corroboration for this opinion, in addition to Partridge's 1830 pamphlet and his 1841 memorial. The inaccurate figures which he cited for the cost of the Academy were quoted again and again, until firmly refuted by the House of Representatives report of March 1844. He helped to organize, and addressed, a number of the "military conventions" held in New England and New York from about 1838 to the Mexican War. One of his pupils edited the short-lived *Citizen Soldier,* a militia periodical launched in Norwich, Vermont in 1840, which lost no opportunity to castigate West Point. Another militia paper, the *New York Military Magazine,* at first praised the Academy but then under different editors began to echo Partridge's sentiments: "We will put the scholars of Captain Partridge against the West Point graduates, and they will be found in point of energy, effectiveness, and sterling worth, much superior as staunch and able officers. But no; as though this was not a free country, favor and duplicity hold the scales . . . , and while such is the case we may never expect to end our wars in Florida." The next issue of the *Military Magazine* carried the news that Partridge had just lectured in Boston and was coming to New York to lecture on "the higher branches of military tactics." Dennis Hart Mahan, a professor at West Point, complained of the article in a letter to the Secretary of War, and blamed Partridge.[11]

In short, much of the organized opposition to the Academy was inspired by Partridge, and may be discounted as proof of nation-wide indignation. He was able to make some headway with various disgruntled groups. The militia officers who attended conventions were gratified by the interest he showed, and eager to listen to assurances that their skill and their claims for financial backing were ignored in favor of West Point. Similarly, Partridge flattered state pride by insisting that the remedy was to replace the Academy with a series of military schools in different corners of the Union. But the effect of his propaganda was limited. Those in official circles dismissed him as a man unhinged by brooding over private wrongs. Most of his arguments, and those of his followers, failed to reckon with the national mood or with the hard facts of American military organization. They deluded themselves, said their critics, with the notion that the United States had or should have a vast military establishment, regular and militia. One proposal by the Academy's enemies was to throw open regular commissions to the entire population. But as Hamilton Fish's committee pointed out, only about a third of those admitted to the Academy usually succeeded in graduating: 36 out of 114, on the average. The 36 was enough to fill the army's vacancies. If the Academy were abolished, the entire nation would be competing each year for 36 chances of commissions; whereas under the present system there were 114 chances of commissions. In the face of such ingenious arithmetic, Partridge's contentions lost their force.

Another devious and ineffective source of hostility to West Point was explained in a letter to the *Army & Navy Chronicle* in 1835. Many cadets were dismissed each year for "deficiency":

A great proportion of these have heretofore been from the West, and have carried back with them tales of *injustice* and *persecution*, with which to solace their disappointed friends, and shelter their own personal pride.

The cause according to this theory lay in the poor facilities for preparatory education available in Western states:

> Some of these persons have returned to the west and become eminent professional men; but the wound . . . to their vanity has never been healed. . . . [They] like to gratify their wounded feelings by injuring the Institution which rejected them. . . .
> The truth is, that the mass of persons who oppose the Academy, are actuated either by some private *pique*, or a desire to make it a *monster*, which they may immortalize themselves in subduing.

Such men did exist. In 1837 for example President Van Buren received a long letter, marked "private and confidential," from a Mr. I. P. Van Antwerp. It is a ferocious assault on the arrogant and anti-Jacksonian behavior of army officers stationed in Indiana. The complainant assures the President that he was once among the Academy's warmest supporters:

> I had been educated at it. . . . I retained my confidence in it, until some of the graduates were sent among the people, to conduct some of their public works. I . . . heard from them an expression of their anti-democratic principles. . . . I then began to lose my confidence in the Academy as a Republican Institution — if such were to be its fruits — And I admit, that my feelings have gained strength with every new occasion when I have come in contact with Graduates.

Mr. Van Antwerp was not a graduate, though to some degree correct in claiming to have been "educated at it." A cadet of his name was admitted to West Point in 1823 but did not manage to stay the course.[12]

THE TRIUMPH OF SYLVANUS THAYER

We shall come back to Partridge in Chapter 8. For the moment it is sufficient to note that, whatever the wrongs done him and the logic of some of his arguments, the clamor against West Point may have been less than universal. It may have been limited to special cases. And second, whatever may be said for Partridge and against his successor, there is no doubt that the high reputation of the Academy dates from Thayer's superintendency. Thayer began in an acrimonious atmosphere. The faculty, in opposing Partridge, were not necessarily willing to subordinate themselves to any other officer. Many of the cadets resisted Thayer's effort to impose his will. There was a furious controversy in 1818 when a committee of five cadets, representing a "combination" of nearly two hundred of their fellows, protested that they had "as a corps in the army, rights to defend; and that as cadets in the Military Academy, they were entitled to a free expression of opinion in regard to its management." Their situation was anomalous: were they students, were they ordinary soldiers, were they embryonic officers? A court-martial held at the Academy evaded the issue, affirming merely that it had no authority to try the five cadets. Thayer persisted in his view that they had willfully disobeyed orders and must be punished. He was upheld by the Attorney General, William Wirt, who ruled in 1819 that cadets ranked as enlisted soldiers. The ruling was confirmed by President Monroe and by the Secretary of War, John C. Calhoun. The cadet ringleaders were dismissed from the Academy.

After this trial of strength Thayer was able to press ahead unchallenged. "The Academy," in the words of one of his admirers, "was suddenly metamorphosed from a drowsy school of supine students to . . . a great seminary of science and military art. The wand of the new Carnot waved over all, educing strength and symmetry from . . . chaos." With the support of Calhoun, Thayer turned West Point into a model school.[13] He added to its engineering and scientific pretensions and built up its other academic departments, so that its four-year course compared favorably with that of any college in the country. Indeed, for the next half-century or so it provided the best engineering instruction in America. He brought on to the staff able young officers like Dennis Mahan (U.S.M.A. 1822). Borrowing from France, Thayer broke the classes into small groups, and required every student to demonstrate constantly at the blackboard what he had learned, or failed to learn. There was a class list, in order of merit; the top five names were printed each year in official reports. Yearly examinations and an awesome final examination were staged in the presence of the Board of Visitors. Students who failed conspicuously in academic work were sent away. Outside the classroom their lives were governed with equal severity. There was an elaborate demerit system: too many demerits led to dismissal.* There were military punishments, such as extra drills, for misdemeanors.

Thayer's reign was not entirely autocratic. The two companies into which he divided cadets had their own cadet officers, though these were appointed by the Academy. Moreover, there were sharp gradations of prestige and authority between the four cadet years. The wretched "Plebes" (Plebeians) of the fourth class — i.e., the first year — were at everybody's mercy, and on merely probationary status. A good half proved incapable of meeting Thayer's rigid standards, and this in spite of their having passed a preliminary entrance examination. The failure rate was progressively smaller in succeeding years, until cadets reached the almost-safe haven of the graduating class, when, as one of them said, "We acquire that air of importance, that show of dignity and condescension to our inferiors, which forms the great characteristic of first class men."[14]

So they passed to the final glory-ordeal of the June examination, when the Academy swarmed with elegant ladies and eminent gentlemen. George Ticknor, professor at Harvard and a Dartmouth classmate of Thayer's, was appointed to the Board of Visitors in 1826. He described the occasion with almost reverent admiration. Staying in Thayer's beautifully regulated house, he was awakened at six by the music of the band, when the cadets began to march. Thayer came in half an hour later. Breakfast was

---

* That paragon among cadets, Robert E. Lee, graduated second in his class in 1829, without a single demerit recorded against him. In contrast, John B. Hood (U.S.M.A. 1853), who graduated second from the bottom of his class, had so many demerits that he barely escaped dismissal. Lee, by then superintendent of the Academy, had to place Hood under arrest at one point and publicly reprimand him.

precisely at seven; then, "a little before eight o'clock, Thayer puts on his full-dress coat and sword, and when the bugle sounds we are always at Mr. Cozzens's [Hotel], where Thayer . . . inquires if the President of the Board is ready to attend at the examination-room; if he is, the Commandant conducts him to it with great ceremony. . . . If he is not ready, Thayer goes without him; he waits for no man."

Thayer sat unmoving in his chair, while the cadets went through their inquisition, from 8 A.M. to 1 P.M., and again from 3 P.M. to 7 P.M.:

> At seven he goes on parade; from half past seven to eight does business with the Cadets, and from eight to nine, or even till eleven, he is liable to have meetings with the Academic Staff. Yet with all this labor, and the whole responsibility of the Institution, the examination, and the accommodation of the Visitors, on his hands, he is always fresh, prompt, ready, and pleasant; never fails to receive me . . . with the same unencumbered and affectionate manner, and seems, in short, as if he were more of a spectator than I am.

Clearly a remarkable man. We can understand why Ticknor endorses the comment of the distinguished engineer officer Joseph G. Totten, one of the few army officers fit to compare with the Superintendent, that "no man would be indiscreet enough to take the place after Thayer; it would be as bad as being President of the Royal Society, after Newton."[15]

WEST POINT IN AMERICAN LIFE

Thayer molded the Academy: the Academy molded its cadets, imbuing them with a strong sense of gentlemanly camaraderie. Captain the Honourable Henry Murray, an English observer not easily impressed, said of the cadets: "You might almost guess the time they had been there by their gentlemanly bearing, a quality which they do not readily lose; for the officers of the American army who have been educated at West Point, enjoy a universal reputation for intelligence and gentlemanly bearing." Indeed, West Point became a standard item on the itinerary of European visitors. From the British foreign secretary George Canning (1823) to the Prince of Wales (1860), they were almost without exception impressed and even startled by the stylish professionalism of the Academy. Another Englishman, camping near the remote Fort Ripley on the upper Mississippi, thought the three officers of its tiny garrison "gentlemanlike, agreeable men, as I have invariably found the officers of the United States army to be." West Pointers, whether with admiration or not, were thought of as gentlemen, and behaved accordingly, conscious of their standing. "A commission," said an anonymous military writer in 1834, "is, unquestionably, a letter of introduction to the envied circles of polite society. . . . The official garb is . . . prima facie evidence of the gentleman and the scholar" — though he warned that "without polished manners, refined sentiments, elegant conversation and a cultivated mind, the votary of the salon will soon find but little support for his military letter-patent of gentility."[16]

Their behavior is the more remarkable in that a fair proportion came from simple homes. D. S. Stanley, who entered West Point in 1852, was struck by the "motley, almost fantastic crowd of boys" from every corner of the Union. There were college graduates "dressed in the height of fashion," together with "rough handed country boys, awkward, uncouth, jeans clad" youngsters from "the Western or Southern farms." One such raw youth, Parmenas T. Turnley of Oak Grove, Tennessee (U.S.M.A. 1846), has left a lively account of his introduction to the Academy. He was plowing on his father's farm when the nomination arrived. He walked most of the four hundred miles to Winchester, Virginia, and from there took his first train ride, to Baltimore. Signing the register of a hotel in New York, he wrote "For West Point" in the remarks column:

I verily believe, had I not added where I was going, that I would have been . . . turned over to the police. Because [of] my appearance, in homespun pants, coat and vest, . . . shoes that had never seen blacking, although well greased with hog's lard, . . . with un-

Artillery exercise at West Point: a hand-colored engraving by J. Hill after George Catlin (1828). The emphasis is on dignity, restraint, efficiency.

kempt hair for I had not seen comb or brush for over three weeks. . . . Altogether I was a rare specimen.

He reached West Point during the annual examination, when the post was crowded with fashionable visitors and a military band played in the lantern-lit dusk. Amazed by the unfamiliar spectacle, he stood bemusedly in a flowerbed until an orderly came and asked him to move.[17]

These were of course not the kind of cadets who excited the indignation of the Academy's critics. West Point, in the words of a typical denunciation (by Representative Sawyer of Ohio, in 1846) catered to "the children of the rich, the powerful and the influential classes, members of Congress and their friends." Such critics were able to document their charges. The Academy's answer was that whatever a cadet's social advantages, he would be treated without fear or favor. One graduate, replying to

Albert G. Hawes, the Kentucky congressman who had proposed the abolition of West Point, maintained:

I have seen a son of the General-in-Chief put down a class lower, whilst his own father was presiding over the Board of Visitors for that examination, when the son of the tailor of the cadets was placed at the head of the same class. I have seen the son of Henry Clay, when the father was "the observed of all observers," sent from the school, and another son retrieve the honour of the name by bearing off the highest honours in his class, when the father had lost all political power.

Alternatively, the Academy could claim that the proportion of privileged entrants was insignificant. This was the intended implication of a summary of cadet family backgrounds compiled for the House Committee on Military Affairs in 1844. The vast majority of cadets declared their parents to be "in moderate circumstances"; a small number described their families as "indigent," and a still smaller as "independent in life." The largest group, about a quarter, were the children of "farmers or planters," while the next largest category was "lawyers, or judges."[18]

Taken on their own terms, these defensive arguments remain unconvincing. Congressman Hawes could still cry privilege after being told that Henry Clay had two sons at West Point. Nor are the Academy's vague statistics impressive, when a category like "farmers or planters" might embrace the extremes of poverty and affluence. There were always cadets from poor families, and equality of treatment did prevail inside the Academy. Admissions therefore never became a flagrant scandal. But an appreciable number of cadets *were* the relatives of the famous and powerful. Leaving aside the polemics of the day, this fact becomes a significant index of the Academy's place in the nation's affairs. West Point nowadays is no doubt more generally praised and taken for granted; but the institution in the second third of the nineteenth century had an importance for prominent American families far beyond its present standing.

The claim deserves to be documented. Here are some instances:

James Monroe, the nephew and namesake of President Monroe, was allowed to graduate in 1815, after a year's study, and later held a snug command at the New York Arsenal. Robert E. Lee, who came to West Point in 1825, was the son of Light-Horse Harry Lee of Revolutionary fame. A testimonial letter in support of his application was signed by no fewer than five senators and three representatives. Abraham Van Buren, the eldest son of Martin Van Buren, graduated in 1827. He resigned in 1837 to act as private secretary to his father, then President, and was re-appointed in the army at the time of the Mexican War. The more successful of Henry Clay's offspring graduated in 1831. Graduates of the following year, 1832, included Henry Swartwout, the son of Samuel Swartwout, a prosperous Jacksonian appointee to the collectorship of the port of New York; and the son and namesake of General Jacob Brown. Two nephews of Senator Lewis Cass, Secretary of War to Andrew Jackson and Democratic presidential candidate in 1848, attended the Academy: George W. Cass (U.S.M.A. 1832), and the wealthy Irvin McDowell (U.S.M.A. 1838), who was to command the Union forces at First Bull Run. Montgomery Blair, the son of Andrew Jackson's powerful supporter Francis P. Blair, entered the Academy in 1832, apparently at Jackson's urging. Jackson's nephews, A. J. and D. S. Donelson, had graduated in 1820 and 1825 respectively. John W. Barry of Kentucky (U.S.M.A. 1830) was the son of William T. Barry, Jackson's Postmaster General. Young Barry, in the role of military attaché, accompanied his father's friend James Buchanan of Pennsylvania to St. Petersburg in 1832, when Buchanan was appointed American minister to Russia. On Buchanan's return to the United States, Barry managed to be transferred as military attaché to the London legation. When Buchanan later became President he used his executive authority to appoint one of his nephews to West Point.

John G. Barnard of Massachusetts (U.S.M.A. 1833) was a relative of General Peter B. Porter, Secretary of War under John Quincy Adams, who got him an Academy place. Barnard's classmate Rufus King of New York was the son of the president of Columbia University, and descendant of a famous family. Robert M. McLane (U.S.M.A. 1837) was the son of Louis McLane,

Jackson's Secretary of State. Henry C. Wayne (U.S.M.A. 1838) was the son of James M. Wayne of Georgia, associate justice of the Supreme Court from 1835 to 1867. John C. Calhoun's son Patrick graduated from West Point in 1841, in company with Alfred, son of the eminent portrait painter Thomas Sully. Among those admitted in the following year, 1842, were two grandsons of President Harrison (one is said to have died of dissipation; the other, Montgomery Pike Harrison, graduated in 1847). Augustus H. Seward (U.S.M.A. 1847) was the son of the New York Whig-Republican leader William H. Seward, who was to be Lincoln's Secretary of State. In 1846 President Polk gave an Academy place to his nephew Lucius Marshall Walker (U.S.M.A. 1850). Another nephew, Marshall T. Polk, was admitted in 1848.[19]

Cadets who graduated in 1850 included Richard Arnold, the son of a Rhode Island ex-governor and Whig congressman; and Gouverneur Kemble Warren, who came from a New York land-owning family. Warren was the protégé of Gouverneur Kemble, owner of the West Point Foundry, an ironworks near the Academy. John B. Hood, later a Confederate general, was appointed to the Academy in 1849 through the agency of an uncle in Congress; his father was a wealthy doctor. Oliver Otis Howard, later a Union general, benefited similarly from a political uncle in 1850, when he was already a student at Bowdoin College. Alexander Stewart Webb (U.S.M.A. 1855) was the son of the New York newspaper proprietor James Watson Webb. One of the cadets in 1860 was the son of Senator Joseph Lane of Oregon, who was running for Vice President on the Democratic ticket with John C. Breckinridge. Among the cadets who resigned in 1861 to join the Confederacy was the son of Senator Gwin of California.[20]

Plenty of other examples could be given. William Tecumseh Sherman entered the Academy in 1836 through the influence of his guardian, Senator Ewing of Ohio; and Ewing's son, Hugh Boyle Ewing, later attended West Point though he left without graduating in 1848. Schuyler Hamilton (U.S.M.A. 1841) was the grandson of Alexander Hamilton, and brother-in-law of Henry Wager Halleck (U.S.M.A. 1839). William L. Crittenden

(U.S.M.A. 1845), executed in Havana for filibustering in 1851, was the nephew of Senator John J. Crittenden of Kentucky; and Senator Crittenden's son, George B. Crittenden, graduated in 1832. Fitzhugh Lee (U.S.M.A. 1856) was the nephew of Robert E. Lee (who was superintendent of the Academy at the time) and of Senator James Mason of Virginia. Horace Porter (U.S.M.A. 1860), a polished young man who became an aide to General Grant, and his devoted follower, was the son of a former governor of Pennsylvania, who in turn was a close friend of James Buchanan. The Delaware industrialist Henry du Pont (U.S.M.A. 1833) had the pleasure of seeing his son, also named Henry, graduate at the head of his class in 1861 (and of following the impressive naval career of his cousin Samuel Francis du Pont).[21]

The network of army connections spread through marriage. One of these families, the Kirby Smiths, has already been cited as having a less than total commitment to military life. Nevertheless they did establish a formidable record of service. Ephraim Kirby of Connecticut was a much-wounded hero of the Revolutionary War, and afterwards colonel of militia. Two of Kirby's sons became army officers. Two of his daughters married officers — one of them Joseph Lee Smith of Connecticut. When he left the army in 1821 Smith settled in Florida. His eldest son, Ephraim Kirby Smith, graduated from West Point in 1826 and made the army his career. Ephraim's sister married a West Pointer, Lucien B. Webster. Their young brother Edmund graduated from the Academy in 1845. Ephraim's son, Joseph Lee Kirby Smith, graduated in the class of 1857. Or there was the Clitz family. John Clitz entered the army from New York in 1814 and served until his death in 1836. One of his sons became a rear admiral in the U. S. Navy; another, Henry B. Clitz (U.S.M.A. 1845) reached the rank of brigadier general in the Civil War. No less than four daughters married army officers — one of whom was Richard H. Anderson of Georgia (U.S.M.A. 1842), who rose to the rank of lieutenant general in the Confederacy, while another, Gustavus A. De Russy of New York, who entered West Point in 1835, became a Union brigadier. Another Civil War general, Fitz-John Porter (U.S.M.A.

1845) of New Hampshire, was a member of a navy family. His father was a navy captain; his uncle was a commodore; his cousin was Admiral David Dixon Porter, who had a distinguished record in the Civil War. And of course West Pointers married the daughters as well as the sisters of army officers. General Zachary Taylor's two daughters were borne off into matrimony by Jefferson Davis and W. W. S. Bliss, both of them military men. "Jeb" Stuart (U.S.M.A. 1854) became the son-in-law of Philip St. George Cooke (U.S.M.A. 1827).[22]

The service world was limited in numbers and in influence. But those who remained in the army were, however defensively, proud of their membership in a professional élite, sharing the same assumptions as the career officers of European armies. Their rapport with one another was symbolized by the signet ring which they wore: class rings, now a common feature of American colleges, appear to have been introduced first at West Point, in the 1830's. Their world was discussed respectfully by members of other American professional classes, if periodicals are a reliable guide. Boston's *North American Review* printed some long, well-informed and sympathetic articles on the army and the Military Academy; and so did the Philadelphia *American Quarterly Review*. A few years later, starting in 1841, the *Southern Literary Messenger* of Richmond, Virginia, featured a number of service articles and memoirs.[23] There were also periodicals devoted exclusively to service matters. The first of these was the monthly *Military and Naval Magazine* (March 1833–February 1836), edited by Benjamin Homans, a Washington bookseller and stationer. It was merged with the weekly, *Army & Navy Chronicle* (January 1835–May 1842), also launched by Homans. The *Chronicle* started up again briefly as the *Army & Navy Chronicle & Scientific Repository* (January 1843–June 1844). True, none of these was able to sustain itself very long. Nor were various later ventures. "Because Mr. Homans of Washington and other gentlemen failed in their endeavors to establish an Army and Navy journal is no argument why others should be so unfortunate": with these brave words a former naval officer in Annapolis,

Maryland, recommended his own new weekly *Civil, Military and Naval Gazette* in September 1850. By March 1851 he had ceased publication. There seemed to be little response to a suggestion by the *Southern Literary Messenger* in 1845 that it should incorporate service material as a permanent feature. The main reason, however, was not apathy but rather the smallness of the service audience. The British *United Service Journal* could count on a readership ten times the size of its American counterparts. As the *Messenger* noted, no American service periodical, even when aimed at the navy as well as the army, had "a reasonable prospect of ever commanding more than one thousand subscribers." In face of this basic difficulty, the interesting fact is that periodicals like the *Army & Navy Chronicle* maintained so respectable a standard for so extended a period.[24]

It should be remembered too that though West Pointers objected to the award of direct commissions to civilians, some of the men appointed in this way were very similar in outlook. William W. Tompkins of New York, commissioned to a captaincy of the 2nd Dragoons in 1836, led his company against the Indians in Florida before resigning in 1838. He reentered the army for the Mexican War as a captain in the 10th Infantry. Though he again resigned, he paid glowing tributes to the army and to West Point while he was editor of the *New York Military Magazine* and the *New York Argus*. Or one might mention Alfred Iverson, the son of Senator Iverson of Georgia, who served as a volunteer officer in the Mexican War and was appointed to the 1st Cavalry in 1855.

Not all of the well-connected soldiers mentioned above remained long in army life. For some, as the previous chapter revealed, West Point was only a steppingstone, the army only a temporary expedient. Cadets who failed to graduate were not invariably well disposed toward the Academy in later life. Edgar Allan Poe did not go out of his way to praise it; nor did Cadet James A. McNeill Whistler, the artist, the son of a regular engineer officer, whose stay at the Academy is commemorated by his remark on failing a chemistry examination, "Had silicon been a gas, I would have been a major-general." Nor were candidates who were unable to secure a nomination at all necessarily friends of the Academy: one such person, a well-known enemy of West Point, was Benjamin F. Butler of Massachusetts. Nevertheless little by little the Academy achieved a remarkable if complex position in American life. A surprisingly long list could be compiled of youths who had *wanted* to go there. Charles Sumner was one case, the songwriter Stephen Foster was another. A later example was the reformer Edward Bellamy. A mere boy during the Civil War, he became enthralled by military affairs. His rejection by West Point in 1867 on medical grounds was a "traumatic disappointment." West Point grew and flour-

Cadet James McNeill Whistler attended the U. S. Military Academy from 1851 to 1854. This elegant lithographed cover of sheet music, dedicated to the graduating class of 1852, exhibits his precocious talent. The slim idealized figures also suggest the completeness of his identification at that time with the world of West Point.

ished in the national imagination. It flourished too in the professional and upper ranks of American society, until its opponents were disposed to believe that the Academy was a monopolistic coterie.[25]

There is no doubt that the army itself came to be dominated by West Point. The Mexican War was the last in which the senior commands were held by non-West Pointers, and after the War of 1812 a substantial majority of army officers were graduates. There were intricate ties between graduates and Congress. Cadets did not hesitate to pull strings in Washington. For instance, when John M. Schofield (U.S.M.A. 1853) was in trouble and about to be dismissed, influential comrades came to the rescue and managed to have him reinstated. Again, George D. Bayard (U.S.M.A. 1856) got an appointment-at-large through the good offices of his father's friend Commodore Stockton, who was then a senator from New Jersey.* In 1854 his father was named a member of the West Point Board of Visitors. Young Bayard told him knowingly: "There is always some intrigue going on in the Board . . . , as to who shall be President of it, and who shall deliver the address to the cadets. Lewis Coryell, of N.Y., your friend, has been here, and I got well acquainted with him. He is a great politician . . . and a great friend of Com. Stockton. He says you will certainly be chosen to address the cadets."

These appointments to the Board of Visitors were yet another link in the chain of West Point influence. On a few occasions some of the politicians and public men chosen for this annual visitation were recalcitrant and submitted critical reports. But they were usually won over by the honor done them and by the glittering charm of West Point in high summer. They swelled the numbers of non-graduates and non-regulars who became admirers and champions of the Academy. The 1829 Board said they would "return to their respective dwellings, fully persuaded that this Institution, even in peace, more than repays its cost to the nation." The 1842 Board, confessing to some initial difference of opinion, ended by declaring their unanimous view that the

---

* Four years later, the year of his son's graduation, the father, Samuel J. Bayard, published a highly appreciative biography of Stockton.

Academy was "an honor to the country." The 1849 Board, whose members included the educator Horace Mann, were equally sure that the Academy, "taking the lead in whatever was liberal and enlightened," had fulfilled all "the great . . . national purposes" for which it was "originally founded."[26]

Former cadets moved into more positions of eminence in civilian life. By 1867 the Academy's graduates totaled 2,218. Of these, 139 pursued careers in education — 26 as presidents of universities and colleges, 23 as principals of academies and schools, and 85 as professors and teachers. Another 334 followed technical careers. This list included

    1 superintendent of the Coast Survey
    6 surveyors general of states and territories
  14 chief engineers of states
  35 presidents of railroads and other corporations
  48 chief engineers of railroads and other public works
  41 superintendents of railroads and other public works
155 civil engineers
  30 manufacturers

In one respect of course they proved nothing as to the Academy's military function. West Point's proud enumeration of its pupils' success in civilian occupations was an ambiguous affair. The resultant gain in prestige was to some extent at the expense of the Academy's military claims. Yet by and large it contributed to the Academy's formidable though rather impalpable standing.* If it could be attacked on a variety of grounds it could be defended on precisely the same grounds. It trained leaders, in all walks of society. Praising the Academy's military prowess in 1848, Colonel Doniphan of Missouri also, and significantly, stressed its civilian importance:

This institution is to the literary system of this country, what the heart is to the human system. It receives the learning, the discoveries

---

* This problem was not unique to the United States. In France the outstanding graduates of the Ecole Polytechnique preferred to enter government service as civil rather than military engineers: the pay was much better. See 36th Congress, 2nd Session, Misc. Doc. no. 3, *Report of the Commission . . . of 1860, to examine . . . West Point*, 38–40.

and attainments of all nations . . . , and having properly digested and improved upon them, sends them forth . . . to all the other institutions of our country. . . . Indeed, to use a homely figure, it is the great city clock by which all the smaller clocks and watches are regulated.

In the nature of American society, the Academy's influence was semi-civilian. But in this very process, West Point spread across the land something of its codes, its polite severity, its tacit faith that an officer was *per se* a gentleman, and a gentleman *per se* the best sort of American. This was not done with any conscious purpose. It was something that accrued, as generation after generation of cadets passed on into service life, into politics, into the professions. A good many of them were the sons and nephews of the successful; a good many others were to become the fathers of the successful. If the regular army was a backwater, the names borne by its officers are to a marked degree names famous in other fields of American experience. And, viewed solely as a military affair, the Civil War provided opportunities for distinction on the grand scale.

The effect of West Point was the greater because the United States was still in a way a small country despite its geographical sprawl. Perhaps the novels of the past whose plots relied so heavily on coincidence were not so improbable after all. Alexis de Tocqueville was astonished to discover how far "the able men in the Union know each other by reputation, many of them personally." A few examples illustrate his point. We would be most unlikely to associate the New York radical journalist Horace Greeley with the Confederate general Braxton Bragg. Yet Greeley came south to Warrenton, North Carolina, in 1836, to marry a Connecticut schoolteacher whom he had first met in the North at a vegetarian boardinghouse. The wedding took place at the house of "Squire" Bragg, Braxton's father. Again, Lincoln's Secretary of War Edwin M. Stanton was not a complete stranger to Lincoln's chief of staff, Henry W. Halleck. They had met in California some years earlier on opposite sides of an acrimonious lawsuit. The memory of it cannot have helped them to work together smoothly. Stanton had also encountered Lincoln, as a minor participant in a law case, and had snubbed him as a provincial nobody. Reading American history in this light, one becomes aware of the wide, fine network of relationships established in part through the existence and extension of the Military Academy.[27]

STORMING OF CERRO GORDO.

JUSTIFICATION BY BATTLE

The Academy still had vociferous opponents in the 1840's. Its military record and its civilian accomplishments were alike open to doubt — the one held to weaken the other. The Mexican War silenced the assertions that the West Pointer was a "kid-glove" gentleman who could not fight. The young officers — Lee, Bragg, Grant, McClellan, Ringgold, Jackson and a score of others — who served with Taylor and Scott had a professional competence that could not be denied by the surliest of amateur soldiers. The units of regulars displayed a steadiness in the face of daunting masses of by no means contemptible Mexican battalions that could only be admired. Indeed, among the volunteer officers, one hundred had attended the Academy though not all had graduated. One-third of the thirty regiments of volunteers were commanded by ex-cadets, including Jefferson Davis of the Mississippi Rifles; and more than one-third of the field officers (those of the rank of major and upward) had had Academy training. Winfield Scott

172

said later that without their services his army, even four times as large, could not have set foot in Mexico City.

A more impartial tribute was paid in 1848 by a war hero, Colonel Doniphan, a member of the Board of Visitors but not a graduate. West Point, he said, had "fought itself into favor": "it challenges the admiration of nations abroad; it has put down opposition at home. Even the heartless demagogue has grown ashamed . . . , and ceased his querulous croakings. Proud old institution; the admiration of her friends, the reproach of her enemies." William Winston Seaton, the Whig editor of the *National Intelligencer*, detested what he took to be an unnecessary and expensive war. One consolation however was "the honor achieved by our arms. . . . How nobly the training at West Point has vindicated itself! This war has settled the wisdom and value of that institution." The Whig diarist Philip Hone, also not enthusiastic about the war as a whole, hoped that after such brilliant victories "the senseless clamor of ignorant fools in Congress . . . will now cease . . . against the noble institution, the Military Academy, at West Point."[28]

STORMING OF MONTEREY.—ATTACK ON THE BISHOP'S PALACE.

One gauge of the nation's attitude to its army was the reaction when energetic secretaries of war sent officers to study in Europe. Immediately after the Napoleonic wars, when French military prowess was almost superstitiously admired, Thayer, Dennis Mahan and one or two others could be despatched to Europe without repercussions. Poinsett, Secretary of War from 1837 to 1841, had a rougher passage: sundry militia conventions protested at this fresh proof of aristocratic privilege. Even so he persisted. Three officers of the 1st Dragoons were sent to Europe in 1839 to examine cavalry tactics. In 1840 five more officers embarked on a grand tour of European military establishments; and three additional dragoon officers were posted across the Atlantic to acquaint themselves with French cavalry training. Then there was a lull, until in the relatively benevolent climate of the post-Mexican years, Secretary of War Jefferson Davis was able to send three officers — G. B. McClellan, Richard Delafield and Alfred Mordecai* — to observe and report on the Crimean War and on various other aspects of European armies: ordnance, fortifications, staff, academics and so on. They accumulated a mass of material, though they reached no very startling conclusions. Their reports were printed as congressional documents in 1860, and reprinted in March 1861 in editions of twenty thousand copies. Solid, informative, abundantly illustrated with diagrams, maps and lithographs, they are impressive testimony to American professional aspirations, and to the educative function of the War Department. Every congressman had his copy, in fact copies to spare. Probably not many men in Washington mastered the contents, or at any rate read them as thoroughly as Jefferson Davis. At least he provided the opportunity. The mere bulk of the three reports conveyed the point that military scholarship was an exacting science.[29]

* Mordecai, who graduated at the head of his class in 1823, is an interesting example of a man who was able to lead a remarkably varied life as an army officer. Being Jewish was clearly no handicap to him. He visited Europe in the commission of 1840–41; as a well-regarded Ordnance officer he had congenial assignments in Washington, Newport and other stations. He was a judge at the New York Crystal Palace Exhibition in 1853 and was sent to Mexico on a confidential mission in the same year. His son graduated from the Academy in 1861, just in time to serve at Bull Run as aide to Oliver Otis Howard. See "The Life of Alfred Mordecai as Related by Himself," ed. James A. Padgett, *North Carolina Historical Review*, XXII (January 1945), 58–108.

Criticism of West Point and of the regular tradition was not entirely dead. To say that the regulars consolidated themselves is not to say that they acquired any real dominance over American society or American affairs. What they achieved was, in the first place, survival; and secondly, an oblique, provisional but some-how tenacious respectability. Only four years after the end of the Mexican War, the president of the Board of Visitors, Marcus C. Hammond, was warning cadets that the army's newfound popu-larity would not last. "There is no prospect of another war," he declared: an interesting comment from a South Carolinian. "The same jealousies will again arise. . . . A decided action towards a reduction, or at all events the denial of a necessary increase, will inevitably follow." He was wrong on several counts. The war did come; and before it came the army had benefited from the addition of more cavalry and from a rise in pay. On their own ground, in the bright air above the Hudson, the West Pointers enjoyed moments of pure pride, in summertime when the music played, when "Old Fuss and Feathers" nodded benignly to the salutes that greeted him, and when New York gentlemen like George Templeton Strong found the climate and the company delightfully congenial.[30]

Hammond was correct, though, in assuming that the regulars needed a war for full acceptance. In the Civil War the supremacy of West Point became undeniable. Its triumph is summarized in an Academy publication, with an understandably gratified tone: "Every important battle . . . was commanded on one or both sides by a graduate — generally both. Out of 60 [listed], contain-ing all the very important battles and campaigns, all but 5 were commanded on both sides by graduates. Of the 5 exceptions, the Army on one side was commanded by a graduate, and in four of these was victorious."

A cynic might argue that this is an equivocal statement: West Pointers must have managed to lose almost as many battles as they won. Yet the Academy's virtual monopoly of high command is a striking fact. While not every American was satisfied with this outcome, there was no doubt that West Point had decisively emerged from its long probation. It might have remained a peripheral or narrowly technical institution, like its English equivalents at Sandhurst and Woolwich. Instead, it successfully asserted a claim to primacy — for the principle of a professionally trained officer class. The British army was far more amateurish in this respect. With no trace of the previous tendency to apologize and qualify, a West Pointer was able to declare in 1863: "If the Greek remembers Marathon; if the Jew lingers at Jerusalem, or the Christian pilgrim grows warm at Bethlehem, so should the American remember West Point."[31]

6

THE AMATEURS: APATHY AND
THE MILITIA

The Congress shall have Power . . .

To provide for calling forth the Militia to execute the Laws of the Union, suppress Insurrections and repel Invasions;

To provide for organizing, arming, and disciplining, the Militia, and for governing such Part of them as may be employed in the Service of the United States, reserving to the States respectively, the Appointment of the Officers, and the Authority of training the Militia according to the discipline prescribed by Congress.

— Constitution, Article I, section 8

A well regulated Militia, being necessary to the security of a free State, the right of the people to keep and bear Arms, shall not be infringed.

— Constitution, Second Amendment

That a well-organized militia is essential to the security of a free people is one of those fine sayings that, like the mild axiomatic truths which adorn Root's system of penmanship, are often copied, but never acted upon. We resolved it at town meetings; we proclaimed it in flaming editorials; it did yeoman-service in many a closely-contested election, on one side or other . . . or on both; orators waxed eloquent upon it . . . ; it was the favorite toast at many a banquet . . . ; Congress rang with it; the Executive endorsed it; it was lugged into the learned opinions of the Judiciary; but nothing came of it.

— *United States Service Magazine,* September 1864

RHETORIC AND REALITY

It was indeed an axiom that America's defense properly rested upon the militia. The militia was, in the time-honored phrases, the nation's "palladium," the "bulwark of liberty." Standing armies, we have seen, were thought dangerous, at least in implication; regular soldiers, in this traditional vocabulary, were hirelings, rascals, "ragamuffins" — the epithet applied to them by John Randolph of Virginia in 1800. The civilian-soldier was the true patriot, most splendidly exemplified in the career of the "American Cincinnatus," George Washington, who had revealed great talents as a general yet retired contentedly into civilian life, like his Roman predecessor, when the war was over. In the legends of American nationalism, we have also seen, it was the amateur soldiers who proved their superiority to the best professionals — Washington's Virginians in the Braddock disaster of 1755, the embattled farmers of Massachusetts in 1775, John Stark's New Englanders at Bennington, "Swamp Fox" Marion in the Carolinas, Jackson's Kentucky riflemen at New Orleans.

Though the significance of these events was given a fond varnish by patriotic chroniclers, they were real events. The colonial militia of early days were in truth accustomed to fend for themselves.[1] And in later days the primacy of the civilian soldier in popular esteem was acknowledged, however sadly, by the regulars. Dennis Hart Mahan's *Complete Treatise on Field Fortification* (1837), one of the first products of West Point professionalism, was dedicated to the militia officers of the United

179

States. Henry Wagner Halleck's *Elements of Military Art and Science* (1846), another highly professional study by a pupil of Mahan's, originated as a set of lectures given in Boston to an audience largely composed of part-time soldiers. The *Army & Navy Chronicle* remarked a little waspishly that Mahan's book might "with equal or rather more propriety have been dedicated to the officers of the regular army," but this service periodical itself bowed to the realities of the American scene by devoting much of its space to militia affairs. Historians reinforced the comforting view that a robust amateur would always beat an effete professional, since amateurs nearly always were robust and professionals effete. This is the lesson imparted in the histories of George Bancroft, John L. Motley and Francis Parkman.[2]

Yet despite the ritual praise of the amateur warrior, the American militia was never put on a satisfactory footing. Lewis Cass, Secretary of War under Andrew Jackson, commented in one of his annual reports that no less than thirty-one executive pronouncements, starting with Washington in 1789, had appealed for an adequately regulated militia — all without effect. It was a topic of some importance, since in theory the liability to militia service touched all American males between the ages of eighteen and forty-five or fifty. But it was one of the topics the nation yawned at. "Bored by the unceasing palaver about a well-regulated militia," said a writer in the *United States Service Magazine* in 1864, Americans had through a "kind of alkaline reaction" been led to conclude that an efficient militia was a contradiction in terms.

In fact the discussion had started before 1789. Congress appointed a committee in April 1783 "to consider what arrangements it will be proper to make in the different departments with reference to a peace." Alexander Hamilton, a member of the committee along with James Madison and others, wrote to General Washington to solicit his "sentiments . . . on such institutions of every kind for the interior defence of these States as may be best adapted to their circumstances and conciliate security with economy and with the principles of our governments." Washington in turn consulted his senior officers, including his chief of artillery, Henry Knox, and his inspector general, Baron von Steuben. Nearly all recommended a small permanent force together with a systematically organized militia. Washington's own report, "Sentiments on a Peace Establishment," emphasized the basic proposition that "every Citizen who enjoys the protection of a free Government, owes not only a proportion of his property, but even of his personal services to the defence of it, and consequently that the Citizens of America (with a few legal and official exceptions) from 18 to 50 years of age should be borne on the Militia Rolls."*

He recommended that this great body should be mustered and inspected not less than once or twice a year. But the real military value would lie in selecting from the mass, as "the Van and flower of the American Forces," the young men aged eighteen to twenty-five who, "from a natural fondness for Military parade (which passion is almost ever prevalent at that period of life) might easily be enlisted or drafted to form a Corps in every State." They would be a "Continental Militia," organized on the same lines as the Continental Army. Though they could be grouped in several ways, Washington's personal preference was for special light companies within existing militia battalions. These would be held in readiness for service, "nearly in the same manner the Minute Men formerly were," and given twelve to twenty-five days of training each year. Drill, uniform and equipment would be standardized. Every state would have its own arsenals. Finally, Washington hoped that the leading characters in the community would "give a countenance to Military improvements, by being present at public reviews and Exhibitions, and by bringing into estimation amongst their fellow Citizens, those who appear fond of cultivating Military knowledge and who excel in the Exercises of Arms." Their example should make it "universally reputable to bear Arms and disgraceful to decline having a share in the performance of Military duties."

* This document is analyzed in detail by John McA. Palmer, *Three War Statesmen: Washington, Lincoln, Wilson* (Garden City, N.Y., 1930), who virtually rediscovered it, and used it to argue that if they had known Washington's true views, Upton and others might have given a very different account of American military policy. His book is an important corrective; but we may doubt whether the professionals would have changed their tune if the document had been available to them.

Congress was too busy to pay close attention to such proposals. In the following year, 1784, when Washington was again a private citizen, trying to resume the life of a Virginia planter, von Steuben published a pamphlet entitled *A Letter on the Subject of an Established Militia*. Like Washington, to whom he sent a draft of his scheme, Steuben admired the Swiss scheme of selective militia service. Unlike Washington, though with his concurrence, Steuben proposed to embody only a small fraction of the enrolled strength of the militia. In contrast to the Swiss, who with their tiny population needed to resort to compulsion (by picking every third man in the relevant age group), Steuben recommended an active militia, numbering only twenty-one thousand in peacetime, to be recruited on a voluntary plan and to serve for three years.[3]

As with Washington's "Sentiments," nothing came of the Steuben scheme. Its practical defect, as Washington had suspected, was that in effect it involved scrapping the general militia, which would offend state pride and outrage hundreds of senior militia appointees by depriving them of their pomp and circumstance. A further "Plan for the General Arrangement of the Militia of the United States," devised by the newly appointed Secretary of War Henry Knox in 1786, took account of these scruples. Knox suggested the retention of the militia as a whole, but would divide it into three age groups: an "advanced corps" of men aged eighteen to twenty; a "main corps" of men aged twenty-one to forty-five; and a "reserved corps" of men aged forty-six to fifty-nine. The youngest age group would be given six weeks of training each year. After a while all American militiamen would thus once have served in the advanced corps, long enough to have become reasonably proficient soldiers. Knox calculated the total militia strength in 1786 as four hundred and fifty thousand and, after revising his figures to allow for exemptions, estimated that his advanced corps would number some thirty-two thousand fit young men. With a force of this size and quality he expected to be able to dispense altogether with a professional standing army.

The Knox plan lay in abeyance for four years. By then he was confirmed as Secretary of War under the new Constitution, and Washington as President. In a message to Congress of August

1789 Washington stressed the importance and urgency of legislation for the governance of the militia. Most members of Congress
would have agreed with Madison that the chief tasks facing
them, in the session which began in January 1790, were "the
plans of revenue and the militia." Washington had already asked
Knox to prepare a militia bill for submission to Congress. Since
Knox was traversing familiar ground, he was able to prepare his
brief before the end of January. His 1790 plan resembled that of
1786, except that the amount of time to be spent by the "advanced corps" in the annual "camps of discipline" was somewhat
reduced. It was now proposed that in each of their first two years
of militia service youngsters should be encamped for thirty days,
and ten days in the third year.

The outcome was sadly disappointing to Washington and his
Secretary. Knox's recommendations were never given close examination in Congress. Various reasons for this neglect can be
offered. One is that congressmen were far more aroused by
Hamilton's plans for national finance, and had little energy to
spare for matters that seemed secondary. Another reason is that
the Knox plan was long and not always felicitously worded. Not
only was Knox clumsy in expression; what he said was apt to
convey the wrong impression. For example, in Knox's letter of
transmittal to the President — the first part of his document,
which therefore caught everyone's eye — he spoke of seeking to
devise a system of defense to meet all crises, "whether arising
from internal or external causes," and went on to say: "The
convulsive events, generated by the inordinate pursuit of riches
or ambition, require that the government should possess a strong
corrective arm." *Internal . . . causes, a strong corrective arm:*
ominous phrases to men concerned to amend the Constitution by
incorporating a Bill of Rights. Knox's old army friend Benjamin
Lincoln told him that though the plan "would make ours the
strongest militia in the world, the people will not adopt it here if I
know Massachusetts." Moreover, in the New England states at
any rate the time-honored militia was still moderately vigorous.
Why overturn it?[4]

The immediate reason for ignoring the plan was that Elias

Boudinot introduced a separate militia bill in Congress a few months afterward which avoided some of the objectionable features of the Knox system. Boudinot reverted to Washington's "Sentiments": liability for all able-bodied men between eighteen and fifty, and separate enrollment of those aged eighteen to twenty-five in "distinct companies . . . which . . . shall form the light infantry or riflemen of each battalion or regiment." They would, however, only train for six days in each year, as against four for the rest of the militia. There would be some degree of federal supervision, though until the national revenue increased militiamen would have to furnish their own arms and equipment.

The Boudinot bill of 1 July 1790, reintroduced later by Jeremiah Wadsworth of Connecticut, underwent drastic alteration in Congress. Boudinot's proposals had already weakened the notion of a genuine classified obligation on the Swiss model. The act which finally emerged in May 1792 still further debilitated the idea; indeed its sponsor Wadsworth voted against it. No provision remained for separating age groups, for specifying any period of training, or for effective federal coordination.* The act of 1792 dodged the issue, as much an oddity in its way as the Second Amendment, with what Walter Millis calls "its seeming *non sequitur* — guaranteeing the right to bear arms to the people because a 'well-regulated Militia,' in which the people took little interest, was necessary." Underlying both was the negative principle that people would rather not be bothered. Stating the point on higher grounds, they resisted the element of compulsion inherent in any scheme for an efficient militia. This after all was one of the most obnoxious aspects of standing armies: the citizen was not truly free if he could be taken away from his home and subjected to an uncongenial discipline.

What the act of 1792 and the Second Amendment also in implication conceded was the supremacy of the states over the federal government, in this particular sphere. The Jeffersonian *National Gazette* praised the new militia system, in revealing

---

* Paradoxically, the Act excluded colored citizens from the militia obligation: Leon F. Litwack, *North of Slavery: The Negro in the Free States, 1790–1860* (Chicago, 1961, 1965), 31.

184

terms, as "the true and equal guardian of freedom and a free country." The Federalist *Gazette of the United States,* on the other hand, said that it would "probably seem a feeble system to many persons versed in military affairs. The great difference of the militia laws of the several states is such, that some will improve, and others perhaps run retrograde in consequence of this law."[5]

So it happened. In practice the state militias were local armies, or at least local agglomerations. The junior officers were, as hitherto, elected by their men; the senior commands were filled at the pleasure of the state governor. The state was required to furnish to the Secretary of War an annual report, including numbers of men enrolled. Even from the outset the reports were scrappy, in some cases nonexistent. During the 1790's certain states were amazingly independent. Vermont and South Carolina sent their own purchasing agents to Europe to buy arms. Massachusetts and South Carolina enlisted men for three years to perform guard duties in Boston and Charleston harbors.[6] There was a collision of authority in the War of 1812. The governors of Massachusetts and Connecticut refused to call out their militia in the federal service; the governor of Vermont resisted the attempt to use his militia outside the boundaries of the state. This constitutional tussle was to be decided (*Martin* v. *Mott,* 1827) in favor of the federal executive; but as Jefferson Davis and Abraham Lincoln were to learn in the Civil War, the states were still assuming that for militia and for volunteer units, the initiative in recruitment and appointment lay with them, not with the federal government.

When the militia were accepted as *de facto* and to some extent *de jure* state forces, the dream of a comprehensive national organization was futile. This feature, while it would produce a patchwork militia system, would not in itself lead to universal decay. The Federalist editor of the *Gazette* expected that some state militias would actually improve while others were running "retrograde." The basic difficulty, to reiterate, was that a casually administered, voluntary militia was militarily useless, while a well-trained, obligatory system was politically unattainable. In peacetime Americans would give only the most grudging, perfunctory assent to Washington's dictum of 1783 that "every Citizen who enjoys the protection of a free Government, owes . . . his personal services to the defence of it." A free government was one that — in every sense of the expression — left its citizens in peace. The result was direly predicted by Knox in the preamble to his 1790 plan. If universal service were not upheld, the alternative must be "a militia of substitutes" like that of Britain: "Wealthy families . . . will prevent their sons from serving . . . ; the plan will degenerate into habitual contempt; a standing army will be introduced, and the liberties of the people subjected to all the contingencies of events."

THE MILITIA BURLESQUED

Knox's worst fears were not realized. In much else he was correct. A militia of substitutes, a militia of farce, a Falstaffian band very soon appeared as almost the only public image of the militia. "Prick him," cries the venial Sir John, in search of his quota, "for we have a number of shadows to fill up the musterbook." The long comedy of hopeless cases and evaded obligations echoed in the American imagination, by descent all the way from Shakespeare. Here is a characteristic allusion from the diary of the New Yorker George Templeton Strong, seventeen years old in 1837 and contemptuously amused by a militia muster: "There were forty warriors, very miscellaneous indeed. Three of them were not serviceable, having sticks instead of guns, and several more were supremely drunk. The gallant captain wore a sword like a scythe blade, and his heroes looked like Sir J. Falstaff's ragged regiment. The line was very crooked; there was an astonishing curvature towards a certain beer room." So much for Washington's hope that the principal "Characters in the Community" would lend tone to the militia.

In this Anglo-American lineage the militia was the immemorial rabble portrayed in Dryden's "Cymon and Iphigenia":

THE AMATEURS: APATHY AND THE MILITIA

The country rings around with loud alarms,
And raw in files the rude militia swarms;
Mouths without hands, maintained at vast expense,
In peace a charge, in war a weak defence. . . .
This was the morn when, issuing on the guard,
Drawn up in rank and file, they stood prepared.
Of seeming arms to make a short assay,
Then hasten to be drunk, the business of the day.

Readers on both sides of the Atlantic would have felt at home with an anecdote related in the *New York Herald* in 1808. It told of an old lady, asked by an enrollment officer whether anyone in her household might be subject to militia duty. Only poor Tommy, she replied, whose age was twenty. "When muster day came she went to the barn, got out the family jackass and led him to the parade ground to answer his name."[7]

Scores of other Americans have left accounts of ludicrous militia musters. One of the best known — fiction but uncomfortably close to the truth — occurs in Augustus Baldwin Longstreet's collection of *Georgia Scenes* (1835). It has a tangled history of borrowings. Longstreet credited the piece to his friend Oliver Hillhouse Prince of Connecticut, and it is said to have been published in a Georgia newspaper around 1813. It was quoted by the British author C. H. Gifford in his *History of the Wars Occasioned by the French Revolution* (1817). Another English author, Thomas Hardy, later inserted the account in his novel *The Trumpet Major* (1879). Hardy had presumably got the story from Gifford. Gifford might have read it in John Lambert's *Travels through Lower Canada and the United States of North America,* a three-volume work published in London in 1810. Lambert's narrative is padded out with extracts from American publications. In his travels, which occupied him from 1806 to 1808, he came across "an excellent satire" on a militia meeting, "published in one of their periodical works," while he was in Charleston, South Carolina. So the legend has an earlier origin than Longstreet remembered. With minor changes of setting it could stand as a description of almost any rural muster in England or America:

[The soldiers] objected to going into these *revolutions* at all, inasmuch as the weather was extremely hot, and they had already been kept in the field upwards of *three quarters* of an hour. They reminded the captain of his repeated promise to be as short as he possibly could, and it was clear he could dispense with all this same wheeling and flourishing if he chose. They were already very thirsty, and if he would not dismiss them, they declared they would go off without dismission, and get something to drink; and he might fine them if that would do him any good; they were able to pay their fine, but could not go without drink to please any body; and they swore they would never *vote* for another captain who wished to be so unreasonably strict.[8]

We can recognize the same situation in the "Militia Muster" sketch performed by the English comedian Charles Mathews after his American tour of 1822–1823. So could his delighted audiences. The "group of American citizens" solemnly practicing "revolutions," with umbrellas for guns, "led by a confused, but meek, Captain, who read the commands from a book" (Steuben's drill manual): this was exactly the pattern of the Prince/Gifford/Longstreet anecdote.[9]

A stock theme in Anglo-American humor, the militia became a favorite subject also in the genre of frontier humor, as Longstreet's sketch indicates. A good example, touching in its blend of hilarity and nostalgia, is *The Puddleford Papers; or, Humors of the West* (1857), by the Massachusetts-born lawyer and author Henry H. Riley. Recalling the lost New England village of his boyhood, Riley laments the decay of its slightly ridiculous yet somehow impressive training day, which "usually opened with a boom from the field-piece, at sunrise, that shook the hills." Later in the day came

the good old continental tunes that were full of fight, played by old fifers and drummers that had been through the wars; men who made a solemn and earnest thing of martial music — who reverenced it as the sacred voice of liberty, not to be trifled with, who thought of Bunker

Hill, until the tears started from their eyes. These old airs, that used to echo among the mountains of New-England — where are they?

Even on that historic ground, says Riley, the militia fell away to nothing. Translated to "the far west," where "there was no attachment to, or veneration for, the past of Puddleford, because Puddleford had no past," the old ceremonies were mere slapstick:

In the fall, the Squire exhibited the first Puddleford Militia Company ever assembled upon parade, to the gaping wonder of its men, women and children. He formed his raw recruits into a line, by the aid of a board fence, which was supposed to be nearly straight. . . . The Squire was a very blood-thirsty looking captain, after he had mounted his regimentals. He had turned up a broad-brimmed felt hat, and tacked the sides by a flaming red cockade, made of flannel, and had fastened an ostrich feather, which he found in the wardrobe of his second wife . . . , in its top, which drooped heavily over his back.

As for the company, it was "as complete a specimen of ragamuffins as were congregated together. There were three guns to the crowd, and the balance of the arms were made up of the most murderous implements within reach, such as axes, pitchforks, &c."[10]

"Squire" Longbow in Riley's sketch, though a figure of fun, was still trying to behave with dignity. In other scenes the militia officer abandoned the effort at discipline. When Hugh McCulloch arrived in Frankfort, Indiana, in 1833 as a young lawyer fresh from New England, he happened upon a backwoods drill. As McCulloch recalled the affair, only the captain was in uniform; otherwise he was as casual as his troops:

As soon as I was observed — "Look there, boss!" called one of the men to the captain; "there comes a stranger; let's have a drink. . . ." The company was dismissed. Whiskey was cheap, and I stood the treat. "He looks kinder stuck up," said one in an undertone, "but he is a d——d good fellow, anyhow." The whiskey produced good feeling in the motley crowd, and I was . . . the hero of the hour.[11]

There was good nature in this double-edged comedy, along with condescension. Frontier vulgarities were implied to possess something admirably American and democratic through their very informality. Military burlesques thus served a number of native, as distinct from Anglo-American, purposes. One was as a form of political maneuver: a means, that is, of poking fun at pompous opponents. The classic attack (which McCulloch knew of and mentioned) was that of the humorously inclined Whig congressman Thomas Corwin of Ohio, in 1840. Corwin, satirizing the military pretensions of a Michigan Democrat who had ventured to question the prowess of the Whig leader General Harrison, convulsed the House of Representatives. He pictured the Michigan warrior at a muster, plumed in chicken feathers, epaulettes slipping about on "shoulders back or sides," mounted on a crop-eared mare, and about to begin the exercises—until interrupted by rain. "Now," Corwin continued, with elaborate sarcasm,

now for the caution wherewith the Roman Fabius foiled the skill and courage of Hannibal. A retreat is ordered, and troops and general . . . are . . . safely bivouacked in a neighboring grocery! But even here the general still has room for the exhibition of heroic deeds. Hot from the field, . . . your general unsheaths his trenchant blade . . . and with remorseless fury he slices the watermelons that lie in heaps around him, and shares them with his surviving friends. Others of the sinews of war are not wanting here. Whisky, Mr. Speaker, that great leveler of modern times, is here also, and the shells of the watermelons are filled to the brim. . . . As the Scandinavian heroes of old . . . drank wine from the skulls of their slaughtered enemies, . . . so now our militia general and his forces, from the skulls of melons . . . in copious draughts of whisky assuage the heroic fire of their souls, after the bloody scenes of a parade-day.[12]

Another, peculiarly American recourse was the burlesquing of actual parades and regulations, in order to laugh the militia system out of existence. Sometimes the muster would turn into a kind of genial mutiny, with the men mocking and mimicking self-important officers. Sometimes burlesque parades were held. Philip Hone, gentleman of New York, watched one such affair in 1831, quite unamused as two or three hundred jokers calling themselves the "Invincible Fantasticals" marched round the city

Invincibles
OR
The New York Militia Muster.

Published at 9 Wall S?

"in motley dresses of every description — Turks, Indians, Bona-
partes, with cabbages for epaulets, band-boxes for helmets, and
broom-sticks for muskets." Abraham Lincoln compared such
spectacles and their effect to the way in which "the institution of
chivalry was ridiculed out of existence by its fictitious votary Don
Quixote." He described a fantastic parade in Springfield, Illinois,
headed by a friend on horseback who carried a wooden sword
nine feet in length and wore a pasteboard cocked hat as big as an
ox-yoke. They bore banners inscribed with facetious mottoes such
as *"We'll fight till we run, and we'll run till we die."* Lincoln
added with satisfaction: "That was the last militia muster here."
Not content with the parade pantomime, the town wits enjoyed
themselves by inventing parodies of militia regulations: "no man
is to wear more than five pounds of cod-fish for epaulets, or more
than thirty yards of bologna sausages for a sash; and no two men
are to dress alike, and if any two should dress alike the one that
dresses most alike is to be fined." Though such buffoonery was a
form of indirect protest, it was obviously relished for its own sake.
For men such as young Lincoln and his colleagues at the bar, one

might almost say that if the militia had not existed it would have been necessary to invent it, in order to supply them with so ideal a target for legalistic mockery. Kindred spirits among the lawyers in Burlington, Vermont (which was then like Springfield, Illinois, the seat of the state legislature) drafted a comic bill in 1851, ostensibly in order to reform the state militia, but also no doubt for the pure fun of the thing. One section decreed: "There shall be at least two officers to every private . . . , provided that any person with curled hair and black whiskers shall be *ex whiskerando* an officer of as high grade as lieutenant-general."[13]

In conventional rhetoric, then, the militia of the United States was the nation's chief defense. Each freeman would spring to arms when summoned, rejoicing in a compulsion that gave him an opportunity to attest his patriotism. His right to bear arms, his duty to do so at call: these were apparently fundamental to the American creed. In practice, this part of the creed became a joke, a bore, a nuisance to the majority of citizens.

ATTEMPTS AT ORGANIZATION

Such disintegration was, as we have seen, not in accordance with the plans of the Founding Fathers. Concerned by the risk of foreign and Indian Wars, and covertly anxious about the control of domestic disorder, they had labored to create an effective part-time army. A law of 1808 provided for an annual expenditure of two hundred thousand dollars for militia weapons; and though this sum was denounced by later critics as absurdly small, it was not in its day an insignificant sum. Before and during the War of 1812, Jefferson and Madison repeatedly urged the establishment of a classified, trained militia. It was obvious that the act of 1792 had little force. In the first five years of the annual appropriation of two hundred thousand dollars for militia arms, of the total available of one million dollars the states had in fact submitted claims amounting to less than one hundred thousand dollars.[14] So the annual messages of Jefferson and Madison revert again and again to the need for improvement. Speaking of the dangers of invasion, in his first annual message of December 1801, Jefferson said that "we should at every session continue to amend the defects . . . in the laws regulating the militia. . . . Nor should we . . . separate until we can say we have done everything for the militia which we could do were our enemy at our door." A year later, in December 1802, he renewed his warning to Congress:

Considering that our regular troops are employed for local purposes, and that the militia is our general reliance for great and sudden emergencies, you will doubtless think this institution worthy of a review, and give it those improvements of which you find it susceptible.

He came back to the subject in 1805, and again in his eighth annual message, of November 1808:

For a people who are free, and who mean to remain so, a well organized and armed militia is their best security. It is therefore incumbent on us at every meeting to revise the condition of the militia, and to ask ourselves if it is prepared to repel a powerful enemy at every point of our territories exposed to invasion. Some of the States have paid a laudable attention to this object, but every degree of neglect is to be found among others.

President Madison took up the theme in his first annual message of November 1809, as in subsequent ones:

193

Whatever may be the course of your deliberations on . . . our military establishments, I should fail in my duty in not recommending to your serious attention the importance of giving to our militia, the great bulwark of our security and resource of our power, an organization the best adapted to eventual situations for which the United States ought to be prepared.

These were generalities. In Madison's 1810 message he was a little more specific:

To give to this great mass . . . the efficiency which it merits, . . . I recommend for the consideration of Congress the expediency of instituting a system which shall in the first instance call into the field at the public expense and for a given time certain portions of the commissioned and noncommissioned officers.

This was one of the proposals for selective training which was to be put forward on several occasions. It was particularly attractive to those who felt that West Point and additional "military seminaries" ought to cater directly to the needs of the militia. A more fundamental reform was in the minds of Jefferson and Madison, in face of the harassments of the Napoleonic wars. The obvious remedy, they began to feel, was that advocated in the Knox plan of 1790: classification. There was no point in enumerating an immense paper army. The numbers eligible for militia service swelled year by year as America's population increased. Sharing with Madison the humiliations of the War of 1812, Jefferson wrote to Secretary of State James Monroe in October 1814 that "we must prepare for interminable war. To this end we should put our house in order, by providing men and money to indefinite extent. The former may be done by classing our militia, and assigning each class to the . . . duties for which it is fit. . . . I trust it is now seen that the refusal to class the militia, when proposed years ago, is the real source of all our misfortunes in this war.[15] In his special message to Congress of the previous month Madison had already delivered a brief but urgent plea for "classing and disciplining" the militia.

Perhaps relief at the relatively successful outcome of the War of 1812 led Madison, in his annual message of December 1815, to confine himself to a tactfully broad observation:

THE AMATEURS: APATHY AND THE MILITIA

If experience has shewn in the recent splendid achievements of militia the value of this resource for the public defense, it has shewn also the importance of that skill in the use of arms and that familiarity with the essential rules of discipline which can not be expected from the regulations now in force.

A year later he was a little less tactful, and ready to bring forward a definite scheme:

The present organization of our militia is universally regarded as less efficient than it ought to be . . ., and no organization can be better calculated to give to it its due force than a classification which will assign the foremost place in the defense of the country to that portion of its citizens whose activity and animation best enable them to rally to its standard.

The plan in question was submitted to Congress by the acting Secretary of War in a few days. Indeed, the House of Representatives had requested such a report. Like the Knox plan, it provided for a division of the enrolled militia into three classes. There were to be annual encampments for the first two. A House committee on military affairs, under the chairmanship of William Henry Harrison, agreed that more training was necessary, and that the younger men in the population were the key group. The committee was, however, uneasy at the practical inconveniences that would be entailed, and so retreated to Madison's initial modest suggestion of improved military instruction in the higher seminaries. Congress contented itself, therefore, by requesting further study of the problem by the Secretary of War.[16]

Nearly ten years passed before there was any detailed discussion of militia reforms. President Monroe, Madison's successor, allotted one sentence to the militia in his first annual message and thereafter said nothing. Nor did the question much concern John Quincy Adams, until he referred in his message of December 1826 to a "board of distinguished officers of the Army and militia," whose report on "the acknowledged defective condition of our militia system" was to accompany his message. The initiative here had been taken by Adams's Secretary of War, James

THE NATION'S BULWARK.

In this print of 1829, the "Nation's Bulwark" can contrive only a ragged muster. Still, the majority have been able to produce weapons of a sort. A decade or two later, even this much evidence of martial spirit was lacking.

Barbour of Virginia, who had convened the board and sent out a questionnaire in advance to governors of states and other interested citizens. Eventually the board recommended, among other things, a reduction of the nation's enrolled militia from the preposterous figure of 1,500,000 to a more manageable 400,000. These were to be raised by state quotas. It was also proposed — though Adams disliked the idea — to set up annual ten-day training camps for militia officers in each state. The 1826 board was thus endorsing the notion of officer education, and a mild form of classification. The result, as before, was inconsiderable. A House committee which looked into the scheme declared its support for the militia in general as the "bulwark of the nation," and in particular for "a well-organized and disciplined Militia," but saw no need or else no possibility of bringing about such a thing.[17]

Andrew Jackson showed that, like his predecessors in the White House, he was aware of what was wrong and what might be done. In his fourth annual message of December 1832 he repeated the commonplace that "the whole subject evidently requires a thorough examination," and suggested that "a plan of classification . . . providing for a system of instruction" might be the answer. Other problems engrossed him in the next couple of years. He returned to the theme in December 1835 with a quite full summary of the issues, and a firm recommendation:

A classification of the population offers the most obvious means of effecting this organization. Such a division may be made as will be just to all by transferring each at a proper period of life from one class to another and by calling first for the services of that class . . . which from age is qualified for the duty and may be called to perform it with the least injury to themselves or to the public. Should the danger ever become so imminent as to require additional force, the other classes in succession would be ready for the call.

Again a futile exercise: in December 1836 Jackson wearily remarked that the necessity "has been so repeatedly presented to Congress . . . that I deem it sufficient . . . to refer to the last annual message and to former Executive communications."

The final effort was made by Martin Van Buren's Secretary of War, Joel R. Poinsett. His plan of 1839–1840 was to divide the country into eight military districts, within each of which there would be a force of 12,500 militia in active service and a secondary reserve, also of 12,500. The nation would thus have an active militia numbering 100,000, and another 100,000 militia auxiliaries. But after a certain amount of debate the Poinsett plan joined all the others, to gather dust in War Department files.[18]

It is worth asking again why scheme after scheme collapsed. Some of the clues are to be found in the ferocious response of Congress in 1814–1815 to two Madison-Monroe bills. These aimed at "filling the ranks of the Regular Army, by classifying the free White Male Population of the United States," and at raising forty new regiments to serve for the duration of the war, and be used to defend the frontiers. Federalist opposition to the War of 1812 accounted for much of the resistance. Even so, the arguments developed were hard to refute. In part the objection was to the principle of compulsion as such; what, for example, would be

197

the position of those with conscientious scruples, such as the Quakers? More vitally, the point was stressed that to federalize the militia was to make it indistinguishable from a standing army. Did Madison not mean to employ it, by legalized press-ganging, as a recruiting mechanism for regular regiments? Here if anywhere, in the control of the conditions of militia service, resided the essence of state sovereignty. Could any true American deny that in certain respects that states *were* sovereign? In 1819 William Theobald Wolfe Tone, son of the Irish patriot, produced a lengthy *Essay on the Necessity of Improving Our National Force.* Tone was an experienced soldier who had served with Napoleon before settling in the United States. If his new country really meant to rely upon the militia, he said, she would have

to withdraw entirely, from the superintendence of [the] respective states, a given portion of the youngest and most active classes, and to commit the power of requiring . . . their service, by rotation, during a portion of every year, the power of appointing their officers, and the whole of their organization, administration, discipline and instruction, to the uniform . . . direction of the central government. A military system founded on this principle, might be rendered most perfect and proper for a republic. But it would be needless to dwell on measures which will not be adopted. The state governments will never commit their militias to the federal executive.[19]

The same kinds of arguments were used against Poinsett's plan. It was challenged as a step to turn the militia into something dangerously akin to a regular army. It was seen as an unconstitutional affront to the sacred rights of the states, in asserting a federal claim to call out the militia for purposes unspecified in the Constitution, and to engage in training which the Constitution prescribed as a state responsibility. "A monstrous project," said Henry Clay. Since 1840 was a presidential election year, the Whigs seized on Poinsett's proposals as a sinister Democratic plot. The Democrats retaliated by reprinting twenty thousand copies of the 1817 House militia report — one of the sources of Poinsett's plan — because its principal author, William H. Harrison, was now the Whig candidate.[20] The difficulties in the way of classification, though not insurmountable and though distorted

THE NEW ERA OR THE EFFECTS OF A STANDING ARMY

A fanciful view of the dreadful consequences that would arise from Secretary of War Poinsett's scheme for a classified, federalized militia.

by political partisanship, were genuine. The line of least resistance — to leave matters alone — was not only the easiest, it seemed to many Americans the most satisfactory expedient.

William Theobald Wolfe Tone's criticism of the existing militia system was related to his thesis that the United States ought to build up a better regular force. A year after writing his pamphlet he secured a commission in the artillery. But some men who were closely acquainted with the existing militia maintained not that no change was possible, but that no change was desirable. A prominent champion of the old militia was William H. Sumner, adjutant general of Massachusetts and a member of Barbour's 1826 militia board. Sumner had already expressed himself weightily in a pamphlet of 1823 on *The Importance of the Militia to a*

Free Commonwealth. Massachusetts was admitted to have the best militia system in the United States — though a cynic might add that the competition was not keen. Nevertheless Sumner was a respected figure — one historian even suggests that he deserves to be called "the Clausewitz of the American citizen soldier," a fascinating honor to contemplate — and he bolstered his own opinions with those of the venerable John Adams:

> These American states have owed their existence to the militia for more than two hundred years. Neither schools, nor colleges, nor town meetings have been more essential to the formation and character of the nation than the militia. . . . Improve its constitution by every prudent means, but never destroy its universality. A select militia will soon become a standing army, or a corps of Manchester yeomanry.

Adams's allusion was to the yeomanry of Manchester, England, who in 1819 with some regular cavalry had made a charge upon a crowd of artisans, killing or injuring so many that the affair became known as the "Peterloo Massacre." Like Adams, Sumner believed it was fatal to entrust military power to any particular segment of the population, including the upper classes.[21]

What then could be done to revivify the standing militia? For all his enthusiasm and knowledge Sumner could produce no solution. Instead he reviewed current criticisms to show they were ill-founded. The common immediate objection was to the recurrence of musters:

> The gentleman complains that they deprive him of the use of his servants, and dismount his coachman from the box when he wants to ride: — the farmer, that . . . they take his men from their labour, when it is most needed; and some of the stock-holders, in the great manufacturing establishments, are opposed to them, because they impede the operations.

Sumner's answer was that the musters were of military value, and provided valuable recreation. He agreed that there was a good deal of drinking on parade days, but maintained that intemperance was a national vice, prevalent everywhere. As for the suggestion that militia officers should be singled ·out for special training, he claimed that this would lower their dignity and in effect reduce them to private soldiers. He objected likewise to the idea of discontinuing drills and instead issuing the militia with rifles, so as to convert them into sharpshooters or guerrillas. This kind of proposal, said Sumner, originated in Western states that had never had a proper militia. Far from strengthening authority, it would promote lawlessness.

In short, the orthodox militia was to Sumner the only conceivable pattern, at any rate in old-established, thickly populated areas. There was the further advantage that the militia hierarchy depended upon the elective franchise, and so was a model of the democratic process. Diligent militia officers "become the objects of civil promotion. It is strictly a republican principle. . . . There are as many men introduced into the municipal, county, and state offices, and into our legislative assemblies, from the militia, as from the bar."

If this type of reasoning represented the higher reaches of militia wisdom, it is easy to see why no large-scale reform could be expected either to emanate from the militia or to be acceptable to them. The transformation, if any, would have to be wrought externally. In fact a gradual redefinition did take place. During and immediately after the War of 1812 sentiment in favor of the militia and against the standing army was strong. Yet as Madison's and Monroe's thinking revealed, neither establishment was conceived as being totally different from the other, at least by the President and his circle of military advisers. It was assumed that regular units would be subordinate to the militia in esteem as well as in weight of numbers.

This attitude became modified, though it is easy to misunderstand what happened. Calhoun as Secretary of War was required to bring about a drastic reduction of the standing army. Viewed in another light, however, he took a crucial step in the consolidation of the professionals. Hitherto the regular army had survived rather than developed. Henceforward its numerical strength was to be, by European standards, insignificant; but its permanence was guaranteed. And its *primacy* was little by little asserted. By 1820, in Calhoun's formulation, the regulars were regarded as the "nucleus" of America's armed forces in an honorific sense. The militia by contrast was envisaged as garrison and second-line troops. Twenty years later, the controversy over Poinsett's plan disguised the truth that on this issue there was little disagreement: the militia were tacitly recognized to be inferior, auxiliary troops. They would *support* the regulars, in an emergency. The regulars, as Poinsett saw their role, would be concentrated as far as possible, even in peacetime, for training in the tasks of war, not dispersed on semi-civilian errands. In wartime the militia would take over such garrison and ancillary duties as had been performed by the professionals.

Poinsett's scheme was repudiated. The American professionals did not become as professional as he would have liked. But some of the attitudes on which the scheme was based aroused far less dissension. The change can be measured in the annual presidential messages and in the accompanying reports from the service departments. Successive Presidents said less and less about the militia. Secretaries of War ignored it, or framed regulations which — like Poinsett's — related the militia to the regulars, and to the garrisoning of the nation's growing quantity of coastal fortifications. In their various annual messages, President Tyler and President Pierce made only one brief reference apiece to the militia. Millard Fillmore was silent on the issue; so was James Buchanan. Through the years, reports from the War Department and Navy Department bulked larger and larger. There were hundreds, thousands of pages on Indian affairs, surveys and improvements by army engineers, harbor defense schemes, details of West Point, activities of naval squadrons, and so on — and only negligible mentions of the militia. To the extent that it was thought by about 1850 to have any serious role, this was to be confined to local and minor purposes. Gone were the visions of the enrolled militia furnishing the "Van and flower of the American Forces."

Another significant alteration of emphasis should be noted. The notion of universal obligation to service had once been taken for granted. In seventeenth-century Massachusetts there was deemed to be no moral basis for individual scruples of conscience: the militiaman was simply to accept "that the Government have good

Reasons to justify their proclaiming and engaging in a war."[22] Opposition to the War of 1812, especially in New England, no doubt helped to undermine this basis. At any rate nineteenth-century America vastly preferred the voluntary principle. In Washington's day independent or volunteer military companies were omitted from the schemes for a classified militia. They were held to operate in a different and somewhat alien context. In 1837, Van Buren's first annual message announced that classification was probably not feasible. In lieu, he recommended instruction for militia officers and "the organization of volunteer corps." This seemingly casual yet fundamental shift of emphasis was made explicit in Tyler's 1843 message. Tyler began with the usual empty statement that "in all cases of emergency the reliance of the country is properly placed in the militia of the several States." But he went on to advise an improved system "looking mainly to the volunteer companies of the Union."

The rise of the volunteer movement is the subject of the next chapter. Its relevance here is as a further stage in the disintegration of the old militia. The change was consummated in the Mexican War, when not embodied militia but *ad hoc* volunteer regiments, such as Jefferson Davis's Mississippi Rifles, formed the bulk of the armies under Scott and Taylor. In his messages on the war, President Polk showered praise on America's citizen-soldiers (and was in comparison distinctly cool in his references to the regulars). But it was the *voluntary* element he extolled. The events of the past few months, he said in December 1846, proved that the United States could "confidently rely" on "an effective force, ready at all times voluntarily to relinquish the comforts of home for the perils and privations of the camp." Two years later, in an extraordinary panegyric, Polk exulted in the proof which the Mexican War afforded of "the military strength of our country." Other powers saw that America had a tiny peacetime regular army of not more than ten thousand; "they held in low repute our militia, and were far from regarding them as an effective force, unless it might be for temporary defensive operations when invaded on our own soil." The victories in Mexico had "undeceived" foreigners, and even some Americans.

From this statement one would expect Polk to proceed to the

achievements of the regulars and the militia. But he was not an admirer of standing armies; and since there was nothing he could justly say in tribute to the militia, his words might in logic be interpreted to mean that its "low repute" was deserved. Instead, however, Polk eulogized the performance of the "volunteer army":

Unlike what would have occurred in any other country, we were under no necessity of resorting to drafts or conscriptions. On the contrary, such was the number of volunteers who patriotically tendered their services that the chief difficulty was in . . . determining who should be compelled to remain at home. . . . Our citizen soldiers are unlike those of any other country. . . . They . . . have been accustomed from their youth to handle and use firearms, and a large proportion . . . are expert marksmen. . . . In battle each private man, as well as every officer, fights not only for his country, but for glory and distinction among his fellow-citizens when he shall return to civil life.

Polk's whole 1848 message constitutes his version of a Farewell Address. It is a sustained sermon on the American gospel — according to the Democratic creed. Within the creed, the rule of spontaneity, improvisation, rugged individualism was now trenchantly applied — if in slightly ambiguous, transitional language — to the creation of armies. The tedious processes of training, formerly said to be essential for the old militia, were superfluous in a country teeming with ardent patriots and dead shots. To judge by results, of course, Polk was not making undue claims for the volunteers. His error lay in slighting the regular contribution, which his ideology obliged him to do. At any rate the term "militia" as he employed it was now without meaning.

Pierce was less imbued with doctrinaire Jacksonianism. The way in which he phrased a request for four new regular regiments, in his second annual message (December 1854), epitomized the double change in emphasis which had half-consciously taken place. He spoke of "the valuable services constantly rendered by the Army and its inestimable importance as the nucleus around which the volunteer forces of the nation can promptly gather in the hour of danger."[23] The permanent professionals and the mushroom volunteers, the one group so few, the other so ephemeral, had between them squeezed out the militia. Or perhaps that is to put the matter too firmly. This had not come about through deliberate policy. We might better say that a vacuum had been filled.

THE MILITIA IN DECLINE

The decline of the militia can be more vividly appreciated at close quarters. To the ordinary American the one or two muster days in each year were a nuisance or worse than a nuisance. The militiaman was still nominally obliged to arm himself, though a handful of states contrived to amass respectable armories. Hence the appearance at musters of ancient, rusty weapons, or — especially in some of the Western states — of make-believe weapons: cornstalks, sticks, umbrellas, ramrods. In theory the deficiency laid the offender open to a fine. The fine was rarely collected but remained an irritation.

More serious was the fine imposed for nonattendance at musters. State law and practice varied; in New York, Pennsylvania and a few others the poor man had a genuine grievance in the decades after the War of 1812. In New York the militia fine was twelve dollars per annum. The prosperous could afford to pay, and regard the sum as a sort of tax. Working men found such a sum considerable; and for nonpayment they were liable to imprisonment as common debtors. In certain areas the fine was ignored or laxly enforced. Elsewhere it was collected, and im-

This is ye GRAND MILITARY Display

A derisive view by an unknown artist of a target shoot. A cow seems to have perished: the target remains unscathed.

prisonment was resorted to. The prison penalty for militia debt attracted the attention of radicals and reformers, who coupled it with the general problem of debtors' prisons and agitated for repeal of the humiliating laws.[24]

The militia obligation was all the more vexatious to the poor man because in fact it was not universal. Exemptions had been prescribed in colonial times. Some of these categories were adopted in the act of 1792 which exempted from service congressmen, seamen, custom house clerks and a few other special groups. Individual states added exempt occupations to their own lists. The Vermont Militia Act of 1818 exempted a large number of categories, including justices of the peace, sheriffs, ministers, deacons, doctors, schoolmasters, ferrymen, millers, and college students and teachers. A few years later manufacturers, founders and their employees joined the company of the exempt. The "citizen soldiers" of Vermont were urged in 1840 to "look around you and see how many *salaried officers* . . ., *professional men,* and . . . others, all of whom have *property,* as well as *persons* to be protected," escaped their responsibilities, "while *you,* who are the *real working men* . . ., are compelled to shoulder your muskets to protect their *persons* and *property.*" Exemptions in Massachusetts were equally generous and equally exasperating to the nonexempt. An unsuccessful attempt was made in 1835 to abolish the "long and cumbrous lists of exempts" in that state, on the ground that "the militia duty has . . . hitherto . . . devolved almost exclusively upon the middle and poorer classes of society," and that "there was no good reason why those who accepted offices, or were voluntarily engaged in professional or literary pursuits, should not contribute by personal service, or pecuniary penalty, to the support of the militia, as well as the merchant, the mechanic, or the laborer."[25]

The well-to-do could escape their obligations by other means. They could accept a militia commission and then swiftly resign; having once held a commission they were free from further service. The reactions of young George Templeton Strong are fairly typical. In 1837 the spectacle of a ragged New York militia drill had vastly amused him. Two years later he was not quite so amused when he noted that "Governor Seward is to review the militia tomorrow; a token fifteen thousand of these unhappy scarecrows are to exhibit themselves." Somehow or other he himself had received a summons to militia duty: "how they caught me I don't know." He declared that he would pay no attention to the summons; he had the excuse that his middle initial was wrong on the document. If pleas for exemption failed he would "get some nominal office for economy's sake." A friend had offered him a chaplaincy, "for it seems the militia chaplains are all laymen, something like Friar Tuck, I suppose, or any other 'hedge priests.'" Strong speculated on what their duties might be — "saying grace at militia suppers" and the like. Apparently he was not required to make the experiment.[26] If he had been even a shade militarily inclined he could also have enrolled as an honorary volunteer in one of the numerous "uniformed" or "independent" companies which are discussed in the next chapter. Whatever their military value, their spread helped to hasten the downfall of the standing militia, by emphasizing the disparity of obligation, the low social status, the dearth of military talent and the comically ill-equipped aspects of the "constitutional force."

On every score, then, the traditional standing militia of the United States had fallen into disrepute by about 1850. As in other areas of government, the federal compromise was apt to produce both overlappings of function, leading to jealousy and deadlock, and hiatuses — areas in which neither the federal government nor the states exercised effective control. Jealousy of federal supremacy led the states to resist any such scheme of classified reform as Poinsett's, which in any case came too late in the day. Boredom and indifference induced both levels of government to pass the problem back to one another. The tangle of worthy and unworthy motives, of prejudice and aspiration, of realism and

The militia at its lowest ebb. In this scathing cartoon the officers' conversation is as hoggish as their demeanor ("Major, I think it best for the officers not to dine with the common sojiers: you see they aint fit 'ciety for the officers — cause they dont know nothing of no refinement." . . . "Well, I think its best for the sojers to dine by themselves, cause when the officers is with em they allways feel a sort a, ashamed").

stolid conservatism, is illustrated in the debate over a bill to reform the Massachusetts militia. Governor Levi Lincoln vetoed the bill, which proposed to organize the militia in volunteer battalions, in March 1833. Supplied with arguments by the indefatigable William H. Sumner, he maintained that the reform would be unconstitutional. The states were bound by the act of 1792 to group their militia into divisions, brigades and regiments; and this establishment would no longer be possible. Moreover, the effect of the bill would be to destroy the historic militia; and for the traditionally minded Lincoln and Sumner, militia duty was still "an exaction of personal service from the Citizen, for the common safety, which he is no more at liberty to refuse than any other tax legitimately imposed." They therefore resisted the sensible observation of a Mr. Daniel Wells, that with respect to the old militia, "the country outgrew its institutions."[27]

In other states which had less of a real militia tradition than Massachusetts, decay and change were accepted more readily, or more cynically. The process was in fact early at work. Some frontier states never developed a militia system worthy of the name. Contrary to cherished American belief, the backwoodsmen — in peacetime at least — were a reluctant, ill-armed soldiery, far less effective than even the doubtful organizations of the seaboard communities. In the backcountry there was no tradition of militia duty and the population was too thinly scattered to be able to meet easily or in sufficient numbers for worthwhile training. The distribution of the annual federal grant of two hundred thousand dollars for the purchase of arms is a case in point. Though adjutant generals concocted militia returns from census figures or other statistics, and though states were proud of their population increase, few seem to have been much concerned to inflate the returns in order to secure the largest possible musket allowance. Frontier states were particularly lax. In the 1850's the distribution formula was changed so that in future it would be proportional to representation in Congress. The device — initiated in Iowa — made little difference. The arsenals that some states had maintained in earlier times dwindled away, their contents neglected or turned over to volunteer companies. Mis-

souri not only declined to buy arms; it rejected a proposal in 1845
to build a state armory to store the arms which had been given to
it. In his gloomy report for 1856, the adjutant general of Louisiana
confessed that there was almost no interest in military affairs in
his state, except in New Orleans and two or three other parishes.
He was not sure what the enrolled militia ought to number. The
arms held by Louisiana amounted to "not more than two thousand
five hundred muskets," most of them ancient and perhaps dangerous old flintlocks. The state's annual quota was fewer than three
hundred muskets. Jacob D. Cox, an Ohio lawyer who was to
have a gallant Civil War career, painted a similar picture.
Though he was a brigadier in the Ohio militia in the 1850's his
commission was "a nominal thing, and in fact I had never worn a
uniform." On the outbreak of the war he went with George B.
McClellan, who had just been given command of Ohio's volunteer troops, to inspect the state arsenal. They found it "simply an
empty storehouse," with a few scraps of worthless equipment.[28]

The grotesque near-fantasy of militia practice is typified in the
method of accountancy for the annual two-hundred-thousand-
dollar expenditure.

The first issues of arms . . . under the act of 1808 being of muskets
only, the apportionment was naturally enough stated in muskets; but
such is the force of routine that after a while when all kinds of arms,
ammunition, and equipments began to be supplied, the accounts were
still kept in terms of muskets.

It was assumed for the sake of convenience that each musket cost
exactly thirteen dollars. In due course there was no musket in use
that cost this amount,

so that this mythical arm existed only in the accounts as a *musket of
calculation*. The quotas . . . had first to be stated in dollars, and then
divided by thirteen to reduce them to muskets of calculation and
fractional muskets of calculation, called *thirteenths*. Then the price of
every arm issued had to be ascertained in dollars and divided by
thirteen, to reduce it to muskets of calculation. . . . [The] system
was neatly rounded off by . . . estimating the cost of the actual
muskets, the manufactured article, at thirteen dollars each, utterly

regardless of their true cost, — sometimes not over nine or ten dollars.[29]

Among the older states, Delaware was conspicuously unmilitary. There the militia fine was abolished as early as 1816, which led to "a total neglect of every appearance of military duty." From the replies to the militia board circular of 1826 it appears that only Massachusetts and Connecticut had much to boast of. William H. Riker suggests that the proportion of annual militia returns submitted to the Secretary of War provides a relative gauge of efficiency. Delaware and Mississippi are at the bottom of his scale, since they hardly ever produced a return. At the head come Massachusetts, Connecticut, Virginia, New Hampshire and New York.[30]

Delaware's lead, if it can be called a lead, was followed by a good many other states. Several abolished imprisonment for non-payment of militia fines when they came to frame or amend their constitutions. This was done by New Jersey (1844), Iowa (1846), California (1849), and Michigan (1850). Others abandoned the punishment though not the law. Compulsory militia service was abolished in Massachusetts (1840); Maine, Vermont and Ohio (1844); Connecticut and New York (1846); Missouri (1847); and New Hampshire (1851). The aim was not an entire retreat from military training, since these were re-formed as volunteer militias. Nor did financial penalties altogether disappear, although they now took the form of a tax or commutation charge, usually less than a dollar, in lieu of military service. Some life remained, as we shall see, in the variegated clusters of volunteer companies grouped under state militia nomenclatures. But the venerable theory of the community in arms was for all real purposes discarded — for a while at least.

The story may be summed up in the situation of New Hampshire. In 1810 the militia of the state was enrolled in thirty-seven regiments, banded into six brigades which in turn were allotted among three divisions. By 1850 this strength had risen to forty-two regiments, totaling in theory more than thirty thousand men. In 1851, however, compulsory militia duty ended. By 1860, in consequence, though the three divisions and six brigades still

A militia muster is the subject of this lithograph by David Claypoole Johnston, ca. 1836. The scene is somewhere in New England, perhaps Boston. The ragged lineup could have been seen almost anywhere in the United States. The only man in uniform is the officer on the right; and he has overdone his finery.

existed on paper, no doubt with their major generals and brigadiers and aides, the thirty thousand had shrunk to one regiment of volunteers, and twelve companies that held aloof from the state system. The militia of New Hampshire, said its adjutant general, "was literally dead."[31] Or, as H. H. Riley wrote in bittersweet recollection of the Massachusetts village of his boyhood, and the changes it had undergone:

Yes, reader, these were training-days in New-England; but the military glory has now actually died out. The last gathering I saw I shall never forget. It was . . . a sorry group, made up of a rusty captain, two or three faded corporals, and a handful of dare-devil privates, who cared no more for their country than so many heathen. The officers looked cowed and heart-broken, and it was evident that the spirit of '76 was on its last legs. I afterwards learned, I am sorry to say, that the captain, in a fit of patriotic rage, broke his sword across his knee, and declared "that he never would turn out again as long as his name was Jones!"[32]

7

THE AMATEURS: ENTHUSIASTIC
VOLUNTEERS

Be it said in praise of your independent companies, that they display a native military genius, a taste in their dress, and an activity and precision in their movements, which would do honor to veterans.

— Colonel Irenée Amelot de Lacroix, *Military and Political Hints,* 1808

THE INDEPENDENT COMPANIES

Though the militia dwindled away in the decades before the Civil War, foreign observers quite often asserted that the United States had a keen military spirit and that every settlement had its company of belligerent amateurs. The *Illustrated London News*, for example, declared in 1859 that there were "at least a million of citizen soldiers" in America, "trained to the use of arms, and ready any moment at the call of duty; and experience proves that the officers are invariably elected for the best reasons, and that the men act with . . . strict obedience" to the officers of their choice.[1]

Any resemblance between this ideal picture and the situation described in the previous chapter would seem purely coincidental. The explanation is twofold. In the first place, foreigners find the lessons they want to find in the behavior of other countries. After the American Revolution, European liberals convinced themselves — as did most Americans, for that matter — that the spontaneous military effort of the citizenry was irresistible. In the first half of the nineteenth century the British, the French and the Americans continued to believe in the various virtues of citizen soldiers, no longer in a revolutionary but in a bourgeois role. They were the army neither of the courts nor of the rabble, but of property-owning citizens: the yeomanry of

A peculiarly hypothetical European portrayal
of a Revolutionary soldier. In this engraving
(Augsburg, ca. 1775) the rough-and-ready
garb of the patriot volunteer has been transformed into something as chic as a ballet
costume.

England, the Garde Nationale of France, equally able (in theory)
to resist a *coup d'état* or to disperse a mob. Europeans believed
that there was something particularly wholesome, and militarily
effective, in the American citizen-soldiery. In the late 1850's,
suddenly alarmed by French belligerence, the British developed a
new volunteer movement. It pleased them to believe that they
could follow American practice and so make themselves invincible.

The second reason is that foreigners tended to confuse the
militia and the volunteers. English travelers saw the gorgeous
array of volunteer companies, and were apt to conclude that they
were a representative sample of an immense militia. As a proof of
the American "fondness for military exercises," a British army
colonel said in 1853, "I have only to refer to their militia and
volunteer corps, which are most creditable. There is not a city or

village in the United States in which the citizens are not enrolled in military companies." They were impressive both in the West and in the cities of the East, where some of the amateur regiments "would reflect no disgrace on the regular service of any nation." The colonel was fascinated by one corps in New York dressed in the same uniform as the British Grenadier Guards:

They marched in sections, with a splendid band at their head; and . . . it would be impossible to find a more military-looking, well-drilled body of men: they were faultless. The same may be said of many other of their corps. . . . Their artillery companies are very effective. . . . The cavalry volunteer corps are . . . well mounted, and equal in every respect to your Yeomanry at home, while the bands, chiefly German, are far superior.[2]

The history of these dazzling volunteer units is complicated to explain, not least because most of them also had militia designations. They were, however, a very different phenomenon from the "common" or "beat" militia, as the word "volunteer" suggests. Militia service was in conception universal and obligatory: the volunteer companies themselves elected to serve, prescribing their own patterns of training, dress and organization. As in other instances, the origin lay in Britain. London's Honourable Artillery Company was founded in 1537. Boston's Ancient and Honorable Artillery Company of 1638 was a direct imitation, and the oldest of the American independent companies. The number multiplied greatly in the eighteenth century. In New England, for example, 1741 saw the foundations of the First Corps of Cadets in Boston, and of Rhode Island's Newport Artillery Company. On the eve of the Revolution and throughout the next troubled generation, volunteer companies mushroomed. A sample includes:

1771	First Company, Governor's Foot Guard	Hartford, Conn.
1774	First "Troup," Philadelphia City Cavalry	Philadelphia, Pa.
1786	Chatham Artillery Company	Savannah, Ga.
1789	Richmond Light Infantry Blues	Richmond, Va.
1807	Pittsburgh Blues	Pittsburgh, Pa.
1807	Washington Light Infantry	Charleston, S.C.

They were usually formed in response to some moment of crisis, and often played a valuable part. The Philadelphia volunteer cavalry gave good service to General Washington. The Washington Light Infantry of Charleston came into being as a patriotic gesture when the British frigate *Leopard* fired upon the U. S. frigate *Chesapeake*. "Remember the *Leopard*" became a company motto, and its members sported a piece of leopardskin on their headgear.[3]

ELITE VOLUNTEERS

These were elite units in several respects. They were, to repeat, volunteer companies existing independently of the statewide systems of militia, and they held themselves aloof from the common mass. They provided their own uniforms, which then as later were nearly always of a dazzling and expensive splendor. A lovingly detailed description of the new Philadelphia Lancer Guard of 1835 may be taken as characteristic:

The dress consists of a coat of rich maroon cloth faced with buff, pantaloons of crimson with a stripe of buff on the outside seams, and a helmet of the lancer shape, the skull of beaten brass, and the crest of crimson with a radiance of silver in front surrounding a golden eagle, the plume is of a snowy white, drooping gracefully from the front peak of the cap, forming together the most elegant and fanciful costume we have seen.

The lance to be carried by the corps, will be polished steel with a light ash staff decorated with a crimson streamer. This species of troops is a novelty in the city, and if gotten up with spirit, will add greatly to the splendor of our parades. We are informed that a Polish Officer of Lancers is engaged to give the necessary instruction in the management of the lance and . . . the sabre.[4]

They followed the international military fashions of the day: riflemen, grenadiers, light artillery, light infantry and general cavalry in the first decades, lancers and dragoons in the 1830's and 1840's. All of these were elite formations in European armies.

218

THE AMATEURS: ENTHUSIASTIC VOLUNTEERS

Light artillery were mounted, specialist units. Cavalry were likewise special units, which accumulated legends of whirlwind charges led by moustachioed noblemen. Volunteer infantry similarly made it clear that they did not belong to the undifferentiated mass of foot soldiers. In European armies the flank companies of infantry battalions consisted of grenadiers and light infantry: men taller and more admired than the rest for their appearance and their skirmishing ability. The American volunteer infantry modeled themselves on this pattern, and like the Europeans affected towering bearskins and other forms of helmet to accentuate their height.

Their uniforms and equipment, their drill instructors and parades and dinners and clubrooms all cost money. The capacity and readiness to pay seemed to guarantee that only the respectable would join their ranks. Indeed the companies were run as exclusive little societies of fifty to a hundred members, screening

applicants and electing their NCO's and officers with an elaborate mixture of democracy and privilege. Among the members of the New England Guards of Boston were young Abbott Lawrence, then merely a clerk in a store but helped on to his later fortune by the corps commander, and Francis Palfrey, who was a Harvard graduate and son of the historian John G. Palfrey. Reviewing the history of the Guards on its fiftieth anniversary in 1862, Charles G. Loring (a former commander) said with satisfaction that it had always "enjoyed a reputation as a military company of gentlemen." The reason for their continued reputation was that the founders "took care that it should be exclusively composed of gentlemen, and men of sound moral character. No man was admitted . . . upon whom the suspicion of any tendency to dissipation rested. . . . Let me tell you that we expelled a member for once having been seen intoxicated in the street. Do you think a Company would do that, and then have unsteady ranks, and officers who could not toe the line?"

In every city, up to the Civil War, there were companies which maintained this genteel quality. A former enlisted man who was employed by the Detroit Light Guard as armorer and musician in 1857 (and stayed with them for thirty-three years) said: "At that time the company got nothing from the State. They had to pay for all they got; uniforms and all. . . . I found the men to be all gentlemen of wealth and prominence, who had joined the company just for the pleasure they would derive by being a soldier." The Putnam Phalanx, formed in 1858 at Hartford, Connecticut, was described two years later by *Harper's Weekly* as "a corps consisting of two companies, numbering together some two hundred and fifty, and composed, for the most part, of the intellectually, physically, and pecuniarily 'solid men' of that city and its neighborhood."[5]

Long before then, the vast majority of volunteer companies had been incorporated within the state militias, at least on paper. The first stage in many cases had been to designate volunteer infantry as flank companies to militia battalions, and volunteer cavalry and artillery as providing those elements for larger militia formations. As the old militia gradually collapsed,

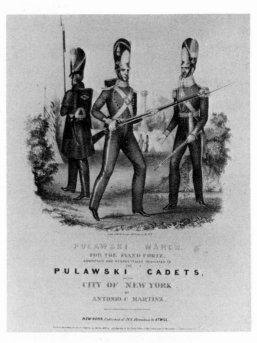

nothing was left but the staff, the skeleton of a theoretical hierarchy of divisions, brigades and regiments, and a miscellany of volunteer units. The next stage, in the states which bothered to initiate reforms, was to constitute the volunteers as the entire effective militia. This was what happened, for example, under a Massachusetts act of 1840. The act provided that all able-bodied white males between eighteen and forty-five (except for exempts) should be enrolled as hitherto, but would no longer be expected to arm or equip themselves or undergo any training. The "active militia," up to the number of ten thousand, was to consist of volunteer corps, which were grouped into militia formations. In some of the larger cities it was possible to recruit several hundred men in one unit: hence the impressive 7th Regiment of New York. But in most cases units were much smaller, and continued to be known mainly by their original name.

They were recognizable too because they continued to choose their own officers and their own style of dress. When the Massachusetts militia paraded in cold weather they had a measure of uniformity, since they wore greatcoats supplied by the state. When they peeled off their coats an astounding variety was revealed. In 1860 the 6th Regiment, Massachusetts Volunteer Militia, consisted of the following characteristic kaleidoscope of companies:

A, of Lowell, organized in 1855 as the Lawrence Cadets, then renamed the National Greys (dress: blue frocks and pantaloons; white crossbelts; tall round caps with white pompons)

B, of Groton, raised in 1775 as the Groton Artillery, which kept two brass field-pieces in its armory (dress: U. S. infantry — dark blue frocks and light blue trousers)

C, the old Mechanic Phalanx of Lowell, organized in 1825 (dress: a gray uniform with yellow trimmings)

D, also of Lowell, organized in 1841 as the City Guards (dress: gray uniform with buff trimmings)

E, of Acton, formed in 1851 as the Davis Guards, in honor of Isaac Davis, an Acton minuteman killed in 1775 (dress: U. S. infantry)

F, of Lawrence, raised in 1855 as the Warren Light Guard, named after General Joseph Warren who was killed at Bunker Hill (dress: U. S. infantry)

G, of Worcester, organized in 1803 as the Worcester Light Infantry (dress: "full dress uniforms of blue")

H, of Lowell, founded in 1851 as the Watson Light Guards (dress: gray uniform)

I, of Lawrence, raised in 1849 as the Lawrence Light Infantry (dress: French infantry — blue frocks, red trousers, kepi)

K, of Boston, formed in 1810 as the Washington Artillery, then renamed the Washington Light Guards (dress: gray uniform).[6]

SOCIAL AND ETHNIC DIVERSITY

As the former name of Company C indicates, another major change had taken place. By the second or third decade of the nineteenth century, the elite companies were joined and swamped by a mass of others, chiefly composed of clerks, artisans and — in the big cities — sometimes of hoodlums. In the West and in country districts generally, there had always been a greater social intermixture, and the volunteers had tended to favor more ferocious names: Invincibles, Avengers, Patriots, Snake Hunters. The most obvious new feature, however, was the proliferation of immigrant companies, especially among the Germans and the Irish. The German companies were to some extent based on the rifle clubs of the old country; for them as for others target shoots were a popular diversion. Some German units styled themselves as Jaegers; in Savannah, Georgia, a company established in 1845 was known as the German Volunteers. Most, though, took an American-sounding name to emphasize their patriotism: the Washington Rifle Corps, say, or the National Greys.

The Irish more commonly advertised their origin. Again in Georgia, Savannah had the Irish Jasper Greens (1842) and Atlanta the Irish Volunteers (1852). The volunteer companies of Philadelphia, along with a Scottish unit — the Caledonian Blues — which wore Highland plaids, and the Riflemen, clad in green fringed hunting shirts, included in 1829 at least two unmistakably Irish formations: the Hibernia Greens and the Montgomery Guards. Orange, New Jersey, together with the Union Blues, the American Continentals and the Liberty Rifles, had in the 1850's an Irish unit called the O'Brien Columbian Rifles. South Carolina in the same decade, together with such companies as the Calhoun Artillery, the Carolina Blues, the Palmetto Rifles, and the German Hussars of Charleston, claimed Irish companies like the Meagher Guards and the Emmet Guards. By 1854 Connecticut had six Irish companies, including the Washington-Erina Guards of New Haven, the Emmet Guards of Hartford, the Jackson Guards of Norwich and the Montgomery Guards of Bridgeport.[7]

Volunteer companies spread in bewildering diversity. New Orleans boasted a Washington Artillery company (1838) and a Bataillon d'Artillerie d'Orléans. In Virginia, among the motley array called out after John Brown's raid,

There might have been seen the modest gray uniform of the Richmond Volunteers mingled with the cerulean blue of those from Alexandria, the glaring buff and yellow of the Valley Continentals, and the indescribably gorgeous crimson of the Southwestern men. In many corps, each gentleman selected his own uniform, and while all seemed affected with a contempt for their citizen's clothes, rarely more than two agreed in the selection of the colors of their military dress. Some wore slouched hats, some military caps, and some stovepipe beavers of the latest style.

The funeral procession of General William Jenkins Worth in New York in 1857 was graced with sixteen volunteer regiments. Pride of place was given to the Irish 69th, led by Colonel Ryan, in cadet

german volunteers / phila.

In Philadelphia, from March 1839 to June 1842, William H. Huddy and his partner Peter S. Duval published a sort of monthly portfolio of colored lithographs, the *Military Magazine, and Record of the Volunteers of the United States of America, together with the Army and Navy* (a nice order of priority). This fluent ink-and-pencil drawing by Huddy is a preliminary sketch of "German volunteers" in Philadelphia. The mounted figure is an officer of the Pennsylvania Light Guard.

gray, striding out to the music of Manahan's Brass Band. Further behind came the 55th Regiment, under Colonel Le Gal, inspired by the La Fayette Guard Band:

The Napoleonic tradition was strong in this regiment, for before the band marched a detachment of full-bearded pioneers, with bearskin busbies, full leather aprons, and axes carried stiffly on the right shoulder. There was even a saucy little *vivandière* with laced pantaloons showing beneath her . . . skirts who carried a small wine keg. . . . The men generally wore the waxed mustachios and small goatees popularized by Napoleon III.

There was also the gentlemanly 7th Regiment, and presumably the Scottish 79th, in kilts.[8]

Almost every age group was represented. There were even companies of children, as recorded in this arch communiqué of 1860: "A petite company, styled the 'Young Riflemen,' paraded in Alexandria, D.C., . . . with a neat uniform and knapsacks. It is composed of boys from ten to fifteen years of age. Young America seems wide awake." So did almost every ethnic group. The *Asmonean*, a New York Jewish weekly, recorded in 1850 that "a fine body of Volunteers, . . . styled the Joseph A. Jackson Guards, after our well-known co-religionist, paraded for target practice on Wednesday last. . . . They presented a soldierly appearance, and deserve credit for their proficiency." Their meeting was more than a passing fad. Eight years later the *Asmonean* noted:

The spirit of the younger and sprightlier portion of our male populations, seems to be centred in the single object of military ardor. Innumerable corps of citizen soldiery daily parade the streets of our metropolis, and the sound of martial music everywhere greets the ear. . . . Our employees, it would seem, have been seized with this "military mania," as they have enrolled themselves into an independent corps.

The corps in question, the Asmonean Guard, included Christians: its secretary's name was J. H. Kelly. Other companies, such as the Empire Hussars (Troop K) and the Young Men's Lafayette Association, seem to have been entirely Jewish. The "military mania" even spread so far that colored military units were proposed in Ohio in 1852. But America was still a white man's country; the proposal appears to have come to nothing.[9]

To some, America was also for the Americans. The spread of "foreign" volunteer units led to a sharp reaction. There was much friction in New Orleans between the "American" and "French" companies; the Washington Artillery changed its name in 1840 to the Native American Artillery. The Irish were still more unpopular and were blatantly discriminated against. A company known as the Columbian Guards, "consisting chiefly of naturalized and native citizens, Irishmen and descendants of Irishmen," was chartered in Boston in the 1830's and incorporated in a militia brigade with the City Guards, the Mechanic Riflemen and other units. When a parade of the brigade was held on Boston Common in 1837, the members of five other companies (except for their officers) broke ranks and walked away in protest. After the parade, or what was left of it, the Montgomery Guards set off for their armory, followed by a mob which pelted them with missiles.

The company was disbanded in 1839. For some years there were no more militia incidents of this kind, though there were violent clashes in Philadelphia between Irish and native American fire companies — which, as we have seen, were often closely linked with volunteer corps. Then as more Irish units came into being, and as the nativist or Know-Nothing movement spread, dissension broke out again. In Boston the Columbian Artillery, organized as far back as 1798, had almost disintegrated in the 1840's. It was revived as an Irish company, to the indignation of nativists who found its presence even more offensive than that of such newly created companies as the Sarsfield Guards. Henry Gardner, the governor-elect of Massachusetts, suddenly announced in January 1855 that it was his intention to "disband all military companies composed of persons of foreign birth." He carried out his threat, though not without resistance. Benjamin F. Butler was colonel of a militia regiment which included an Irish company — the Jackson Musketeers of Lowell. He refused to obey the disbanding order and challenged Gardner to court-martial him. The governor evaded the issue by a comprehensive and chaotic gerrymandering maneuver: all militia regiments were reconstituted so that there was no place for the Irish companies or for their champion Butler.

Countermaneuvers in this sordid comic opera almost restored the *status quo*. Butler was soon reelected to a militia command, this time as brigadier general. The Mongomery and Sarsfield Guards continued in existence as "associations" for "literary and military purposes."

But the insult stung. It was felt again a few months later when the Know-Nothing governor of Connecticut, William T. Minor, followed Gardner's example. Six Irish units were disbanded on the plea that "Military Companies organized as foreign Companies, and composed entirely of the foreign born, are believed to be detrimental to the military interests of our State, and their continuance inconsistant with the spirit of our Institutions." A German company, the New Haven City Guards, was allowed to remain: its members were mainly Protestant. Again the governor's action was contested. Two adjutant generals declined to promulgate his order. The *New Haven Register* pointed out that the Washington-Erina Guards was an exemplary company whose commander was native-born. The *Bridgeport Farmer* revealed that Captain Coates of the disbanded Montgomery Guards had formerly served in the U. S. Army. Ironically, he was "a very zealous Whig, and in all party matters, was particularly intimate with Mr. John M. Wilson, now one of the principal managers of the Know-Nothing Inquisition in this city." A couple of years later, with Minor's departure, the ban ended.[10]

Similar half-ugly, half-ludicrous machinations went on in New York and some other states including Wisconsin, though no serious attempt was made to disband Irish units. Instead the nativists strove to create "pure" American companies. In the 1840's Poughkeepsie had an American Citizens Corps. New York City's first nativist regiment was the American Rifles. On their first parade the commander of one of the companies was so incensed to learn that a "foreigner" had managed to worm his way into the battalion that he "threw up his commission." The American Rifles came into the militia structure as the 71st Regiment in 1852.

There was much play with the words imputed to George Washington during one of the most critical periods of the American Revolution: *Put none but Americans on guard to-night.*

There were sundry other petty upheavals in the intricate lineage of the New York state militia. Thus the 9th Regiment, mainly Irish, was disbanded in 1858; its members transferred to the clamantly Irish 69th Regiment. A new 9th Regiment was formed from a wing of the 55th, whose main wing consisted of French immigrants. The minority group, a mixture of native Americans and Swiss, had striven to assert its separateness by wearing trousers of a different color; "while efforts had been made to harmonize this incongruity, no settlement could be effected, for neither side would yield the point." Secession seemed to agree with the minority wing, if we can credit the fulsome account of a militia periodical which described the new 9th as "like a thorough-bred black spanish cock, with his broad, bright, red comb, glossy, dark plumage, and gallant mien, swelling much larger and grander than his weight (numbers) would seem to justify."[11]

The final explosion of anti-Irish sentiment was produced by the conduct of Colonel Michael Corcoran, when he resisted the order to parade the 69th Regiment to welcome the visit of the Prince of Wales in 1860. In the words of a wildly cheered oration by Thomas Meagher, Corcoran "refused lawfully as a citizen, courageously as a soldier, indignantly as an Irishman." Native American opinion was very different. There were proposals to disband the 69th, and Corcoran would have been court-martialed if the Civil War had not supervened. *Harper's Weekly* warned the Irish not to presume on American hospitality, and cast doubt on their military prowess:

As militiamen and soldiers they have not infrequently been an absolute nuisance. It is not worth while to repeat the story . . . of the Irishmen who deserted from our army and constituted the battalion of San Patricio, in the Mexican War. . . . The spectacle of the ignominious surrender of the Irishmen in Lamoriciere's army, who had volunteered to assist the Pope in keeping down his Italian subjects, has not yet been forgotten. Before our Irishmen thrust themselves anew under

229

the public notice they should allow the effluvia of this transaction to pass away.[12]

These disputes shrank away in the heat of 1861. The companies and regiments of Massachusetts, Connecticut and New York were transformed without question into war formations. Corcoran redeemed himself by rushing from a sickbed — in the popular story — to lead the 69th at Bull Run; wounded and captured, he became a hero. For Irish-Americans at any rate his actions were consecrated by his later death in the field in December 1863.*

THE SOCIAL FUNCTION OF VOLUNTEER SOLDIERING

It is clear that whatever its military uses the volunteer movement fulfilled a number of other purposes. The companies were clubs, conferring status and identity. Their members also acquired a kind of second identity. On parade, or dining together and applauding florid toasts, they were liberated from domestic and commercial preoccupations, and transformed by magnificent costume. They could feel patriotic, and therefore democratic, and yet elevated into a romantic-genteel realm where one might talk without embarrassment of nobility, honor, chivalry, gallantry. A Charleston pamphleteer fell easily into this language, praising the spirit of the volunteers "where discipline comes as easily as did in days of yore the page's obedience to his mistress."

The volunteer movement established convivial and honorific ties within the amorphous general community. It appealed as much to immigrants, seeking to find the community, as to native Americans seeking to preserve what they imagined the community

* All was not quite forgotten or forgiven. The colonel of a New York regiment, serving in Virginia in April 1863, challenged a mounted group which rode into his lines in the dark and would not give the countersign. He was shot dead by one of the party — who turned out to be Brigadier General Corcoran. His men threatened to go and take revenge. Corcoran's not very convincing (or contrite) explanation was accepted by the authorities. He was killed by falling off his horse in a similar night ride a few months later. The implication is that he may have been drunk on both occasions. See Matthew J. Graham, *The Ninth Regiment New York Volunteers: Hawkins' Zouaves* (New York, 1900), 411–419.

to be. In this sense it is an early example of the American joining habit, a forerunner of the Elks, Red Men, Lions and Rotarians of a later generation. Volunteer companies, like these service clubs, developed an extensive network of relationships. The chronicles of the volunteer militia abound in examples of friendly visits between company and company, striving to outdo one another in deportment and hospitality. The pattern was much the same in all parts of the country. Nor did it change through the decades, except that improved communications made longer journeys possible. In Illinois in 1835 the two Springfield companies were invited to Jacksonville. The Jacksonville newspaper showered praise on their "rich and showy" uniforms, their "arms bright as sunbeams," their "gallant, military-looking" officers. There was a welcoming dinner with "brimming bumpers, compliments and comic songs." Next day came a review, another dinner "with the usual finale of good wine, good toasts and good feeling," a sham battle, and a military ball "which for numbers, music, decorations, brilliancy

Ladies' tickets, to admit the "fair sex" to festivities organized by
two New York companies, the high-toned Benson Cadets and the
Governor's Guard — the latter a more politically minded body, to
judge from its place of meeting.

The Gulick Guards led a double life, made explicit in the design of their ball-ticket, and in their motto:

Firemen with Pleasure,
Soldiers at Leisure.

The martial pretensions of the volunteer movement are well brought out in the elaborate card of the National Cadets.

of dress and beauty of belles, has never been equalled, we make bold to say, in this state." Three months later the Springfield companies entertained the warriors of Jacksonville. Once again the climax was a "military ball," intertwining bravery and sentiment. Longing to preserve the mood of the previous night, some of the ladies of Springfield escorted the Jacksonville visitors for several miles on their homeward ride. At the moment of parting they formed a ring with the Jacksonville girls, hand in hand, and sang tender songs to one another while the men glittered in the offing.

Most visits were more strictly male in emphasis, as when ninety-five members of the Savannah Blues came by sea to New York in 1860 to visit the City Guard.[13] But every company delighted in displaying its uniform at dinners and dances as well as on parade and in camp. Scores of specially composed marches and waltzes were dedicated to particular companies. This sheet music with its lithographed bravura is a charmingly overblown survival of the 1830's, 1840's and 1850's. So are the invitations and programs to innumerable forgotten balls and soirees organized by the citizen soldiery.

The volunteer companies were of course a movement for young men. Apart from the romantic opportunities they offered, they supplied something that did not exist until college life and organized athletics developed widely in the United States. Volunteer companies anticipated a number of features of collegiate behavior: special dress and gestures, forms of fraternity, hazing, ritual, abracadabra partly in joke and partly in earnest. Thus in 1822 the Boston Light Infantry visited the Salem Light Infantry. In the course of some horseplay a Salem volunteer exclaimed to one of the Bostonians, "Oh! you Tiger." This became a catchword; it was then "an easy stage to adopt the growl of a tiger, and at the conclusion of the three cheers, a 'Tiger' was invariably called for." We are told that when the Boston company visited New York in 1826 they "astonished the Gothamites by giving the genuine growl." Here perhaps is the origin of the cheerleading of American football; and the college and high school bands, with their elaborate countermarching, may also hark back to the antebellum days when spectacle, athletic activity and rivalry were furnished by military companies.* Certainly the flavor is reminiscent. Like college athletes, the volunteers alternated between buffoonery and an almost fanatical absorption in the details of training and equipment. Indeed, one historian suggests that there was a direct correlation between the rise of sports — cricket, baseball, rowing, boxing — at the end of the 1850's, and the decline of military companies. He is no doubt correct on the first point, but wrong on the second. There had never been so many companies in existence as in 1859 and 1860. If some youngsters abandoned their volunteer units to march with the Wide-Awakes, they were after all not engaged in anything very different.[14]

MILITARY EFFICIENCY

The military efficiency of the volunteers is problematical. Their weaknesses in this respect are obvious. Their enthusiasm was sartorial, fanciful, social rather than warlike. Their chronicles often dwelt upon ludicrous minutiae. In an account of the New York 7th Regiment we find such unconscious gems as *During the whole history of the Regiment no subject of that character has ever provoked so fierce and bitter controversy as the proposed change in the uniform hat;* and *Another trouble during the Richmond trip was the mutinous conduct of Band-Master Noll and his musicians. The fatigues of the journey, the heat of the weather, and perhaps the free flow of wine and lager-beer, had demoralized the band* . . . Many companies endured for only a few years, or had little continuity of membership. Most, outside New York and a few other large centers, were too small to have

* When the S.S. *Lafayette* sailed from Philadelphia for Liverpool in 1851, some delay and alarm was caused by mechanical breakdowns. On several evenings the captain sought to distract the male passengers by drilling them on deck "in the true militia style." They enjoyed the experience, and finally "presented the skipper with a huge *wooden* sword, as a token of our appreciation of his services as commander-in-chief of the Lafayette Guards. It was sport, if nothing else; and while we were so engaged, we were not thinking of our broken engines." Benjamin Moran, *The Footpath and Highway; or, Wanderings of an American* (Philadelphia, 1853), 22.

any military value: thirty or forty men made an insignificant unit, however awesome their regalia. Their magnificence, Frederick P. Todd points out, was sometimes more apparent than real. Their muskets were often merely on loan from state arsenals, and their horses hired or borrowed. Even active companies tended to confine their loyalty to the company itself. Some of the volunteers in Boston, declared a report of 1857, "when they parade as companies, do so with great numbers, and make a splendid appearance, but when they parade with the regiment they do not take the same interest." Militia formations were fragmented, even in the few states like Massachusetts which had taken pains to create a genuine militia organization.[15]

But there is a good deal to be said on the other side. In the first place, the volunteers functioned as a police.* Slave-patrolling in some parts of the South and action against city mobs in the North gave them a quasi-military *raison d'être*. More important, the volunteer militia offered an outlet to quite large numbers of men with genuine military appetites. Some may have become prominent in the Civil War through unflagging ambition rather than talent. Writing after the Civil War, to justify and glorify themselves, they may have exaggerated their prewar military preparation. But allowing for this, the record is still not negligible. Here are some cases:

In Philadelphia three generations of the Cadwalader family were active amateur soldiers. John Cadwalader fought in the Revolution. His son Thomas became a major general of Pennsylvania militia. Thomas's son George Cadwalader served as a brigadier general with Scott in the Mexican War. Before then he had formed and trained two volunteer companies, one of infantry and one of artillery. His artillery company became famous and he was reputed to be "the best amateur officer in the United States."[16]

One of the Springfield, Illinois, companies of the 1830's, the

---

* In riots like those of Philadelphia in 1844 the volunteers were essential to the restoration of order. They acted as police on many minor occasions. In 1839, for instance, the Washington Branch Railroad gave some Baltimore volunteers a complimentary ride "for the prompt and efficient aid they had rendered the Company in quelling the disturbances which had arisen between the laborers on the lines" (*Military Magazine* [Philadelphia], I [August 1839], facing plate 15).

Sharp Shooters, was raised by a young man named E. D. Baker who had served as a private in the Black Hawk War. In the Mexican War he commanded a volunteer regiment as a colonel. A Whig and later Republican politician and an old friend of Abraham Lincoln, he moved out to Oregon. He was a senator when the Civil War began, secured a volunteer colonel's commission, and was killed in 1861 at Ball's Bluff — an incident which deeply shocked Lincoln and stimulated Congress to establish the Joint Committee on the Conduct of the War. Their conviction was that he had been no military novice.[17]

John A. Quitman of Mississippi, who like Cadwalader attained high rank in the Mexican War, was born in Rhinebeck, New York, in 1798. As a young man he went to Ohio to practice law, and became a lieutenant in a rifle company. Before long he moved to Mississippi where he was appointed a brigade inspector of militia; "you see," he wrote, "my winter evenings" in Ohio, "studying tactics and the art of war, are already available." He formed and commanded the Natchez Fencibles. He prepared a new militia system for the state and took pride in his appointment as a militia brigadier. He entered the House of Representatives in 1855; appointed chairman of the committee on military affairs, he was an energetic supporter of the regular army, and introduced a bill to increase army pay. One of the most revealing of Quitman's remarks was made in the course of a tour of Europe in 1839. He saw a version of the Battle of Waterloo staged by 12,000 British regulars. Profoundly impressed — he talked about it for months afterward — Quitman wrote: "Oh, let me see a field like this, and let me die." Perhaps the Civil War would have satisfied this longing; he died in 1858.[18]

In the North, a man with a military craving as entire as Quitman's was Philip Kearny. The nephew of the soldier Stephen Watts Kearny, he was born in New York "to great wealth and distinguished social position." Though his family would not let him attend West Point, in 1837 he managed to secure a direct commission in his uncle's regiment, the 1st Dragoons. He had a spell in France, studying cavalry tactics, and in 1840 served in Algeria with the Chasseurs d'Afrique. In 1846 he resigned his commission, but almost at once rejoined, recruited a squadron and fought in the Mexican War. Kearny resigned again in 1851 (he had been badly wounded and had lost an arm in Mexico), and settled on an estate in New Jersey after a trip around the world. In 1859 he was back in France and, attached to the French army, saw its battles at Magenta and Solferino. He returned to the United States at the beginning of the Civil War and served in the Union army with distinction until he was killed in action in September 1862.[19]

Another Northerner of fewer social advantages was John White Geary, who also had a passion for military affairs. At sixteen Geary was a lieutenant in the militia. When the Mexican War started he was elected lieutenant colonel of a Pennsylvania volunteer battalion, while in his middle twenties. He was subsequently mayor of San Francisco and governor of Kansas, in both of which he experienced his share of violence. In the Civil War he fought bravely, was twice wounded, and ended up as a brevet major general.[20]

Alpheus S. Williams of Connecticut, like Kearny, came of a prosperous family. He graduated from Yale in 1831 and made an extended tour of Europe. Settling in Detroit to practice law in 1836, he at once joined the Brady Guards, an elite volunteer company which for several months was called into service to patrol the Canadian border. After ten years he was still in the Brady Guards and had become its captain. In the Mexican War, Williams was appointed lieutenant colonel of a Michigan regiment. Back in Detroit again, he immersed himself in militia activities, ending up as major in the large and thriving Light Guard mentioned earlier in this chapter. When the Civil War began, Williams had spent a quarter of a century in one military organization or another. He ran a school of military instruction for a few months, until in August 1861 he was appointed brigadier general of U. S. Volunteers. He served throughout the war as a competent division commander and temporary corps commander.[21]

At the time that Williams's unit was keeping an eye on the Canadian frontier, some hundreds of swashbuckling Americans were attempting to assist William Lyon Mackenzie's abortive rebellion in Ontario. One such group was led by a melodramatic militiaman and mayor of Akron, Ohio, named Lucius Verus Bierce. He sought to pass on his warlike appetites to his nephew Ambrose Bierce by sending the boy to study at Kentucky Military Institute. Though Ambrose's stories of the Civil War (*Can Such Things Be?* and *Tales of Soldiers and Civilians*) helped to earn him the nickname of "Bitter Bierce," he was himself a brave and devoted officer, as fascinated as he was horrified by armies and warfare.[22]

Lew Wallace, best known today as the author of *Ben Hur*, was born in Indiana in 1827. His father, a West Point graduate, had resigned his commission to follow law and politics and became governor of Indiana. Lew was a restless boy; at nineteen, enthralled by the Mexican War, he raised a volunteer company and fought with it in Mexico as part of the 1st Indiana Infantry. In the 1850's he organized a company at Crawfordsville and trained it so efficiently that "most of its members became officers in the Civil War." Wallace himself served as a major general at Shiloh and on other fields.[23]

The military aspirations of Benjamin F. Butler have been previously referred to. His father had raised a company of light dragoons in the War of 1812. Butler's widowed mother tried hard to get him a West Point nomination in 1836, when he was eighteen. He was "horribly disappointed" to be told that there were no vacancies for their district in Massachusetts. He consoled himself, while working as an attorney in Lowell, by plunging into militia activities. Like Alpheus Williams, though eventually in a more exalted capacity as a militia general, he spent the entire quarter-century before the Civil War in part-time soldiering.[24]

Hiram G. Berry, born in Maine in 1824, also wished to attend the Military Academy. Unlike Butler he secured an appointment, only to be forced by his mother to decline. He too thereupon solaced himself, when he was not otherwise occupied as a successful businessman and mayor of Rockland, as captain of the Rockland City Guards and as a divisional inspector of militia with the rank of lieutenant colonel. He considered himself well prepared for his rise in the Civil War to a major generalcy.[25]

One of the Union's most talked-of commanders in the Civil

War was Daniel Butterfield, the composer of the bugle call "Taps," the designer of striking corps badges for the Army of the Potomac, and Meade's chief of staff at Gettysburg, where he was severely wounded. Butterfield, who remained in the regular army at the end of the war as a colonel, was born in Utica in 1831. An undergraduate at Union College, he was also a private in the Utica Citizens' Corps. When he moved to New York to practice law he joined the somewhat nativist 71st Regiment, rising to become its lieutenant colonel. In 1859 he was elected colonel in full command of the New York 12th Regiment. His account of his doings is not overmodest and is tinged with hindsight. Nevertheless, since he was a confident and resourceful wartime soldier, some weight may be attached to his claim that he had "long been impressed . . . that war was inevitable on the slavery issue. . . . I fitted myself in every way possible, so that I had nothing to learn concerning tactics or discharge of duties in the positions I held."[26]

A few more instances will help to fill out the picture. William Sprague, the youthful governor of Rhode Island who accompanied his state's soldiery at Bull Run, had poured his boyish energies into a fashionable company known as the Rhode Island Marine Artillery. He was one of the Americans who were lured to Europe in 1859 by the chance to witness the fighting between the French and Austrians in Northern Italy. Though he never achieved the major general's commission he sought in the Civil War, and refused a lesser rank, Sprague certainly entered the conflict with dreams of glory nurtured by his richly accoutered years as a militia colonel. If he had not become entangled in Washington politics as a senator and son-in-law of Salmon P. Chase, he would probably have persevered in his desire to be a real general.[27]

A more solidly impressive record was that of Alfred H. Terry of Connecticut, who had a brilliant Civil War career from Bull Run, where he was colonel of the 2nd Connecticut, to his seizure of Fort Fisher in January 1865, as a corps commander. After graduating from Yale he was admitted to the bar in 1849 and became clerk to the New Haven county court. According to John A.

Logan, the champion of volunteer soldiering, while Terry was "driving away at the law, the real bent of his genius" was toward a military life. From 1854 to 1861 he commanded a Connecticut militia regiment. John M. Schofield, a regular soldier and so a more impartial witness, reinforces Logan. Terry, he says, was "a ripe scholar, a thorough lawyer, a very laborious student of the art and science of war, — more so than most West Point graduates."[28]

One final biographical note on an amateur soldier, George Lee Thurston of Lancaster, Massachusetts, who died as a result of war service in December 1862, is representative of the prewar enthusiasms of a sizable number of young Americans:

His father as adjutant of the old Lancaster regiment was noted for efficiency and soldierly bearing. George . . . always assumed command of the boy militia companies that were casually improvised at school, or noisily organized and paraded during vacations. In earliest manhood, wherever his business located him, he . . . became a leading spirit in some independent military organization. . . . At Boston he was a member of the "Tigers"; at Ogdensburg he was lieutenant in an infantry company; at Chicago he was sergeant in the famous Light Guard. Returning to his birthplace shortly before the civil war, he joined the Clinton Light Guard, as lieutenant.[29]

ELMER ELLSWORTH

But another case is worth looking at: that of Elmer E. Ellsworth, "the first martyr of the Civil War," who is so perfect an epitome of the volunteer psychology as to be almost a caricature.[30] Ellsworth was born in New York State in 1837, of poor and unschooled parents. Typically, he wished to enter West Point; but he was unable to prepare to the proper educational standard. He had to be satisfied with amateur soldiering, and in Stillwater, New York, organized a company with the extravagant yet typical enough name of the Black Plumed Riflemen. When his family moved out to Chicago, Ellsworth sought a suitable company, but being still wretchedly poor could not afford to join the ones he admired. Then he met a Frenchman who had served with a Zouave regiment in the Crimea, and who taught him the peculiar Zouave drill. Having made a few friends among the militia he was able to find part-time work as a drillmaster in Illinois and Wisconsin. He was a small man, but wiry and quick, and so much in earnest that he soon knew far more about soldier-ing than his acquaintances. He also fell in love and became engaged to Miss Carrie Spafford.

His prospective father-in-law, a banker, was understandably not impressed by Ellsworth's career thus far. The young man was penniless and obviously could not make a living by teaching drill to sundry volunteer companies. Mr. Spafford made Ellsworth promise to study law. For some while he rubbed along on the margin of starvation, picking up a few dollars as a law copyist, with only one suit to wear and no bed to sleep on. The contrast between his meager, obscure existence and that of Mr. Spafford or of his prosperous young contemporaries was nearly unbear-able. He was sustained by a comprehensive fantasy of martial excellence. The lawbooks on his table would enable him to draft a complete system for a reformed militia. His wretched diet and his bare room, rightly understood, were signs not of civilian failure but of soldierly austerity. The easygoing young clubmen with whom he consorted were to be the instruments of his ambition.

His chance came in 1859 when these companions elected him captain of a moribund company, the National Guard Cadets of Chicago. No doubt Mr. Spafford disapproved, but Ellsworth saw the situation as a challenge. He reorganized the company as the United States Zouave Cadets: a grander name and one embody-ing a novel idea, since this was the first Zouave unit in the whole country. They adopted the picturesque Zouave costume – red cap, sash and loose trousers – and those who were hairy enough grew moustaches and goatee beards. He devised a strict code of conduct – no drinking while in uniform, or gambling or billiards or swearing. Unconsciously they anticipated the penitential na-tional mood of two years later.

Ellsworth taught his men the complicated Zouave drill, a kind

of rapid gymnastics, and thanks to his fanatical zeal they began to attract attention. A Zouave, said a Chicago newspaper, is a fellow "who can climb a greased pole feet first, carrying a barrel of pork in his teeth — that is a Zouave. A fellow who . . . can take a five-shooting revolver in each hand and knock the spots out of the ten of diamonds at 80 paces, turning somersaults all the time and firing every shot in the air — that is a Zouave." Someone else said that whenever Ellsworth's "dazzling company" appeared in Chicago, the street at once filled with spectators: "At double-quick and at the call of the bugle, these sixty or more young athletes would form figures of crosses, double crosses, squares, triangles, like the dissolving figures of the kaleidoscope." The bugle notes replaced shouted words of command, and as they perfected their drill Ellsworth was able even to dispense with the bugle. They adopted too a special Zouave yell, in which may perhaps be recognized the old ritual of the Boston Light Infantry, and the genesis of subsequent cheerleading techniques: "Each man doffed his cap, and jerked it up and down in front of him with a pump-handle movement, shouting in chorus at the same time, 'One! two! three! four! five! six!' and winding up with an Indian-like shout of 'Zouave! tig-e-r-r!' "

Two events now transformed Ellsworth's existence. First, he met Abraham Lincoln in Springfield, became a nominal student in the law firm of Lincoln & Herndon, and watched the friendly lawyer blossom in 1860 into a presidential candidate. Here was luck at last, after a run of family misfortunes. The candidate might well be elected, as Ellsworth was no doubt assured by a new friend, John G. Nicolay of the Springfield Grays, who was to become one of Lincoln's private secretaries. Then at last Ellsworth would have some backing, a bed to sleep in, a more sustaining menu than dry biscuits, and something tangible to present to the hardheaded Mr. Spafford, not to mention father-dominated Miss Carrie. He began to urge on Lincoln the idea of a Bureau of Militia, to be established within the Department of War. He submitted an elaborate draft of a militia bill to the Illinois legislature.

The second event was for the moment more astounding. In the summer of 1860 Colonel Ellsworth — he had by now acquired this militia title — took his company on a drill tour of twenty American cities. The tour did not cost very much; the railroads offered excursion rates and hospitality was provided by volunteer companies along the way.

The tour was a sensation. The Zouaves traveled from Adrian, Michigan, to Detroit, to Cleveland, to Niagara Falls, to Rochester, to Syracuse, to Utica, Troy, Albany. At each point they challenged the local companies to compete in drill. Their own display, which lasted from three to four hours, was so scintillating that the newspapers, and tens of thousands of spectators as well as more official judges, agreed that the Chicago Zouaves were unrivaled. At Albany the elegant Burgesses Corps was most impressed. Huge, excited crowds applauded them in New York City. Lincoln's other private secretary, John Hay, said that Ellsworth's portrait "sold like wildfire in every city of the land. Schoolgirls dreamed over the graceful wave of his curls, and shop-boys tried to reproduce the *Grand Seigneur* air of his attitude. Zouave corps, brilliant in crimson and gold, sprang up, phosphorescently, in his wake, making bright the track of his journey." A Zouave company, for example, immediately appeared in Albany, and others in places North and South that Ellsworth never visited. The Irish-born poet Fitz-James O'Brien (who died of a Civil War wound in 1862) wrote a poem on the Zouaves in seven stanzas, apparently after watching the Chicago company perform in New York. The poem pictures French Zouaves in an encounter with a "sallow Arab troop" whom they vanquish. The first stanza reads:

> To bugle-note and beat of drum
> They come — the gallant Zouaves come!
> With gleams of blue and glints of red;
> With airy, light elastic tread;
> With dashing, wild, insouciant air;
> With figures sinewy, lithe, and spare;
> With gait replete with fiery grace;
> With cloudless eye and boyish face,
> And agile play of feet and hands,
> Swift as a Bedouin of the sands,
> They come — the gay Zouaves!

The final stanza declares:

> Your Zouave corps, O haughty France!
> We looked on as a wild romance,
> And many a voice was heard to scoff
> At Algiers and at Malakoff;
> Nor did we Yankees credit quite
> Their evolutions in the fight.
> But now we're very sure what they
> Have done can here be done to-day,
> When thus before our sight deploys
> The gallant corps from Illinois, —
> American Zouaves![31]

Ellsworth's team moved on to acclaim in Boston and Salem (where the Light Infantry was quickly transmuted into the Salem Zouaves). Their severest test came at West Point, where they showed their familiarity with the official army style as well as with Zouave methods. In Philadelphia and Baltimore they continued to dazzle large audiences with drilling, marching, firing and dexterous bayonet play. In Washington, President Buchanan declared that he had never seen such precision. They were "public benefactors"; if other Americans were equally prepared to defend their country, "we may defy a world in arms." The same scenes were enacted in Pittsburgh and in Cincinnati, where an orator assured them, "Our hearts have thrilled with pride . . . as we saw the chivalric Zouaves of Chicago fling down the glove before the corps d'élite of the imperial cities of the Atlantic seaboard and beheld them emerge . . . with no blot or blemish on their bright escutcheon." By way of St. Louis and Springfield they returned to Chicago and a heroes' welcome: fireworks, speeches, a torchlight procession.

Ellsworth had come a long distance from Mechanicville, N.Y. He had given a prodigious stimulus to the volunteer movement. Discarding the "stiff buckram strut of martial tradition," said Hay (perhaps borrowing from O'Brien), "he educated them to move with the loafing *insouciance* of the Indian, or the graceful ease of the panther." Though the style was French, Americans could persuade themselves that it had been theirs all along, especially when introduced to them from what a volunteer speaker from the imperial city of Philadelphia described as "the far West."

Ellsworth's patron was duly elected in November 1860 and he accompanied the President-elect to Washington as bodyguard. Some of his high and probably ordinate hopes were dashed. Denied the chief clerkship of the War Department, and the headship of his dreamed-of militia bureau, he settled for a regular second lieutenant's commission. Then came Fort Sumter, and Ellsworth's third great chance. Resigning his commission for grander vistas, he raised a Zouave regiment among the firemen of New York, bringing 1,100 of them in their brand-new baggy outfits to Washington.

He was soon ordered to advance across the Potomac into Virginia and occupy the town of Alexandria. He and his men enjoyed the assignment, which they carried out without trouble in the early morning of 23 May 1861. It was, so to speak, the early morning of the Civil War itself — a time before Bull Run, before the slaughter and the weariness had set in, a time for bravura.

Young Ellsworth, in his moment of easy triumph, saw a Confederate flag defiantly flying from the roof of a hotel known as the Marshall House. Accompanied by a few men and a delighted newspaper correspondent from the *New York Tribune,* he ran into the building and cut down the flag. As they were descending the stairs with their trophy, exuberance turned to horror. The proprietor of the hotel suddenly confronted them and fired a shotgun point-blank at Ellsworth, who dropped dead with a "heavy . . . headlong weight." His men avenged themselves on the proprietor. Too late: the adored little colonel was dead.[32]

His body was brought to the White House for the funeral service. John Hay sent an eloquent tribute to the *Atlantic Monthly.* It was agreed that the Union's "first martyr" might have developed into a great soldier. For a little while, until more resounding disasters demanded attention, he was remembered and discussed. The public sighed for his bereaved parents and for his presumably heartbroken fiancée, Carrie Spafford of Illinois.

VOLUNTEERS ON THE EVE OF WAR

The abrupt end of Ellsworth leaves us with an enigma, the enigma of all volunteer soldiering in prewar America. What did it amount to? Was the busy talk of militia reform mere self-important posturing, or cynical political maneuver? Were the thousands of volunteer companies engaged in anything more than Shriners' antics, American Legion horseplay? Did Ellsworth and ardent young Americans of his stamp, thirsting for adventure and recognition, have any real conception of what they meant to do and be? Was there any military value in the Zouave gymnastics?

Was the enthusiasm they engendered more than a temporary fad? Various Zouave units in the Union and Confederate armies persisted well into the war; none achieved special renown. The New York Fire Zouaves had already caused trouble in Washington through their raucous indiscipline. Was Ellsworth himself a hopeless juvenile?

Perhaps no person or corps in the volunteer movement deserves to be taken at his or its own valuation. There is a thread of make-believe running through the whole affair. The huge warriors, bold as brass, seem only half-size when they are in their drab usual clothes. The people gazing on them from the sidewalk are never quite sure whether to cheer or to guffaw. The sashed and epauletted dancers, calculated to melt the heart of any girl, have lapsed next morning into extreme ordinariness. The talk of knights and escutcheons might appear preposterous in the era of the railroad, the telegraph and the cheap newspaper — as preposterous as it was to appear a generation afterward to Mark Twain's Connecticut Yankee. Yet Twain and his Yankee were not wholehearted in their ridicule; and they ought to have perceived that warfare, mediaeval or modern, professional or amateur, is in its nature somewhat ephemeral, factitious, absurd. The American volunteers, as later chapters may reveal, had a good deal in common with their regular contemporaries. The members of the Cleveland Greys or the Sing Sing Guard who subscribed to Huddy and Duval's *Military Magazine* for the narcissistic pleasure of seeing themselves rendered in its sumptuous plates were no more self-consciously vain than was Winfield Scott. Their uniform was not more gorgeous than his — though of course he would have resented any claim to parity in button and braid.*

Nor should the overblown, semi-farcical aspects of the volunteer movement, or its seeming inadequacy as a preparation for the ordeals of the Civil War, blind us to its potential merit. In a few

* A facetious contributor to the *Army & Navy Chronicle* (IX [7 November 1839], 299–300) said that in all his travels he had never seen a more gorgeous sight than "the Pacificator of the East, of the West, of the North, and of the South," Winfield Scott, "dressed in the full costume d'armée of a major general," with his cockade, cocked hat, tassels, yellow swan feathers, blue-and-brimstone coat, epaulettes, sky-blue sash, sword-knot, belt plate, spurs, etc., etc.

states, notably New York, Massachusetts and Connecticut, the disintegration of the old militia was accompanied by a genuine reform, through the regrouping and encouragement of volunteer companies. The adjutant general of New York, speaking in 1860, reminded his audience of the lamentable previous situation: "You remember the 'general training' with its booths, its drunkenness, and its harlequinry; the pompous captain, with his tall plume and incongruous uniform, strutting . . . before a tatterdemalion throng; the importunate marshal, with his list of fines imposed by ignorance." But then the state militia was reorganized: "In lieu of countless divisions, brigades and regiments of men on paper, or in tatters, we have now but eight divisions, [comprising] sixty-four regiments of bona-fide men, uniformed, armed and equipped, and passably well drilled." True, there were still many deficiencies. The state had no weapons available for twenty-five recently created companies. The commutation tax was difficult to collect, and produced too small a sum to meet military expenditure. Even so, sixty-four regiments — each with several hundred men — were no mean force.

The military associations and conventions which began to meet in the 1830's have a patchy and abortive history. Early meetings were mainly concerned to destroy the old militia, or to pass resolutions attacking West Point. The associations of the 1850's, in New York, New Jersey and some other states, were not able to accomplish a great deal. But they served as a focus for discussion. Thus the New York Association's 1860 meeting, held at Newburgh, took note of a letter from a Michigan major general of militia, praising the New York volunteers and describing attempts to follow suit. In the writer's division, "We have forty companies, now organized, and in a fair state of discipline . . ., and applications . . . for the organization of the additional companies, which for want of arms must lie over until next summer. Our troops are all armed with the latest rifled muskets." And there was a significant debate on the need to give a fresh identity to the volunteer movement. They did not quite arrive at the term National Guard, though this was familiar from French usage and had indeed been appropriated by one of the New York volunteer regiments. But what they had in mind was almost exactly the National Guard of a subsequent era: "The Volunteer Militia, uniformed, armed and disciplined, should no longer be associated, even in name, with the rudely formed bodies of former years. It should have a specific name. *State Guards* is suggested, with qualifying name of the State — as the New York Guards. The term Militia, would then be properly applicable to the troops of last resort."[33]

The change, as the Association realized, could only be made general by Congress; and it would have led no doubt to an interminable wrangle over state and federal authority. But it was a sensible and necessary proposal. So was Ellsworth's related scheme for a Bureau of Militia in Washington. One sees from the pages of militia periodicals such as the New York *Military Gazette,* which grew out of the Association's activities and ran from 1858 until 1861, that there were in America groups of reasonably well-informed and responsible amateur soldiers groping toward an adequate semi-federalized volunteer force. They ought not to be dismissed as clowns in fancy dress, even if their debates were both tedious and premature.

One further aspect of their efforts should be mentioned. In 1849 Massachusetts introduced annual encampments for its volunteer militia. The idea was not new: many independent companies had gone under canvas for two or three days each year, to enjoy a round of barbecues and target shoots. But the scale of the endeavor was novel, and its success led other states to do the same. The Massachusetts adjutant general said that in 1857, of the one hundred and two companies in existence, sixty-three had come into being since the encampment law was passed. He doubted whether more than ten of the older companies would have survived without the stimulus it offered. In 1857, for example, a battalion of some two hundred volunteers under the command of the enterprising Ben Perley Poore pitched tents at his farm in West Newbury. "On this occasion, the Major had caused an entrenchment to be thrown up . . . with bastions, at

The Grand Review of Camp Massachusetts near Concord, September 9, 1859.

each . . . angle . . . , which made the encampment look much like a fortified camp. . . . Not only was the camp opened to visitors, but the Major's hospitality extended into his mansion house — in fact, there were no doors closed."

Politically minded officers like Poore and Ben Butler saw in the encampments an ideal opportunity to win friends and influence people. But they were justified in claiming, as Butler did, that in the annual encampments of 1857–1860, "in fact I had commanded a larger body of troops, duly uniformed and equipped, than any general of the United States army then living except General Scott." Indeed, the six thousand men of the 1860 camp, Butler said, exceeded Scott's Mexican War force.[34] Certainly they were conspicuous features of the autumn landscape. "Our plains were overrun the other day," Thoreau recorded dourly in his journal in October 1859, "with a flock of adjutant-generals, as if a brood of cockerels had been let loose there, waiting to use their spurs in what sort of glorious cause, I ask."*

New York was not to be outdone. The 7th Regiment, camping in style at Kingston in July 1855, issued a daily newspaper, the *Camp Worth Journal*. A few weeks later they were followed by two thousand men from another division of state militia, for whom some enterprising publisher in Kingston produced the *Camp Ward Journal*.[35]

The tensions of 1859–1860 perhaps did more than anything else to stimulate volunteer activity, North and South. Nelson A. Miles, who rose to the rank of divisional commander within a few years, was working as a lad in a Boston crockery store. Observing "the undisguised preparations which were going forward in the Southern States," he began to devote himself to the study of military history and tactics. He also attended classes given by a French veteran, Colonel Salignac. "So capable and so popular was this French officer of the old school that the size of the corps . . . grew . . . from a small company of the young men of Boston" to a body of over three thousand men, "among whom were many officers of Massachusetts regiments destined to serve with distinction." After Lincoln's election, says Miles, the tempo increased. Volunteer companies were recruited to full strength. Other organizations sprang up to learn drill from Mexican War veterans or French officers who had lately served at Magenta and Solferino. "During all the months between the election and inauguration of Mr. Lincoln, in the winter of 1860 and '61, military armories were crowded."[36]

These martial preparations may seem not to square with the stories of Northern confusion at Bull Run, or with subsequent despairing analyses of muddle and lack of preparation. Our final question must again be whether the volunteer movement made any genuine contribution to the Union effort in the Civil War.

* *Journal of Henry David Thoreau*, ed. Bradford Torrey and Francis H. Allen (14 vols., Boston, 1906), XII, 404. Like other prophets, Thoreau was not invariably right. The rest of the journal entry, which refers to John Brown's raid on Harpers Ferry, shows that he expected the Massachusetts militia to be used in repressing the slaves.

What happened for instance to the sixty-four regiments from New York: could they not have been sent *en masse* to Washington after Fort Sumter?

The answer is not simple. In part, it is that the volunteers were after all not on a war footing. Instant readiness for protracted service was an impossible idea. It had never even worked with the Massachusetts minutemen, despite the fame they acquired at Lexington and Concord. Massachusetts allowed the idea to lapse and no other colony adopted it.[37] The companies and regiments of the late 1850's were in most cases not psychologically or actually prepared for more than a ninety-day stint — the usual call made upon the old militia. Some had more pomp than circumstance.

However, they provided at least some training for the Williamses and Terrys who were the officer material of the Union armies. Even if they did not serve as complete units, or did not serve very effectively, they contributed thousands of eager recruits at the outset of the war. New York's 7th Regiment supplied 662 men to the Union army and navy, the great majority as officers. Sixty were killed or died from wounds and disease. A large number of the remainder suffered wounds.[38]

Some regiments did indeed answer the call *en bloc*, keeping their designations intact except that — as in the case of the New York 69th — they dropped the word "militia" from their title. Those states which had genuine as opposed to paper militia organizations were the promptest and most useful in supplying men. It was no accident that in the critical days after Sumter, the units which hurried through Baltimore on the way to an almost beleaguered Washington came from New York and Massachusetts. Ben Butler did not produce his regiment of deliverers out of a hat but from an existing system.

The system in most states either broke down or was transformed by wartime emergency. In the pandemonium the volunteer militia receded from view, and historians have paid little attention to its obliterated structure. Yet in some states the foundations were fairly substantial. If the Union had called at once for regiments to serve for the duration instead of for three months, and if when it later sought to create a more solid basis for an army, it had been able to cope with the rush, it might have got on to a war footing with less waste, chaos and delay. If the demand had been made upon the volunteer militia, and they had then been accepted instead of being turned away in droves, Emory Upton might not have been able to draw so unflattering a portrait of the enthusiastic amateur.

8

PROFESSIONALS AND AMATEURS: A BALANCED VIEW

No, No, the brave PROFESSION MILITAR
Is not learnt, Sir, by *Fancy* in the *Schoole*,
   Dreaming, contemplating, to *spelling* held;
But *seeing, sweating, fighting* in the FIELD.
     — Sir Richard Fanshawe's translation
       of Camoëns, *The Lusiads*, 1655

I have seen enough on this march to convince me that Volunteers and Volunteer Generals wont do. I have repeatedly seen a Second Lieutenant of the regular army exercise more authority over the Volunteers — *officers and privates* — than a Mustang General.
     — *The Mexican War Diary of George B. McClellan*

Let us not then be reminded of a Curius, a Regulus, a Cincinnatus, and of all those worthy Romans who repeatedly left the plough to assume the command of the legions. In the first place the art of war was then in its infancy. How long would the legions of Rome have stood the attack of a modern army with its artillery?
     — William Theobald Wolfe Tone, *Essay on the Necessity of Improving*
                         Our National Forces, 1819

The regular troops looked with contempt upon the unprofessional movements of the militia; the militia railed at the dilatory and useless formalities of the regulars. Each avowed . . . that matters could be much better conducted without the other.
     — Mrs. John H. Kinzie, *Wau-bun: The Early Day in the Northwest*, 1856

THE CASE FOR PARTRIDGE

Previous chapters have presented apparently contradictory views of the status and quality both of the professional and of the amateur soldier. It ought now to be possible to draw together this material and arrive at a balanced view.

We may begin by looking again at Alden Partridge, and by considering whether he and other opponents of the Academy did not have genuine criticisms to offer. The memoirs of his chief, the weakly amiable Joseph Swift, offer a further clue to the reasons for Partridge's dismissal from West Point. At this stage French military prestige stood extremely high. The performance of American soldiers in the War of 1812, as Madison was well aware, had not been uniformly impressive. A proposal that gained currency during these years was to establish one or perhaps two additional military academies. Alexander Hamilton had envisaged several. In 1808 Colonel Irenée Amelot de Lacroix, an emigré soldier from France, had recommended the establishment of a central military school at Philadelphia "and two more at the extremities of this vast republic": he did not even mention West Point. The idea was mooted in Madison's second annual message, in December 1810, though Congress did not act on the suggestion. Madison had a particular desire to build up the elite Corps of Engineers and a more general belief that military "seminaries" were an inexpensive way of imparting the art of war "without actual war." Swift was in agreement. In January 1814, at the request of the Governor of Ohio, "I gave him a plan to form a military academy in that growing State. My view of the use of such institutions in the several States is that it is the best mode to interest militia officers to train no larger body of militia than a battalion. . . . The duty of a freeman to defend his country could best be initiated at such schools. But by no means to interfere with the Military Academy at West Point."

Partridge too was thinking of some such plan while he was still entrenched at the Academy. In May 1815 he proposed to the acting Secretary of War the founding of two additional military schools. They were to cater to naval officers — Annapolis, we should recall, did not come into existence until the 1840's — and to students not intending to enter the services, who would pay for their education. They were to be of the same size as West Point; one was to be in or near Washington, and the other at Pittsburgh or some similar Western town. Comparable proposals were often put forward in the next thirty years.[1]

The problem, in Madison's words of 1810, was to train military personnel "without the expense of extensive and standing armies." The obvious place for such personnel, as Partridge and his associates continued to argue, was in the militia, since the regular army would not be able to absorb them all. But West Point was itself liable to produce a surplus of trained personnel. Should these not also be used to pass instruction on to the militia? If so, was not the Academy's function a dual one? Some West Pointers appeared to accept the notion. As late as 1860 Dennis Mahan assured some volunteer soldiers that he had always looked on the Academy as part of the militia organization. "Its value to the regular service," he said, "is far less than to our Militia. Such at least is my view of it, and such I believe was the view taken of it by the Father of the Republic." There is nothing surprising in this statement. The idea was certainly compatible with Calhoun's conception of an expansible army, and the Academy was accustomed to thinking of itself as a minor term in the American military equation. There was therefore also a case, as Partridge maintained, for running the Academy flexibly. For example, did every cadet need to remain for four whole years?[2]

By the end of the War of 1812 Madison and his successive Secretaries of War, James Monroe and William H. Crawford, were strongly impressed by military professionalism. Awed like the rest of their generation by the achievements of Napoleon's

258

armies, they looked to France for guidance. The French military schools, St. Cyr and the École Polytechnique, seemed ideal models. Indeed, Americans were prepared to go further. At one point they thought of making West Point purely an engineering school under the control of French officers. In January 1816 Swift had several conversations with Madison and Crawford on improvements to the Academy, "with a view to inviting . . . some officers from the military schools of France. The question was whether to place these officers as professors at the Academy, or to attach them to the corps of engineers in a bill about to be prepared by the military committee of Congress."[3]

As it happened these schemes were never fully implemented. But the French model continued to fascinate the American government[*] — and some American soldiers, including Winfield Scott who was at the time on leave in France. Sylvanus Thayer seemed the appropriate person to introduce the Napoleonic system. Returning from his study of French military engineering schools, the "new Carnot" was installed at West Point. When Partridge was dismissed in 1817, so was the alternative, possibly vague and yet quite respectable "American" view of the Academy as a training center for regulars *and* militia. What replaced it was an incomplete move toward professionalism on the French plan. The result was somewhat anomalous. West Point was to be both a specialist engineering school, under the aegis of the Corps of Engineers, and a general military academy. It was reasonable to argue that the Academy could not be both, and that whenever a choice had to be made the preference would be given to professionalism.

Partridge may in truth have been a poor administrator. In later life his hostility to the Academy may have grown rabid, especially when he failed to secure regular commissions for graduates

[*] In 1816 Congress authorized the appointment of Simon Bernard, one of Napoleon's engineer officers, to a brigadier generalcy in the American army. He thus outranked Colonel Swift. Bernard remained in his privileged post for fifteen years. Within two years of his arrival Swift and another senior engineer, Lieutenant Colonel William McRee, resigned in protest. Partridge was not the only victim of military Francophilia. See *D.A.B.*, II, 223, and George W. Cullum, *Campaigns of the War of 1812 . . . with Brief Biographies of the American Engineers* (New York, 1879), 177–186.

of his own foundation, Norwich University. He memorialized Congress to this effect in 1841, arguing that although Norwich-trained cadets were, "to say the least, as well qualified for commissions . . . as those of any institution in the country, and have also obtained the necessary qualification at their own expense, they are virtually excluded therefrom by the *arbitrary* and *monopolizing* regulations" of West Point.[4] But his views were consistent over a considerable period. Nor was he opposed to all French influence: under his regime the Academy had appointed a French professor of engineering, Claudius Crozet. Nevertheless Partridge had some grounds for believing not only that he personally had been victimized, but that the Academy was being turned in the wrong direction out of an excessive enthusiasm for French method. In the long run Thayer and his supporters may have been correct: but there was nothing inevitable in the process.

THE CASE AGAINST THAYER

Moreover, though Thayer has become a revered figure in the Academy's annals, it is possible to query whether his rule was in fact impeccable. Academy chroniclers concede that Thayer's initial relations with the staff were not much happier than Partridge's and that many cadets were angered by his severity. The usual explanation is that Thayer inherited a lax administration and had to stiffen it. So he had to court-martial the five cadets who in 1818, representing nearly two hundred of their fellows, demanded a say in the management of the Academy. He had to insist on a clarification of cadet status, and had to ask for their expulsion from West Point.

The affair is complicated. Thayer may have felt that he could not negotiate with a junto of legalistic cadets: they might destroy his authority. But their grievances, set out with impressive clarity, show that they resented the harshness and arbitrariness of the new regime. Thayer himself argued that the radical cause of the trouble was the "erroneous and unmilitary" idea cadets had "imbibed at an inauspicious period of the Institution": namely, under Partridge. They denied this: only Ragland of the five "ringleaders" had been present at West Point at the moment when Partridge and Thayer were disputing the title to the superintendency. In a memorial to Congress the dismissed cadets requested an investigation of the Academy, "which, if allowed to be governed according to the monarchical ideas of its present ruler, will, in a short time, be so advanced in depravity as to require nothing less than its complete extinction."[5]

One may sympathize with Thayer. The cadets were an unruly lot. In the great Christmas riot of 1826, thwarted in a scheme to prepare a quantity of eggnog, a band of cadets hurled stovewood at the staff and one of them tried to shoot an officer. Nineteen of the rioters were court-martialed and dismissed, including the roommate of Jefferson Davis. Davis himself was put under arrest and was lucky to escape expulsion. But he and other cadets such as Leonidas Polk felt that such troubles would never have arisen if Thayer had had the sense to relax his rigid supervision now and then. Polk (U.S.M.A. 1827) complained that Thayer encouraged post employees to inform on cadets, and was capricious in distributing punishments. Another graduate, Francis H. Smith (U.S.M.A. 1833), also thought that even when Thayer was firmly entrenched, his discipline was too harsh. Smith is an important witness, for as superintendent of the Virginia Military Institute he too maintained a high standard of discipline. Even so, looking back in the course of a reunion address when we might expect him to have expressed rosier sentiments, Smith said of Thayer's reign: "It was useless to attempt to awaken tender emotions in him. He was not without feeling, but he never displayed it in his *office*. That office . . . comes up to me to-day as a judgment hall, which no cadet entered without a sentiment of awe, or left without a feeling of relief."

Thayer's last years were thorny. We are told that his authority was flouted by Andrew Jackson, who went over his head in reinstating cadets whom the Superintendent had been forced to dismiss. One pardoned cadet, says G. W. Cullum, "erected a hickory pole in front of the barracks as the signal of his triumph over authority." A notorious offender, Thomas W. Gibson (the roommate of Cadet Edgar Allan Poe), is said to have been convicted by several court-martials, twice for drunkenness and twice for setting fire to buildings, and yet to have been returned to duty by Jackson's Secretary of War. Finally, according to the Academy version, Thayer resigned in disgust in 1833.°

Perhaps Thayer was right in his view that armies depend on obedience. The Jacksonian climate of opinion cannot have made his task easy. While he was refining his scheme of ranking cadets annually in order of merit, similar systems were being abolished as undemocratic at Dartmouth and Bowdoin. An anecdote offered by Francis H. Smith would seem to reflect the hopelessness of Thayer's struggle. Perhaps it was the occasion of his resignation. In 1833 one of Smith's classmates, Willoughby Anderson, was dismissed for drunkenness after a visit to the forbidden Benny Haven's tavern. Several well-connected cadets, among them Smith and the son of Secretary of State McLane, wrote letters on Anderson's behalf. With their aid he was able to arrange an interview with President Jackson and was reinstated.

However, the point of the anecdote for Smith was that Anderson should never have been dismissed in the first place. The real trouble was not that Jackson was too lenient but that Thayer was too strict. He was a martinet, insisting on an impossibly austere level of conduct.[6]

If this is so, the criticisms of the Academy made by dismissed cadets, as well as by Alden Partridge, may rest on more than childish pique. Why *not* try to bring regulars and militia into

° It may be significant that Jackson's nephew A. J. Donelson was a cadet in 1818–19, at the time of the arrest and trial of Ragland and the other four cadet spokesmen. Donelson joined other cadets in signing various documents to indicate his support of the spokesmen, and his belief that the Academy was being mismanaged. He appears to have conveyed his impressions to his uncle. At the 1819 court-martial Ragland, a Virginian, quoted what seems to have been a letter from Jackson, saying that if the charges against Thayer were substantiated, "there can be no doubt but that [he] will be reprimanded, if not dismissed." Thomas Ragland, *Defence before a General Court-Martial, Held at West Point* (pamphlet, Newburgh, N.Y., 1819), 13–14.

closer rapport? It was not enough to answer, as some defenders of the Academy did, that men trained at West Point quite often became prominent in militia or volunteer organizations; this was a haphazard, not a planned affair. Why *not* accept, at least in some degree, Partridge's belief that the Academy was intended to train militia officers? Why *not* establish additional academies? Though they were obviously not needed to supply the modest needs of the regular army, two more such federal institutions, one perhaps situated in the West and one in the South, might well have been of value in providing a more widespread semi-military, semi-scientific education. Their existence might have broadened the basis of entry into the commissioned ranks of the regular army, and moderated the feeling that West Point was a monopoly akin to the Second Bank of the United States. Or why not, following an idea canvassed in the 1830's, appeal to state pride by raising a regular regiment from each state?*

One can see objections to all these possibilities. State and sectional pride was likely to reject the idea of being associated with a federal organization; we recall the opposition to Poinsett's plan of 1840 for a graded national militia to be trained in the same drills as the regular army. After V.M.I. set the pattern for state-sponsored military schools there was less and less support for schools at the federal level. Appointing a regular regiment from each state would have meant enlarging the army to a perhaps unacceptable degree. It might have entailed a partial surrender of federal control to that of the states. As with other recommendations, reform might have led to squabbling over political patronage. Still, a number of thoughtful suggestions were put forward, only to be rejected or ignored. They remained below the surface of American life as buried alternatives, and so as buried resentments. Justly or not, since no major changes were attempted or even seriously discussed, critics of the regular army became convinced that they were dealing with a selfish coterie.

* One of the verses of "Benny Havens, O!" as printed in the *Army & Navy Chronicle*, VII (4 October 1838), 215–16, includes the lines:

> Award each State a regiment of regulars that know
> Their officers were chosen chums of Benny Havens, O!

VOICES FROM THE RANKS

An associated complaint, already mentioned in Chapter 4, was that enlisted men in the regulars had almost no chance of a commission. The evidence presented earlier may have implied that practically none were suitable: that educated rankers were misfits and alcoholics, and less educated men were too uncouth to hold command. The majority of the foreign-born recruits who made up a higher and higher proportion were disqualified in other ways. Some commentators see the distinction between officers and men as something more basic than snobbery. Samuel P. Huntington argues that as armies were professionalized in the nineteenth century, the gulf became one of function. The officer was acquiring a *profession,* the enlisted man merely a *trade*. The distinction was thus between the "management" and the "application" of violence. Or were the Americans, consciously or otherwise, following the British instead of the French? In *The Ruling Class,* Gaetano Mosca points out that Britain and the United States were almost alone in the Western world in raising their armies by voluntary recruitment rather than by conscription. The volunteers they enrolled were mostly from the unemployed poor. Class distinctions between officers and privates were therefore more conspicuous than in the widely representative armies of continental Europe. The result, Mosca believes, is that by virtue of family connections and education these army officers retained "close ties with the minority which by birth, culture and wealth stands at the peak of the social pyramid."[7]

PROFESSIONALS AND AMATEURS: A BALANCED VIEW

There is some truth in these observations. But for the American army at any rate, a small but vocal minority of enlisted men, backed by some civilian opinion, refused to accept so static a conception of society in the United States. They could not see why their nation should not follow French practice in automatically opening say one-third of the army commissions to enlisted men. Who were the officers of the army, an NCO asked in 1834: "Are they not those whose fathers, through fortunate circumstances, happened to get them to West Point? And . . . are there not . . . very many, equally deserving, in the Army, who cannot rise by dint of every perseverance . . . to that eminence?" Educated young men entered the ranks either because of "the frowns of fortune" or through a real wish to become soldiers, only to find themselves stuck in the non-commissioned grades. In every European army (except the British, he might have noted), "the *private* MAY rise to eminence. But to the *United States* soldier, it is denied to him, let his conduct be what it will." A letter in another service periodical five years later pleaded the same case, citing General Gaines as a keen advocate of the principle: "No pay that the Government will give its soldiery, will induce good American citizens . . . to join the army in time of peace. A number of officers, and some of high rank, are of the opinion that the good of our army would be vastly promoted if the . . . meritorious soldier should have . . . the chance of arriving to the distinction of a commission."

Occasionally the chance came. In 1838, after eighteen years' service, a sergeant major in the 1st Infantry was promoted to second lieutenant. But his promotion, hardly precipitate, was rare enough to be a news item.[8] According to one disgruntled soldier of the period, "There is just as almighty a difference preserved between a *Sergeant-Major,* who is the highest non-commissioned officer in the service, and a *Brevet Second Lieutenant,* who is the lowest commissioned officer, . . . as though it were sacrilege in the former to presume to approach the latter in a familiar way."

This complaint comes from a volume of anonymous and fictional *Recollections of the United States Army* (1845), which may have been meant to perform the same service for the common soldier, in exposing his miseries, that had been accomplished for

265

the ordinary seaman by Richard H. Dana's *Two Years Before the Mast* (1840). The nature of his grievance becomes clearer when we compare the book with a second exposé of service life, *Dragoon Campaigns to the Rocky Mountains* (1836), supposedly written by one James Hildreth. Both books contend that respectable Americans have been induced to enlist, especially in the new mounted regiments, with the understanding that they will then qualify for commissions. Many men, says Hildreth, "were enlisted only on the express declaration that they were to rank with the cadets at the military academy, and under the belief that they were rather to be considered as a volunteer corps. . . . Many were told . . . that they would have nothing to do but to ride on horseback . . . , to explore the western prairies and forests . . . ; and . . . often was the remark made, that it would disgrace a dragoon even to speak with an infantry soldier." There is other evidence to bear out their claim that something of the kind was done, probably by recruiting officers in the hope of filling their ranks with native Americans of good stock.* The treatment accorded such men seems to have been shabby. No wonder that they accused West Point of having become "an engine of *favouritism,* mainly filled with the pets of scheming and other influential men," which *"exclusively* furnishes all the commissioned officers . . . , or, in many cases, the *things* which are intended to represent officers."[9]

A few West Point graduates agreed with the dissatisfied enlisted men. Isaac I. Stevens (U.S.M.A. 1839), a lieutenant of engineers at the time, said in a private letter of 1848 that the Academy could be much improved. Discipline was too strict; it should concentrate on producing officers for "the Staff and Scientific Corps — including in the latter both engineers and Artillery"; and officers should be commissioned direct from the ranks, a democratic step which would be "in harmony with our institutions." Every enlisted man "should feel that by training and close

* For a later instance of discontent, see the laconic reference in A. G. Brackett, *History of the U.S. Cavalry* (New York, 1865), 123, to the situation in 1848 at the end of the Mexican War, when "it was deemed advisable to discharge the enlisted men of the regiment of Mounted Riflemen, who had found some pretext, through the medium of certain legal advisers, to annul their obligations with government. As a consequence of this, it required some time to again fill up that regiment."

attention to duty he can become an officer." Oliver Otis Howard, an instructor at West Point in the late 1850's, was troubled by "a class distinction which seemed too intense for our republican ideas, and . . . made the army disliked by the people at large." He gave a talk to his brother officers advocating a milder and more generous spirit, and had it published as an article in a New York magazine. The memoirs of some enlisted men indeed show that certain officers treated them courteously.

But reformers like Stevens and Howard were in the minority. Stevens wrote that he was pleased by the long-overdue legislation in the 1846–1847 session of Congress which authorized the President to promote NCO's to brevet second lieutenancies for gallantry in action. President Polk, however, noted in his diary in May 1847 that while he was anxious to make such appointments, he was being resisted by the adjutant general and other regular officers who were urging the superior claims of former Academy graduates. And Howard states that his article "caused quite a commotion at West Point. . . . Even the superintendent was annoyed because he thought that I reflected upon his management of affairs. Some agreed with my sentiments, but the majority said that they were contrary to a proper military spirit."[10]

THE LONG-SUFFERING REGULARS

A *proper military spirit*: did the West Point interpretation of this involve snobbery and favoritism, and help to make the army "disliked by the people at large"? It is not easy to avoid taking sides in the ancient quarrel between the professionals and the amateurs. But the effort is worth making, even at the risk of repetition.

On the army's side, we may sympathize with their irritation at the coarse Jacksonian rhetoric. In this rhetoric, "workingman" was a vague yet powerful term, so powerful that it seemed to oblige those against whom it was used to insist that they were of the same company. Their defensive exasperation is well brought out in the protest of a regular officer made in 1836: "let us . . . finish this miserable cant of aristocracy, as thrown out against the army. . . . The writer of this notice also claims to be one of the people. Like every graduate of the Military Academy, he claims to belong to that important and only respectable and useful class, the workingmen of the land."[11]

Again, we may sympathize with the regulars' conviction that the militia and volunteers performed badly in most of the campaigns they took part in. There is a scathing account of one such campaign — the Black Hawk War in Illinois, in 1831 — by Philip St. George Cooke (U.S.M.A. 1827). The volunteers were, he maintains, noisy, slow and panicky. They lost their rations; their supply columns were "incredibly timid and unmanageable," they ran away from a small band of Indians and then reported "a bloody battle with 1,500 warriors"; and on top of all this, Cooke had the chagrin of reading in a newspaper which had been brought into camp "a speech made by a Western senator, who branded the regular army as the 'sweepings of cities,' etc. etc., and extolled the frontier men — militia — rangers (our friends, the volunteers), as infinitely superior; men who would be 'here tonight, and to-morrow fifty miles off;' who would 'subsist themselves,' etc. Verily, your politician excels in humbug!"[12]

The army's annoyance was more sharply stated a few years later in the campaigning against the Florida Seminoles. One much-discussed incident concerned the behavior of Missouri volunteers in a mixed force under Zachary Taylor. According to one regular account, Colonel Gentry was mortally wounded in trying to rally his fleeing Missourians: "He told Col. Taylor that his men had deserted him, and he had been sacrificed." This is repeated in a letter from an army surgeon:

Thus have been fought three battles since the war commenced. . . . In *all* the regulars have done the fighting — in *all* the irregulars have been false — leaving the honor and the loss chiefly to the army. . . . You will see in the New Orleans papers some denials of the conduct of the volunteers under Col. Taylor. I have heard it repeatedly from respectable authority that the dying commander of the volunteers said to Col. T. "my men have not sustained me but spare them." I have never heard this denied. . . .

The letter goes on:

However delicate this subject may be in the ears of the politicians, it ought to be known that henceforth we may trust more to what will sustain us in the field, and less to rapacious men who come for plunder, for negroes, and run as soon as an Indian fires a rifle at them.

In the Mexican War John Sedgwick (U.S.M.A. 1837), a lieutenant in the 2nd Artillery, had a similar story to tell of the fighting at Monterey. He says that though the Texans fought well, as a rule "one regiment of regulars is worth three of volunteers":

Mr. Polk, in parting with Colonel Watson and his Baltimore regiment is reported to have said, "Remember that you are not the hirelings of Government, but brave defenders, ready to step into the trench," etc. And now the papers say the brave Watson was killed fifty yards in advance of his men, which was true; but they might have added that his men broke and ran and left him, and with few exceptions, did not get again into the battle. It is to be hoped that such defenders will be kept to protect Washington, and that they may be as successful as they were in the last war.

Eighteen months later Sedgwick still had to admit:

No very good feeling exists here between the old army and . . . the volunteers. The old army (officers) feel they have had the brunt of the fighting. . . . But when letter after letter comes from the States

269

claiming all the credit of every action, and often when there was not a volunteer there, it has . . . led to some sharp words.[13]

It is clear from these accounts that the regulars detested volunteer troops not only for their inefficiency but for their brutality, especially where Indians were concerned. Many regulars shared Philip St. George Cooke's feeling that the Indians had been cheated of their birthright. He found the Illinois country of the Black Hawk War very beautiful. He could well understand why this landscape, "bound to the very heartstrings of the Indians, . . . should possess for him fatal attractions." Fatal, that is, "when the dollar and cent interests of the unsympathizing whites demand the letter of the hard-driven, if not fraudulent bargain." In various situations the regulars had the distasteful task of dispossessing Indian tribes, and of trying to protect them against white settlers. Brigadier General John E. Wool, charged with the preservation of the peace in the Cherokee country in 1836–1837, was accused by the governor and legislature of Alabama of having usurped the powers of civil tribunals, disturbed the peace of the community and "trampled upon the rights of the citizens." He was cleared by a court of inquiry whose proceedings showed that poor Wool had been given a thankless and delicate assignment, and had become convinced that the Indians were in need of protection while they were in process of ceding their lands. "With these people." he told the Secretary of War, "it really seems to be no crime to kill an Indian. They do not look to the probable consequences. This circumstance, together with the daily efforts of the whites to dispossess the Indians of their houses and lands, has created a state of feverish excitement, which it will be exceedingly difficult to repress when the hour of their departure arrives."[14]

Wool was at loggerheads with the civilian authorities nearly twenty years later, in Oregon and Washington; and again one feels that he was in the right. According to a partisan account, Wool "made our people more the objects of his *resentment*, than the Heathen murderers, to whom he seemed to yield all his sympathies. The Volunteers who *improvized* a substitute for his

270

neglected duty — provoked his bitter hate." Joseph Lane of Oregon, speaking in the House of Representatives, condemned Wool as "a tactician after the fashion of the military fogies of Europe," despite the "utter inadaptation" of these tactics to Indian warfare. Wool was admittedly a cantankerous and rather unspectacular soldier, perhaps too old to be active (he was seventy-two at the time). In his own account, which however carries conviction, there was no need for activity. The people of the Northwest were determined to exterminate the Indians remaining in the area and to make the U. S. Treasury pay for the sport. At federal expense they had raised two regiments of mounted volunteers in Oregon and one in Washington. They had provoked a fight with the Walla Walla Indians, murdered the chief when he appeared under flag of truce, and sent bits of his scalp, his ears and his hands "as trophies to their friends." When four hundred harmless Indians were moved from one reservation to another, escorted by two companies of regulars, the captain in charge said "it took a large part of his command to prevent the citizens from murdering those four hundred." When the party finally set out, they were trailed by a white settler "who shot one of the Indians, declaring . . . he intended to follow them and kill all he could. Many and similar cases have been reported." For his opposition to the "inhuman and barbarous practice," and to the "wholesale plundering of the treasury of the United States," Wool said, "I have been denounced by the Governors of both Territories and the Legislature of Oregon. The latter has demanded . . . my removal from the command of the Pacific Department."[15]

In this perspective it becomes easier to understand why regular officers, from Winfield Scott downward, behaved so irascibly in the face of what they regarded as vicious civilian interference. Thanks to the civilians, they believed, even the forts they occupied were badly chosen. Ethan Allen Hitchcock protested to the Secretary of War in 1842 that Fort Wayne, "Cherokee Nation," ought to be abandoned. The presence of a garrison brought whiskey shops, which were not allowed in the Cherokee area, and the consumption of alcohol brought trouble. John Pope (U.S.M.A. 1842) of the Topographical Engineers made a vigor-

271

ous report on the same theme to Secretary of War John B. Floyd in 1859. Many army posts in the Southwest were, he argued, useless. Settlers demanded them as a source of profit, and pleaded their necessity by brazenly or hysterically exaggerating the danger of Indian atrocities. Most of these so-called "atrocities" were merely a desperate response to murders and insults from the whites. The soldiers were disgusted to be embroiled in such affairs.[16]

Scott and his subordinates felt victimized in a situation in which nothing was clearly defined. It was roughly understood that the President was commander in chief, the Secretary of War his expert civilian representative, and the general in chief his military head. But the relations between Secretary of War and general in chief were hazy; the role of such other figures as the adjutant general was open to debate; staff work was amateurish, communication so slow and uncertain that endless muddle and friction could be caused — for example, when Scott or some other figure got word of a change affecting him through private correspondence or the newspapers, perhaps in garbled form, before his official orders arrived. Army headquarters was more or less where the general in chief wanted it to be; and for much of his career Scott chose to be in New York instead of Washington. When an energetic, punctilious and touchy Secretary of War like Jefferson Davis arrived in office a collision was inevitable.

By the standards of a later day, Scott, Gaines and the rest were deplorably insubordinate. Serving officers were forbidden to utter criticism of the President, their commander in chief; by extension, they should not have engaged in public controversy with the President's executive head, the Secretary of War. After a special order of 1825 they were debarred from writing for publication on controversial service matters. The rule was ignored by senior officers, and their juniors, sometimes instigated from on high, took the cue. Every time there was military activity there was an accompanying battle in the newspapers, to represent the feuding factions between the army and the volunteers (or within the army). A court of inquiry was held at Frederick, Maryland, in 1837, under the presidency of General Macomb, to look into "the tendency of such . . . publications." Two officers who had been

272

prominent newspaper writers, Captain Hitchcock and Captain George A. McCall, were asked to explain themselves. They offered skillful defenses which indicate the handicaps under which they labored — and perhaps the extent to which they were "civilian" in outlook. Hitchcock's argument was that liberty of speech and freedom of the press impelled every American now and then to publish his views. Whatever army regulations might prescribe, "I cannot but think that a rule of Mr. Jefferson's . . . is . . . applicable . . . — that, error is not dangerous when truth is left to combat it." Captain McCall's line was that in the United States, "where the liberty of the press is enjoyed in the fullest sense of the word, the rapid dissemination of every description of account of military. . . operations, even while the army is in the field, may be expected. Where the militia constitutes the principal numerical force . . . ," amateur soldiers would for all sorts of reasons send news back home. Such reports "are circulated in a thousand ways, and tend to impress improperly the public mind." Their inaccuracy and sensationalism could best be countered by accurate, signed statements contributed by experienced soldiers.[17] Though the court of inquiry accepted these explanations, regulars continued to be somewhat inhibited in writing for publication, at least in comparison with volunteers.

McCall's oblique criticism of the militia is a reminder that Scott suffered severely from civilian soldiers during the Mexican War. Much of his irritability can be forgiven when we recall that Scott, a soldier of nearly forty years' experience, was burdened by Polk with major generals like Gideon Pillow — a Tennessee lawyer and friend of the President — whose military training was nil. Pillow, treated politely by Scott at first, responded by compiling outrageously boastful battle reports, by attacking Scott in private correspondence with Polk and others, and by printing anonymous correspondence to the same effect in newspapers. Still more galling was Polk's readiness to make Senator Benton of Missouri a lieutenant general: a rank that did not then exist, but which would have placed Benton over Scott at the head of the army.* Benton was innocent of military knowledge, except for

* Other aspects of these matters are discussed in Chapter 9.

273

fairly brief service in the War of 1812. Though he was one of West Point's principal critics, he had to confess that he had never seen the place. Benton did not get his command; but the threat hung over Scott, and Congress came quite near to passing the bill to authorize the lieutenant generalcy.[18]

Taking all these factors together, one sees that the regulars had fairly good grounds for condemning, so far as they were publicly able to do so, the national emphasis upon the enthusiastic amateur. To the regular, the amateur soldier was very much as Emory Upton portrayed the situation: incompetent, erratic, boastful, wasteful.

THE INSUFFERABLE REGULARS

What is to be said on the other side? We have seen that even some regular officers, and some enlisted men, believed West Pointers to be disagreeably snobbish, and too fastidious to be real warriors. The image persisted in the popular mind into the Civil War. In the closing stages of that conflict the Union general Henry W. Slocum got into conversation with a Confederate prisoner and asked for his opinion of his former leader, Wade Hampton. The prisoner replied that Hampton was "a sort of dandy gentleman, one of those fellows from West Point." Slocum, himself an Academy graduate, agreed that "some of the West Pointers did not know enough to straddle a horse." The joke was the more enjoyable because in fact Hampton was not a West Pointer and had had no formal military training.

But was the popular conception merely a joking matter, based on ignorance? In an earlier chapter mention was made of the insulting treatment of two West Point instructors, Maury and McClellan, pushed into the pauper pews at a church service by a sexton who mistook them for enlisted men. It is perhaps significant that neither officer saw any serious implications. "To us," Maury says, "it was only a funny incident."[19]

A similar insensitivity is apparent in other anecdotes. Philip St. George Cooke's description of the Black Hawk volunteers, though amusing and probably accurate enough, is tinged with condescension at the blunders of "these raw fellows, who had no more idea of the first principles of military respect and subordination, than they had of Frederick's campaigns." It does not occur to him to wonder why a backwoodsman *should* know anything about the campaigns of Frederick of Prussia. Or if we look again at the complaints of the Western democrat Van Antwerp, we begin to understand his annoyance at the Whiggish tone of the officers he has met. Allowing for political partisanship, there is something recognizable, and age-old in his picture of the lordly West Pointers:

The terms "Mobocracy," "vulgar rabble," "ignorant herd" etc. etc. are as common among these gentlemen as household words; and I venture to assert that three of them can not be got together, at any time and place, and the subject introduced, without there escaping from at least two of them, as applied to the name of Mr. Jefferson, the epithet "d——d demagogue," "mobocrat," or something equally complimentary; while those of "d——d old fool," "scoundrel" etc. etc. will just as certainly be appended to that of General Jackson.

The tone can be detected too in the memoirs of Alfred Mordecai (U.S.M.A. 1823). He recalls that when he was an assistant professor at the Academy in 1824, "a shout, almost of derision" greeted the announcement that Andrew Jackson was a candidate for the presidency. "One of the stories of the day was that, when it was mentioned to the General himself, he exclaimed: 'A Hell of a President *I* should make.' Perhaps many people afterwards thought that his anticipations were realized." In 1829 Mordecai was in Richmond while the Virginia constitutional convention was in session. The convention, he noted, lowered the qualifications for voters and prepared the way for universal suffrage — "unhappily as I think." And an officer writing in 1839 protests that "uneducated and misinformed people," influenced by demagogues, "actually think that the officers of the regular army are their *servants*": "We, for one, cannot subscribe to this loco-foco doctrine. . . . We cannot consent that every *sans culotte* we meet in the street, should look on us as his *servant*. . . . [W]hile we hold a commission in the United States Army, . . . we do not feel a very oppressive sense of gratitude to the *'people'* as . . . spoken of . . . by the demagogue."[20]

There is nothing very sinister in these comments. To dislike Andrew Jackson was not necessarily to be an "aristocrat" — whatever that expression might mean in the American context. The dislike of regulars and volunteers for one another is to be found in other countries and in other periods. In the United States its lineage stretches at least as far back as Braddock's defeat in 1755, with the American regulars inheriting the role of the British redcoats. The charges leveled by both sides are hoary with age. The regular is a tenderfoot, a dude, a snob; the amateur is a comic or vicious ignoramus. One is too clean, the other too dirty. One has an unreal vision of discipline and precision; the other, greedy and unscrupulous, is probably selling rifles and firewater to the Indians. The pattern of mutual contempt and incomprehension has been repeated in a thousand films and television programs. Generally speaking the regulars have come off best in these fictional reenactments. In this respect the balance has been redressed so completely that it is hard for us to see the amateurs' case. Granted that the regular army never exercised a powerfully bad influence, there is still some validity in the view that a professional near-monopoly existed, and that the ways of the regular army left something to be desired.

It was after all an army officer, Braxton Bragg, who in his articles in the *Southern Literary Messenger* pointed out how absurdly high a proportion of his fellows were serving in staff appointments: far more, he claimed, than in European armies. And though the regular navy came less under attack it was even more vulnerable. Thus, Representative Sawyer of Ohio contended in 1846 that of sixty-seven captains on the navy list, no fewer than thirty-six were "waiting orders." In other words they were on shore leave, doing nothing but draw their pay, or as Sawyer put it, "feasting on fat dinners, living at their ease, reading the papers, and discussing politics." His suggestion was that these idlers were somehow — "discussing politics" — a menace to the state. "The hardy, industrious, enterprising pioneers of the Far West and the Southwest," he asserted, "know not how to account for this system of extravagance and folly." A ripely demagogic performance; yet his facts were true. Until the system was reformed by an act of 1855 there was no proper retired list. Promotion went by seniority. The navy's officers formed an inert mass of largely redundant personnel. According to one scholar, the Secretary of the Navy "never sent to sea those officers who had become incapacitated by age, disease, or the accidents of their profession; but gave them nominal shore-duty, or else no duty at all with leave-of-absence pay." One captain had been unemployed for thirty-six of his fifty-four years of service; another had spent only two of his thirty years as a captain at sea. "In 1848 a certain commander had not been to sea for more than 41 years." The navy list was swollen with unnecessary appointments; "many statesmen . . . left memorials of their families . . . by making midshipmen of sundry sons, grandsons, nephews, and cousins." We have discussed a similar tendency in the case of West Point nominations, and have seen that wealthy and well-connected officers like Ethan Allen Hitchcock managed to avoid unpleasant duties. Expenditure on the services was not a negligible item in the national budget. Men of Sawyer's stamp were, then, not talking entire nonsense when they grumbled at the wastefulness and laxity of service organization. Jefferson Davis was not behaving merely as a fussy bureaucrat when he resisted Winfield Scott's claim for eight years of brevet back pay.[21]

In short, though criticisms of the army were often ill-informed and cliché-ridden and illogical, there were things to criticize. There was, for instance, something unresolved and sometimes objectionable in the special place accorded to the Corps of Engineers. Resentments built up inside and outside the army; and two queer but not completely absurd books by John J. Lenney show that these resentments lingered on long after the Civil War. Denied a commission after serving as an enlisted man in the 1890's, Lenney labored for many years to prove in chapter and verse that the army had since the early nineteenth century depended upon a caste system, with the ordinary soldier at the bottom and the Corps of Engineers ensconced at the top — operating from the privileged sanctum of West Point. Two men played "leading and baleful roles" in this un-American development, according to Lenney: John C. Calhoun, as Secretary of War, and Superintendent Sylvanus Thayer.[22]

Richard Taylor, the son of Zachary Taylor, was well disposed toward the army though not a West Pointer. Writing after the Civil War, he could still criticize the results of assigning the ablest graduates to the Engineers and Ordnance. After a few years, he said, "they become scientists, perhaps pedants, but not soldiers." The remedy was to require all officers to serve in each branch of the army, and to compel staff officers to take tours of regimental duty. Until this was done there would be an unhealthy gap between the staff and the line, between theory and practice.

With the outbreak of the Civil War there began a fresh outcrop of complaints against the regular army. Aggrieved and suspicious civilians maintained that there must be something amiss at West Point, and in the spirit of the old army, when so many graduates flocked to the Confederacy. It was widely believed that the best officers had deserted the Union, and that those who remained usually did so from "accidental indifference" or from "want of courage and decision at the proper moment." Jacob D. Cox, an amateur soldier with a distinguished record, said that the regulars were "confessedly soldiers of fortune." Like their brethren in the British army, they subscribed to such prudent mottoes as "Volunteering brings bad luck," or to Talleyrand's famous injunction, *"surtout, point de zèle": above all, no enthusiasm.* An angry civilian who styled himself "Adjutant of the 210th Pennsylvania Volunteers" claimed in 1864 that the war would have gone far better

had the nation been unencumbered by this ruin of a Regular Army, that has given us little else than a tremendous array of officers, many of them of the Pigeon-hole and Paper order, — beggarly lists of Privates — routine that must be carried out at any cost . . . — and Red Tape that everywhere represses patriotism.

How long, he asked, "must these sneaking Catilines in high places abuse our patience?"

But what can be expected from officers who are not in the service from patriotic motives, but rather from prospects of pay and position? End the war, and you will have men who are now unworthy Major and Brigadier Generals, subsiding into Captains and Lieutenants. Their movements indicate that *they* realize their position fully; but when will the country realize that "strategy" is played out?

Alpheus S. Williams, another civilian soldier who like Cox proved his worth in the Civil War, summed up peacetime experience in the old army as "at least fifteen years as a *clerk* in an army bureau or on duty at a frontier post as a lieutenant to a command of a dozen men, where there are no books, no drill, no military duty, nothing but a vast amount of whiskey drinking, card playing, and terrific, profane swearing; and where, as a consequence, men forget in a year or so all they could learn in four years, and acquire habits of the most indolent and unambitious and dissolute kind."

Of course these are prejudiced comments. But they are not utterly unfounded. They are borne out by at least one regular, Oliver Otis Howard, who was stationed in Florida in 1856–1857 when sporadic fighting went on against the Seminoles. His companions led an existence of yawning vacuity, punctuated by practical jokes and heavy drinking. They had little faith in the war itself: "It was a frequent remark by our regular officers: 'We haven't lost any Indians.'" They did their duty, "but without much ardour." The volunteers who fought beside them were by contrast active, murderous, unscrupulous. The two styles clashed.

They continued to clash. The army's sentiments were as a whole conservative. Many officers had served in the South; some, like Walter H. Stevens of New York (U.S.M.A. 1848) had married into Southern families and were to join the Confederacy. The professional demeanor was a little languid.[*] In the secession winter of 1860–1861 Howard was on duty at West Point. As late as 23 February 1861 a Northern regular, urging him to accept the offer of a professorship in North Carolina, could write: "As an officer of the army, I presume, of course, that you entertain no views on the peculiar institution [slavery] which would be objectionable to a Southern community." When one of Howard's companions accepted the colonelcy of an Ohio volunteer regiment, an officer from Kentucky declared indignantly that "a West Point man who goes into the volunteers to fight against the South forgets every sentiment of honor." Howard explains why regulars initially were reluctant to transfer to the volunteers. The idea disturbed their conventional notions of status. Senior officers, determined to keep the regular enclave intact, resisted the process. Even after Bull Run, though the cabinet had decided to release one hundred regular officers for volunteer service, Adjutant General Thomas told an applicant that "if he had his way not a single officer of the Regular Army would go into the Volunteer service." But other forms of conservatism held the regulars back. They would, Howard said, have put the matter thus: "We belong to the whole nation, we do not want it divided; we propose to stand by it forever, but we do hate this civil strife; we will not be eager to enter the lists . . . ; certainly not merely for the sake of promotion. We do hope and pray that the difference will be settled without bloodshed."[23]

These hesitations did not last. But as the war dragged on, certain civilians still believed that West Pointers were largely to

---

[*] Richard S. Ewell (U.S.M.A. 1840), soon to become a Confederate cavalry leader, was serving in New Mexico in January 1861. He wrote to his niece: "Officers generally are very much averse to anything like civil war, though some of the younger ones are a little warlike. The truth is in the army there are no sectional feelings and many from extreme ends of the Union are the most intimate friends." *The Making of a Soldier* (Richmond, Va., 1935), 97.

blame for the Union's reverses, and that the West Point coterie was exercising gross favoritism. Alpheus Williams, in the letter cited above, discussed why so little opportunity was being given to the volunteer general Nathaniel P. Banks. His conclusion was that "the whole West Point influence is against any man who did not happen to spend four years of his life in that institution." A second civilian-soldier, Benjamin F. Butler, afterward said bitterly: "The results of the discipline and teachings at West Point . . . inflicted upon me more injury than mortal man ever did before or thank God, mortal man can do again. I felt it from the 16th day of April, 1861, until the 8th day of November, 1865. It constantly overshadowed and enveloped me and clouded my path." Butler, it will be recalled, could claim that at the annual encampments of Massachusetts militia he had had the opportunity to handle more troops than the average regular ever saw assembled together.* A third civilian-soldier, John A. Logan, who like Banks had fought in the Mexican War, had an almost obsessive grievance against West Pointers. He was commanding a corps and expected to be given command of the Army of the Tennessee, only to see the appointment awarded to O. O. Howard; and Howard, whatever his other qualities, was not the most inspiring of leaders.

Some of the political aspects of this antagonism will be considered in the next chapter. The point here is that Academy graduates did appear to give preference to one another, and that in military prowess the difference between regulars and volunteers was not always readily discernible. If a number of volunteer generals displayed mediocre talent, so did the majority of West Pointers, especially those who had hung on in the regular army on obscure or purely technological assignments. Volunteer or regular, the problem was to find men who would fight, and who could control large-scale operations. The capacity of an officer to profit from experience was the vital factor. There was no arcane body of doctrine revealed only to regulars as the reward of a lifetime of study. As Cox remarked, the principles of war were in

* Butler's remarks were made in the House of Representatives, 14 February 1871, in a debate on the proposed expulsion of some West Point cadets. It is worth noting that he recommended leniency.

essence so brief and simple that they could be printed on the back of a visiting card. He would have applauded the comment of Lloyd George, on the tendency of the British service chiefs in World War I to regard themselves as the sole qualified arbiters on military policy: "War is not an exact science like chemistry or mathematics where it would be presumption on the part of anyone ignorant of its first rudiments to express an opinion contrary to those who had thoroughly mastered its principles. War is an art, proficiency in which depends more on experience than on study, and more on natural aptitude and judgment than on either."[24]

The relations between professionals and amateurs were strained because there were faults and virtues on both sides, and because each was imprisoned in ancient attitudes. Neither could be impartial. As the distinction between them grew less sharp with the prolongation of the Civil War, antagonisms were both softened and exacerbated. Since then the claims of the volunteers, peevish and excessive though they are, have been too quickly dismissed. John A. Logan deserves a hearing no less than Emory Upton.

DANGERS OF A STANDING ARMY

There remains a final, complex issue in seeking a fair assessment of the regular army before the Civil War. How far did Americans genuinely continue to believe that it was "dangerous to liberty"? Politicians used the argument so often and auto-

matically that it might appear to have become meaningless. Defenders of the regulars ridiculed the belief that an army of fifteen thousand could subvert a nation of fifteen million. Yet we may be wrong to assume that the prejudice, however baseless, had lost its effect, or that it was confined to political utterance.*
The New England clergyman Lyman Beecher, reminiscing a generation afterward on the crises of the War of 1812, placed high among them the threat of military despotism: "The militia was our only safeguard . . . ; it was the people, spread over the land, armed and organized for defense. The militia can not usurp, nor be surprised and subdued, and in no way could the liberties of the nation be betrayed but by the general government taking the militia from the control of the states as material of a standing army. This was attempted, but the danger was foreseen and averted." Beecher goes on to praise Governor Griswold of Connecticut, "of immortal memory," for refusing to allow the state's militia to be called into the national service. The thesis was settled, he maintains, "that the militia was a state force for state defense."[25] He was in fact wrong about this: the interesting feature is that he continued to believe that the militia was essentially a local force.

Beecher was not attacking the regular army for any inherent tendency to exceed its powers. His complaint was against the encroachments of the federal government. This was a recurrent fear, and a good deal more than a rhetorical device on the part of a political opposition casting about for a stigma. In a number of national emergencies, the administration's policy was not merely disliked, it was quite profoundly distrusted. This is not to say that politicians never exaggerated; they played upon deep-seated American suspicions. "Standing army" was an evocative phrase.

* A late example is provided by the bimetallist pamphleteer "Coin" Harvey, who in 1899 declared his fear that the expansionism stimulated by the Spanish-American War might leave the United States with a standing army of 100,000 men; and that these "mercenaries" might be employed to impose a monarchy upon the country. See Richard Hofstadter, *The Paranoid Style in American Politics* (New York, 1965), 306–307. Such fears were not allayed by occasional unguarded remarks from conservatively minded Americans. One of these, a New York corporation lawyer, was heard to exclaim as he watched a military parade in honor of Admiral Dewey that it would "show these anarchists and socialists that there is an armed force in this country able to defend property against the rabble." See Ray Ginger, *Atgeld's America* (New York, 1958), 186.

The standing army was certainly a live issue during the later 1790's. Alarm at Federalist policy in establishing the provisional army of 1798–1799 was one of the factors that led to John Adams's defeat in the 1800 election. The Republican argument was repeated in the 1804 presidential election:

As soon as the weight of WASHINGTON's character was removed out of the way of the aristocratic faction, a Standing Army, with HAMILTON at its head, became an avowed object. Though to give a countenance to the project, WASHINGTON was *named* Commander in Chief, yet he was never to see the camp, unless the country should be actually invaded.

The anonymous pamphleteer insists that the Federalists still seek a war with France and Spain, and that they sacrificed Adams when he resisted them and was "instrumental" in disbanding a "useless and expensive army":

We wish union in the choice of JEFFERSON as President, because such an union will tend to the subversion of the hopes, which that restless Party yet entertain, of involving us in a war — of raising a Standing Army — or changing our Constitution — or of dividing our union.[26]

At this stage the fear of what a repressive administration might do with the aid of a standing army was not quite baseless. The immediate consideration was that the country might, once it had an army, be dragged into war. There was the belief, likewise resting on some foundation, that a standing army was one of the social institutions admired by those who wished to model the United States upon the class hierarchies of Europe; and that a fair number of Americans fancied a gentleman's career in the regular services. Hamilton was a conspicuous example — in Republican eyes and to some extent in reality — of an able adventurer with military instincts. There was the allied fear that an administration with military commissions in its gift would have a powerful weapon of patronage.

A decade later the parties had changed position. It was now the Federalists, protesting against the War of 1812, who made dark allegations against the Jeffersonians. Once more, after discounting partisan bias, one cannot help feeling that they have a case. The heart of the case, indeed, is *patronage*. In asking for an extension of the regular army Madison was — in the indignant phrases of John Randolph of Roanoke, himself a Republican — building up a "vast structure of patronage," a "mighty apparatus of favoritism." Suspicion was all the stronger when the distinction between professionals and amateurs was still so vague. The Federalists at the beginning of 1813 accused Madison of planning to place at the head of a vastly expanded army one of his cabinet members, James Monroe. Monroe was acting Secretary of War; he was also Secretary of State, and the most likely candidate to succeed Madison as President. "What a grasp at power is this!" cried the Federalist politician Josiah Quincy of Massachusetts. Though Monroe did not take a military rank on this occasion, his correspondence shows that Quincy's guess was not far out. Much of the Federalist rancor of course arose from being shut out from this patronage, whether in regular or volunteer regiments. Winfield Scott, then a Jeffersonian Republican, testified that "Federalists were almost entirely excluded from selection, though great numbers were eager for the field, and in the New England and some other states, there were but very few educated Republicans."

A similar situation prevailed in the Mexican War. A general suspicion of standing armies embraced a particular complaint that the Democrats under James K. Polk were exploiting the opportunity of a war to strengthen themselves politically. By the beginning of 1848 the fighting in Mexico was over. Fifty thousand men, regulars and volunteers, had already been mustered. Many of the regiments in the field were below strength. Polk was nevertheless asking for another thirty thousand men in *new* regiments, of which ten were to be regular. These ten regular regiments, said an angry Whig Congressman from Polk's own state of Tennessee,

will place in his hands additional appointments to the number of, at least, five hundred and forty officers, of various descriptions — from generals and colonels down to second lieutenants. He has already much greater patronage than Washington, Madison, Jackson, or any other of his predecessors possessed, and I cannot . . . believe that the interests or honor of the country would be advanced by increasing it.

Why was Polk acting thus? The ironical answer:

I may be allowed to say, that an important election is approaching, and that five or six hundred additional electioneerers, thrown into different towns and counties of this Union, under captivating military titles, might possibly be able to increase the strength of the Administration.[27]

Such patronage was also applied in some degree to volunteer commissions. But with volunteer regiments patronage was distributed among the states, not concentrated in Washington. Only the senior generals' appointments rested with the President, though he might express his opinion on less senior commissions. In any case, volunteer rank was temporary and held less prestige among the aspiring. True, if precedent were followed the regular army would always be reduced at the end of a war. Nevertheless the President's power to mold an army in his own political image was bitterly contested; and there was no certainty that he would not try to keep an inflated army in being to secure a party advantage. If this became by degrees the true meaning of the constant warnings against the menace of standing armies, it was enough to constitute a significant item in the list of reasons why Americans tended to insist that the only good soldier was a semi-civilian.

9

POLITICS AND MILITARY AFFAIRS

A more egregious error never took possession of the mind of an American than the notion that a military officer should take no part in political affairs. . . . If a military officer feels no interest in the important political struggles of the day, . . . he acknowledges himself at once to be a mere machine, . . . a hireling.

— "ALCIBIADES," in Army & Navy Chronicle, 1836

A citizen of the United States, on accepting a commission in the military or naval service, must surrender for the time being, his right of political action.

— "JUSTICE," in Army & Navy Chronicle, 1836

For God's and your country's sake, come out of Washington!

— Sherman to Grant, March 1864

From what I know of them, I would not trust an ordinary politician with my grandmother's toothbrush.

— Major General Lord Baden-Powell

POLITICAL INNOCENCE

It is commonly asserted in American military histories and memoirs that the regular army has steered clear of politics. Unlike the militia and volunteers, professional officers are said to have been politically innocent. This does not mean that politics have had no effect upon them. Congress is seen to have either neglected and insulted them, or else at times of national emergency such as the Mexican and Civil Wars, to have foisted off on them flagrantly incompetent "political" generals like Gideon Pillow and Benjamin F. Butler. Either way the regular army was supposedly victimized.

There is no doubt that professional officers felt victimized. Previous references have shown how annoyed they were by political orations on the dangerous and mercenary character of standing armies, or by the congressional habit of cutting down the military establishment. They had grievances concerning pay, allowances, promotions, furlough. As in all armies they blamed the politicians even more than they blamed the service bureaucrats. They had contempt for the distant men in Washington who did not themselves risk danger or disgrace.

It is also true that many officers took little interest in party politics. At West Point the military theorist Dennis Mahan taught nearly all the cadets who became senior commanders in the Civil War. He led a cloistered existence, never voting in a civil election. A second soldier, Winfield Scott, said in 1839 that during thirty-one years of service he had not been to the polls or attended a party meeting: he had not, as he put it, "committed the indecency of blending party feelings with public duty." Twenty years later, discussing the 1860 election with President Buchanan, he declared that while he was in sympathy with the Bell-Everett (Constitutional Union) ticket, "From a sense of propriety, as a soldier, I have taken no part in the pending canvass, and, as always heretofore, mean to stay away from the polls." Either indifference or the same sense of propriety might account for George B. McClellan's ignorance of what he called "practical politics"; he did not vote in a presidential election until he cast a ballot for Stephen Douglas in 1860.[1]

The West Pointer knew that he was meant in some way to stand above politics. Cadet George D. Bayard told his father in 1852: "A member of our class leaves us on Monday; G——l, the nephew of the illustrious candidate for the Presidency. Not finding West Point suited to his taste, he has resigned, and I think it about the best thing he could have done, for the place is exceedingly conservative and abolitionists are not favored. But politics here, are eschewed, and the politician is in no esteem." Parmenas T. Turnley says that he was unusual among officers in being concerned with political events. He gives an illustration of "the utter ignorance of the average army officers on the distant frontiers in March, 1860, of what politicians had in store for them."[2] The occasion was a dinner at Camp Floyd, in Mormon territory, presided over by Brigadier General Albert Sidney Johnston of Kentucky, one of the Army's most admired figures. The other guests included Fitz-John Porter. Turnley was much teased as "the advanced political prophet." With mock gravity, a colonel asked him to "enlighten the company on what the political future has in store for our country and the army." Turnley, aware that he was being baited, hesitated before answering that the Union would split and that there might be a war within two years. There was a burst of laughter. Johnston carried the joke further by requesting to be told which side Turnley, a Tennessean, would join. Turnley said he did not know. Johnston, who was to become the shining light of the early Confederacy, said primly, "Well, I am sorry you should feel any doubts on the subject. I should suppose that every military officer would have no hesitation in being with his government."*

Professionals appear then to have eschewed politics and despised politicians. They were convinced that they had good reason for their dislike. In their view, which has gained fairly general acceptance, the Civil War was imperiled for the Union by "politics." It was won largely because "politics" were at last brought under control: West Pointers were gradually able to assume the chief commands, with appropriately beneficial results. In this view, "politics" embraced various features: the interference of President Lincoln and Secretary of War Stanton in military problems; the appointment of "political generals" (or "warrior statesmen" as they preferred to be described) — B. F. Butler, N. P. Banks, Carl Schurz, John A. McClernand — who were either members of Congress or men with political influence in particular states, but in either case devoid of military talent; the infusion of state politics into recruiting and promotion; the primacy of political over military considerations (for example, Lincoln's desire for a victory in the fall of 1862, to preface the announcement of his decision to abolish slavery in the Confederacy; or the furlough he gave to General Logan of Illinois to go home and "campaign" for Lincoln's reelection); and the widespread and virulent meddling by Congress, especially through the Joint Committee on the Conduct of the War, which in effect sought to establish political tests for the holding of military office. "Politics" was baneful, and best avoided.

The letters of Civil War soldiers are full of the theme. Southern success was widely attributed to freedom from "politics." A staff officer reported in his diary the opinions of his chief, David Hunter (U.S.M.A. 1822), commander of the Army of West Virginia, in July 1864: "General Hunter says that Jeff Davis was the only Secretary of War who ignored politics and political appoint-

---

* Turnley made a bet that there would be a war and that Johnston would not stay with the Union. A Union bullet at Shiloh in 1862 ended any chance that Johnston might pay him his winnings.

ments. His management of the Southern armies has shown the value of these principles, while the United States Government has nearly destroyed the vast resources of the people. Thousands and thousands of lives and millions of property have been sacrificed to the filthy demon of politics."* Emory Upton, the leading exponent of professionalism, was sure his own military career had been impeded by politics. Graduating from West Point in 1861, a year early on account of the crisis, he rose rapidly in rank. But though he was commanding a brigade in the Army of the Potomac by the spring of 1864 he was still not a brigadier general. He wrote disgustedly to his sister in April: "My long-expected promotion is not forthcoming. General Meade has informed me that without 'political' influence I will never be promoted. . . . The recommendations of those officers whose lives have been periled in every battle of the war have been overweighted by . . . the paltry politicians." Upton was in fact promoted two months later. But for the rest of his life he was convinced that the civilian direction of the war, and especially the power of Secretary of War Stanton, had been almost fatal. He told his friend and classmate Colonel Henry A. du Pont in 1879: "If you want to know who was the cause of a three years' war after we created a disciplined army of six hundred thousand men, it was Stanton." By then Upton was busy with the manuscript of his book on American military policy. "I began the book," he also said in 1879, "with the intention of avoiding politics; but it is impossible."[3]

* The Northern idea of a politically pure Southern army was of course an illusion. See Chapter 10; and for the moment, consider the reaction of Colonel Lafayette McLaws (U.S.M.A. 1842), on hearing in September 1861 that two politicians from his home state Georgia had been given Confederate commissions: "I am getting much disposed to come home. The Cobbs are coming over to the Peninsula. . . . And report says Howell will come as a Brigadier General. I do not wish to be under any politician, nor will if it can be helped." Horace Montgomery, *Howell Cobb's Confederate Career* (Tuscaloosa, Ala., 1959; *Confederate Centennial Studies*, no. 10), 38–39. Braxton Bragg complained loudly that fellow regulars were being slighted in the Confederate army: see Don C. Seitz, *Braxton Bragg* (Columbia, S.C., 1924), 47,55.

MILITIA AND VOLUNTEERS

It is indeed impossible to avoid politics in discussing American military affairs, though not quite in the sense Upton meant. He and his fellow regulars were correct enough in asserting that the militia were associated with politicking. Andrew Jackson's initial interest in the Tennessee militia seems to have been mainly in pursuit of social and political advancement. In Georgia a generation afterward, we are told, no person who expected to go far in politics "neglected to get himself made a colonel, at least"; the militia muster with its captive audience was "a first-rate political instrument." The path to advancement was the same in the North. Chester A. Arthur of New York, for example, as an ambitious young lawyer-politician joined the militia to enlarge his acquaintance. He secured the impressive-sounding post of judge advocate general of the Second Brigade of the New York State Militia, and in 1860, as a reward for assisting in the reelection of Governor Morgan, was given a decorative assignment as engineer in chief on the Governor's staff. The situation infuriated men with a genuine interest in military affairs. One such enthusiast in Chester Arthur's state was the gentlemanly John Watts de Peyster, who had a total though perhaps naïve attachment to soldiering. "In 1850–1851," he testifies with a comprehensible if unsophisticated indignation,

I had been very instrumental in passing a Militia bill. . . . I was well-known to Thurlow Weed through my friend, Senator Beekman. I had accomplished the creation of the office of Inspector-General. I was to have it. Thurlow Weed asked me if I was an adroit politician, good stump-speaker, and aware of the opportunities afforded by the office, if given to a cunning politician, who . . . had an excuse for visiting every township in the State.[4]

Weed the party boss and de Peyster the amateur warrior did not see eye to eye, in fact did not speak the same language:

I answered, "I am neither a wire-puller nor a stump-speaker, but a soldier, by instinct and experience." Thereupon he compelled [Governor] Washington Hunt to appoint Benjamin F. Bruce Inspector-General, a slab-sided wash-basket. You will understand the simile if you have ever seen . . . a loose-knit wash-basket in a seaway. It gives out and takes in water, and twists and squirms as if it had no normal shape.*

The independent volunteer companies of peacetime were no less affected by political considerations. Some could be called parapolitical as well as paramilitary organizations. In the political battles of the 1790's rival companies paraded on behalf of rival parties. The followers of Washington and John Adams in Newark, New Jersey, rallied round the Federal Blues, while the supporters of Jefferson and Madison marched with a company known as the Republican Fusiliers.[5] In Worcester, Massachusetts, two separate parades were held to celebrate the Fourth of July in 1812. The Federalist parade was escorted by a Federalist unit, the Worcester Light Infantry, and the Republican one by a Republican unit, the Worcester Artillery. By 1840 the Light Infantry had changed its complexion; it had become so Democratic that the Whig members seceded and formed their own company. They called themselves the Worcester Guards. But they had been tempted to adopt the name of Worcester Harrison Independent Guards, so that the initials would read WHIG on their knapsacks, and abandoned the idea only because the full name would have

---

* To console and possibly to get rid of him, de Peyster was named Military Agent to Europe for his state. He went to Europe and reported exhaustively on European militia systems.

been inconveniently long. There were precedents of a sort: the Mechanic Light Infantry of Salem, Massachusetts, had a uniform button inscribed "True Whigs of 76 and 34" (1776 and 1834). In Richmond, Virginia, the Light Infantry Blues were so Whiggish that when they were required to assemble for a visit by the Democratic President Van Buren they did so under protest: "Resolved that the Company parade tomorrow and escort the President of the United States to his quarters, and it is *distinctly* understand that the honor is paid to the office and not to the man."[6]

Some of this is close to slapstick. But political partisanship persisted in sterner circumstances. A Whig amateur soldier says of his election to the colonelcy of the 1st Tennessee Volunteers in the Mexican War: "The old political companies were called for by the Govr and it so happened that 3-4 of those in my Regt are democratic officers, but there is a majority of 200 Democrats of the rank and file [of an enlisted strength of 960], yet I beat a [militia] Major Genl and a Democrat 169 votes. So you see I out ran the Whig strength." One could not find a clearer avowal of the political basis of volunteer service. Nor were politics a joking matter. Within a month the colonel discovered that "politics is somewhat in my way as all my field officers are Democrats and are somewhat jealous of any character I may acquire." He went on ruefully: "I hope I shall never again have any desire to ingage in any political contest." Things began to improve soon after. Nevertheless this volunteer colonel continued in his letters to treat politics and soldiering as almost interchangeable.[7]

POLITICS AND PROFESSIONALS

The regular army was far less directly involved in politics. But there was merely a difference of degree, not of kind, despite the protestations of innocence and of victimization. As we have seen, politics entered from the outset of an officer's career, whether his nomination to West Point was put forward by the President, the

Secretary of War, or a congressman. George Crook (U.S.M.A. 1852), it will be recalled, owed his nomination to his Whig congressman from Ohio, Robert C. Schenck. Schenck was guided by the reflection that Crook's father was "a fine old Whig farmer." Direct appointments to commissions were even more a matter of party favor. Even the thirty army and thirty-four navy chaplaincies, it was said in the 1850's, were liable to be filled by "political wire-pullers, with very little, if any, reference to the appropriate qualifications" of the candidate.

Once cadets were at the Academy they had little to do with party politics, except in the feverish months that preceded the Civil War. But those who had strings to tug at tugged them uninhibitedly, sometimes to rescue friends in distress, more often to aid their own budding careers. When Cadet John M. Schofield of Illinois (U.S.M.A. 1853) was dismissed for misconduct, he "proposed to go straight to Washington and lay the facts before the government. Then I realized . . . what it meant to have friends. All my classmates and many other cadets came forward with letters to their congressmen, and many of them to senators whom they happened to know, and other influential men in Washington." Schofield, who was to become a well-esteemed general, was finally saved through the intercession of Senator Stephen Douglas.[8]

As for personal advancement, evidence is candidly supplied in Samuel Bayard's memoir of his son George, whose useful New Jersey connections were noted in Chapter 5. Places in the more dashing branches of the service were eagerly sought after. George Bayard, due to graduate in June 1856, already had his eye on the main chance in the previous September. He informed his father that "there will be a terrible scramble for the mounted regiments":

Indeed many will have their friends at work before, to secure appointments in the dragoons or cavalry. You must do what you can for me at Washington. With the aid of [Senator] Thomson and the Iowa senators, and others you can induce to back me, I ought not to fail.

In the following June he was hot on the trail:

I shall go to Washington immediately after graduating and urge my claims to a lieutenant's brevet either in the Dragoons or Cavalry. I wish, father, in the meantime you would ask your friends in Congress — the senators with whom you are on the proper terms, and the members of Congress from New Jersey, to back my application.

Young Bayard continued to take advantage of his connections. In December 1857, hearing that six new regiments were to be authorized, he instructed his father to try and procure him a captaincy in one of them: "With senator Thomson's aid, and that of the N.J. members, there can be no difficulty." This time he overreached himself and was unsuccessful. But in 1860 he appealed to his father to secure him a post in the cavalry department at West Point, by lobbying Secretary of War Floyd and President Buchanan; and eventually got what he wanted. By April 1862, after a year of the Civil War, Bayard was colonel of a Pennsylvania cavalry regiment. He informed his father that he had come up to Washington from his post at Aquia Creek: "General McDowell took me to the President, Secretary of War and Treasury and demanded that I should be made a Brigadier-general. The Secretary of War says my nomination shall go in in a couple of days. . . . If I find there is any need of it, I will see Senators Harris, Thomson and Ten Eyck."* The appointment *was* confirmed.[9]

Bayard was an exceptionally well-placed and, it must be said, able soldier. (He was killed at Fredericksburg in December 1862.) But his case was not unique. Thus, the father of John F. Reynolds, another capable regular (U.S.M.A. 1841), was prominent in Pennsylvania Democratic politics. He was a friend of Senator (later President) Buchanan, who furnished a West Point nomination for John Reynolds and a midshipman's appointment for John's brother. In the Mexican War, Buchanan was solicited to help John Reynolds to a brevet promotion. He replied smoothly, "I shall take good care of John when the time arrives." Buchanan kept his promise; John was given *two* brevets, so that

---

* Harris, Thomson and Ten Eyck were senators from New York and New Jersey. The Bayard family had lived in Iowa during the 1840's: hence the previous reference to "the Iowa senators."

by 1848 he was a brevet major. Then came the postwar doldrums, when promotion was scarce. Reynolds grumbled to his father in 1855: "In the Army, merit is no recommendation and political influence is everything." Reynolds was mollified when in 1860 he was appointed commandant of cadets at West Point, a favor he may well have owed to Buchanan. Braxton Bragg was another regular with a grievance. He resigned his commission in January 1856 in disgust; he had hoped that President Pierce and Secretary of War Jefferson Davis, whom he had known in the Mexican War, would reward his Democratic fealty by granting him privileged army assignments. In a plaintive letter of 1856 Bragg says that Davis "could drive me from the army but not from my party."*

The system was certainly uneven in operation. Grant and Sherman, for example, were both out of the regular army in the spring of 1861. Grant had no influence: Sherman's brother John was a congressman. When Grant wrote to the Adjutant General suggesting his competence to command a regiment of infantry, his letter went unanswered. Sherman, aided by his brother, became colonel of the 13th Infantry — a new regular regiment.[10] We begin to see what army officers may have meant by "politics": it was what *other people* successfully practiced. As the occasion arose, regulars like other Americans turned instinctively to Washington.

The case of Pierre G. T. Beauregard is instructive. Graduating second in his West Point class in 1838, he was able to select the Corps of Engineers as his arm of service. Except for the Mexican War he was thereafter stationed mainly in his home state Louisiana, where he was in charge of "Mississippi and Lake defences," and then (1853–1860) superintending engineer for the construction of the New Orleans customhouse. He was ambitious to the point of chicanery. He sought help from anyone who might give it, including the Mississippi soldier-politician John A. Quitman and his own brother-in-law Senator John Slidell, the political boss of Louisiana. When Franklin Pierce achieved the Democratic

---

* An odd comment in the light of the subsequent belief, widely held in the Confederacy, that President Davis was sheltering Bragg from much-justified criticism.

presidential nomination in 1852, Beauregard, trading like Bragg on a Mexican War acquaintanceship, hastened to hitch his wagon to the new star by sending a fulsome congratulatory letter. He strengthened his claim to Pierce's gratitude by contributing several pseudonymous letters to a New Orleans paper in praise of Pierce's military reputation — which one might not have expected a regular to regard very highly. In 1854 Beauregard attempted to wangle the colonelcy of a new infantry regiment through political influence. Four years later he did not allow his military rank to deter him from running for office as mayor of New Orleans — though he would presumably have left the army if he had won.

At the end of 1860 Beauregard was invoking the help of Slidell and others to gain the superintendency of West Point. Their efforts carried the day, although he resigned almost immediately because of the threat of war. The negotiations led him to write a curious letter in October 1860 to an engineer crony, John G. Barnard: "After much reflection . . . , I have consented to sacrifice $5000 a year* & allow my name to be presented for the position [at West Point], & to do all I can to have you put in charge of the New Custom House here, *on the condition* that you will resign it in my favor whenever I return . . . for I attach much importance to finishing it." As a Confederate general Beauregard continued to use political allies to get his own way against Jefferson Davis.[11]

Beauregard ought not to be singled out. He was only doing what others did when they had the means. Moreover his situation, like that of most engineer officers, was peculiar. They had distinguished themselves academically and were held in esteem. They were entrusted with important tasks in a semi-civilian capacity. The nature of their work often obliged them to cultivate friendly relations with powerful civilians. It is not surprising that they became expert in the art of political persuasion. William B. Franklin of Pennsylvania (U.S.M.A. 1843), who graduated at the head of his class, was tied to Washington in more ways than one.

---

* This probably refers to extra pay and perquisites. But his special pay for the customhouse work was only eight dollars per day.

At the outbreak of the Civil War he was superintending architect of the U. S. Treasury. His father was clerk of the House of Representatives, and he married a girl whose father succeeded Mr. Franklin in the clerkship. Captain Montgomery C. Meigs of Pennsylvania (U.S.M.A. 1836), another able engineer officer, was responsible in the same period for work upon the Washington Aqueduct and the Capitol, in close touch with Congress and the Executive. In Pierce's administration Meigs got on well, as a Philadelphia gentleman who was also a Democrat, with Secretary of War Jefferson Davis. When under Buchanan he found himself thwarted by the new Secretary, Floyd, he constantly appealed for support to friends in Congress, Davis among them.[12]

Whether army officers were specialists or not, the border line between civil and military functions was ill-drawn. Regulars understood that, as in Britain, their uniformed presence at polling stations was unwelcome. An officer who lent some artillery pieces to be fired in celebration of a "party triumph" — possibly Van Buren's accession to the presidency in 1837 — drew a sharp reprimand. But Secretary of War Poinsett's additional comments suggest that political involvement was not always avoided:

The Department condemns all interference, on the part of the officers of the Army, with the party politics which, from the nature of our institutions, so often agitate the country. If they take an active part in political strife, passions and prejudices will be enlisted for or against them, and their condition become dependent upon the success or defeat of a party; engendering a state of feeling fatal to the standing, as well as to the discipline, of the Army.

Indeed, there had been a lively correspondence on the problem in the *Army & Navy Chronicle* in 1836. One officer, signing himself "OLIVE BRANCH," was convinced that regulars must act with complete integrity and impartiality. "No man," he said, "would be fit to serve his country . . . who would chain himself to the car of any man, civil or military, or who would blindly follow the dictation of any mortal." On the other hand "ALCIBIADES" believed: "The feeling and the opinion that an officer should take no part in politics are conceived in the most servile spirit, and inculcated by heartless military aristocrats, whose interest it is to hold the minds of their subordinates in entire subjection to their domineering propensities." "ARISTIDES," a naval officer, agreed with "ALCIBIADES" that officers both naturally and as a matter of right should be politically conscious. A fourth correspondent, "JUSTICE," sharply disagreed. The 5th Article of War, he said, and the officer's oath on being commissioned, barred the way.* True, they did not expressly forbid the expression of political opinions; but, said "JUSTICE":

We will suppose . . . that a President is a candidate for re-election; a portion of the army are so much in favor of some other candidate, and so much opposed to the President . . . , that their political enthusiasm leads them to the place of election . . . ; in doing which, it would be necessary . . . for them to defame and traduce the character and conduct of the President, in proportion as they would extol and applaud their favorite; and consequently . . . would . . . lay themselves liable to the penalties awarded by the rules and articles of war.[13]

Though "JUSTICE" probably had the best of the argument the discussion was inconclusive. This was partly because it raised matters for which there is no satisfactory solution. Again, the argument for political virginity among the military depends on ready obedience and the habit of subordination; and in the American context these could not be strictly enforced. Poinsett, no doubt wisely, did not cashier or court-martial the officer who lent the artillery — in spite of the 5th Article of War. While opposed to one another on some grounds, "OLIVE BRANCH" and "ALCIBIADES" unite in denouncing the "dictation" of superiors, civil or military, and perhaps especially military: "heartless military aristocrats" is the phrase of "ALCIBIADES." "OLIVE BRANCH" sounds high-minded in his plea for individual integrity. But

---

* The 5th Article read: "Any officer . . . who shall use contemptuous or disrespectful words against the President of the United States, against the Vice President thereof, against the Congress of the United States, or against the Chief Magistrate, or Legislature of any of the United States in which he may be quartered; if a commissioned officer, shall be cashiered, or otherwise punished as a court martial shall direct." The officer's oath required him to swear to "bear true faith and allegiance to the United States of America" and to "observe and obey the orders of the President" and of "the officers appointed over me."

where would this leave the Bayards and Beauregards, not to mention the Scotts, struggling to further their careers? The problem was exactly that stated by Poinsett. Army officers did not engage in politics as a group activity. But they believed they had a right, and a positive necessity, to use political connections. Despite Poinsett, many believed that their own careers *were* "dependent upon the success or defeat of a party."

The senior officers, especially after the War of 1812, at times plunged into political intrigue in their own interests – for their very survival, as they saw it. Their professionalism was contingent. They had observed men like James Monroe and John Armstrong who in the War of 1812 apparently perceived no essential difference between high civil and high military rank. They usually won their initial appointments through party favor: Winfield Scott had Republican friends in Virginia to thank not only for his first commission but also for his subsequent promotions up to the rank of lieutenant colonel. They caught the habit of insubordination, as was illustrated in Chapter 4. Scott after a mere two years of service was court-martialed and then suspended for a year as a punishment for publicly criticizing his superior, General Wilkinson. A small group in the War of 1812 – Scott, Gaines, Brown, Macomb, and of course Andrew Jackson – showed extreme bravery. They got on fast. They were praised in Congress; medals were struck for them, they were presented with tastefully inscribed swords at public banquets. Scott, handsome and vain, was toasted in 1816 as "The Personification of Glory." They were assured that they were the saviors of their country: nothing was too good for them.[14]

Then came the long frustrating years in an army too small to contain so much vaunting ambition. Each became fixated on his chances of preferment;* and everything, in peacetime, depended on having friends at court. After his appointment as general in

---

* It was not possible to rise higher in rank than a major generalcy. Scott's promotion to lieutenant general was only a brevet rank. Grant's appointment as lieutenant general in 1864 was regarded as a personal promotion, not a precedent. Only George Washington, in American military tradition, was deemed worthy of the ultimate rank – though the Confederacy was to be somewhat more generous. The situation was still more cramped in the navy, where until the Civil War there were only three officer grades.

chief in 1821, the year of Jackson's retirement from the army, Jacob Brown looked ahead to the presidential election of 1824, hoping for a sympathetic master. President John Quincy Adams, the victor in 1824, grew intensely irritated with Brown's greedy meddling in politics. And under Brown were the two implacable rivals Scott and Gaines, each equally concerned over the struggle for the presidency. Each believed he had the ear of a leading contender, John C. Calhoun; each was mistaken. Their interminable controversy over precedence in rank flared up in response to the political atmosphere; it was in the election year 1824 that Scott challenged Gaines to a duel. Four years later, when Adams passed over both of them on the death of Jacob Brown, and appointed their relatively inoffensive junior Alexander Macomb to the post of general in chief, he would have liked to court-martial the pair and push them out of the army. But they were too eminent, too vituperative, too close to the political scene.

Scott and Gaines remained enemies until the latter's death in 1849. Scott could have no hopes of preferential treatment from another old adversary, Andrew Jackson, who to his chagrin occupied the White House from 1829 to 1837. What could he expect of a President who had once almost fought a duel with him? For a while Scott and Gaines were too immersed in campaigning against the Seminoles and against each other to raise their ambitions to a higher scene.

But now came the grand political temptation for American senior soldiers — one to which most of them succumbed. Scott was much praised for his tactful handling of the Cherokee removal and of the crises along the Canadian border. He had evolved apparently into a soldier-statesman: a position to which he had aspired as far back as 1822, when he suggested to President Monroe that he would make an excellent diplomatist, preferably as minister to France. At the beginning of 1839 a friend, the editor Charles King of the *New York American,* proposed him as a Whig presidential candidate. This is the background of Scott's assurance to the Democratic Secretary of War Poinsett in February 1839 that in his many years of service he had not once voted or attended a party meeting. At that stage he was perhaps sincere. But willy-nilly he *was* a possible candidate. Even if Scott had not been politically ambitious, the seeming indications of popularity might have begun to convince him that the nation needed him. Gouverneur Kemble of New York provided Poinsett with a mocking account of Scott's behavior in June of that year. Kemble found himself traveling with Scott on the Hudson River steamboat from New York to West Point. When Scott disembarked, the passengers gave him three cheers — "all of which," Kemble observed, "was of course taken very kindly and graciously, but he professed to deprecate being held up as a candidate for the presidency at this, or *any future time* — it is a hard part for him to play, but he does it with more discretion than some would have expected of him, and only overacts sometimes."

Scott was politically naïve. He failed to realize that he was being used by the Whig managers for a variety of purposes and was not in their estimate a serious candidate for 1840. Still, he was drawn into the arena and developed the insidious presidential virus, which has affected shrewder men than he. Though Scott had not voted for thirty years, he remedied the omission in 1840. In the words of his biographer, from 1839 onward he was "unquestionably a politician as well as a soldier." Seeing the Whigs choose General Harrison, a "warrior statesman" (whom he incidentally despised), and seeing Harrison triumph, he naturally enough concluded that the public would be even more enthusiastic over General Scott. When Harrison died in office Scott began to look ahead to 1844. Though he was again not the Whig choice he continued to figure in their political equations. In 1848 he was again tantalized and chagrined when the Whigs fastened upon a military hero, his rival Zachary Taylor. At last in 1852 Scott had his chance, when the Whigs nominated him to run against the Democratic contender, Franklin Pierce. Both were portrayed as military heroes, though Pierce was a New Hampshire politico whose exploits were confined to a fairly brief experience under Scott in the Mexican War. Since 1841, or through most of these years of yearning for the presidency, Scott had been general in chief.[15]

STORMING OF CHAPULTEPEC.

THE MEXICAN WAR

At the upper levels of the army, politics and soldiering were intertwined. The Mexican War offers an extraordinary example of the confusion in American civil-military relations. This is not to gainsay the victories won by the American columns, or the fairly incisive direction of the war effort by President Polk. In comparison with the Mexicans, the Americans were paragons of efficiency and plain dealing. Even so, certain of the civil-military aspects verged on the preposterous, and certain others on the outrageous.

Polk's problems were vexing in the spring and summer of 1846, as the confrontation along the Rio Grande turned into formally declared war. Something of a dark-horse candidate, he was a suspect figure to many Democrats, let alone to those of the Whig persuasion. For the sake of party cohesion — a vital matter to one who was a devout Democrat — Polk had to seek to placate such Van Buren Democrats as Senator Thomas Hart Benton of Missouri. He had to reckon with the frustrated anger of the Whigs, many of whom regarded the Mexican War as the result of deliberate American provocation, and who yet dared not jeopardize the safety of Zachary Taylor's army or their own careers by hindering the military buildup. Polk had a genuine antipathy to professional armies. He also had genuine and not unreasonable misgivings as to the caliber of his senior professional officers. Taylor, on whom the war's first battles depended, was a rough old

305

warrior of limited experience and perhaps capacity. Winfield Scott, the general in chief, was notoriously grandiloquent and quarrelsome. Scott's inveterate enemy, Edmund P. Gaines, behaved so rashly in the early stages of the war that Polk was probably right to remove him from active command. Though the national mood was bellicose in 1846, the war was expensive. One setback might be enough to swing sentiment against Polk. He was determined to "conquer a peace" in the quite literal sense of meaning to conquer and acquire the Mexican provinces of California and New Mexico. But he could not declare his intentions too openly. A suitable strategy was not easy to formulate; nor was the appropriate blend of military and diplomatic action. A limited penetration of Mexican territory, of the kind soon achieved by Taylor, had the advantages of economy and prudence. The disadvantage was that it would fail to satisfy the popular craving for spectacular, swift victory, and that it would be unlikely to induce the Mexicans to sue for peace. These aims might be accomplished by carrying the war into the heart of Mexico — as was done with Scott's landing at Vera Cruz, in the spring of 1847, and the subsequent advance on Mexico City. But the risk of humiliating defeat, and of prolonging the war, was correspondingly greater.

These were questions of policy and morale which would have faced almost any President in the circumstances. What aggravated them was Polk's temperament and the spleen of partisan politics. Personally honest, single-minded and energetic, Polk was also — like his revered predecessor and fellow Tennessean Andrew Jackson — a man of fierce and narrow prejudice. Mixed up with his real doubts as to the competence of Scott, Taylor and Gaines was the fact that they were known Whigs, and the Whigs had seized the presidency in 1840 by nominating a military hero as candidate. If Taylor's troops were too successful, and Taylor got the credit, he would be an obvious candidate for 1848. Indeed, the Whig politico Thurlow Weed swiftly discerned the possibility. Taylor might wreck his chances through ignorance and stupidity; but this same stupidity might lead him into military disaster, which in turn could do irreparable harm to the Democrats. Comparable considerations affected Polk's view of

Winfield Scott. Scott had after all been a likely contender for the Whig nomination in 1844, although eventually the choice fell upon Henry Clay. As President, as an American, as a man with an imperial mission, Polk wanted his armies to triumph. As a deep-dyed Democrat he meant to secure the credit for his party and deny it to the Whigs — or "Federalists" as he persisted in labeling them in the diary that he filled, night after night, at the end of exhausting labors. Senator Benton later summed things up: the administration "wanted a small war, just large enough to require a treaty of peace and not large enough to make military reputations dangerous for the presidency."[16]

Nothing that Taylor could achieve altered Polk's low opinion of his military ability. Polk became increasingly exasperated by what he interpreted as dilatoriness, a tendency to disobey orders, and growing political ambition. In a typical diary entry, of January 1847, the President called Taylor "a vindictive & ignorant political partisan" who had allowed himself to be "controlled and managed by bad men for political purposes." On his side Taylor was convinced that he was being victimized. In the first months of command his suspicions were confined to Polk and Secretary of War William Marcy. Before the end of 1846 he had added Winfield Scott to his list of chief persecutors.

The two men had previously been on good terms. Scott had troubles of his own to engross him, though he was magnanimous enough to give what support he could to Taylor.

Polk grudgingly offered Scott command in the field in May 1846. Almost at once he was angered to discover that Scott, immersed in a mass of administrative work, did not plan to leave Washington until the end of the summer. In a few days their relations were strained to breaking point. Polk was shown a copy of a private letter from Scott to a senator who had inquired about commissions in the newly authorized regiment of Mounted Rifles. "The proposed Riflemen," Scott indiscreetly though not altogether inaccurately answered, "are intended by western men to give commissions . . . to western democrats." He was sure that no "eastern man," West Pointer or Whig "would obtain a place." Polk was furious at the Whiggishness of this answer. Scott for his part was furious because, without consulting him, Marcy had asked the Senate Military Affairs committee (whose chairman was Thomas Hart Benton) to add to a war measures bill a clause providing for two new regular major generals and four brigadiers. He sent a long, resentful letter to Marcy, indicating his conviction that the President was hostile to him. He told a friend that the proposed appointments were designed "first, to supersede me, and, at the *end* of the war, say in six or eight or twelve months, disband every general who would not place Democracy above God's country."

The clause was whittled down by Whig opposition. Scott's rashness, however, led the President to withdraw his offer of command in the field. For several months the general in chief, chastened, worked away in Washington. Meanwhile Democrat after Democrat was being named to volunteer commissions as major generals and brigadiers. All were from civilian life, though one or two such as William O. Butler of Kentucky, Robert Patterson of Pennsylvania and John A. Quitman of Mississippi had previous military experience. Most of them, notably Gideon J. Pillow of Tennessee, Polk's onetime law partner, were active politicians. Pillow was to keep Polk supplied with confidential information and opinions, hot from Mexico.

By October 1846 the administration had decided on a seaborne expedition aimed at Mexico City, and Marcy was now convinced that Scott should lead it. In November, Polk, still hoping to find a substitute "with the interests of the administration at heart," tried to persuade himself and his cabinet that Patterson would do. Another and bolder plan was also in the air. Polk had begun to accept military advice from Senator Benton. The advice was freely proffered. Benton was a large sonorous man, with a special stake in the war because of the activities of his son-in-law Colonel John C. Frémont. On 10 November 1846 the President sought Benton's views on the forthcoming expedition. They agreed that Taylor was not adequate:

I asked who would be the proper officer to command. . . . [Benton] did not answer. I spoke of Gen'l Scott. He said he had no confidence in him. . . . He then said there ought to be a Lieutenant General of the army who should be commander in chief. He said it required a man of talents and resources as well as a military man for such a command, & that with a view to obtain peace more depended upon the talents & energy of the officer than upon mere bravery. He then said that if such an office was created by Congress, he would be willing to accept the office himself. I remarked Generally that I would have confidence in him and would be pleased to see him at the head of the army in such an expedition. He alluded to what was apparent to every one, that the Whigs were endeavouring to turn this war to party & political account.[17]

It might seem hard to believe that Polk could have written the final sentence with a straight face, or that he could have sanctioned Benton's grandiose suggestion. Polk was however in earnest, as nearly always. He knew that most of the opposition to the war came from the Whigs. The war was the major fact in political calculations for both sides. He thought himself justified in appointing Democrats to senior posts because he mistrusted men of the rival party and because it was almost impossible to find anyone who had no previous political allegiance. In a volunteer army, war was truly, though not in the sense Clausewitz intended, "politics carried on by other means." Polk could claim that in the early stages he had tried to make appointments impartially — only to find that fellow Democrats would not tolerate such laxity.

On 19 November, after further cabinet discussion, Polk reluctantly took the plunge and gave the command of the Vera Cruz operation to General Scott. The general in chief was overjoyed, and by the end of the month was en route for Texas. What he did not know, or did not for some time believe, was that Polk was still eager to create the rank of lieutenant general in order to place Benton in supreme command. For the next two months the President and Benton busily pushed the scheme in Congress. They managed to gain House approval and were thwarted only by a quite small majority in the Senate. In March 1847 Polk took the opportunity to make Benton a major general. Benton replied that "he had no desire to go to Mexico simply to have a plume &

bunch of feathers in his hat; which I understood to mean that if he could be General in-chief of the army he would accept, but not otherwise."[18] Benton also made it known that he wished to be invested with diplomatic as well as military powers. Polk was prepared to consider putting Benton in command with this lower rank, even at the price of recalling all four major generals — Scott, Taylor, Butler and Patterson — who would be senior to him. The cabinet demurred. Even then, Polk was ready to supersede Scott and Taylor; since Butler and Patterson would remain senior to Benton, however, the appointment eventually fell through. Before long Polk and Benton were in disagreement on sundry other matters. In the President's diary "General" Benton, as he had begun to style him, was demoted to his old (War of 1812) rank as "Colonel" Benton, or merely designated as "Senator" Benton.

In order to launch his campaign Scott had to deprive Taylor of some of his best troops. Taylor took the necessity as a deliberate plan to rob him of the chance of glory. He was wrong to believe that Scott was scheming against him. He was correct in supposing that the step reflected on his own generalship. Other observers, whether or not they credited the administration with Machiavellian intentions, saw that the result of the "second front" in Mexico would be to create a break between the two Whig generals.[19] Scott's efforts to soothe Taylor's hurt pride were unavailing. Through most of 1847 and all of 1848 he and Taylor were at loggerheads.

Polk continued to find fault with nearly everything that both men did. When Scott was compelled to arrest an insubordinate officer, Colonel William Selby Harney, with whom Taylor had also had trouble, Polk typically sought an explanation in political terms: none other seemed as real to him. Harney (a Tennessean like Polk and Pillow) was deemed a good officer: he was, however, Polk wrote in February 1847,

a Democrat . . ., was one of Gen'l Jackson's personal friends, and was appointed by him. I can conceive of no reason but this for the arbitrary and tyrannical conduct of Gen'l Scott. . . . Gen'l Taylor had acted with the same proscriptive spirit, not only towards Col. Harney, but other gallant Democratic officers. I have myself been wholly uninfluenced by any reference to the political opinions of the officers of the army in the conduct of the war. [!] It has not been so with the Federal commanders in the field. I have good reason to believe that Gen'l Taylor's camp has been converted into a political arena.

An opposite view of Taylor and his army was presented by another Tennessean, Colonel William B. Campbell, who happened to be a Whig. Writing from Monterrey in November 1846 in praise of Taylor, Campbell said:

Most of the other high in rank officers are out here on a political tour to gain reputation to give them importance when they shall return home. . . . They are all jealous of each other and . . . all these Democratic Gen's, and Col's, and Major's and officer's [sic] and men are striking at Genl. Taylor whom they fear may be taken up for the Presidency. . . . I feel myself not safe amongst men who seem to have no other object here but to advance the political party to which they owe their elevation. . . . any poor Whig who fell under their power would fare badly.[20]

But then again, not all the partisan enthusiasm was confined to the Democrats. Captain Robert Anderson,* a regular officer serving with Scott, wrote fervently in February 1847: "Great anxiety is entertained here by Genl. Scott's friends relative to a bill before Congress to make a Lt. Genl., as we know it is aimed at Genl. S. and designed to place some politician above him. If Genl. S. can take the field with a strong force, carry Vera Cruz . . . and then establish himself safely in the interior . . . , before the arrival of the Lt. Genl., his being superseded will make him President, in spite of the manoeuvres of politicians." The "politicians" were behaving wickedly; yet it did not occur to Anderson to consider Scott's aspirations for the presidency as political. As for Colonel Campbell, who had meanwhile joined Scott's army, he too assumed as a matter of course that military victory would lead to political victory. Campbell, writing in March 1847, was jubilant

* Fourteen years later, as a major, Anderson became famous as the commander of Fort Sumter.

at the news of Taylor's triumph over Santa Anna at the hard-fought battle of Buena Vista: "His fame is now complete . . . and he will be the next President by acclamation. He will make a good President, and I am for him or for Scott or any Whig who may be our nominee." Campbell's main worry, voiced a week later, was that the administration would "excite a rivalry between Scott and Taylor."[21]

In such an atmosphere of accusation and counteraccusation one can almost forgive Polk his meager comments on Buena Vista and subsequent American successes. Taylor, he thought, had been "constantly blundering into difficulties" and had got out of them "with very severe loss." He believed that not Taylor's generalship but only "the indomitable bravery of our army" saved the day at Buena Vista. This conclusion was doubly acceptable to Polk in that Taylor's army consisted mainly of volunteer regiments. If Taylor had been defeated, Polk observed sourly, "he would have been universally execrated." But the Whigs would now strive to make him a candidate. "They care nothing for political principle. The Spoils of office are all that they care for."

Polk continued to react in the same grudging way to Scott's advance on Mexico City. He recorded Scott's victory at Cerro Gordo in a couple of joyless sentences. A previous entry, while he was awaiting news of the battle, shows that he had already decided on a comforting formula: "Our forces are the best troops in the world and will gain victories over superior forces of the enemy, if there was not an officer among them. This proves the injustice of giving all the credit of our victories to the commanding General and none to his inferior officers and men."[22]

In the next few months Polk's dislike of Taylor and Scott grew even stronger, and his corresponding desire to recall one if not both of them. Some of his irritation with Scott was understandable; the general in chief had taken umbrage when the administration sent to Mexico a civilian diplomat to arrange peace terms with Mexico. This figure was Nicholas Trist, chief clerk of the State Department. Before long the President was annoyed with Trist also, for apparently exceeding his instructions. Moreover Trist (who had attended West Point, though he had not

graduated) and Scott became so well disposed toward one another that Polk had a fresh cause for annoyance. When the news
reached Washington of Scott's culminating victories outside Mexico City, and of the Americans' occupation of the "Halls of
Montezuma," Polk once more revealed his petulance and suspicion. He noted merely that the American casualties had been
heavy; that among the wounded was his friend and confidant
Gideon Pillow; and that he was "much disappointed" not to have
received official dispatches from Scott.[23]

Pillow proved not to be badly wounded; in fact some of his
critics alleged that his wound was largely imaginary. Other,
emotional wounds were soon under discussion, in a protracted
affair which did little credit to Pillow, Scott, Polk or another of
the principals, Brevet Major General Worth. The trouble arose
over various letters which began to appear in American newspapers describing the recent campaigns. Of these the most notorious was printed in the *New Orleans Delta* in September 1847,
over the signature "LEONIDAS." Most of the newspaper contributions claimed a lion's share of the credit for various division
commanders. Some by implication depicted Scott as supernu-
merary or even incompetent. The "LEONIDAS" letter praised Pillow for his "masterly military genius." It had obviously been inspired by Pillow, and rushed into print.

Scott was justifiably annoyed. He had already had occasion to
offer mild criticism of Pillow's dispatches as being flamboyant
and self-centered. Pillow had answered affably but declined to
modify his language. Years later in his autobiography Scott was
able to characterize Pillow in a dispassionate paragraph as "an
anomaly, — without the least malignity in his nature — amiable,
and possessed of some acuteness, but the only person I have ever
known who was wholly indifferent in the choice between truth
and falsehood, honesty and dishonesty."[24] It was a pity that this
time, knowing well how close Pillow was to Polk, Scott could not
contain his temper. He issued a resounding general order, in his
worst fustian style, reprimanding the guilty officers without
naming them. Though Pillow lay low for a while, Scott immediately provoked a truculent response from Worth and from an-

other regular officer, Lieutenant Colonel Duncan. Worth had once been Scott's protégé; as recently as 1840 he had christened his son Winfield Scott Worth. But like Harney he suffered from the ingrained American military habit of denouncing the plans of his superior officers. He had become disaffected, and after the fuss was over rechristened his son William.

Scott placed Worth, Duncan and Pillow under arrest. Hearing of the wrangle, Polk not surprisingly decided it was caused by "the vanity and tyrannical temper" of the general in chief, who was bent on "persecuting Gen'l Pillow and others who are supposed to be friendly to me." The President seized the opportunity to supersede Scott in command, to institute a court of inquiry instead of a court-martial, and to replace Scott not with Taylor but with William O. Butler — a soldier who agreed "with me in his General opinions" and so could be relied on "to carry out my . . . plans in good faith."[25]

The court of inquiry, opening in Mexico in October 1847, dragged on until 1 July 1848; the later stages were held in the United States, at Frederick, Maryland. Since Worth dropped his charges against Scott and Duncan was a minor participant, the main contest was between Winfield Scott and Gideon Pillow. The proceedings and supplementary documents cover 635 pages of small print. Scott was no stranger to such inquisitions; nor were his fellow officers, in an army given to professional litigation. To the Mexicans the inquiry was baffling in the extreme. They were used to intrigue; bad faith between Santa Anna, Valencia and others had helped to bring about their defeat. What they could not easily understand was the role of Scott. They had come to admire him as a gifted soldier and a firm but humane and honest overlord. Yet Scott, it appeared, was as much on trial as Pillow.

The court heard testimony from scores of witnesses: officers, enlisted men, and civilians, including a number of journalists. Pillow had ingenious if not very convincing answers for the charges leveled against him. The "LEONIDAS" letter was shown to be in the handwriting of another officer, a paymaster named Burns who insisted that he had on his own initiative composed it and placed it in the mailbag of Freaner, the *Delta* correspondent.

Though the testimony of Freaner and others was highly skeptical, the story could not be disproved. Once Pillow had managed to disavow responsibility for some of the extravagant claims as to his military prowess which had got into the newspapers, much of the laborious cross-examination lost its force. Thus, he was supposed to have killed a Mexican cavalry officer at close quarters. Scott summoned witness after witness to show that in fact Pillow had merely taken a shot at a fleeing prisoner. The most he could demonstrate was that Pillow had been lauded — by himself, or by others — for an episode whose circumstances were confused. As for the impropriety of encouraging newspapers to print stories flattering to Pillow and critical of other generals, the Tennessean countered by producing a long letter from Scott's confidant Hitchcock which had ended up in the *New York Sun.* True, the letter constituted a sharp indictment of Pillow which appeared to tell against him in the court record. "The grand difficulty" with Pillow, said Hitchcock, was his "impudence and falsehood, in writing letters to the newspapers, puffing himself for deeds he never performed, and then denying all knowledge of the letters; and, finally, by eluding, always, what an honorable man would seize upon to allow, the truth to appear before a proper court. Some scoundrel has attempted to get up an idea that the regular officers are persecuting this contemptible son of Tennessee." Hitchcock enjoyed himself by going on to analyze the supposed leg wound received by Pillow at Chapultepec; he asserted that eyewitnesses as reputable as Captain Robert E. Lee had failed to detect any damage worse than a mild bruise. True also, Pillow's attempt to reveal that Nicholas P. Trist was biased against him, and in favor of Scott, apparently did him more harm than good. The attempt involved reading out a letter sent by Trist to Secretary of State Buchanan, in which Pillow was compared to Santa Anna ("the same low craving for distinction, . . . the same happy facility in deviating from the ways of truth") and described as having a character "such as to qualify him for shining at a county court bar, in defence of a fellow charged with horse stealing, particularly if the case were a bad one and required dexterous tampering with witnesses."[26]

315

A less thick-skinned man than Pillow might have preferred to suppress material of this kind. His point, however, was that he had done nothing unusual in encouraging accounts of himself to be printed in the newspapers, or in corresponding with friends in Washington. If he used Major Burns as his intermediary, Scott could be argued to have done the same with Colonel Hitchcock. If Pillow corresponded with the President, to Scott's detriment, then Scott's friend Trist had corresponded with the Secretary of State to Pillow's detriment.

The cases were of course not strictly comparable. Scott was Pillow's commander; Hitchcock's letter, unlike those inspired by Pillow, was not explicitly devised for publication; Scott's dispatches, unlike those of Pillow, were relatively modest in tone and generous to other officers. A court of inquiry held a century afterward would probably not have contented itself, as this one did, with gentle disapprobation of Pillow's conduct on one matter. But the whole issue was in 1847–1848 hopelessly confused. There were no clear grounds for censuring Pillow.

Above all, he was Polk's friend. Polk, in common with many Americans of the period, understood the factions within the army not simply in political terms, but as proceeding from politics. He erred in doing so, but not totally. He was unfair to suppose, as he wrote in his diary at the end of the long controversy, that "Gen'l. Pillow is a gallant and highly meritorious officer [who] has been greatly persecuted by Gen'l Scott, for no other known reason than that he is a Democrat in his politics and was supposed to be my personal and political friend." Scott had no difficulty with other Democratic volunteer generals like Quitman and Shields. Pillow was a braggart and an intriguer, whose lack of military talent was to be dismally confirmed in his subsequent service with the Confederacy, when he abandoned his troops at Fort Donelson and left them to a leaderless surrender. Yet political calculations *were* inescapable and sometimes dominant during the Mexican War. Scott and Taylor *were* potential Whig candidates; Taylor *did* become President a couple of years afterward. Nor could it be said that volunteer officers were the only troublemakers. Worth and Duncan were as fractious as Pillow, if less devious. Regular soldiers attached to the staffs of volunteer generals were apt to display a partisan spirit which though not necessarily "political," at any rate showed a ready disposition to stake their own advancement on supporting their military patron. Captain Joseph Hooker (U.S.M.A. 1837), who served as Pillow's chief of staff, no doubt deserved the praise his commander bestowed upon him; he reciprocated by upholding Pillow at the court of inquiry. Some regulars and some volunteers held aloof from controversy. For the rest, there was no marked difference between the professional warrior and the amateur.

The story of the Mexican War is unedifying. It must be said that, by the test of previous experience, Americans may have felt that they could afford so much dissension. The British in the Revolutionary War and the Mexicans in 1846–1848 revealed after all an even more unedifying degree of dissension — and elements of corruption. If the War of 1812 terminated luckily, it could be taken as additional proof that the Almighty had the United States under protection.

More importantly, it must be stressed that in none of the four major wars — 1776–1783, 1812–1814, 1846–1848, 1861–1865 — spanned by this book could military considerations simply outweigh others. The Revolutionary War, like that of 1861–1865, was a civil war in which every military problem was bound to have other overtones. The War of 1812 and the Mexican War, if not exactly civil wars, were nevertheless highly unpopular. Each was condemned on more than mere partisan grounds by the opposition party — Federalist, Whig. In 1812, we recall, more than two out of every five congressmen voted against the proposed declaration of war. In 1846, fourteen representatives and two senators rejected Polk's war message; three more senators, including John C. Calhoun, abstained. In the House, sixty-seven Whigs voted against the first war appropriation bill. A Kentucky congressman cried: "It is our own President who began this war."

We can see why in the War of 1812 "Federalists were almost entirely excluded" when it came to awarding army commissions.*

* Scott, *Memoirs* (2 vols., New York, 1864), I, 35. Writing long after the event, Scott, originally a Jeffersonian Republican, deplored this party vendetta. One wonders how he himself would have reacted at the time, if there had been a large influx of Federalist officers.

We can see why, with this national aura of mistrust, Polk should have leaned so heavily upon Democratic military appointees. Political patronage is not the entire answer; there was something rabid in the wartime atmosphere. Congressional rhetoric was floridly classical in the decades leading up to 1865. Much of the allusion to treason and tyranny, Caesar and Catiline can be discounted as oratorical ornament; yet not all. The country *was* divided; the division *was* taken seriously.

THE CIVIL WAR

Such considerations apply even more to *the* Civil War of 1861–1865. To them must be added the persisting confusion of responsibility. Codes of behavior and chains of command were, as we have seen, equally ill-defined. There was a rough recognition that the President was commander in chief, and that if he were strong-willed, like Polk, he might assume a great deal of authority. The Secretary of War was his civilian representative. But a Secretary of War such as Edwin Stanton could contrive to influence policy in ways not necessarily in accord with those of the President. The relations between the Secretary of War and the general in chief were even less well defined and less satisfactory, if possible, than in equivalent situations in European countries. Secretary of War Jefferson Davis and General in Chief Winfield Scott were on the worst of terms. The role of such officials as the adjutant general was open to debate. Though a surprisingly high proportion of regular soldiers were on staff duties, even in peacetime, the notion of staff work was hazy in the extreme. When Halleck was created general in chief in 1862, neither he nor the

President nor anyone else was quite sure what he could do or ought to do. Despite the growing use of the telegraph, communications were erratic. Information which ought to have been confidential was broadcast, or never reached the intended recipient. On the eve of the Peninsula Campaign, McClellan first learned from a newspaper of Lincoln's order of March 8, 1862, divesting him of the general-in-chiefship and restricting him to command of the Army of the Potomac. Fitz-John Porter, court-martialed a few months later, was left in ignorance of the verdict and had to glean the news of his disgrace from a journalist encountered in the street.[27] Muddle and resentment were occasioned in many other instances, when some senior officer got word of a change affecting him through the press or through private correspondence, sometimes in garbled form, before official orders reached him. Fantastic rumors were current in the war years, often of plots aiming at military dictatorship, and gained credence by appearing in print.

The Union army did have legitimate grievances against politics and politicians in the Civil War, at least according to its own lights. There were the initial and continuing senior appointments dished out to the Bankses, the Butlers, the Schenckses, the McClernands. There was the prodigious politicking, at all levels, of the (predominantly) volunteer army: the elections within units to choose company officers, the power left in the hands of state governors to nominate field officers, the maneuvers of congressmen to promote their friends and demote their enemies. There was the constant interference with the formations fighting near to Washington. Given the muddled American military heritage, and his own consequent uncertainty, it is hard not to sympathize with McClellan in 1861–1862. Whatever his failings, he behaved no worse, to say the least, than his predecessor Scott might have done in similarly trying circumstances. He was not the first or the last soldier to complain that the damned civilians were trying to run him. Those who came after, when matters were somewhat better regulated, still detested their proximity to Washington. John Sedgwick, as a corps commander under General George G. Meade, received a letter in November 1863 from an old lady

This lithograph is a jibe at General McClellan, shown daydreaming at his Harrison's Landing headquarters during the Peninsula campaign of 1862. The caption pointedly adds: "See evidence before Committee on conduct of the War."

which concluded: "May God preserve you from all dangers in the battle field and in the camp, and especially from commanding the Army of the Potomac." Sedgwick commented that from this last danger he was safe: "I know my name has been mentioned, . . . but nothing could induce me to take it. Meade is twenty years older than when he took command."[28]

Above all, regulars within reach of Washington — which in greater or lesser degrees meant most of them — had cause to fear and loathe the activities of the Committee on the Conduct of the War which Congress established in December 1861. Its terms of reference were sweeping. Its members were not only unversed in military affairs: they looked with suspicion on any soldier who had been at West Point. They were the spokesmen of the extreme, radical wing of the Republican party; the Committee's two Democratic members were largely ignored. The ferocity of the radicals is displayed in a typical subsequent utterance of one of the Committee, George W. Julian of Indiana:

Democratic policy, in the year 1861, gave us as commanders of our three great military departments McClellan, Halleck, and Buell, whose military administrations have so terribly cursed the country; while it impressed upon our volunteer forces in the field such officers as Fitz-John Porter, General Nelson, General Stone, and very many more whose sympathies with the rebels were well known throughout the country.

Porter and Charles Stone were of course regulars. William ("Old Bull") Nelson was a former naval officer — obligingly removed from the Committee's list by an aggrieved comrade who shot him dead in September 1862. Julian went on:

Of the major- and brigadier-generals in our armies Democratic policy has favored the Republican administration, if I am not mistaken, with over four-fifths, — certainly an overwhelming majority; while those great hives of military patronage the Adjutant-general's Department, the Quartermaster's Department, the Commissary Department, the Ordnance Department, and the Pay Department are all under Democratic control and have been during the war.[29]

Senator Benjamin F. Wade, Senator Zachariah Chandler, Representative Julian and the other prime movers on the Committee were supported by a good many members of Congress, by influential newspapers such as Greeley's *New York Tribune* and Raymond's *New York Times,* and by a large section of the public. They regarded Lincoln as weak, evasive, and lukewarm on the slavery issue. They convinced themselves that the army, thanks largely to West Point, was beset with apathy and defeatism, and that any officer known to be a Democrat was guilty of these sins until proved innocent.

Stanton shared their creed, and gave audience to Wade and Chandler every day that Congress was in session. It was Stanton who clapped General Charles P. Stone under arrest, and then denied him a fair hearing, after the fiasco at Ball's Bluff which led to the establishment of the Committee. Its members, eager to believe the worst, decided that Stone was guilty of treasonable relations with the enemy, and harried an innocent man into ignominy and imprisonment. Stone was released after six months and served again, but never in positions of responsibility. After the war he was almost a man without a country. His wanderings took him to Egypt, where he became chief of staff of the Khedive's army. Pasha Stone eventually returned to the United States and in his closing days, with an irony that cannot have been lost on him, was entrusted with the construction of the pedestal for the Statue of Liberty in New York harbor.[30]

The Committee treated other suspect generals with the same scant ceremony. Witnesses appeared alone, sometimes to find they were being interrogated by only one or two members of the Committee. Relevant testimony was withheld; they did not know whether they were merely witnesses or whether like Stone they had been selected as victims. At least, soldiers who were under suspicion of "disloyalty" were handled in this fashion; the Committee maintained a dossier of the known or supposed political views of senior officers. It opposed the promotion or recommended the dismissal of men who did not meet its requirements. The Committee was by contrast heavily biased in favor of "reliable" citizen-soldiers such as Benjamin Butler, Lew Wallace and John C. Frémont. It encouraged officers thought to be radical in sentiment, planned military policy so as to push these officers forward, and thus helped to split the army into rival factions by setting one commander against another.

In vain might McClellan protest that his Democratic leanings held no military significance. As the spring of 1862 approached without apparent signs of haste on his part, the Committee grew almost morbidly suspicious. His plan to withdraw from the Washington front and advance on Richmond from the east, by way of the James Peninsula, struck them as not merely weak but possibly treacherous. At their insistence Lincoln ordered McClellan to regroup the twelve divisions of the Army of the Potomac into four corps under the senior division commanders, Irvin McDowell, S. P. Heintzelman, E. V. Sumner and Erasmus Keyes. The first three men had voted against McClellan's scheme at a previous conference, while Keyes had supported it only with reservations. All four, moreover, were considered "radicals," whereas the other divisional commanders — now to be their juniors — were for the most part politically "conservative," and strong supporters of McClellan. The immediate defenses of Washington were placed under the command of a political appointee, Brigadier General James S. Wadsworth of New York. Another political general, Nathaniel P. Banks of Massachusetts, was to be entrusted with a separate corps created from the forces in the Harpers Ferry–Shenandoah Valley area.[31] The radicals and Stanton also convinced Lincoln that McClellan had unduly weakened the defensive line covering Washington. On their urging he decided to withhold McDowell's corps from McClellan's Peninsula expedition. It is conceivable that the Committee may have had ulterior, party motives, akin to those of Polk in the Mexican War. According to this theory, the radicals did not believe that the capital was in serious danger: they hoped to give their man McDowell a chance to dash forward and capture Richmond while McClellan was embroiled elsewhere with the main Confederate army.

The Peninsula Campaign proved inconclusive. The radicals then backed John Pope, and ensured his promotion over McClellan in the summer of 1862. The defeat at Second Bull Run destroyed most of Pope's glamour, but he was let off lightly. Popular hostility was directed instead at Fitz-John Porter, a warm admirer of McClellan. Porter, serving as a corps commander in the Bull Run battle, was denounced by Pope and by McDowell (another corps commander). Accused of deliberately sabotaging Pope's maneuvers, Porter was found guilty at a court-martial arranged by Stanton, and cashiered. This miscarriage of justice, on a level with the deplorable treatment of General Stone, was not finally corrected until 1886.

The Committee's desire for vengeance was aroused by the

further Union defeat at Fredericksburg in December 1862.* Four Committee members descended on the camp of Pope's successor, Ambrose Burnside, to collect testimony. Burnside was a friend of McClellan. But he escaped their wrath by revising his opinions: he assured his inquisitors that far from condoning slavery he was working to end it. Reassured that Burnside's heart, and so presumably his head, was in the right place, the Committee sought another scapegoat for the Fredericksburg disaster. They found an acceptable victim in one of Burnside's generals, William B. Franklin. Though Franklin was more fortunate than Stone or Porter, he was never again given an important command. Once a highly regarded professional, he resigned from the army in despair in 1866.

Committee members were, following the familiar pattern, lenient with General Joe Hooker, a fellow radical; they allowed him to escape censure after his inglorious performance at Chancellorsville in May 1863. They were less inclined to look kindly upon Hooker's successor George Meade (a conservative). Though they could not demand Meade's dismissal for his generalship at Gettysburg in July 1863, they criticized his subsequent slowness and gradually began to hound him: hence the force of Sedgwick's remark that "Meade is twenty years older than when he took command." They were not sure what to make of General Grant. Then he too incurred their displeasure for the inconclusive and bloody Wilderness Campaign of 1864, and they urged the President to add Grant's name to the dismal roll of rejected generals.

There could well have been a committee to investigate the conduct of the Committee on the Conduct of the War. Or so some of the Union's luckless generals might have felt. There was some substance, along with exaggeration, in the comment of *The Times* of London that America's Jacobins were repeating the extremist tendencies of the French Revolution: "The denunciation is precisely the same as those launched against the Girondins by the Mountain in the old French Convention. Disasters in the field

* Politics of another sort may have been involved in the removal from their commands in November 1862 of McClellan, Porter and Buell, all Democrats. Their fall was not announced until after the midterm congressional elections. Warren G. Hassler, *McClellan: Shield of the Union* (Baton Rouge, 1957), 314–322.

have divided the Republican Party, and the zealots impute the reverses, not to the want of generals able to win victories, but to lack of faith in a principle."[32] Vigilantism was rife. But then, the crisis was acute; and not all the faults were on one side.

This was, to reiterate, a civil war, with some of the elements of a revolution. In the confusion, opportunities for corruption abounded; it is hardly surprising that the venal side of politics — bribery, toadying, influence-peddling — flourished. Yet many Americans regarded politics in a higher spirit. It was one of the mechanisms which might enable the Union to wrest victory out of dire emergency. The New Yorker George Templeton Strong, an active member of the Sanitary Commission, recorded in his diary an argument at the Union League Club, shortly before the 1864 presidential election. The Club had drawn up a resolution that its duty was to use its influence to promote the reelection of Lincoln. A few members objected on the ground that this would convert the Club into a "mere political machine." Strong exploded: "A 'mere political machine,' indeed! What subject of human thought and action is higher than politics, except only religion? What political issues have arisen for centuries more momentous than those dependent on this election? They are to determine the destinies . . . of the millions and millions who are to live on this continent for many generations to come."

Politics was in this sense far more than a corrupt game. The crisis was deeper and deadlier in its divisiveness than that of the Mexican War. The response was inevitably more alarmist. If the congressional radicals exceeded the proper limits of their authority, so by normal standards did the President — by expending money without previous sanction, by suppressing newspapers and arresting civilians. Accusation and counteraccusation were therefore virulent in the extreme. Stanton and the Committee on the Conduct of the War suspected McClellan of treasonable sloth: McClellan in his memoirs charged Stanton with "treasonable conspiracy."[33]

Even for those who behaved more coolly, political could not be separated from military issues. Should the war be pressed hard against the South? Against all parts, or against certain regions?

Should the border states be treated gently, in order not to drive them into the Confederacy? What should be done about slavery, not merely in the abstract but as a practical and urgent problem facing Union commanders? Should they respect Southern property, and return escaped slaves to their owners? Or should they treat the runaways as "contraband of war" (Butler's solution), or declare them liberated (Frémont's view)? Should the aim be to reach a settlement with the South and seek a swift end to the fighting, or to shatter the slavocracy as the only sure means of reconstituting its social base? Should Northern morale be sustained by the avoidance of heavy casualties, or by waging aggressive warfare? There was unanimity neither in the government nor in the army on such thorny and fundamental questions.

From the standpoint of energetic Union men, a number of propositions seemed incontrovertible. The training of regular soldiers, in this view, made them too deliberate, too fortification-minded. Second, regulars were by training and association committed to a warped idea of the Union. The annual Boards of Visitors had kept on assuring the American public that West Point imbued cadets with a love of the Union. But a large number of West Pointers had joined the rebellion. The affection they appeared to show was for one another: an affection that made Northern West Pointers reluctant to strike hard against their Confederate fraternity.* Hence the recurrent rumor that such-and-such a Union general, under criticism for sluggishness, had actually slipped across the lines to consort with the enemy commander. In the third place, it was assumed that most Democrats were untrustworthy, and could only exculpate themselves — like Benjamin F. Butler — by displaying the fanaticism of the newly converted. A Democrat was a potential Copperhead; some Democrats, such as Manton Marble, editor of the *New York World*, were regarded as vicious traitors. It followed, fourthly, that the most dangerous of Union commanders was a West Point

* The radicals would have been angered but not surprised if they could have read the diary entry for 6 May 1861 of the retired soldier Ethan Allen Hitchcock: "Many friends urge my return to the army. But I have no heart for engaging in a civil war. . . . If fighting could preserve the Union (or restore it) I might consider what I could do to take part — but when did fighting make friends?" *Fifty Years in Camp and Field*, ed. W. A. Croffut (New York, 1909), 430.

graduate who admitted to being a Democrat and who had close social or family ties with the Confederacy. According to this rough yet not entirely absurd formula, several Union commanders were objects of legitimate suspicion. Don Carlos Buell, for example, was a cousin of old Daniel Twiggs, the general who surrendered the Department of Texas to the Confederacy in 1861 and then joined the rebellion. George Meade was the brother-in-law of the Confederate general Henry A. Wise, the former governor of Virginia. A cousin of McClellan served as chief of staff to the Confederate generals J. E. B. Stuart and Wade Hampton.

Such prejudice was not confined to Northern radicals. Indeed the very term "radical" is misleading. The Committee on the Conduct of the War was not the only voice of vehement Republicanism. Secretary of War Stanton was at least as implacable as the Committee. Lincoln, though attacked by extreme antislavery men as weak and conservative, was himself impatient with McClellan and other generals who seemed to be dragging their feet. So was his Secretary of the Treasury, Salmon P. Chase, who was not much impressed by Stanton or Lincoln. Though the reports of the Committee no doubt inflamed public opinion, members of the public such as G. T. Strong were already disposed to share their restless inquisitorial attitudes. After the defeat at Fredericksburg Strong expressed his fear that "Franklin and many of his brethren are, like the late General Fitz-John Porter, bad cases of blood poisoning and paralysis from hypertrophied McClellanism." As late as November 1864, Strong was still an enthusiastic admirer of Benjamin Butler. Butler might not have won brilliant victories: the important thing was that he was a true Union man, a "terrier" well able to deal with Copperhead "rats."[34]

The Committee, in other words, typified a fairly widespread Northern viewpoint. To see this as a contest between Republican zealots or intriguers and hapless West Pointers is to distort and oversimplify. Not all "political" generals were upheld: though the loyalty of N. P. Banks was not considered doubtful, he became as unpopular with the Committee on military grounds as were certain of the regulars. Nor were the regulars uniformly castigated. The Committee, in common with many American civilians, refused to accept the claim that professional training was an essential prerequisite for generalship. But at various times it eagerly urged the claims of regulars deemed to be of the right stamp: William S. Rosecrans in the West, McDowell, Pope and Hooker in the East.

Possibly the regulars were contaminated by the political atmosphere. One may argue that they were forced into partnership by the realization that the only chance of promotion, and sometimes of survival, lay in a real or apparent conversion to radicalism. Similarly, one may contend that as in the Mexican War, the more prominent generals were forced into political awareness by being openly discussed as presidential timber. This could be seen as McClellan's fate, when he became the somewhat reluctant Democratic nominee in 1864. Certainly political strategists knew that any general who achieved conspicuous success in an important command, especially in the East, was automatically entered for the presidential stakes. Lincoln's famous letter to Hooker of January 1863, appointing him commander of the Army of the Potomac, may be interpreted in this light. Lincoln praised Hooker as one who did not "mix politics with your profession." He went on: "I have heard, in such a way as to believe it, of your recently saying that both the Army and the Government needed a Dictator. . . . Only those generals who gain successes, can set up dictators. What I now ask of you is military success, and I will risk the dictatorship." A letter full of the humorous sagacity for which Lincoln is justly admired. Yet it is also a sharp warning to Hooker *not* to meddle with President-making, on the assumption that he is very likely to be impelled to do so if he gains a victory. A few months later, when a successor to Hooker was being sought, the administration may have been stimulated to prefer Meade to John F. Reynolds on the ground that Meade, having been born abroad (his father was in the consular service), was thereby disqualified from becoming a presidential possibility. In 1864 Grant was being boosted for the White House; the *New York Herald* acclaimed him as "the man who knows how to tan leather, politicians and the hides of rebels." According to one account Lincoln delayed naming Grant to the command of the

Union armies until he had received an assurance — via J. Russell Jones, the U. S. marshal in Chicago and a confidant of Grant's — that the general had no intention of trying for the presidency, despite the encouraging chorus from Democratic newspapers.[35]

Grant and Sherman were unusual among Union commanders in their distaste for political intrigue. This is not to say that they had no awareness of political nuances. Grant was after all only renouncing his chance of nomination for the coming election of 1864. The next time round, 1868, he was in fact the Republican candidate. Even in 1864 he could hardly fail to realize how much was at stake in Lincoln's campaign for reelection. He and other generals responded readily to the administration's appeal to send soldiers home on leave to sway the vote in doubtful states. Some states allowed their soldiers to vote in the field. Whether or not generals acquiesced, there is evidence that these votes were rigged to ensure Republican victory. Grant dispatched a telegram to Lincoln the day after polling to inform him that the Sixth Corps had turned in a Republican majority of over twenty thousand. One biographer of Grant, citing the telegram, adds: "he was practically Jim Farley." Not quite; still, the point is worth making.[36]

Most Union generals, through whatever mixture of conviction and self-interest, displayed rather than disguised their political leanings. Burnside, Halleck, Hooker, McClellan, Rosecrans, Sherman, Stone and Grant were among the regulars who had left the army before the war. Some of them — including McClellan, a railroad executive and a Douglas Democrat — had quite well-defined political opinions. Ambrose Burnside, who resigned his commission in 1853, had run unsuccessfully as a Democratic candidate for Congress in Rhode Island before joining his friend McClellan in the Illinois Central. In the growing sectional crisis they could not help but form "views" — views which as civilians they were perfectly entitled to hold and express. Hooker, who also resigned in 1853, had particular reasons to regard himself as a civilian. He had taken Pillow's side in the Pillow-Scott controversy during the Mexican War. When he first offered his services to the army in 1861 he was snubbed by the War Department. The most plausible explanation was that he was being victimized by General Scott's regular subordinates. A number of serving regulars held or developed firm political convictions.

So while the Committee on the Conduct of the War may be blamed for forcing political alignments upon the Union generals, it cannot be said that the soldiers themselves were utterly apolitical. As we have noted, McDowell, Pope, Hooker, David Hunter and others declared themselves to be radical. McClellan insisted in his memoirs that he was innocent of political ambition. No doubt this was true at the outset. Yet despite himself he followed the path of Winfield Scott. He was a hero; he began to believe what he was told by his admirers, or by people who shared his resentment at the Republican administration — that he was a genius whose country needed him at the head of its councils. Once he was sufficiently famous he was automatically a candidate for the presidency. As with Scott, his very fall from favor not only spurred his ambition and rancor but also made him the more attractive to the opposition party.

The most balanced assessment of the situation is that of Jacob Dolson Cox. This Ohio politician, who became a major general and a corps commander, was a former brigadier general of militia. Though he had never worn a uniform in peacetime he claims to have long been interested in tactics and strategy. The volunteer battalions had, he concedes, many defects; they often went wrong, for example, in their initial choice of officers. But the worst errors were remedied, and the mass of young volunteer officers showed both ability and adaptability. As for the so-called "political generals," he wisely remarks:

In an armed struggle which grew out of a great political contest, it was inevitable that eager political partisans should be among the most active in the new volunteer organizations. They called meetings, addressed the people to arouse their enthusiasm, urged enlistments, and often set the example by enrolling their own names first. . . . It was a foregone conclusion that popular leaders of all grades must largely officer the new troops. . . . It was the application of the old Yankee story, "If the Lord *will* have a church in Paxton, he must take *sech as ther' be* for deacons."

Cox admits that in a sense "the whole organization of the volunteer force might be said to be political," but that "we heard more of 'political generals' than we did of political captains or lieutenants."[37] The infusion of politics at all levels, from the narrow matter of party patronage to the broadest and highest matters of Union policy, was thus not merely inevitable but even desirable.

On the question of patronage appointments, the West Point complaint was that senior commands were entrusted to men of no military talent, some of whom had got in by the door marked "push" and some by the door marked "pull." Could *anything* be said in praise of a Banks or a Butler, a McClernand, a Daniel Sickles, a Franz Sigel, or (on the Confederate side) a Gideon Pillow, a Howell Cobb or a Felix Zollicoffer? The most obvious answer is that Lincoln (and Davis, to a lesser extent) were obliged to appoint such men, or to accept them on pressing recommendation. There were not enough West Pointers to go round. Lincoln needed Sigel because Sigel was German-born and a leader in the St. Louis community. As such he was a valuable bellwether for German-Americans: "I fights mit Sigel" was said to be their slogan. Moreover, Sigel was a graduate of a military academy and had served in the German army. He had been active in the militia since he arrived in the United States. It was reasonable until events proved otherwise to assume that Sigel might be another Steuben or de Kalb. Benjamin Butler's prewar militia experience, his energy and confidence, and his standing as a War Democrat made him too important to be brushed aside. Banks, a former congressman and governor of Massachusetts, sounded like a politico and had a somewhat unimpressive war record, culminating in his resignation after the Red River fiasco in 1864. But he was a man of courage who held a series of thankless commands, and who had some grounds (like General John A. Logan, the former Democratic congressman from Illinois) for believing that he was discriminated against by a West Point coterie. James S. Wadsworth was a radical Republican who interrupted his military service to run unsuccessfully for the governorship of New York: he was also a gallant leader who returned to the army, commanded a division at Chancellorsville and Gettysburg, and was mortally wounded in the Wilderness in 1864. The overriding fact, as Butler and Logan were to insist in later years, was that long before the end of the war every important command was in the hands of a regular soldier. The most that "political" or "civilian" soldiers could hope for was a subordinate role, or command of an unpromising sideshow like the Red River campaign. In other words, the professionals had no more reason to complain of this political feature of the war than of radical efforts to determine strategy.

The Committee on the Conduct of the War did behave arbitrarily. But insofar as there *was* a "West Point mentality," the Committee and its supporters were not entirely wrong to equate this with sluggishness. Though the wrong men — Buell, Porter — may have been hounded, there was a case for punishing a few commanders *pour encourager les autres.* Insofar as the West Pointers shared the same uncertainties and prejudices — including political ones — as the rest of their countrymen, the Committee was not entirely wrong in treating them accordingly.

While there was therefore a kind of *esprit de corps* among regulars, before and during the Civil War, its effects were limited. The professionals sometimes thought of themselves as an entity when they were threatened *as an entity* by outsiders, or believed they were. Their chief complaint was against politics and politicians because these were convenient shorthand terms. "Politics" covered a multitude of actual or fancied forms of neglect, ingratitude, injustice, disappointment. Like soldiers in other armies, who have looked forward to peacetime "in order to get back to real soldiering," they attributed to the military sphere everything that was simple, clear, honest and heroic, and to the political sphere everything that was tangled, discordant, frustrating and treacherous.

They were in fact, of course, far from united on most issues. In the Civil War the Union seemed at moments to be more at war with itself than with the Confederacy. They bickered over minor points, they split wide apart on the major issues of the war. Their factious quarrels spilled out in courts of inquiry, court-martials and even occasional duels. They were following the confused tradition of American civil-military relations.

The regular officers were then not a caste apart, absorbed in their craft and unaware of political contexts. It must be added though that their behavior was as a whole healthily strident. As the articles in the *Army & Navy Chronicle* of 1836–1837 had revealed, there were at least two sides to the problem of the involvement of soldiers in politics. The pure, apolitical professional was apt to be too much cut off from the life of his country. He could degenerate into the outlook of a mercenary. Or, through disdain and conceit, he could conceive of himself as a privileged and powerful janissary. At the other extreme, the too thoroughly civilianized soldier was equally dangerous: nonmilitary factors played too large a part in his thinking.

Both of these extreme tendencies could be seen in other countries. The United States has not had "men on horseback" though it has had a number of generals in the White House. Among presidential aspirants, only the semi-civilian soldiers have carried the day. Those with vainglorious, proconsular temperaments have failed to satisfy the electorate. The public has, to use a distinction drawn by T. Harry Williams, preferred the "Ikes" to the "Macs" — Taylor to Scott, Grant to McClellan. Bearing in mind the deficiencies of Scott and McClellan, we may be glad that Democratic intrigue ruined the chances of the one, and Republican intrigue the chances of the other; if Polk and Lincoln, and their henchmen, had acted with high-minded generosity toward these contenders, it is conceivable that both generals might have gained the presidency. It is almost certain that they would have made bad Presidents. It is, however, also almost certain that neither would have indulged his grandiose egotism to the extent of subverting the Constitution. Though their heads were turned by ambition and flattery, they were still sane. In the 1860's there was a great deal of talk in the North, among soldiers and civilians alike, of the need for a strong man, a leader, a Cromwell, to save the Union. The need remained a matter of talk. None of the putative Napoleons took any positive step to assume control. When challenged, the men on horseback were quick to dismount. There was no real threat of a *coup d' état*. None went even as far toward power as France's abortive hero of the 1870's, General Boulanger.[38]

Neither before nor during the Civil War did America solve the problem of how to steer neatly between the extremes of civilianness and militarism. But then, no other country has discovered the exact range of appropriate compromises. This is a problem without a perfect solution. The American answer leaned toward civilianness. In the words of "Alcibiades," writing in the *Army & Navy Chronicle* in January 1836:

> If a military officer feels no interest in the important political struggles of the day, . . . he acknowledges himself at once to be . . . a hireling . . . who would serve the *Russian Autocrat*, the British King, or even Louis Philippe, provided the pay and rank were sufficient temptation.
>
> Nearly every officer of any distinction, at the commencement of the American Revolution, was a politician. . . . Politics filled our early councils with those who had . . . wielded the sword against the enemies of liberty. . . . Look to the late war with England! Were not many of the most distinguished officers of that period politicians, most of whom still live to prove the truth of the assertion?

The West Pointers were professional to the extent that they thought themselves better than amateurs, and gave preference to their own kind where they had the opportunity, as Sherman did in picking O. O. Howard rather than John A. Logan to command the Army of the Tennessee after the death in action of James B. McPherson. Otherwise they were quite deeply immersed in civilianness. If they had not been, perhaps fewer would have abandoned the Union and gone over to the Confederacy. But their critics were inconsistent in reproaching them simultaneously for being an aristocratic coterie *and* for responding so representatively to the emotions that swayed their fellow countrymen. Many of the professional politicians were amateur soldiers. Many of the professional soldiers were amateur politicians. The interfusion made things awkward; it helped to prevent them from becoming catastrophic.

10

A SOUTHERN MILITARY TRADITION?

You and I see already rising in the West, where military feeling is rife, a spirit which will not brook much longer the insults already cast upon the flag of the country. . . . If you have any misapprehension about the Northern people — if you suppose that because . . . they are not fired by your hot blood, they will not perform their duty . . ., you are very much mistaken. We are the equals of each other; we are of the same blood, the same parentage, the same character.

> — John Sherman, House of Representatives, 18 January 1861

At the wedding breakfast given for General Magruder's niece at the mansion of the governor-general of Canada, the governor asked [General Pickett] to what he attributed the failure of the Confederates at Gettysburg. With a twinkle in his eyes, he replied, "Well, I think the Yankees had a little something to do with it."

> — *The Heart of a Soldier: As Revealed in the Intimate Letters of Genl. George Pickett, C.S.A.*, New York, 1913; introduction by Mrs. La Salle Corbell Pickett

---

In all the southern states, they have succeeded in impressing the public mind that the North is governed by a mob (of which unfortunately there is too much truth) and in the South that all is chivalry and gentility.

> — William T. Sherman, 17 August 1861

The cry was in the air that the North only won by brute force; that the generalship and valor were with the South. This has gone into history, with so many other illusions.

> — Ulysses S. Grant, in John R. Young, *Around the World with General Grant*, 1879

HISTORIANS AND THE TRADITION

It has been suggested in the two previous chapters that some of the familiar generalizations of American military history are of doubtful value. There is a further generalization, more widely accepted and more comprehensively documented: namely, that insofar as the antebellum United States had a military tradition, this was largely confined to the South.

The theme of Southern militance has been developed by a numerous company of scholars. In an article published in *Current History* (1929), Robert D. Meade asserted that Southerners "started" the War of 1812 and the Mexican War. "To the Mexican War the South supplied over 46,000 troops, or twice as many as did the North, and in both wars almost all the outstanding Generals." The Southern military tradition was most conspicuous in Virginia and South Carolina. Virginia might be called the "Mother of Generals," since its products included George Washington, William Henry Harrison, Winfield Scott, Zachary Taylor, J. E. B. Stuart, Thomas J. Jackson, G. H. Thomas, Joseph E. Johnston and Robert E. Lee. The main reason for this preponderance was that "before the Civil War the Southern aristocracy considered only the learned professions, agriculture or soldiering as fit employment for their sons." A habit of several generations thus gave the South a disproportionate place in the officer class of the regular army. The contrast between North and South could be dramatized by comparing, through the whole nineteenth century, the careers followed by prominent families in Massachusetts and in Virginia. Seven "representative" Massachusetts families — Channing, Brooks, Cabot, Wendell, Lee, Lowell, Phillips — contributed only nine army officers. In Virginia the Lees alone "furnished ten officers, four of whom later attained in the Confederate Army the rank of Major General." The Randolphs of Virginia produced ten army officers in the same period.

Meade's argument is taken further in a subsequent article by James C. Bonner, in the *Georgia Review* (1955), which adds the reflection that "of all the presidents of the United States born in the South, eighty per cent had seen military service prior to their election. . . . In direct contrast, of those born elsewhere eighty per cent were without military experience of any kind."[1]

Similar propositions are offered by a literary historian, Willard Thorp, in a 1955 anthology entitled *A Southern Reader*. Thorp traces the Southern military tradition back into colonial times, with their recurrent Indian wars. He adds that it was nourished not only by the formation of Texas and the contest with Mexico, but also by "the Southerner's acceptance of violence as part of life, by the aristocratic duel and the frontier gouging. And it was perpetuated by the survival of the militia system from colonial days. The county militia enrolled every able-bodied man and expected him to keep ready at home a musket and ammunition." In such an atmosphere it was natural for the Southerner to believe that "military discipline was moral discipline, that it taught diligence, order, and restraint and was as necessary to the development of the successful gentleman as the training of the mind given by the more academic studies." Hence the spread of military academies: V.M.I., the Citadel, Georgia Military Institute.

According to Thorp, literature contributed to the tradition:

The Southerner, partly out of a subconscious need to find justification for a distinctly feudal social and economic system, read heavily in [Sir Walter] Scott, and in such Southern novels as Carruthers's *Knights of the Golden Horseshoe*, Kennedy's *Horseshoe Robinson*,

Simms's *The Partisan*. In them he found . . . an idealized picture of chivalric warfare which went far to make acceptable the dashing bravado of such men as Jeb Stuart and the perhaps overgenerous chivalry of Lee.[2]

Aspects of Southern chivalry, including duels and tournaments, are analyzed in an earlier work, *Romanticism and Nationalism in the Old South* (1949), by Rollin G. Osterweis, with much the same conclusions. He does not go quite as far as Mark Twain, who maintained in *Life on the Mississippi* that Sir Walter Scott "had so large a hand in making Southern character, as it existed before the War, that he is in great measure responsible for the War." Osterweis does not believe that there was a "Sir Walter disease." Nevertheless he devotes a chapter to Scott and other influences in literary romanticism, in order to demonstrate that the South responded readily to notions of knighthood and of clannish patriotism. From Scott, apparently, came the word "Southron" which gentlemen of the slave states took for their own — though it was in fact used by Scott's heroes as a term of contempt. From Scott, Osterweis believes, came the Southern tendency to refer to Northerners as "Saxons" (men of low birth) and themselves as "Normans" (a knightly, warrior society). A Southern poem in praise of a gallant horse named Grey Bayard echoes the name of Fitz-James's charger in Scott's *Lady of the Lake*. In a tournament staged at Fauquier White Sulphur Springs, Virginia, in 1845, the contestants enrolled under such sobriquets as "Brian de Bois-Guilbert" and "Wilfred of Ivanhoe."[3]

Details of these neomediaeval pastimes are given in *The Ring Tournament in the United States* (1936), by Esther J. Crooks and Ruth W. Crooks. Nearly all the examples they cite are of jousts in the South — not of rider against rider, but of riders competing to carry off small suspended rings on the end of their lance. One of the first tournaments seems to have taken place in Maryland in 1840. "Knights" rode at the ring at Fauquier Springs, Virginia, as early as 1841. The entertainment was apparently introduced in North Carolina, South Carolina and Georgia in 1856–1857.[4]

The most circumstantial analysis is that of John Hope Franklin,

The Militant South, 1800–1861 (1956). By 1860, says Franklin, "the South claimed to be the fountainhead of martial spirit in the United States." It argued that Southern soldiers had figured decisively in the nation's wars, and that Southern theorists such as Dennis Hart Mahan and William J. Hardee furnished the treatises for the U. S. regular army. These formal skills thrived within a generally "militant" context: a context of violence, whether rough or ritualized. The man of the South was "the product of his experiences as a frontiersman, Indian fighter, slaveholder, self-sufficient yeoman, poor white, and Negro. He gladly fought, even if only to preserve his reputation as fighter." In oratory and literature, in dreams of Southern expansionism, in militia patrols and volunteer parades, in brawls and duels, at West Point and the sundry academies that Franklin calls "West Points of the South," the Southerner is held to have demonstrated his militance. With each decade the Southern predilection for violence and for military display grew more prominent, until by 1861 Southerners, in Franklin's concluding words, "were ready to fight, and this is what they would do."[5]

A political scientist, Samuel P. Huntington, substantiates some of these contentions in *The Soldier and the State* (1957), an examination of various models of civil-military relationships. Huntington maintains that "a 'Southern military tradition' existed in a way in which there was never a New England, Middle Western or Rocky Mountain military tradition." As with previous scholars, he believes that the sources of this lay in continuing Indian warfare (climaxed by the Florida war of 1836–1842), in the fear of slave revolts, in the cult of romantic chivalry and in the social patterns of an agrarian economy. More important was the conservatism of Southern thought, which "furnished a sympathetic environment for the growth of the professional ideal and channeled the military concern aroused by the other aspects of Southern life into an active recognition of the nature of the military profession and a preference for that profession as a career." The course of the Civil War revealed the different attitudes of the two sections. Whereas the Union, at least in the beginning, passed over the claims of serving officers in favor of men from civil life, the South made immediate and eager use of its professionals. Nearly two-thirds of the regular officers who joined the Confederacy became generals, as against less than one-third of those who stayed with the Union.

Southern influence was dominant in prewar military and naval matters. Secretaries of War (including Jefferson Davis under Pierce and John B. Floyd under Buchanan) were often Southerners, as were Secretaries of the Navy and congressional leaders in military affairs. A disproportionate number of West Point cadets came from the South, and the Academy acquired a strong "Southern" tinge. In the army list of 1837, three of the four active generals were Virginians; nine of the thirteen colonels of the line were Southern. Officers entrenched in senior posts were usually from the South. Among them — all Virginians — were Winfield Scott, general in chief from 1841 to 1861; Roger Jones, adjutant general from 1825 to 1852, and T. S. Jesup, quartermaster general from 1815 to 1850.

Huntington attributes to Southern enthusiasm the emergence of an "American Military Enlightenment" in the years 1832–1846. Though stimulated by the consolidation of West Point, this flowering of military scholarship was most in evidence among Southerners and in the South. It witnessed the publication of periodicals such as the *Army & Navy Chronicle,* and acknowledged the primacy of the *Southern Literary Messenger,* which by 1844 is said to have become "a sort of organ of the United States Army and Navy." The foundation of Southern military schools testified to the new interest in military professionalism. A Virginian, Dennis Mahan, established himself as the nation's foremost military theorist. Another Virginian, Matthew Fontaine Maury, was the most vigorous writer on naval reform.[6]

The same line of reasoning, as Huntington hints, is held to explain at least the initial stages of the Civil War. A typical statement is that of Benjamin P. Thomas in his well-received biography of Abraham Lincoln (1953):

The South was better prepared than the disorganized North. From the first the seceding states had foreseen the possibility of war and had begun to amass war materials and enlist troops. The Confederacy enjoyed the best of military leadership. So many careers were open in the North that Northern officers frequently resigned from the army to enter other fields; Southerners, with fewer occupations available in civil life, more often made the army a career. From the outset the Confederacy commanded the services and West Point training of such men as Robert E. Lee, Albert Sidney Johnston, Pierre G. T. Beauregard, Joseph E. Johnston, "Stonewall" Jackson, J. E. B. Stuart, James Longstreet, and A. P. Hill. Bereft of the services of many of the army's ablest officers, Lincoln had to experiment with leadership.[7]

In contrast with that glittering list of Southerners, we recall the generals whom Lincoln promoted and discarded in heartbreaking succession. We remember that the most famous — McClellan, Grant, Sherman — had quit the army several years before, and were struggling along in civilian life, shabby and obscure like Grant biding his time in Galena, or else were prosperous, like the railroad executive McClellan; but in either case they had abandoned the effort to sustain a professional military career.

CONTEMPORARY OPINION

The idea of a distinctive Southern military tradition is not a latter-day invention. It was believed in by plenty of Americans of the Civil War era, and earlier. Daniel Tyler of Connecticut (U.S.M.A. 1819) made himself an expert on artillery. He resigned from the army in 1834, having failed to secure a captaincy in the new Ordnance Corps. Invited to rejoin by Secretary of War Poinsett, Tyler replied: "My Army life has been without any reward, and I have lost all ambition to be connected with the service where politics and prejudice ruled, and where the fact that a man was not born in the South was a bar to promotion." His allusion was to the reorganized Ordnance Corps, in which all the officers but five had been selected from the South.

The Massachusetts-born Erasmus Keyes (U.S.M.A. 1832), who served at three different periods as aide to Winfield Scott, convinced himself that his chief was biased against Northern officers.

A SOUTHERN MILITARY TRADITION?

In an angry letter to President-elect Lincoln, dated 26 November 1860, Keyes begged him to appoint a Northerner as Secretary of War. He suggested Benjamin Wade or John Sherman as men who would "proceed to build up Northern officers and place them in commands proportionate with the population of the North." Southern holders of the office, Keyes alleged, had used their powers to the utmost "to build up and fit for command the young officers of Southern birth, while those from the North have been treated with neglect and contempt." A year later he repeated his charges at a Washington breakfast party attended by Secretary of the Treasury Salmon P. Chase. Similar opinions were being voiced during February and March of 1861, in far-off New Mexico. John Van Deusen Du Bois (U.S.M.A. 1855), a subaltern from New York stationed at Fort Union, must have found its name derisory. He noted in his journal on February 12 that only three of the officers were thoroughly loyal. On March 15 he wrote: "Very few officers would not prefer to serve the South, who have always treated us well, to the north who have always abused us." Two weeks later he added: "If we could only keep the West Pointers true there would be very little fighting in the south, for they could not organize and equip an army. But Jeff Davis will take with him many of our best men. The north have not a political friend in the army."[8]

Southerners themselves appeared sure of their superior military prowess. Daniel Hundley, a young Alabama lawyer, published an analysis of *Social Relations in Our Southern States* in 1860. He was no stranger to the North, for he had been to Harvard and had lived for a while in Chicago. Hundley compares the activities of Northerners, who have turned chiefly to "commerce, manufacturers, literature, and the like," with the Southern interest in "agriculture mainly, political economy, and the nurture of an adventurous and military race." The Southern gentleman obliged to follow a career is "most enamoured of politics and the Army; and it is owing to this cause, that the South has furnished us with all our great generals, from Washington to Scott, as well as most of our leading statesmen, from Jefferson to Calhoun."

Southern newspapers stated the matter more vehemently. The

Raleigh (N.C.) *Banner* of 29 April 1861 declared: "The army of the South will be composed of the best material that ever yet made up an army; whilst that of Lincoln will be gathered from the sewers of the cities — the degraded, beastly offscourings of all quarters of the world, who will serve for pay, and run away . . . when danger threatens them." The *Charleston Mercury* of 2 June 1861 explained that "our raw troops are far superior to the raw troops of the United States. Our people are used to arms. They are accustomed to the gun and the horse. The people of the North can neither shoot a rifle nor ride a horse, unless trained."[9]

A good many Northern soldiers and civilians were apparently ready to accept the Southern estimate, however reluctantly. Major Philip Kearny told an acquaintance in 1860 that while he believed the North would eventually triumph in the impending contest, they labored under serious disadvantages. They were "ignorant of the art of war"; they despised "every trained soldier as a charlatan." Man for man, the Southerners were, "I acknowledge, . . . the best soldiers." William Wetmore Story, the American sculptor, contributed a passionate plea for the Union to the London *Daily News* in 1862. He was certain that Northern genius would in time produce great amateur soldiers. For the moment, however, the South benefited greatly from "the general superiority of its officers, many of whom were trained in the North, and educated at West Point. The South, having had the lion's share of patronage, has in this as in other branches of preferment got the better of the North." After the failure of McClellan's Peninsula campaign, General John Sedgwick wrote dispiritedly to his sister in September 1862:

The army are now around Washington, occupying nearly the same positions they did last winter. The enemy have outgeneralled us. Their hearts are in the cause; our men are perfectly indifferent, think of nothing but marauding and plundering, and the officers are worse than the men. . . . On our part it has been a war of politicians; on theirs it has been one conducted by a despot and carried out by able Generals.

As late as 1864 another Union officer was almost equally angry and discouraged. The North had made little use of West Point, sending the wrong kinds of young men there:

344

in the Loyal States, the profession of arms had fallen . . . into disrepute previously to the outbreak of the Rebellion, and instead of being known as a respectable vocation was considered as none at all. Had military training . . . been connected with the common school education of the land, we would . . . have been provided with an able array of officers for our noble army of Volunteers. Among the other preparations for their infamous revolt, the Rebels did not fail to give this especial prominence.[10]

Among the other preparations . . . Most Northerners, confronted with secession, discerned signs that the South had focused its military tendencies in the service of some deep-laid plan of campaign. William T. Sherman, on his way down the Mississippi in October 1859 to take charge of the Louisiana State Seminary of Learning and Military Academy, explained in a letter to his wife that in the event of trouble he would of course not remain with the secessionists. "I merely allude to these things now," he said, "because I have heard a good deal lately about such things, and generally that the southern states, by military colleges and organizations, were looking to a dissolution of the Union." President Buchanan and his doughface cabinet, above all his Secretary of War Floyd, were considered alarmingly complaisant and perhaps treacherous. Emory Upton, a cadet in his final year at West Point, wrote home on 21 December 1860:

Floyd has sent twenty-five thousand stand of arms to different Southern posts within the past year, and for what? Certainly not for the use of soldiers garrisoning them. What, then, is the inference? That they shall be convenient for *secession*. The Administration must be deeply implicated. Its conduct can not be explained otherwise.

The charge against Floyd, investigated by the House Committee on Military Affairs, was even more weighty than Upton indicated. The accusation was that Floyd, anticipating the secession crisis, had in the spring of 1860 sent no less than 115,000 muskets and rifles to be stored in Southern arsenals. A further accusation was that he had actually disposed of 22,500 muskets by sale to various Southern states, after Lincoln's election. By the beginning of February 1861, when the Committee's report was published, Floyd had been forced from office on other charges — of financial irregularity. The report exonerated him and, by implication, Buchanan's administration. But what ardent Unionist could believe it?[11]

In 1836 a minor pseudonymous novel, *The Partisan Leader: A Tale of the Future,* was published in Washington. The actual author was a Virginian, Nathaniel Beverley Tucker, who imagined a Virginia rising in 1848–1849 against Northern oppression. In 1861 it suddenly seemed to be more than idle speculation. A New York reprint of that year carried an introduction citing the novel as evidence that "the fratricidal contest into which our country has been led is not a thing of chance but of deliberate design, and that it has been gradually preparing for almost thirty years."

A final example may be given of Northern belief that the South had conspired to turn its innate militancy to the cause of secession. In June 1864 a Union army under General David Hunter raided down the Shenandoah Valley. They destroyed much property associated with the Confederate war effort. Hunter's chief of staff, D. H. Strother, was consulted on what should be destroyed, including the Virginia Military Institute at Lexington. Strother's testimony is doubly interesting since he was a Virginia Unionist. He told General Hunter that he regarded V.M.I. as "a most dangerous establishment where treason was systematically taught." He believed "the States Rights conspirators had with subtlety and forethought established . . . the school for the express purpose of educating the youth of the country into such opinions as would render them ready . . . tools wherewith to overthrow the government . . . when the hour . . . arrived."[12]

The Thinking Bayonet was the title of a Civil War novel published in 1865 by the New England author James K. Hosmer. In it a Southern aristocrat, deriding the Northern workingmen as meek Saxons, declares: "I belong to these Normans — tamers we are! We have tamed those Saxon boors; we will tame these negroes, and some day tame still other races."[13] What Hosmer offers with hostile intent as a version of Southern character would have been maintained with pride by Southerners themselves. On this point the sections appeared to be in agreement.

ASPECTS OF MILITANCE

In face of so much assertion, there might seem no sound reason to deny the existence of a distinctive Southern military tradition, however we define the term. Some of the arguments are obviously stronger than others. We may detect a tendency to claim too much — if W. H. Harrison of Ohio (Virginia-born) was a "Southern" president, why not also A. Lincoln of Illinois (Kentucky-born)? — and still feel that the general point is valid. We do not need to accept the theory of a Southern conspiracy, including Floyd or not including Floyd, to accept the view that the slave states had a heartier appetite for violence and warfare than did the free states.

The problem is not so straightforward. For reasons which will be considered later, the story has been presented incompletely. Once "Southernness" was accepted as a fact, chroniclers and scholars were content to corroborate the familiar picture. It is not that they have falsified the record, but that they have failed to consider whether phenomena allocated to Southernness might not also be found in the North. If so, Southern distinctiveness might prove somewhat indistinct. Thus we have been told that ring tournaments, perhaps deriving indirectly from enthusiasm for *Ivanhoe* and other works of Scott, were a special feature of the South. No doubt this has been true of the South since 1865: was it true of the prewar decades? The Crookses' book on the subject is entitled *The Ring Tournament in the United States*. Yet it is confined almost entirely to the South. Were there tournaments in the North? Yes, the authors concede: there have been tournaments in various "states bordering the Southern states," among them Ohio, Pennsylvania, Delaware, New Jersey and New York — the last two of which are not usually defined as border states. Being Southerners, on the trail of what they hold to be a Southern pastime, the authors feel no need to go into these Northern fringe activities. Indeed, they add, "it does not seem necessary to comment, since the tournaments in these surrounding states have been promoted largely by persons who have come from the South."

As for Walter Scott, most accounts of his popularity begin by mentioning how eagerly his books were reprinted by American publishers, whose headquarters were in the North, but then dwell exclusively upon his *Southern* appeal. But among the Northern and subsequently abolitionist Beecher family, the appeal was equally powerful. Harriet Beecher Stowe recalled that when she was a girl "one summer we went through Ivanhoe seven times," until they were able to recite many of its episodes verbatim.[*] The Massachusetts writer Catharine Maria Sedgwick said of Scott's *Kenilworth* in 1822: "I salute it with as much enthusiasm as a Catholic would a holy relic." In 1833 Rufus Choate delivered a much-discussed lecture in Salem, Massachusetts, on "The Importance of Illustrating New-England History by a Series of Romances like the Waverley Novels." Though Choate's aim was not so much to praise Scott as to develop a New England literature, he took for granted that the audience shared his own admiration for and close knowledge of Scott's writings. American travelers in Scotland invariably made a pilgrimage to Scott's home, Abbotsford. Samuel S. Cox of Ohio did so in 1851 with three American friends. They also paid tribute to Scott's grave at

---

[*] The popularity of *Ivanhoe* did not die in New England. As late as 1912, the Yale graduating class of that year cited *Ivanhoe* as its favorite novel. Paul Rosenfeld, *Port of New York*, introduction by Sherman Paul (Urbana, Ill., 1966), vii.

Dryburgh Abbey. Scott lay there, Cox noted with emotion: "But Marmion, Waverley, Ivanhoe and Old Mortality were not interred in Dryburgh on that day. They form a part of the deathless spirit and creative mind of him who shed at once so much lustre upon his country's legends and history, and so much benignity upon mankind. We gathered a twig near his tomb."[14]

Material for questioning other assumptions of Southern uniqueness has been presented in previous chapters. A recapitulation of certain elements is worthwhile.

THE MARTIAL SPIRIT IN GENERAL

In his *Southern Reader* Willard Thorp says of the American Revolution that it typified the Southern fighting tradition, since the colonies were "led to victory by a Virginian experienced in the Indian fighting, and it was in Virginia that Cornwallis surrendered." He and Robert D. Meade stress the dominant Southern role in the War of 1812 and the Mexican War. These are dubious contentions. It is true that George Washington was a Virginian: it is not true that the South in other respects shouldered more than its share of military responsibility. Of Washington's principal native-born commanders, Philip Schuyler was from New York, Nathanael Greene from Rhode Island, John Sullivan from New Hampshire, Benedict Arnold from Connecticut; Anthony Wayne was a Pennsylvanian, while Benjamin Lincoln and Henry Knox were Massachusetts men. There was no preponderance of Southerners in the Continental line. The important engagements of the war chiefly took place on Northern soil. In American military history battle-names like Trenton and Princeton, Brandywine and Germantown, Bennington and Saratoga (all in the North) are more vividly prominent than such Southern fields as Cowpens and King's Mountain. The place of greatest symbolic importance was and continued to be West Point on the Hudson River in New York.[15]

A Southern chronicler, yielding this much, might answer that Northern martial ardor waned rapidly after the Revolution, as its leading citizens and institutions began to be shaped by commercial and manufacturing demands. He might well reiterate that the South responded far more readily to the War of 1812 and the Mexican War. But the process was not apparent to everyone. Early in 1801, at the time of the disputed Jefferson-Burr presidential election, when sectional feeling ran high, the *Washington Federalist* boasted bloodthirstily of what the Massachusetts militia, "consisting of 70,000 in arms — with those of New Hampshire and Connecticut united almost to a man," could do to the "factious foreigners in Pennsylvania or a few *fighting* bacchanals of Virginia . . . farcically performing the manual exercise with *cornstalks* instead of muskets."[16] The War of 1812 proves little: the Northeastern states dragged their feet because, with some justification, they thought it an unnecessary conflict, brought on by an administration whose economic policy had already seriously harmed them. They had equally cogent reasons, shared by many Southern Whigs, for disapproving of the Mexican War. In that war, recruiting logistics in any case made it simpler to draw upon the Southern states. Those who supported the Mexican War did so with equal excitement North and South. The enlistment and casualty figures reveal that it was not waged entirely by

Southern regiments, and certainly not by the Old South. Altogether 1,053 American soldiers were killed in action; another 508 died of wounds. Of this total of 1,561 fatal battle casualties, 944 were incurred by the regulars, who were recruited chiefly from the North. Of the remaining 617 deaths through battle, suffered by volunteer troops, 371 appear to have come from slave states and 242 from free states. Illinois lost more men among the volunteers (98) than any other state. The most substantial Northern contingents, from Illinois (6,123), Ohio (5,536), and Indiana (4,585), though smaller than the chief Southern contingents from Texas, Louisiana and Missouri (all over 7,000), were considerably more numerous than the contingents from Georgia (2,132), Virginia (1,320) or South Carolina (1,077). Indeed all three of these were exceeded by New York's 2,396 volunteers. Though South Carolina lost 56 men as against New York's 43, Georgia lost only 6 men in battle and Virginia none at all. Taking the regulars into account, there were more Northern than Southern names in the obituaries.[17]

To make such a claim is to come near to the kind of blurred exaggeration characteristic of some Southern versions. A more significant observation may be that peace advocates, and others worried in the 1830's and 1840's by the spread of violence, drew no distinction between slave and free states. In Lincoln's Springfield Lyceum address of 1838, he emphasized that such outbreaks were not confined to the slave or to the free states: *Whatever . . . their cause may be, it is common to the whole country.* Lynching and vigilantism were "Western" rather than specifically "Southern" phenomena. Yet the violence of thinly settled frontier communities was no worse than that of mobs in thickly settled Eastern areas. We have seen that every large city in the United States had its history of murderous disorder, and that Southern patriots like W. J. Grayson were at pains to contrast Northern urban violence with the tranquil atmosphere of the South. John Brown with his 21-man "army" at Harpers Ferry was as foolhardy and ferocious as any Southern filibusterer yearning to carve out a Caribbean empire.

MILITARY SCHOOLS

Franklin and other scholars have instanced the spread of these in the prewar South. It cannot be denied that such schools became a noticeable feature of Southern education. Virginia Military Institute (1839) and the Citadel (1842) firmly established themselves. V.M.I. has derived particular glory because "Stonewall" Jackson was a member of its faculty. But it is worth reiterating that the military school was actually a Northern invention, the brainchild of Alden Partridge, whose academy in Norwich, Vermont, began life in 1819. Partridge and his graduates, as explained in Chapter 3, founded a large number of other academies patterned upon Norwich. Though the majority were established in the South, a fair proportion were Northern. Those in the North fared as well, or as badly, as those in the South. The factors that determined their success were largely nonmilitary. Since the Southern educational system was inferior to that of the free states, any school was both more needed and more jeopardized by lack of funds. The formula that determined the success of V.M.I. and the Citadel — that of allotting a military appropriation for educational purposes — was at least as much a sign of poverty or parsimony as of military zeal. In any event, it guaranteed a degree of permanence denied to many private ventures. Even so, a number of Northern military schools had a quite long lease of life. Why have such institutions as Mount Pleasant Academy, in New York, sunk from view, while we continue to stress the prevalence of Southern counterparts? One answer is that the fashion for military academies developed after the Civil War (for example, in the Shenandoah Valley), and has been assumed to be equally vigorous before the war. A wider reason is that, as with Sir Walter Scott, military academies have come to be regarded as a feature of the South, or rather of *the idea of the South*. They have hence been regarded as *not-Northern*, and have had no significance attached to them. The boys at V.M.I. have been highly visible in the eyes of posterity; those in cadet gray at Mount Pleasant, New York, or Highland Military Academy in Worcester, Massachusetts, or in Hamden, Connecticut, have been well-nigh invisible.

THE MILITARY "ENLIGHTENMENT"

Samuel Huntington has usefully drawn attention to the development during the 1830's and 1840's of a quantity of writing on American military affairs. But the case is hardly proven that this was a Southern monopoly. Within the army the center of intellectual interest was West Point. The most distinguished theorist was a Northern engineer officer, Henry Wager Halleck of New York (U.S.M.A. 1839). He studied fortifications in France. His official *Report on the Means of National Defence* (1845) won him a deserved reputation. Invited to deliver the Lowell Lectures in Boston, he published the result in a solid treatise, *Elements of Military Art and Science* (1846), which was of much greater general interest than Mahan on *Advanced Guard, Out Post, and Detachment Service of Troops,* or Hardee on *Rifle and Light Infantry Tactics.* Huntington calls it "the most sophisticated volume written by an American military man prior to the Civil War": a fair comment on a book which begins with a reasoned answer to pacifist arguments and ranges widely over military problems in America and Europe. A few years later, for his own edification, Halleck translated Jomini's military biography of Napoleon. The nickname of "Old Brains," which he acquired in the Civil War, was not altogether complimentary. He has often been ridiculed as a soldier-intellectual, pedantic and indecisive. Some of his own previous words could be turned against him; deploring the mistakes of the War of 1812, he asked in 1846:

> In the event of another war, . . . shall we again exhume the veterans of former days, and again place at the head of our armies respectable and aged inefficiency; or shall we seek out youthful enterprise and activity combined with military science and instruction? The results of the war, the honor of the country, the glory of our arms, depend, in a great measure, upon the answer that will be given to this question.

Yet Halleck, eight years younger than Robert E. Lee, was far from senile when the Civil War broke out. He was probably the most erudite soldier in the country. General Grant praised him in 1862 as "a man of gigantic intellect and well studied in the profession of arms." Sherman recalled Halleck's "indomitable industry" when they had sailed round storm-ridden Cape Horn on the way to California. He and other officers played cards: Halleck, lashed to his berth and equipped with a pile of books, was "boning harder than you ever did at West Point." Struggling in what he called the "political Hell" of wartime Washington, he may have been unjustly maligned by his contemporaries and by historians. In any case his standing as a theorist is beyond dispute. If there was an American military enlightenment, he was its prime example. To point out, as Huntington does, that Halleck was Mahan's pupil and that he was socially conservative is not to make him a Southerner.[18]

Nor was there anything particularly Southern in the matter of military periodicals. The principal service publications, the *Military and Naval Magazine* (1833–1836) and the *Army & Navy Chronicle* (1835–1842), were produced in Washington, D.C. Though the *Southern Literary Messenger* of Richmond, Virginia, featured a number of military contributions in the 1840's, it was preceded by substantial military articles in Boston's *North Amer-*

ican Review and Philadelphia's *American Quarterly Review.* These are ignored by historians of the South.*

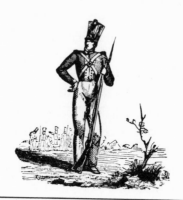

MILITIA AND VOLUNTEERS

Historians have even more casually brushed aside the possibility that amateur soldiering existed on much the same terms North and South. John Hope Franklin's material in *The Militant South* is admirably full — on the South. He has followed Osterweis and others in assuming that the Southern pattern was unique. He has been followed by historians content to reiterate the conventional story.[19] But Chapters 6 and 7 have indicated how much North and South had in common. Most of the nation's militia periodicals were published in the North. Below the Mason-Dixon line there was nothing to compare with such New York publications as the *Éclaireur* (1853–1858), "devoted to the Army and Militia of the United States," mainly under the editorship of John Watts de Peyster, or the *Military Gazette* (1858–1861), "devoted to Military Literature." Though they naturally gave space to New York's military affairs, they also attempted to cover the national, indeed the world scene. There was plenty of com-

* Leonard D. White, *The Jeffersonians,* 1801–1829 (New York, 1951), 211, draws attention to an article of 1826 in the *North American Review* — "the first discussion of the military policy of the United States in a journal of opinion that has come to our notice."

plaint in them as to the deficiencies of New York's volunteer militia; yet no indication that they recognized the South's training and organization as in any way remarkable.

Nor was it. As Chapter 6 revealed, the decline of the old militia was a nation-wide phenomenon. As Chapter 7 revealed, the volunteer movement also was national in scope. It was, however, most conspicuous in states which had once had a coherent militia structure, and in cities: in other words, in states such as Massachusetts and New York. Old-established Southern cities — New Orleans, Charleston, Savannah, Richmond — had their clusters of brightly uniformed volunteer companies. But these were rivaled, and outmatched in number and variety, by equivalent companies in the North. Isabella Lucy Bird, an Englishwoman traveling in America in 1854, found herself in Detroit on the day of the State Fair:

Military bands playing "The Star-spangled Banner," and "Hail Columbia," were constantly passing and re-passing, and the whole population seemed on the *qui vive*. Squadrons of cavalry continually passed my window, the men in gorgeous uniforms, with high waving plumes. . . . Two regiments of foot followed the cavalry. . . . The privates had a more independent air than our own regulars, and were principally the sons of respectable citizens. They appeared to have been well drilled, and were superior in appearance to our militia.

In New York a few weeks later she was struck by the "militia regiments in many-coloured uniforms, marching in and out of the city all day." New York's Seventh Regiment made a profound impression when it paid a visit to Richmond in 1859. Among the spectators was young John S. Wise, the son of Virginia's Governor Wise: "I stood agape at every evolution. The Virginia troops, which I had theretofore regarded as perfection itself, seemed to me now a mere incongruous lot of painted toys, contrasted with this homogeneous mass of military, neat, brilliant in cleanliness, and absolutely without gaudiness." Volunteer companies, together with military periodicals and associations, were if anything more prominent features of the North than of the South. F. L. Olmsted, observing the Southern scene in the 1850's, felt that

This colored lithograph, after C. H. Beers, offers a charmingly stylized view of the Suffolk Guards of Sag Harbor, New York, ca. 1835. In their immaculate refinement, attended by equally immaculate ladies, they declare themselves a match for the gentlemen of West Point or of any volunteer company throughout the Union.

the "Cotton Kingdom" was deficient in most amenities, including not only libraries and debating societies but also military companies.[20]

It might be answered that the South began to arm and prepare in the *late* 1850's, and so by 1860 presented a martial appearance contrasting with that of the North. But this was not the case in Richmond as late as 1859; nor in other states whose militia systems were moribund. John Hope Franklin refers to new companies organized on the eve of the Civil War. The same surge of enthusiasm was evident in the free states. Nelson Miles of Boston, speaking of the activities of the Salignac Drill Club in that city, recalled that in the secession winter of 1860–1861 "military armories were crowded" with eager young men like himself, determined "to prepare themselves for whatever struggle might lie ahead." The Zouave craze, a feature of the immediate prewar scene, originated not in the South but in Chicago, and spread through the North in response to the tour of Elmer Ellsworth's company. Ellsworth epitomizes a military ardor — a military romanticism — which was no Southern monopoly, and in this form perhaps not even as prevalent in the slave as in the free states.

Taking the general assessment of "militance," what are we left with of a distinctively Southern character? A greater propensity to dueling and brawling, perhaps. But most of the violence in the United States could be attributed to Western frontier, or to urban (and so mainly Northeastern) mob behavior. Military schools were perhaps more common in the South, but not to an extraordinary degree. The same may be said of military titles. The "Kentucky colonel" is to some extent a post–Civil War creation. We must remember that the hero in Dickens's *Martin Chuzzlewit*, staying in New York, discovered that the other occupants of his boardinghouse apparently consisted of *four majors . . . , two colonels, one general, and a captain:* a concentration that could hardly have been surpassed in any Southern boardinghouse. We must remember the remark of the army surgeon Rodney Glisan: *Let any person try the experiment of calling out "halloo, colonel!" . . . in a large crowd, assembled for any purposes in our cities, and he will be surprised at the number of responses.* The militia collapsed as ignominiously in the supposedly militant South as in the supposedly commercial North. One of the classic farcical accounts of a militia muster is to be found in a Southern book, A. B. Longstreet's *Georgia Scenes*. The volunteer companies flourished most in the cities, and therefore most in the North. Ring tournaments and Walter Scott? Once again the evidence fails to support the notion of a different, chivalrously warlike prewar South.

A Maryland Zouave company on the eve of the Civil War, imitating the style set by Elmer Ellsworth's Chicago Zouave Cadets.

More volunteer elegance, this time from Savannah, Georgia.

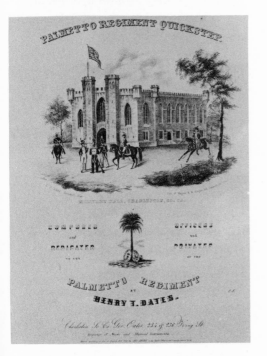

One of the hundreds of pieces of sheet music produced for the gratification of volunteer companies. This one is dedicated to the Palmetto Regiment of Charleston, South Carolina.

THE QUESTION OF THE REGULARS

One large problem remains to be investigated: the problem of whether the regular army was really a Southern preserve. We have seen that contemporaries believed this and that historians agree with them. They have offered convincing detail in support of their contention. If they are right, there may still be irrefutable grounds for speaking of America's military tradition as a Southern tradition.

Their documentation may seem overwhelming. In *The Volunteer Soldier of America* (1887), John A. Logan produces figures on admissions to West Point, from 1802 to 1861, which stand as follows:

Non-slaveholding states	2,278
Slaveholding states	1,710
Territories (New Mexico, Utah, Washington)	8
District of Columbia	109
Appointments "at large"	307
Unknown	26
	4,438

Logan considers the 109 cadets admitted from the District of Columbia "chargeable" to the slave states. Leaving out the territories and the "at large" appointments, this gives him a figure of 1,819 from slaveholding areas as against 2,278 from free areas. He could have strengthened his thesis by assuming that a high proportion of the "at large" appointments, being in the gift of pro-Southern administrations, would have been bestowed upon the South. Logan notes that the total population of the free states in 1860 was 18,978,000, as against 12,240,000 in the slave states. Another way of stating the matter — for instance, in Lloyd Lewis's biography of General Sherman (1932)—was that between 1802 and 1861 the Academy held one cadet for every 5,757 persons in the Southern states and only one for every 8,330 Northerners.

Franklin provides further ammunition by disclosing that between 1802 and 1829 there were 1,913 Southern candidates for admission, and only 2,160 from the more populous North. In 1820, Southerners constituted 53 per cent of the graduating class, at a time when the slave states claimed a bare half of the country's total population. In 1850, when the South had only 35 per cent of the population, Southerners represented 47 per cent of the graduating class.

Moreover, nearly a quarter of the serving regular officers in 1860 — 259 out of 1,080 — had been appointed to commissions from civil life; and 130 of the 259, just over half, were from the South. Northern West Pointers numbered 491, as against 330 Southerners. Thus 460 of the army's 1,080 officers were Southern.[21]

The figures cited in secondary works and in such compilations as G. W. Cullum's *Biographical Register of . . . the U. S. Military Academy* do not, however, always square with one another. They prove difficult to interpret, in part because they are often brought forward, as in Logan, to bolster a presupposition. It must be observed in the first place that the number of cadets *admitted* is a very different thing from the number *graduated*. There seems to be evidence that the proportion of Southerners seeking admission was higher, taking other factors into account, than that of Northerners. But the explanation is not straightforward. A plausible consideration may be that the South suffered from a relative dearth of good colleges, which would lead Southerners ambitious for an education to look northward. Another, less probable hypothesis is that since the South was relatively less wealthy than the North, the free education furnished by West Point would be a relatively greater attraction.

Whatever the explanation, it seems that those admitted from slave states were more likely to be dismissed before graduation than those from free states. The tables opposite illustrate the point for a fifteen-year period. Of those admitted from the North, 54.6 per cent graduated, as against only 38 per cent of those from the South. It will be seen that in the five North-western states of Illinois, Indiana, Iowa, Michigan and Wisconsin, only 27 graduated out of 63 candidates, or 43 per cent. This suggests that for the North at any rate cadets from newer states were at a disadvantage, either because of inferior preparatory education, or because they were more unruly, or both. Southern cadets may have labored under the same disadvantages, though the discrepancy between older and newer states is less apparent. Various nonmilitary considerations enter into an assessment. On their own, these figures certainly do not sustain the view that Southern boys took more readily than Northern ones to the military life as led at West Point.

Nor do the examples cited in Chapter 4 reveal any marked difference between Northern and Southern cadets, and their families, when they came to assess their reactions to a prospective military career. We recall that Jubal Early of Virginia (U.S.M.A. 1837) shared his family's conviction that the Academy ought not to be regarded as an entry to the army but to such "desirable occupations" as law or medicine; and that he resigned his commission a year after graduating: namely, at the earliest opportunity. We recall too that another Virginian cadet, Thomas J. Jackson (U.S.M.A. 1846), declared: *I intend to remain in the army no longer than I can get rid of it with honor, and means to commence some professional business at home.*

Not surprisingly, Southern cadets by no means dominated the Academy's class lists. Likewise, as the table at the top of page 364 — compiled from Cullum — indicates, there is no indication of a

West Point Admissions and Graduations, 1829–1843[22] *

Free States	Admitted	Graduated
Connecticut	32	14
Illinois	19	6
Indiana	29	14
Iowa	2	1
Maine	30	21
Massachusetts	61	35
Michigan	10	5
New Hampshire	25	15
New Jersey	34	19
New York	159	95
Ohio	70	34
Pennsylvania	126	67
Rhode Island	15	7
Vermont	22	14
Wisconsin	3	1
	637	348

Slave States	Admitted	Graduated
Alabama	28	6
Arkansas	5	1
Delaware	12	7
Florida	8	2
Georgia	52	13
Kentucky	58	29
Louisiana	21	4
Maryland	43	26
Mississippi	12	5
Missouri	9	5
North Carolina	67	20
South Carolina	54	18
Tennessee	63	22
Virginia	112	49
	544	207

* Cadets admitted from the District of Columbia and "at large" are omitted. The figures for these are: D.C., *admitted,* 36, *graduated,* 19; "at large," *admitted,* 200, *graduated,* 36.

363

SOLDIERS AND CIVILIANS

U.S.M.A. Graduating Classes, 1820–1860
(First Five Places)

Class	Southerners	Northerners
1820	3	2
1825	1	4
1830*	2	2
1835	–	5
1840†	2 or 3	2 or 3
1845	3	2
1850	–	5
1855	1	4
1860 (5-year course)	–	5

* Plus 1 cadet from Washington, D.C.
† Doubtful case of Charles P. Kingsbury, born in New York and appointed from North Carolina. Kingsbury remained with the Union in the Civil War.

growing tendency to Southern academic dominance through the decades. As the table below shows, the statistics on *graduating* as distinct from *admitted* cadets — again taken from Cullum — give a much less "Southern" picture than in Logan. Reckoning the numbers by the states from which they were appointed, from 1802 to 1861 the North contributed 1,133 graduates and the South 627 (including 194 graduates from the four states which did not secede). Approximately 64 per cent of West Point graduates thus came from the North. In order of rank the first twenty-five states (free states italicized) were:

State	Number of Graduates
1. *New York*	317
2. *Pennsylvania*	187
3. Virginia	142
4. *Massachusetts*	124
5. *Ohio*	106
6. Kentucky	77
7. Maryland	77

8. *Vermont*	73	
9. North Carolina	64	
10. South Carolina	59	
11. *Connecticut*	56	
12. Tennessee	55	
13. *Maine*	51	
14. *New Jersey*	48	
15. *Indiana*	47	
16. *New Hampshire*	45	
17. Georgia	44	
18. *Illinois*	28	
19. Alabama	26	
20. Missouri	22	
21. *Rhode Island*	19	
22. Delaware	18	
23. *Michigan*	16	
24. Louisiana	15	
25. Mississippi	14	

Another 49 graduates came from the District of Columbia, and 123 had been appointed "at large." Even if a majority of these were Southern, there was still a Northern preponderance much of the order one would expect from the relative populations of the two sections, and from the fact that most cadets were nominated from congressional districts, whose boundaries were determined by the census figures.

A closer look at selected graduating classes reinforces the picture:

Class	Northerners	Southerners	Doubtful	Total
1820	14	15	1	30
1825	22	15	–	37
1830	22	17	3	42
1835	32	22	2	56
1840	28	10	4	42
1845	26	14	1	41
1850	23	20	1	44
1855	28	5	1	34
1860	27	11	3	41

Such figures go some way to correct the impression of an Academy under Southern sway.* But they would still not destroy the conventional picture if it were possible to show that the army itself was dominated by Southerners.

A principal argument along these lines is that Southerners tended to remain in the army, unlike Northerners; they enjoyed the life, we are told, and had fewer nonmilitary professional opportunities open to them. There is little evidence for this contention. We have seen that 64 per cent of the Academy's graduates from 1802 to 1861 were Northern, if we leave out appointments at large and from the District of Columbia. Even on the unlikely assumption that every one of these additional cadets was a Southerner, the percentage of Northerners would still be nearly 59 per cent. These figures may be set against the summary in R. E. Dupuy's *Compact History of the U. S. Army*, according to which the ratio of Northern to Southern serving West Point officers in 1861 was 491 to 330, or approximately 60 to 40.

Actual cases bring the figures to life. "Stonewall" Jackson and Braxton Bragg are examples of famous figures who left the army some years before the Civil War — though Jackson, because he took a post as a professor at V.M.I., is often spoken of as though he were still in the army in 1861. It is commonly said that able Northern West Pointers, having become army engineers, were easily tempted into careers as civil engineers. To the extent that more Northerners than Southerners graduated at the top of the Academy list there may be some truth in this. True, too, there were more opportunities for railroad construction and other forms of engineering in the North. But graduates were after all not confined to their own section. Plenty of Northerners took up such employment in the South, and to a lesser extent this happened in reverse.

In the large Academy class of 1835 there were many resignations, in part through low morale and in part because of the

* Note that the class of 1850, cited by Franklin, contained an unusually high proportion of Southerners.

attractions of civil employment during the "internal improvements" boom. The routes taken by Southern graduates closely resemble those of their Northern classmates. Four of the first five cadets on the list, all from the North, resigned a year after graduating. Four of the five — George W. Morell and John H. Martindale of New York, Charles H. Bigelow of Massachusetts and Charles J. Whiting of Maine — became engineers. Four Southerners — Alfred Herbert of Maryland, Arnoldus V. Brumby of North Carolina, and Robert M. Renick and James N. Ellis of Virginia, who graduated sixth, seventh, eleventh, and thirteenth respectively — resigned within a couple of years and took up engineering. The same process can be traced all the way down the list. Herman Haupt of Pennsylvania gave up his commission for civil engineering; so did William H. Griffin of South Carolina and Alexander M. Mitchell of North Carolina. Others, like James M. Withers of Alabama and Hugh McLeod of Georgia, left to become lawyers and merchants. Even Joseph E. Johnston (U.S.M.A. 1829), the most professional of Southern soldiers, left the army for a year in 1837 to try his hand at civil engineering. Albert Sidney Johnston (U.S.M.A. 1826), equally celebrated in Southern military annals, resigned his commission in 1834; though he fought in Texas and in the Mexican War, he did not rejoin the regular army until 1849, when he had to endure six years as a paymaster before securing the colonelcy of a new cavalry regiment. The talented Hébert brothers, Paul and Louis, graduated in 1840 and 1845, first and third respectively in their classes. This class rank led them into the Corps of Engineers. Paul resigned in 1845 to become chief engineer of their native state, Louisiana. Louis Hébert resigned in 1847 and eventually succeeded his brother in the chief engineership.

We must conclude that there was no marked tendency for Southern West Pointers to remain in the service.

Another principal argument is that Southerners were politically favored and so came to occupy an excessive proportion of senior military posts. Alexander H. Stephens of Georgia, Vice President of the Confederacy, believed this was so. Arguing at the Georgia convention of November 1860 that there was no need for the South to secede, he tried to demonstrate how firmly his section had held the reins of power:

> We have had a majority of the Presidents . . . as well as control and management of those chosen from the North. . . . So of the Judges of the Supreme Court, we have had eighteen from the South, and but eleven from the North. . . .
>
> In choosing the Presidents (*pro tem*) of the Senate, we have had twenty-four to their eleven. Speakers of the House, we have had twenty-three and they twelve. . . . Attorney-Generals, we have had fourteen while the North have had but five. . . .
>
> *We have had a vast majority of the higher officers of both army and navy* while a larger proportion of the soldiers and sailors were drawn from the North. Equally so of Clerks, Auditors and Comptrollers filling the Executive Department, the records show for the last fifty years that of the 3,000 employed, we have had more than two-thirds, while we have had but one-third of the white population of the Republic.[23]

Stephens could easily substantiate his remark about the higher officers in the army. In the 1850's, Jefferson Davis of Mississippi was followed by John B. Floyd of Virginia as Secretary of War. From 1852 the command at West Point was held by Southerners: Robert E. Lee and William J. Hardee. Virginians headed the medical corps and the topographical bureau. Two of the army's three brigadier generals were Southerners, and all but one of the commanders of the army's geographical divisions. The general in chief, Winfield Scott, was a Virginian. When four new regiments, two of cavalry and two of infantry, were established in 1855, eleven of the sixteen field officers were Southerners. In one of them, the 2nd Cavalry, thirty-one out of fifty officers were from the slave states.

Yet once again the picture alters when it is scrutinized. Ezra J. Warner, a recent military historian, points out the significance of two factors: "slow promotion" and "the enormous relative increase in population of the free states after 1840."[24] By 1860 the ratio of Northern to Southern population was 61 to 39 (the Southern total including three and a half million slaves). But, Warner observes, much of this disproportion occurred after 1840;

and the senior posts in the army remained in the same hands for a great many years. The Quartermaster General and Commissary Generals had remained ensconced ever since 1818, the two chief engineer officers since 1838, and two of the four generals of the line since 1841. Nineteen colonels of the line were veterans of the War of 1812; the oldest of them, Colonel Whistler of the 4th Infantry, had been commissioned into the army in 1801.

Warner has analyzed the *Army Register* for 1860. Excluding medical officers and military storekeepers, he estimates that there were 950 serving officers in the staff and line. Of the 950, there were 555 from free and 395 from slave states (including the District of Columbia and the non-seceding states). The percentages were thus 58.4 as against 41.6.

Only in the cavalry was there a Southern preponderance. In other branches the North held a clear majority. Warner's findings can be summarized in the following table:

	North	South
Cavalry	72	104
Artillery	142	67
Infantry	200	139
Staff (including engineers and ordnance)	141	85
Field grade line officers	46	30

It thus appears that only one of the familiar legends of Southern professional military prowess — that of excellence in mounted warfare — has much substance.* Any other overweighting of Southern influence can be accounted for either as the effect of inertia, or by considering Alexander Stephen's claim. His speech was a protest *against* secession. He maintained that the South had managed to retain a disproportionate share of power in

---

* "Southern and Western men are accustomed to horseback riding, and the War Department evidently acted upon the thought that better cavalrymen could be procured from those two sections. The Northern States, if memory serves me correctly, had a majority of the officers in the two infantry regiments organized at the same time." Richard W. Johnson, *A Soldier's Reminiscences in Peace and War* (Philadelphia, 1886), 97. Johnson (U.S.M.A. 1849), a Kentuckian, fought in the Union army.

the face of the census returns. This was obviously the result of minority pressure. The American political system is to a surprising degree at the mercy of organized minority opinion, where this is conservative in expression. The complaisance of the majority, and the special situation of the Senate, allowed the South to assert rights to political if not economic parity, and thus to seize more than its fair share of Federal patronage, in *civil* as well as in *military* appointments. To the extent that the South was a self-conscious minority it was determined to take what it could, and could not help exaggerating what it had got.

Within the army, the chief favor it secured was a generous share of direct commissions. Of the 259 officers serving in 1861 who had been appointed from civilian life, and had not gone through West Point, 130 — or just over 50 per cent — were from the South. There are indications that the South had always done well out of direct commissions, for example in the 1830's. Their effect was minor, however: a high proportion of civil appointees subsequently resigned their commissions, and in any case they made up only a quarter of the army's commissioned strength in 1861.

Otherwise, the following should now be clear:

If Southerners applied for admission to West Point in disproportionate numbers, the disproportion was corrected by dismissals before graduation.

Southern graduates showed no disproportionate tendency to remain in army life.

Only in one arm of service, the cavalry, were Southerners conspicuous in numbers.

A large majority of enlisted men were Northern (including of course foreign-born recruits).

There remains the final question of whether Southerners were not even so "the best soldiers," as Philip Kearny believed. The course of the Civil War would appear to bear this out. It is commonly believed that the South — though outmanned — outfought and outgeneraled the North.* This view has two main

---

* A further possible explanation for the tendency to believe that Southern commanders were of higher caliber than those of the North is that, because of the Confederacy's system of grades, they seemed to hold higher rank. Until Grant

aspects. First, there is the fact that a considerable number of professional soldiers joined the Confederacy, and the notion that they represented the cream of the old army. Second, there is the idea that something in Southern temperament and society made Johnny Reb a more formidable adversary than Billy Yank.

The first point also carries an assumption that the Southern war effort was less weakened by "politics" than in the North. The example of Beauregard, discussed in Chapter 9, suggests that this was not so. True, the Confederacy had no opposition party, no precise equivalent to the Northern Copperheads, no turmoil over midterm or presidential elections. But Eric McKitrick believes that such apparent unity was a source of weakness rather than of strength.[25] There was no lack of discord in other forms. Nor was the infusion of West Pointers an unmixed blessing. Many in the Union complained at the rigidity and the coterie spirit of the Academy's products, and thought it sapped the Union's war spirit. The same complaint was voiced in the Confederacy. Indeed, John S. Wise said that "the Confederacy felt this influence far more than the United States":

> Mr. Davis, our President, was a West Point graduate, as was everybody else connected with our military organization. General Bragg, his favorite military counselor, was the martinet of the old army; and Generals Hardee and Cooper, the leading advisers at headquarters, and Generals Lee and Johnston, the commanders in the field, were all West Point graduates.
>
> I am not belittling the great advantages secured to the Confederacy by service of a number of very superior West Point officers . . . ; but with them came also a very inefficient and inferior lot, unfit for the high commands to which they were assigned, — men who stood in the way of better officers, and who were appointed and retained merely through favoritism.[26]

It is impossible to prove that the best of the Confederate commanders were *not* abler than their Union opponents. Scores

---

became a lieutenant general in 1864, no Union soldier stood above the rank of major general. In the Confederacy, on the other hand, there were altogether eight full generals, seventeen lieutenant generals and seventy-two major generals. See Ezra J. Warner, *Generals in Gray* (Baton Rouge, La., 1959), xxiv–xxv.

of volumes have been devoted to discussion of their relative merits. But once Lee and Jackson, Grant and Sherman have been left out of the balance, the Confederate roll is not strikingly impressive. Was Stuart a better cavalryman than Sheridan? Were Beauregard, Bragg or the two Johnstons finer soldiers than the generals who opposed them? Not in the eyes of two British military historians, W. B. Wood and J. E. Edmonds, who speak of the "strange impression" that Confederate West Pointers were better than those in the Union:

> Sherman was much better served by his subordinates, and the Corps commanders in the Army of the Potomac were probably superior to their "opposite numbers" in Lee's army. At first they fell short of Grant's exacting standard, but under his guidance they improved. Grant and Sherman seem to have got better results from their subordinates because they maintained a stricter discipline.

As to the second point, that Johnny Reb's environment made him a tougher fighting man than Billy Yank, this tends to rest on various vague generalizations, e.g., that Southerners were country boys, accustomed to riding and shooting, whereas the urban Northerners lacked these basic skills. Such generalizations are unconvincing. It is true that a higher proportion of Union soldiers were city-dwellers. But in both sections rural exceeded urban population. Farmers North and South were equally versed in riding and shooting. Moreover, as Theodore Ropp observes, "some city men, even in the South, made better soldiers than the men from very poor country districts. A man's general educational level played a surprising part in his fitness for battle."[27] These theories were not palatable to Southerners at the outset of the war, nor afterwards. Here and there, though, one encounters an admission which amounts to a reversal of the usual Cavalier-Yankee dualism. Lloyd Lewis instances a couple discovered in the course of research on his unfinished biography of U. S. Grant. The English politician Charles Wentworth Dilke, traveling in the South in 1868, was told by a planter: "Our officers were good, but considering that our rank and file were just white trash and they had to fight regiments of New England Yankee volunteers, with

all their best blood in the ranks, and Western sharpshooters together, it is only wonderful we weren't whipped sooner." Lewis,
querying whether the Northern army was not *more* aristocratic
than the Southern, in wealth and education, goes on to relate an
anecdote from a Massachusetts major, wounded in the Wilderness
beside General Wadsworth, "the immensely rich New Yorker.
Rebel soldiers kept coming up to look at the dying general and
on learning who he was, saying 'I'd never believe that they had
such men as that in their army.' "[28]

In short, yet another set of cherished beliefs is — to say the
least — open to question.

FURTHER EXPLANATIONS

No matter how much we throw into doubt the received version
of the militant South, it is still necessary to explain why the
version seemed true not merely to historians but to men of both
sections at the time of the Civil War.

The first part of the explanation has to do with West Point. In
addition to the 129 Southerners with direct commissions who
joined the Confederacy, 184 serving West Point graduates did
so — 16 of these from the North. As officer after officer resigned
his commission and "went South," shock and outrage spread
through the Union. Republican leaders, knowing or suspecting
that only a small minority of West Pointers were sympathetic to
their party, quickly convinced themselves that the Academy was
a hotbed of Southern sentiment. Had not these officers sworn
loyalty to the Union? What could they have been taught that
made them take their allegiance so lightly? Why did they rush to
resign? Why were their resignations so promptly accepted? Secretary of War Simon Cameron, in his first annual report of July
1861, declared that "but for this startling defection, the rebellion
never could have assumed formidable proportions." The place of
birth of the disloyal cadets was not enough to account for their
conduct. In view of such "extraordinary treachery," Cameron

suggested that the cause must lie in "a radical defect in the system of education itself." Alluding to the recent and critical report of the Board of Visitors, he drew the inference that West Point instruction ignored "the essential distinction between acts wrong in themselves and acts wrong because prohibited by special regulations."

Many Union men agreed with him. Chandler of Michigan declared in the Senate that within half a century the Academy had bred more traitors "than all the institutions of learning and education that have existed since Judas Iscariot's time." As late as January 1863, urging the abolition of West Point, Senator James H. Lane of Kansas said that if the North were defeated an appropriate epitaph would be: "Died of West Point pro-slaveryism."

By then most of the initial anger and alarm had abated; the move to close the Academy was defeated by 29 votes to 10. Union men were readier to listen to the defenders of West Point. They could take comfort from the fact that all of the 16 Northern graduates who joined the Confederacy were married into Southern families; or, more positively, that 162 of the 330 Southern serving graduates had remained loyal, whereas only 1 of the 130 Southerners appointed from civil life had done so. They could begin to see the force of such replies to Cameron as that of Major J. G. Barnard, printed in the *National Intelligencer* on 10 July 1861, which reminded the citizens of Washington that defections to the South were not confined to the army but were still more conspicuous in the Cabinet and in Congress, and even in the case of a justice of the Supreme Court — that sanctum of Americanism.[29]

Nevertheless, the suspicion persisted. It took on new life with the legend that secession had actually been taught at West Point, or at least condoned in one of the Academy textbooks.* It was

* The legend was not simply a figment of the Northern imagination. For different reasons it appealed also to the Southern imagination and was therefore propagated by Confederates. Captain Pickett of Virginia (U.S.M.A. 1846) asserted in September 1861 that "the right of secession was taught in our text-book at West Point." (It is perhaps worth adding Pickett graduated bottom of his class, and that he was initially opposed to disunion.) See *The Heart of a Soldier: As Revealed in the Intimate Letters of Genl. George Pickett, C.S.A.* (New York, 1913), 34.

revived and reemphasized in the postwar crop of memoirs and histories of the conflict. In 1884 the public could read in the autobiography of Winfield Scott's aide, Erasmus Keyes, that the old army was permeated with Southernness. Three years later, John A. Logan's treatise-cum-reminiscence, *The Volunteer Soldier of America*, repeated Cameron's charge verbatim and added his own gloss: "It was the traitorous defenders of the Government that made the Rebellion practicable. Had they kept the faith of soldiers . . . there would have been no Rebellion, and the nation would not have been called upon to endure the sacrifices of blood and treasure which followed as a direct consequence of their treason."[30]

And of course the lingering belief in West Point disloyalty or indifference was absorbed in the larger belief, during the war and for a generation after, that there had been some sort of Southern conspiracy, military and otherwise, to shatter the Union. For Logan, the author of *The Great Conspiracy* (1886), and other "bloody-shirt" chroniclers, theories of iniquitous Southern militancy long continued to answer the query of why the North took four years to restore the Union. Such theories were all the more essential to anguished Union men in the grim years of the war. This amalgam of suspicions and rationalizations, nearly all of them unfounded and disproved, had its permanent effect upon historical interpretation. One by one the more extravagant items in the story were dispelled. It was shown that West Point had *not* inculcated secession. It was demonstrated that Floyd had *not* flooded the South with arms: the rifles and muskets he transferred to Southern arsenals were nearly all obsolete and surplus; those sold to Southern states were taken from stocks in Southern arsenals. No matter: to remove the more garish legends was only to make it harder to account for the power of Southern resistance without positing an innately martial Southern disposition.

Other factors account for the North's almost superstitious regard for Southern prowess. Though the Confederacy had its doubts and dissensions, these *seemed* far worse in the Union, especially in the first half of the war. Secession came as an appalling shock. It threatened the fabric of the Union in subtle as well as obvious ways. Secession confirmed the secret fear that

American society was unstable, and based on wrong principles. The fear was particularly acute among the Northern gentry. George Templeton Strong wrote in his diary in December 1858 that America was degenerating into lawless barbarism. "Our civilization," he lamented, "is decaying. We are in our decadence. An explosion and crash must be at hand."

Strong was a staunch Unionist when the crash came. Indeed he was among those who welcomed the war, once it was under way, because it would enable the heroic temper to reassert itself in a society hitherto obsessed with moneymaking. The aristocrat might step into his rightful inheritance, ousting the demagogue and the speculator. The North was being punished, perhaps by God, for materialistic and democratic excesses. Perhaps (the Northern gentleman might uneasily feel) democracy had never really worked, or not when put to any severe strain. Democracy spoke with too many mouths, was self-indulgent, cowardly and corrupt. Among military leaders the North had no one to match Robert E. Lee in dignity and firmness. Jefferson Davis the planter-soldier seemed to some a considerably more imposing figure than Lincoln the lawyer-politico, ungainly and crude. Southern unity seemed to contrast with the babble, discord and hesitancy of the Union. If the war could only be won by unity and leadership, the Confederacy appeared irresistible. Only there was the principle of aristocracy openly avowed. Educated Northerners, covertly attracted by the vision of an undemocratic, hierarchical Southern society, were vulnerable to every criticism of their own shapelessly egalitarian order and every assertion of Southern strength. Much of the disapproval of Lincoln among such Northerners can be understood if we view him through their eyes as a person deficient in the aristocratic virtues — including valor. When Ralph Waldo Emerson complains in 1863 that "you cannot refine Mr. Lincoln's taste, extend his horizon, or clear his judgment: he will not walk dignifiedly through the traditional part of the President of America," one almost feels that he has Jefferson Davis in mind as a model of what Lincoln *ought* to have been.[31]

Apart from these anxieties, the Northern war effort was actually weakened and retarded by the sheer difficulty of defining war aims and pursuing them wholeheartedly. Lincoln put the problem very well in a letter to some Missouri radicals in October 1863:

We are in civil war. In such cases there is always a main question; but in this case that question is a perplexing compound — Union and Slavery. It thus becomes a question not of two sides merely, but of at least four sides, even amongst those who are for the Union, saying nothing of those who are against it. Thus, those who are for the Union *with,* but not *without,* slavery — those for it *without,* but not *with* — those for it *with* or *without,* but prefer it *with* — and those for it *with* or *without,* but prefer it *without.*

There were still more subdivisions which he listed before continuing with an analysis of the strife entailed by such differences:

At once sincerity is questioned and motives are assailed; actual war coming, blood grows hot and blood is spilled. Thought is forced from old channels into confusion. Deception breeds and thrives. Confidence dies, and universal suspicion reigns. Each man feels an impulse to kill his neighbor, lest he be first killed by him.[32]

Here Lincoln is addressing himself to the exacerbated problems of a border state. But his remarks may be taken as an eloquent reminder of the psychological handicaps of the Union: handicaps which inhibited the war effort and disposed Northerners to fancy that their Southern enemies were fighting on surer ground, for more coherent and more easily attainable if for less admirable aims. This, to repeat, is a double factor. It helps to explain why the North required so long to defeat the South, and why — then and later — the North was willing to credit the legend of a solid, militant South.

Another reason why it took four years to defeat the Confederacy was the Union's misuse of skilled manpower resources. The South did attempt to establish a regular army in 1861, but no more than five companies were ever enrolled in it; the effort was soon abandoned and well-nigh forgotten.[33] In the North, on the other hand, a regular army was in being; and as in the Mexican

War, official policy was to keep this body intact, officers and all.

At the outbreak of the Civil War, for example, Captain George Crook (U.S.M.A. 1852) came east from his post in California to get into the fighting. His plan was to transfer from the regulars into the volunteers. Crook gained the support of his Ohio congressman, R. C. Schenck, who was himself by now a brigadier general of volunteers. They learned that at a cabinet meeting it had been decided to allow one hundred regular officers to take service in volunteer regiments. Then they called upon Adjutant General Thomas:

When Gen. Schenck told him the object of our visit, he acknowledged the action of the Cabinet the day previous, and volunteered the remark that if he had his way not a single officer of the Regular Army would go into the Volunteer service. Whereupon Schenck told him that thank the Lord he didn't have his own way, and talked very sharp to him.[34]

Crook got his release, and the colonelcy of the 36th Ohio Infantry. Other regulars were less lucky. John M. Schofield (U.S.M.A. 1853) attributed the length of the war to this single cause. The North, he said, had many more competent military men than the South. "The difference was that the South used the few they had to the best advantage, while the North so used only a very few of their many." Scores of young officers were left "to drag along four years in the discharge of duties several grades below their qualifications." General Grant became aware of the waste entailed when he was stationed at Cairo, Illinois, in 1862. He often met Confederate officers under flags of truce, and saw how quickly they had moved into senior posts. "In this way what there was of military . . . training was distributed throughout their whole army. The whole loaf was leavened."* Not so in the Union army:

* Even so, the Confederate loaf was not leavened equitably enough to satisfy all West Pointers. Braxton Bragg complained to the Confederate Secretary of War in September 1861: "For some time a growing dissatisfaction has existed . . . among the regular officers of the Army of the old United States service, which has culminated in a number of resignations. They have seen themselves overlooked by their Government, while their juniors . . . were put over them in rank." Bragg renewed his complaint to the Confederate Adjutant General a month later. Don C. Seitz, *Bragg* (Columbia, S.C., 1924), 47, 55.

A SOUTHERN MILITARY TRADITION?

The North had a greater number of educated and trained soldiers, but the bulk of them were still in the army and were retained, generally with their old commands and rank, until the war had lasted many months. In the Army of the Potomac there was what was known as the "regular brigade," in which from the commanding officer down to the youngest second lieutenant, every one was educated to his profession. So, too, with many of the batteries; all the officers, generally four . . . to each, were men educated for their profession. Some of these went into battle at the beginning under division commanders who were entirely without military training.

One of the victims was "Phil" Sheridan (U.S.M.A. 1853), who as late as May 1862 was still only a captain. Grant, McClellan and Emory Upton all agreed that the Union was gravely in error in not breaking up the regular army and distributing its personnel among new volunteer regiments.[35]

Bewildered, anguished, beset by actual and imaginary difficulties, the North was a ready prey to doubt. Hesitant Unionists could not easily convince themselves that it would ever be possible to put Humpty-Dumpty together again. The creed of democratic nationalism, to which nearly all Americans subscribed, taught that — as in the Revolutionary War — any people determined to achieve independence by force of arms would generate an irresistible martial fervor. The struggle of Greece against the Turks, the dazzling campaign of Garibaldi's Redshirts in Italy, bore witness to this "truth" of history. No wonder that immediately after Bull Run the Lincoln administration offered Garibaldi a senior command in the Union army (though the scheme never matured).[36]

Passionate Unionists, while they might suppress such disheartening thoughts, were equally disposed to exaggerate the extent of Southern preparedness and military talent — if only to argue that to gain victory the Union must emulate the Confederacy. The Brahmin historian Francis Parkman, in a series of trenchant letters to the *Boston Advertiser*, deplored the "emasculate" mediocrity of Northern life, praised what he took to be the Southern emphasis on "military honor," and delighted in signs of the emergence of a Northern military elite composed of gentlemen.

Parkman's picture of the South was fanciful. Even the West

Point cadets from the South were less uniformly "aristocratic" than might be supposed. D. S. Stanley, a Northern cadet of the class of 1852, said that "in the South a farm is called a plantation, but plantation boys in my class told me that they worked alongside of the niggers in the cotton fields."[37] Such disclosures were powerless in face of the accepted image of a land of warriors presided over by haughty planter-chieftains. Northern military setbacks in the first two years of the war reinforced the image.

It had of course a long history. In Blackstone's *Commentaries* professional soldiering is described as a species of slavery. The equation was sometimes reversed by Northern reformers, so as to argue that a slave society was a military society. This is apparent, for example, in the 1825 report of the Massachusetts Peace Society, which refers to "the *slave-making* and the *slave-holding* system" as "the Military System." By extension, Northern critics of slavery could thus convince themselves that the South was per se "military" or "militant," whether or not the facts bore out the belief.[38]

Parkman was no abolitionist, yet he had inherited the general Northern view of a "Cavalier" South. The idea mattered more than the reality — and to Southerners as well as Northerners. Once the Civil War was launched, the "Cavalier" concept became as vital to Confederate morale as it was daunting to Union morale. More than ever the South belonged in the realm of mythology. In the words of David Bertelson, it was not "a social reality, but rather a concept existing only in the realm of values." With the *idea* of the South were associated a miscellany of qualities, reprehensible or admirable, which conferred upon the section a distinctiveness it had in fact never entirely or exclusively possessed. In particular, as William R. Taylor has shown, the complex, unstable, defensive American gentry idea was attributed to the South: an idea by turns odious, undemocratic, forbidden, enviable, charming. Ring tournaments and Sir Walter Scottism were romantic aspects of this gentry idea. Upper-class Northerners could not quite stomach and could not quite repudiate what it entailed. For different reasons, they found the mythology of Southernness as useful as did Southerners.

A SOUTHERN MILITARY TRADITION?

They found the place of West Pointers especially difficult to interpret. So of course did some Northern graduates of the Academy. The prewar gentry idea, being more explicit and more extolled in the South, was apt to be defined *as* "Southern." Some Northern officers fancied that they were accorded more recognition in the South. Remembering their hour of glory in the Mexican War, or their years of service elsewhere on Southern frontiers, they too sometimes envisaged the United States as being geographically rather than metaphorically divided into "Cavalier" and "Yankee" realms. Temperament and training left few of them radically inclined. In general they favored the *status quo,* like other Americans with upper-class leanings; and so were not so much proslavery as anti-abolitionist. There is a fine but important distinction to be drawn. They were not biased toward the South, but toward styles which are commonly though inaccurately regarded as "Southern." These styles pertained to both sections; they were merely more overt below the Mason-Dixon line. They were dark stars in the Northern sky.[39]

The lineaments of the Old South acquired sharper definition during the Civil War, and far sharper meaning when the war was lost. It is possible to argue that the Old South is largely a post-1865 invention. To most Northerners after 1865 the idea of the bygone South, stripped of sinister attributes, survived as pure fragrance. To most Southerners the idea was still more poignant. In defeat, ex-Confederates stood deeply in need of consolation. Their best consolation was the faith that the Old South had been a gracious civilization which had gone down to a defeat of utmost gallantry.

Both sides were therefore prepared to subscribe to the semi-legendary version of a Cavalier or militant South. Within the Confederacy the *recherche du temps perdu* was an extraordinary feature of the postwar years. An internally contrived "Reconstruction" coexisted with that imposed externally by the victorious North. One example is the Georgia plantation house which Tom Watson's father began to build on his return from the army, when he no longer needed or could afford such a luxury. His need was symbolic, his gesture insane but perhaps a device to preserve

381

sanity. Equally striking is the quantity of tournaments staged in the South *after* the war — in some cases during the summer of 1865. One suspects that these performances were more frequent after Appomattox than in the antebellum years.

So with other elements in the Southern legend. In the retrospective process romantic chivalry came to be thought of as a uniquely Southern manifestation. A good illustration is the story in T. Harry Williams's *Beauregard* of the making of the first Confederate "stars-and-bars" battle flags. "They were manufactured," says Williams, "in the best tradition of Southern romance" — out of silk from ladies' dresses. In the best *tradition;* for in truth there was nothing especially Southern about the event. Women have been immemorially associated with war in such displays of sentiment. Among the flags presented to Ellsworth's Fire Zouaves in April 1861 were a great crimson silk banner from Mrs. John Jacob Astor, Jr., and a flag from the actress Laura Keene. All over the Confederacy *and* the Union women were sewing and embroidering colors to be borne into action.[40]

After the war the Lost Cause continued to acquire glamour. Robert E. Lee was virtually canonized; the Richmond church where he had worshipped attracted *his* worshippers, and the Lexington college over which he presided became another of his shrines. Jackson, Stuart and others of the Southern dead joined the pantheon. The sanctifying of certain of the survivors would have gone ahead more rapidly if they had not, like their Northern ex-opponents, yielded to the temptation to squabble over their military reputations. Northern military history was on the whole written in a magnanimous spirit. The achievements of Northern arms seemed perhaps to gain in luster if Southern prowess was given at least its share of attention.

Preoccupied in the Gilded Age by other things than war, the North was willing to permit the South to lay claim to the nation's military tradition — the more so when Southerners actually began to fill the regular officer corps in disproportionate numbers. Scholars soothed Southern pride, and did not wound that of the North, by reiterating the hallowed anecdotes of Cavalierdom. Warlike Virginia was contrasted once more with its ancient

antithesis, Yankee Massachusetts. In fact the contrast was heightened by assuming that the spirit of antebellum Massachusetts
was typified by such Transcendental figures as Emerson and
Thoreau. If the contrast is fair, there is certainly a startling
difference between Lee and Jackson on the one hand, and Emerson and Thoreau on the other. But the Transcendentalists were
hardly representative figures. Nor for that matter was Massachusetts any more representative of the varied Northern scene
than Virginia of the Southern scene.* If the contrast has to be
drawn, however, Massachusetts was by no means devoid of military enthusiasm. It had one of the best militia organizations in the
country. Among the officers of the old army none was more tough
than Edwin Vose Sumner of Boston, Massachusetts. Commissioned from civil life in 1819, Sumner was a veteran cavalry
officer who won further renown in the Mexican War. One of his
sons became a brigadier general in the regular army; another rose
to the rank of major general in the Civil War. A son of the
Massachusetts clergyman-historian John Gorham Palfrey graduated from West Point in 1857 at the head of his class, after having
graduated from Harvard in 1853, and served with distinction as
an engineer officer in the Civil War. Charles Russell Lowell, who
graduated from Harvard a year after J. C. Palfrey (offering a
valedictory oration on "The Reverence Due from Old Men to
Young"), spent two adventurous years in Algeria and Italy, im-
mersing himself in military experiences. After Fort Sumter he
applied to Senator Charles Sumner for a commission. "Whether
the Union stands or falls," he wrote, "I believe the profession of
arms will henceforth be more desirable and more respected than
it has been hitherto." Lowell, killed in action in 1864, was among
Sheridan's most brilliant cavalry colonels. Men of this stamp

---

* We might also ask whether "Stonewall" Jackson was a representative Southern
figure — apart from his surprising military talent. He was not a planter-aristocrat;
he was clumsy, irritable, and imbued with the notions on dietary reform and the
like which are usually taken to represent Northern faddism. Though a less un-
balanced person, he has something in common with John Brown, at whose execu-
tion Jackson was present in command of a squad of V.M.I. cadets. The opinion of
Ulysses S. Grant is interesting. Jackson, he said, "impressed me always as a man of
the Cromwell stamp, a Puritan — much more of the New Englander than the
Virginian." John R. Young, *Around the World with General Grant* (2 vols., New
York, 1879), II, 212.

convinced Francis Parkman that the North had not gone soft; Harvard boys were a match for the best the South could bring against them.†

The South remembered its youthful heroes and wove their legend into the larger legend of a unique Southern military tradition. The North, having other things to do, could spare its heroes no more than a portion, and an apparently incongruous one, in its own special legend of triumphant manufacturers and impatient pioneers. Neither told the whole truth, although both intended to.

† Sumner and Palfrey are described in *D.A.B.* On Lowell see *Memoirs of the War of '61: Colonel Charles Russell Lowell, Friends and Cousins* (Boston, 1920), 1–12. In a foreword, Elizabeth C. Putnam said that at the beginning of the Civil War photographs of these young Bostonians were sent to English acquaintances. "Placed on their drawing-room table in London, the portraits helped to convince their friends that our army was not made up of 'mere mercenaries.'" Among the cousins were Oliver Wendell Holmes, Jr., and Francis Lee Higginson.

11

THE AMERICAN MILITARY ETHOS

Et j'ai grande allégresse
quand je vois en campagne rangés
chevaliers et chevaux armés
— Bertrand de Born

By the rude bridge that arched the flood,
Their flag to April's breeze unfurled,
Here once the embattled farmers stood
And fired the shot heard round the world.
— Ralph Waldo Emerson, "Concord Hymn"

I join with you most cordially in rejoicing at the return of Peace. I hope it will be lasting, and that Mankind will at length, as they call themselves reasonable Creatures, have Reason and Sense enough to settle their Differences without cutting Throats; for, in my opinion, *there never was a good War, or a bad Peace*. What vast additions to the Conveniences and Comforts of Living might Mankind have acquired, if the Money spent in Wars had been employed in Works of public utility!
— Benjamin Franklin to Sir Joseph Banks, July 1783

RECAPITULATION

The story so far presented is confusing and somewhat contradictory. To recapitulate in brief:

The American regular army (like the navy) was by European standards insignificant in numbers and status, and was disliked by many citizens on principle and in practice. Life in the ranks was so unattractive that by 1860 the majority of recruits were young immigrants. Few remained in the army for long; they deserted in quantity. Prospects for the officers were so limited that many resigned their commissions at the earliest opportunity. Whether they stayed in the army or left it, American regular officers retained civilian characteristics to a considerable degree. Though generally indifferent to political issues, they were quick to make use of political connections, and tended to regard their congressman as their particular patron — not surprisingly, since most owed their Academy nomination to him, and to his knowledge of their family's political affiliation. One reason why few officers supported the Republicans in the 1850's was that this was a new party whose network of patronage was not yet developed. Engineer officers often undertook construction work which brought them into intimate contact with federal and state politics. Whatever their branch of service, American officers would have felt some sympathy with the caustic estimate of a British observer, the Hon. Grantley F. Berkeley, condoling with his friend Lieutenant George D. Bayard of the 1st Cavalry in May 1861:

The privates composing [your] army are foreigners, and though splendidly officered, by American gentlemen, the enlistment for a short period mars the drill; while at the same time pay and promotion for the gallant gentlemen of the profession are so low and slow, that really insulted as they are by the assumed rank above them of the [militia] generals, colonels and captains *I saw*, Heaven save the mark! I only wonder at the officers whose acquaintance I made at Fort Riley, including Col. Sumner, having taken to the profession of arms.[1]

On the other hand, as Berkeley attested, the officers — especially in a regiment like Edwin Vose Sumner's 1st Cavalry — were recognizably "gentlemen." They were, in the words of Morris Schaff of Ohio (U.S.M.A. 1862), the "sons of the leaders in business, political influence, and social standing."[2] Though the Academy was much criticized, appointments were eagerly sought after; much of the criticism was the product of envy. Between 1825 and 1860 West Point acquired a remarkable prestige. This was in part social, in part academic. The military consequences were indirect, yet far from negligible. Little by little professional training came to be accepted as an inevitable feature — some would have said an essential feature — of the American officer cadre. The army was thus professionalized at the same time that it appeared to become increasingly civilianized. The gap between officers and men widened, decisively and perhaps disagreeably. Precariously, this abused yet admired elite entrenched itself, claiming more than it got but actually achieving more renown and even power than one might have anticipated, given the ostensibly practical, egalitarian tone of Jacksonian America.

Then there were the citizen-soldiers. The organized militia degenerated into a pretense, a joke — an almost too easy theme for cartoonists and humorists. Yet within the militia were men who clung to the decayed ideal of a citizen army. Such men attacked the regular army on occasion not because they hated soldiering but because they felt they represented a rival martial principle. These men, the John A. Quitmans and Benjamin F. Butlers of the nation, turned to amateur soldiering from a variety of motives: vanity, political ambition, and also a thirst for splendor, distinction, heroism. In their hands the volunteer movement, ephemeral and prodigal in its manifestations, embodied a martial aspiration of some force.

Despite mutual hostility, regulars and amateurs had a good deal in common. There were likewise more similarities than differences between North and South. In greater or lesser degrees, all revealed an attachment to certain native attitudes, and to others which had been inherited or were still being borrowed from Europe.

INTERNATIONAL ASPECTS

The first point to emphasize is that no complex society of the past couple of hundred years has had a wholly harmonious, efficient and acceptable military system. In Britain, from which the United States took a great deal, the militia and volunteers were as comical and vainglorious as their transatlantic counterparts. The British regular army was criticized for being both too big and too small, too costly and too parsimoniously provided for. The rank and file, voluntarily recruited as in America, were on the whole regarded — much like American rankers — as the mudsill of society. Irishmen, the English equivalent of America's immigrants, provided the mainstay of the bulk of regiments. If the American fault was too short enlistments, a frequent complaint in Britain was that the soldier had to sign half his life away in committing himself to serve for twenty years and more. As for officers, if the American species could be accused of being too "scientifically" trained, the persistent reproach against their British confrères was lack of training, since as a rule only the engineers and artillery subjected officers to preliminary professional instruction; the rest began service as arrant amateurs. Staff and supply services were almost scandalously deficient. The weaknesses of the British army were uncovered in the Crimean War of 1854–1856: displays of courage were not always enough to offset indecisive generals, ignorant officers, muddled orders and administrative chaos.

The French in the Crimea and in other nineteenth-century campaigns seemed far more competent. It seemed that the Americans were correct to imitate French methods and graft these on to the older, British formulas on which General Washington's

Continental Army had necessarily been based. Some American military critics argued that the imitation had not gone far enough. Why not select a generous proportion of enlisted men for commissions, as in the French army?

Yet the French system had its abuses (and proved no match for the Prussian war machine in 1870–1871). It depended on a socially objectionable form of selective compulsory service. The long terms of enlistment gave France, Denis Brogan has said, "a force of long-service mercenary soldiers, totally cut off from civil life, blindly loyal and officered chiefly by semi-literate, recklessly brave, unintelligent ranker officers of the type Zola was to depict in La Débâcle."[3] France's civilian soldiery of the Garde Nationale were actually about on a par with American volunteer militia, but paraded more grudgingly. And the history of Prussia suggested that if Britain and France *had* maintained more perfect military institutions, this might have been at the expense of desirable *un*military elements in their civilizations.

The second point to emphasize is that American professional soldiers, and citizen soldiers to a lesser degree, belonged to an international military realm. They drew their historical allusions from a common stock. Alexander, Hannibal, Caesar, Cromwell, Frederick the Great were examples as familiar to them as to European students of war. For contemporary sources and models, they also turned to Europe and to the campaigns of the European powers all over the world. Organization and administration, tactics and armament, uniforms and accoutrements, were the stock in trade of service periodicals. American examples were at the time less discussed in Europe. For the moment the United States drew upon rather than contributed to universal military lore. All professional bodies have this international tendency, though it is not always fully conscious. Military professionalism exhibits the tendency in an extreme form. Armies mirror their own societies in all sorts of ways; they also grow to resemble one another more and more, at least outwardly, through the cameraderie of hypothetical enmity.

In talking about the American army of the nineteenth century, we must therefore remind ourselves that it was a blend of older

THE BRAVE VOLUNTEER.
(ZOUAVE.)
617

British and newer French practice, and that the British and French in turn were borrowers from other military orders. McClellan's official report on his travels to and from the Crimean War was republished by J. B. Lippincott and Company of Philadelphia in 1861 with a title that exemplifies the process: *The Armies of Europe: Comprising Descriptions in Detail of the Military System of England, France, Russia, Prussia, Austria, and Sardinia, Adapting Their Advantages to All Arms of the United States Service, and Embodying the Report of Observations in Europe During the Crimean War, as Military Commissioner from the United States Government in 1855–56.* In his report McClellan described the Zouave troops which the French had established in their army after facing such opponents in North Africa. Zouave units swiftly appeared in the United States — though not, it is true, within the regular army. As an instructor at West Point, McClellan delivered an elaborate lecture on Napoleon's Russian campaign, contemplated another on the Thirty Years' War, and adapted a French manual of bayonet exercise. He was one of many West Pointers who imbibed nearly all their ideas from the Swiss-French military theorist Baron Jomini. American amateur warriors such as John Watts de Peyster strove to demonstrate that they were as widely schooled as the professionals.[4]

THE AMERICAN MILITARY ETHOS

The American military ethos involves a wide range of attitudes and assumptions, some native and some forming part of a climate of opinion shared with Europe. They include incompatible ideas, since the ethos was somewhat discordant.

One element is the prominence of warfare in the literature, classical and modern, of the Western world.

The first essay theme required of Wendell Phillips as a Harvard freshman in 1827 was "A Knight Errant of the Middle Ages, Compared with Achilles, Theseus, or Hercules, and with a Modern Soldier." It would be hard to find a more perfect epitome of the eclectic classical-romantic concerns of the age. From this period onward the dominant subjects in American schoolbooks, according to Ruth Miller Elson, were "heroism, death, illness, decay, a mystical nationalism, a transcendental approach to nature, and the process of winning success against great odds."

Similar material filled European texts and anthologies. There was one important difference of approach. American nationalism sought to draw a contrast between the flawed heroes of antiquity, or of more recent European history, and the superior products of native virtue. E. D. Mansfield, for example, declared in 1847 that "no young man ever pursued a career of ambition, without having in his mind . . . some personified FIGURE OF GLORY":

The Poems of Homer have been the study, and his heroes the admiration of all ambitious conquerors, down to the last Christian ages. They were studied by Alexander, and read by Napoleon; they have fired the martial enthusiasm of thousands of youth. But, are the Poems of Homer, written in the dark ages . . ., filled with the imaginary gods of Paganism, and with all the sentiments of cruel Usurpation . . ; are these to furnish Heroes for the imitation of American Youth?

Homer would not suffice, said Mansfield; nor would Bonaparte, "a man without a true idea of Equity or Justice." It was a mistake to seek America's vision of personified greatness in antiquity, or across the Atlantic:

He is an American. France produced in Napoleon the greatest genius for war in the Modern World. Prussia produced the greatest General, in the actual field, in the person of Frederick the Great; but to America was reserved the right of furnishing, in WASHINGTON, the MODEL HERO of all Modern Times: A HERO by right of his character; by right of his country; by right of his times; and by right of his performances.[5]

Washington, like Benjamin Franklin — the other great hero for nineteenth-century America — was thus admired for other qualities than purely military ones. But his courage and his leadership were vital factors. Unlike Franklin, George Washington was a hero who was also heroic. The formative legends of American nationalism were to a large extent legends of heroism in war.

Liberty presupposed liberators. The air breathed in by newly independent Americans had a scent of gunpowder. Seventy years after the Revolution, students in the debating society of a Virginia college decided by a majority of 14 to 12 that in the winning of independence even more honor was due to the nation's soldiers than to her statesmen.

The same verdict would no doubt have been rendered throughout the country. There appeared to be no conflict of interests: battlefield and council chamber complemented one another.

To celebrate the United States was among other things to celebrate its soldiers and sailors, its battles on land and on sea. It would be ridiculous to describe Walt Whitman's *Leaves of Grass* as war poetry. But vignettes of war occur fairly often in the principal poem, "Song of Myself":

Cadets at West Point were trained in drawing by such well-established artists as Charles R. Leslie, Seth Eastman and (after 1834) Robert Weir. Their "copies from the antique" were usually of classical warriors. Cadet Jefferson Davis (U.S.M.A. 1828) exhibits a cold proficiency in his rendering.

The slaying of a centaur — a subject unconsciously prophetic of William T. Sherman's mortal blow at the Confederacy in 1864–1865 — is the theme of the copy-drawing that he made at the Academy in 1838.

I am an old artillerist — I tell of my fort's bombardments,
I am there again . . . .

. . . . .

Again gurgles the mouth of my dying general — he furiously waves
> *with his hand,*
He gasps through the clot, Mind not me — mind — the entrench-
ments.

Elsewhere in the poem Whitman describes the massacre at the
Alamo. Again, he asks "Did you read in the sea-books of the old-
fashioned frigate fight?" and offers a lovingly detailed account
of the celebrated victory of 1779 in which the *Bonhomme Richard,* commanded by John Paul Jones, compelled the surrender of
His Majesty's ship *Serapis* ("We have not struck, . . . We have
just begun our part of the fighting").

Whitman could have taken his material from a score of popular
military and naval histories by such authors as Charles J. Peterson, Thomas Wilson and Jacob Neff. He could have consulted the
ambitious *History of the Navy* (1839) by the novelist James
Fenimore Cooper, who had once been a midshipman.

Among the more distinguished historians, Francis Parkman had
a lifelong enthusiasm for feats of valor. Ancestors had fought at
Ticonderoga, and at Lexington and Concord; his younger brother
held a commission in the navy. Parkman believed that the military instincts "are always strongest in the strongest and richest
nature." Less belligerent, William H. Prescott was less inclined to
extol the military instincts. As a Whig he was distressed by the
Mexican War. But he was not opposed to all combat. Disagreeing
with a peace advocate who contended that wars were dishonorable, Prescott made a vigorous reply: "No! by all those who fell at
Marathon; by those who fell at Morgantown and Bannockburn;
by those who fought and bled at Bunker's Hill; in the war of the
Low Countries against Philip the Second, — in all those wars
which have had — which are *yet* to have — freedom for their
object, — I can't acquiesce in your sweeping denunciation, my
good friend."[6]

Some of the most popular paintings of the naval encounters of the War of 1812 were the work of the English-born artist Thomas Birch. An unknown artist of the early nineteenth century took a look at Birch's portrayals of Perry's victory on Lake Erie. His crude version manages to be both homely and heroic, and was no doubt much discussed and admired by his neighbors.

In the big histories that had claim, then, to literary distinction, as well as in more journalistic fare, the American public was treated to a rich diet of blood and thunder. Parkman's volumes on the French and English in North America formed a record of almost continuous conflict. Prescott's histories of the Spanish conquests in Mexico and Peru were a chronicle of bloodshed. So with John L. Motley's *Rise of the Dutch Republic* and *History of the United Netherlands*. None of the three intended to glorify warfare as such. Prescott and Motley indicated that much of this killing was barbarous and dreadful. Both assumed though that men must *fight* for their liberties and that eventually they would carry the day. An intimate connection was implied between patriotism and warfare, democracy and heroism, progress and military prowess — even if the prowess was improvised and temporary. They discerned a grand movement of mankind in which the higher forms of society triumphed over the lower; virtue proved both morally *and* militarily stronger than vice. So the Christian Spaniards defeated the pagan Incas and Aztecs; the Protestant Dutch withstood the Catholic Spanish; the freedom-loving American colonists worsted the semi-corrupt Englishmen of the mother country; the "Teuton" or "Saxon" proved finer than the "Latin" or "Celt."

The unashamed truculence of this nineteenth-century sentiment is well brought out in the words of Eli Thayer, the New England colonizer of Kansas, written late in his life:

> The Latin races claim that their founders were nursed by a wolf. The Saxons have a higher origin. Their founder was nursed by a polar bear. Deep in the nature of this race is found that untamable ferocity, which fears nothing, but can endure everything. . . .
>
> These qualities may be usually concealed under all the Christian amenities . . . but under . . . this gentle and genial exterior, there slumbers the grizzly ferocity. It is in every Saxon breast . . . a hundred baptisms cannot drown it; a thousand sacraments cannot eliminate it. It was with Cromwell and his Ironsides. Wellington felt it as he stood . . . at Waterloo and received unmoved the repeated charges of Ney and the Imperial Guard. In peace and in war, this quality is found wherever there is Saxon blood. . . . It will govern the world.[7]

The doctrine was harsh, stern. Thayer maintained that Saxon sculptors, if they instead of Latins had carved Prometheus and Laocoön, would not have depicted them writhing in pain but showing "a calm and defiant endurance." Parkman, who had doubts as to the efficacy of a democratic social order, wrote with especial sympathy of the plight of Coriolanus-like heroes such as La Salle, bearing intolerable burdens of responsibility and betrayed by weak or treacherous underlings. *Noblesse oblige:* pride of race, pride of family sustained the natural leader when nothing else availed. For the many who still felt the force of the old

Calvinist religious faith there was a penitential side to the on-ward movement of the race. Emory Upton, who spent a year in the radically religious atmosphere of Oberlin College before entering West Point, assured his sister in 1860 that America had incurred God's displeasure by succumbing to the assorted evils of Mormonism, spiritualism, intemperance, slavery and corruption in politics. "Few there are," he said, "who have not bowed the knee to Baal. . . . Why should we expect tolerance when God suffered such calamities to befall his own chosen people? He scourged them with war, and he will punish us likewise." Upton's solace was that if war came he would play his part without reluctance, "for I believe that I shall be on the side of right." War might be a purgative.[8]

There was a further comfort. Despite the horror and suffering of the battlefield, on which peace writers dwelt with grisly particularity, war *did* to most of Upton's contemporaries appear to advance the level of mankind; and in the process there were dazzling opportunities for individual heroism. To young men dreaming of romantic glory, history presented the inspiring lesson that in the space of a day one single battle could decide the fate of empires. On that single battlefield, one individual with one great stroke of daring could determine the day's outcome. Could anyone doubt that it was the genius of Alexander of Macedon which carried his small army across half the known world? In a few hours General Wolfe had settled the future of Canada and gained immortal fame upon the Heights of Abraham. George Washington had restored the patriot cause by one consummate move when he crossed the Delaware and routed the Hessians at Trenton. The lesson was developed by Sir Edward Creasy in his influential book *Fifteen Decisive Battles of the World* (1851). His examples seemed undeniably valid. At Tours, for instance, Charles Martel had freed Europe from the Moslem yoke. At Hastings in 1066 William of Normandy had won a kingdom and changed the course of English history. The defeat of the Armada in 1588 destroyed the hope of restoring the authority of the Roman church in England. At Saratoga in 1777 the Americans secured the alliance with France which virtually guaranteed eventual independence. At Valmy in 1792 the French upheld their determination to carry through their own revolution. And at Waterloo in 1815 Napoleon, the most dangerous man in Europe, was at last struck down.

Napoleon, as E. D. Mansfield and others insisted, was a depraved, "European" figure, a Lucifer among the select company of the truly heroic at whose head stood Washington. But his astounding rise to fame, his role as enemy of the overweening British, his combination of insignificant stature, burning ambition, fierce will, courage and intelligence and unorthodoxy, and even the element of ruthless cruelty, made him the outstanding romantic hero in the eyes of two or three generations of young Americans, aching to transcend their everyday surroundings.

For American professional soldiers, of course, Napoleon's was a career demanding minute study and if possible imitation. It has been said that every youthful general in the early stages of the Civil War secretly saw himself as a potential Napoleon. McClellan and Beauregard were both no doubt pleased to be compared to the Frenchman. Whenever West Pointers sought to justify the Academy as a repository of military science they could not help but invoke the name of Napoleon. In his 1847 observations, before reaching the conventional judgment on Bonaparte's failings, Mansfield delivered a panegyric on Napoleon as "the Representative of modern SCIENCE IN ACTION . . . the Impersonation of Modern Intellect! — Clear as the Sun; — strong as the blasts of the Tempest . . ."[9]

Perhaps Mansfield lifted some of his notions from Emerson, who had lectured on Napoleon in his "Representative Men" series in Boston during 1845–1846. Emerson's view, though on a far higher plane, reveals a similarly equivocal response to this demonic personage. But the passion for Napoleon originated earlier, and was more pervasive. Andrew Jackson was rendered by artists in Napoleonic poses and even with a Napoleonic hair style. In 1839, when John A. Quitman of Mississippi went to Europe, he followed a conventional itinerary in touring the battlefield of Waterloo. "I have had a chart of this ground in my head for years," he noted; "it seems to have been specially designed for a great battle. It is but the surface of the earth, but it appears to me higher than the Pyramids."

Enthusiasm for Napoleon, and for inspecting Waterloo, was stimulated by the publication of Joel Headley's *Napoleon and His Marshals* (1846), which had reached its fiftieth edition by the Civil War. The fashion was catered for also in the 1850's when *Harper's Monthly* serialized J. S. C. Abbott's leisurely *History of Napoleon Buonaparte*, with woodcuts to enliven the text.[10]

Whatever the source of interest, there was no doubt that it existed. Two parties of Americans have left record of their reactions to Waterloo on visits made in 1851. One group of Tennesseans, including Governor N. S. Brown, apparently concluded that Wellington had the advantage of the ground and would have been beaten if Napoleon had been able to meet him on equal terms. Benjamin Silliman, a Yale professor among a party of Northerners, contented himself with a more poetic response. Though they had traveled overnight from Cologne to Brussels, says Silliman, "we allowed ourselves no time for repose. . . . A more exciting object was in view, and we made, as early as possible, the necessary arrangements for an excursion to a place more memorable than Marathon and Thermopylae, and which will be visited and explored until time shall cease to count the hours." T. J. Jackson, who thought Napoleon the greatest of commanders, managed to see Waterloo for himself on a tour in 1846. Puzzled by Napoleon's defeat, he supposed "God intended him to stop right there."[11]

It was not necessary to make the pilgrimage to Europe in order to catch the excitement. As a boy, General Philip Kearny used to sleep under an engraving of Napoleon at Lodi — one of the dazzling battles of the young general's Italian campaign. Emory Upton was stirred to thoughts of a military career at the age of fourteen by reading a life of Napoleon.[12]

A cult so extensive must have many meanings, some of which are only in the loosest sense "military." For Emerson, Napoleon was a military genius but also, and perhaps preeminently, the "agent or attorney of the middle class," the idol of "the young, ardent, and active men, everywhere," the supreme epitome of confident common sense who changed "old, iron-bound, feudal France" into "a young Ohio or New York." He is almost Hank Morgan in Mark Twain's *Connecticut Yankee*. But this is a peculiarly Emersonian version, which like Twain's novel fails to answer the problem of whether what Emerson called the "absorbing egotism" of the great leader is compatible with democratic society.

Abraham Lincoln approached the problem in his Springfield Lyceum address of 1838. Pointing to the signs of social unrest in America, he asked how men of "ambition and talents" could be content with mere elective office:

> What! think you these places would satisfy an Alexander, a Ceasar, or a Napoleon? Never! Towering genius disdains a beaten path. It seeks regions hitherto unexplored. . . . It thirsts and burns for distinction. . . . Is it unreasonable then to expect, that some man possessed of the loftiest genius, coupled with ambition sufficient to push it to its utmost stretch, will at some time, spring up amongst us?

In *Patriotic Gore* Edmund Wilson suggests that the effect of this is ambiguous: Lincoln has "projected himself into the role" against which he warns his audience. Few American public men have revealed less of the lust for power and its trappings than this modest, gangling Middle Westerner. Yet he *was* ambitious. In his way Lincoln too thirsted and burned for distinction. It is most unlikely that he had any conscious desire to achieve Napoleonic authority, and almost certainly not by success in the military sphere. But as a man of his time he was susceptible to the vocabulary of romantic individualism. There was a contradiction, though not usually a painful one, between "equality" and "achievement," to use the terms of Seymour Martin Lipset. In a related form the conflict was between the idea of community and the idea of the individual, or between the useful and the splendid. In his Springfield address Lincoln implies that there was no such discord between communal and individual aspiration in the early days of the republic: the one subsumed the other. But now the individual craving for glory is separate, and strong. How can it be gratified?[13]

No solution could be found. There was no proper place in American life for the professional elitism, the social hauteur, the aristocratic recklessness associated with European armies. In several of the grand surveys of human evolution drawn up in the nineteenth century — by Auguste Comte, Herbert Spencer, Lewis H. Morgan or Brooks Adams, for example — mankind is seen as having evolved through various phases, one of which is the military phase. The warrior is thus consigned to the past, as an outmoded type. Yet there was still a place for military heroes, if only it could be defined. There was still a need to uphold the nation's independence and to carry forward its manifest destiny. There was a strong though oblique romantic conviction that men had somehow been better in the military phase. Their passions then had been direct, wholehearted and noncommercial.[14]

Since this craving for glory could not be satisfied institutionally within the United States, it existed somewhat clandestinely inside the enclave of the regular army and navy, or found outlets elsewhere — in the imaginative literature of Sir Walter Scott and Lord Byron, and later in Tennyson's *Idylls of the King*, which Elmer Ellsworth loved to quote; in the grand historical subjects painters were expected to produce; in the national appetite for uniforms, titles, military soirees and parades; in the imperial fantasies of the Knights of the Golden Circle and the filibustering raids of William Walker (who went under the Napoleonic designation of the "Grey-Eyed Man of Destiny").

The supreme romantic image was of a young man, perhaps of mysterious and probably of aristocratic lineage, alone or at any rate in the lead, in peril, driven forward by some compelling, noble purpose. Longfellow's enormously popular poem "Excelsior" is one illustration. The hero of the poem is an unnamed youth; he bears a banner with a strange device; his aspiration is both literally and figuratively upward; he endangers himself; and he perishes. A more strictly military vision, no less haunting to the imagination of the era, was of some beautiful young officer, mounted, at the head of a cavalry charge, or else on foot, sword held aloft, leading what was evocatively called a "forlorn hope." There was an infinite pathos in the death of such heroes, expiring

THE SOLDIERS ADIEU.

nobly on the battlefield, urging on their comrades, breathing out a
last message to mothers and sweethearts. The Revolutionary War
and the War of 1812 furnished plenty of incidents, as Whitman's
lines reveal; and the fighting in Texas and Mexico renewed the
stock.

The way in which they were rendered in popular literature and
art — for instance, in Currier or Kellogg lithographs — was often
surprisingly "aristocratic." These prints luxuriate in gentlemanly-
romantic sentiment. Dapper young officers in gloves pledge their
troth to ringleted ladies under rose-covered eaves, while soldier-
servants at a discreet distance hold the steeds which are to bear
them away to danger, to fame, perhaps to death. If they die they
die immaculately, like Major Ringgold at Palo Alto or Colonel
Clay at Buena Vista, in the arms of politely aghast comrades.

403

Nor of course was this romantic mode confined to regular soldiers. Volunteer units comported themselves, or liked to think they did, in the same mode. Indeed, the opportunities for sentimental flourishes were greater. In 1859 Ellsworth's Zouave Cadets made a trip from Chicago to Fond du Lac, Wisconsin, to celebrate the opening of the North Western Railroad. Two hundred young ladies who accompanied them each contributed a ribbon to make up a perfumed bouquet of colored silk. Next year a sterner moment threatened to arrive. The company was ordered to turn out in expectation of a Chicago election riot. "The hour of the expected disturbances was at hand," wrote Ellsworth. So he "brought the men to attention and commenced to march them slowly about the room, when . . . with one accord" they began to sing "Annie Laurie," "and shaded in the expression by the sober feeling at that moment pervading the company I never heard anything sound so inexpressibly sweet."[15]

Keepsakes, ribbons, "Annie Laurie," gift-album poetry: these romantic flourishes were harmless enough, and not to be taken as proof that all young Americans wanted to be soldiers or aristocrats or both. The point is that the romantic mode delighted in images of gallantry and chivalry; that these were not confined to the South, though they were sometimes described as "Southern"; and that their connotations were to some extent at odds with the robust, matter-of-fact, egalitarian tone of Jacksonian America. This does not mean that they were un-American, or unimportant. It means that we have tended to overlook them, because their operation was indirect and because they seem at first glance not to accord with our sense of American ideology.

DREAMS OF GLORY

Dreams express hidden fancies, suppressed longings. The dream, which usually ends with the dreamer returning with relief or regret to the real world, is a literary device characteristic of romantic thought; and often these are dreams of glory. Whitman's *Leaves of Grass* may be regarded as a series of dream fragments. But less familiar and more fantastic examples are to be found. Thus, Colonel William Falkner, great-grandfather of the American novelist, published two verse epics (or would-be epics) in 1851, *The Spanish Heroine* and *The Siege of Monterey*. Both deal with the Mexican War, but bizarrely. The American officers in *The Siege of Monterey*, including Jefferson Davis and Braxton Bragg, are portrayed as Homeric heroes; they ride in chariots, wear plumes, and are armed with shields, swords and spears.

A better, in fact a perfect example of the dream-device survives in a volume of essays entitled *A Gallop among American Scenery; or, Sketches of American Scenes and of Military Adventure* (1843). The author, Augustus Silliman, was the brother of the Yale professor Benjamin Silliman who some years later was to explore the battlefield of Waterloo. The whole volume is a casebook of romantic, gentrified attitudes. It is written in a hectic, mannered prose, with amazing pretensions to worldly cultivation. The sketches cover visits to London, to Canada, to the South and so on; fishing off Newport, excursions in the White Mountains;

DEATH OF COL. CLAY,
BATTLE OF BUENA VISTA, FEB. 23. 1847.

When shot down a second time he drew a brace of pistols from his belt, handed them to Capt. Cutler, and requested him to deliver them to his father, with this message. "Say to him that he gave them to me, and that I have done all that I can with them and now return them to him".

LITH. & PUB. BY J. BAILLIE. Entered according to act of Congress in the year 1846, by J. Baillie, in the Clerks Office, in the District court for the southern district of New York. 118. NASSAU.

MAJOR RINGGOLD, MORTALLY WOUNDED

At the BATTLE of PALO ALTO, May 8th 1846.   When the gallant Major fell, Capt.ain Duncan offered to take charge of him.   "No replied he "You have more important duties to attend to   I shall be taken care of."

and many anecdotes of battles and naval engagements, related with a solemnity quite different from the whimsical-jocular style of other sections. Not surprisingly, the gentleman-author praises West Point: "Well would it be, in this disorganizing age, if, instead of prostrating the Academy, every State had within her borders a similar institution as a nucleus of order, discipline, and obedience." Examining British soldiers in Montreal, Silliman admires as a gentleman and deplores as an American. "How well these Englishmen sit their horses," he exclaims ecstatically.

"See that gentleman — with what delicate hand he reins the fiery blood that treads as if on feathers beneath him." *Gentleman, delicate hand:* we are in the world of colored prints where every lady and gentleman has tiny, tapered hands and feet. "How picturesque," he sighs (*picturesque:* another pet word of the period) — "how picturesque appear . . . these red-coated soldiers." Then however Americanism reasserts itself: "Picturesque! I like them not — they indicate a subjugated people."

Silliman reinforces this impression by interrogating a soldier whose brightly polished gorget is inscribed with the regiment's battle honors: Badajos, Salamanca, Vittoria, Waterloo. He discovers that the man does not know what they stand for: " 'Tis well. Thou art the machine . . . that they require — Verily, thy daily wage of sixpence, and thy ration, are full compensation for thy service." There follows a homily on the world's oppressed masses who are beginning to demand freedom. Silliman urges the ignorant redcoat to learn what is afoot and how to play his part in throwing off the shackles. But in a footnote he shows himself more militarily inclined than the English soldier:

The custom of emblazoning . . . the actions in which they have signalized themselves, obtaining in the British and other European services, is not now allowed in that of the United States, on the score of its aristocratic tendency! Although, perhaps, in the instance alluded to, the stupidity of the individual prevented him from understanding their meaning; still, to the more intelligent of the soldiers, they are no doubt a great incentive to uphold the honour of the regiment.

The sketch most worthy of study in Silliman's indeterminate volume is a romantic medley called "Old Trinity Steeple." It is an account by a young nob of his elegant New York lodgings, where he is tended by a faithful old Negro servant, Scipio, and distracts himself with a collection of fine books, clothes, wine, pipes and cigars. He falls asleep amid this dandified clutter. In sleep he dreams successively that he is up on the weathercock of Trinity Church, whirling on skates to the North Pole, aboard a ship sucked into the Maelstrom, plucked away to a tropical paradise, and cast into a dungeon where he is guarded by a venerable knight with a long sword — dream sequences in the idiom of Edgar Allan Poe or Herman Melville. He escapes from the dungeon and is plunged into another scene:

My noble white charger leaped clear of the earth, as he felt my weight in the saddle, — I was at the head of an immense army — my bold cuirassiers formed a moving mass of iron around me. The bugle sounded the signal for engagement; — peal after peal of musketry flashed from the dark masses, — the rattling reverberating roar rolled from right to left, — the gaping throats of the cannon announced in broad flashes the departure of their messengers upon the journey of death. On we rushed — battalion on battalion, — we stormed the redoubt, — "Charge," I shouted, — "Charge the villains — men of the fifth legion — follow your leader — hurrah — they bear back." I seized the standard from a fallen soldier, — I planted it upon the blood-stained parapet — Hah! brave comrade beware! — his bayonet is at thy shoulder — 'tis buried in thy heart. — I will revenge thee,! I dashed upon him, — we fought like tigers, — we rolled upon the ground, — I seized my dagger — the bright steel glittered — thousands of deep hoarse voices wildly roared — "The mine — the mine — beware — beware!" Flash — roar — bodies — earth — rocks — horses — tumbrils, — all descending, covered me — and — and . . ."

— and he awakes, finding he has pulled on top of himself the fender and fire irons, table, lamps and tea set, while his dog howls in alarm and fellow lodgers laugh at him from the doorway.[16] A burlesque? In a way, yes: the essence of the essayist's genre is to be not wholly serious. But Silliman is not laughing at the ingredients of his dream. He is confessing to a hidden appetite, yet also congratulating himself, for he knows that the appetite is widespread, honorable, and appropriate for a young gentleman in easy circumstances. The idiom is somewhat British: it smacks of Charles Lever's "rollicking" stories of *Harry Lorrequer* (1837) and *Charles O'Malley* (1840). The incidents are largely French. No matter. Romanticism was not concerned with national frontiers; Napoleon's legions were so to speak in the public domain. In dreams at least it was possible for every American to wear the orders of nobility and chivalry.

A second example is worth quoting in full, because it is more unexpected and because it shows how in this dream form an American expressed a deep pride in his martial heritage as well as a reformer's hope that the heritage might be transformed. It is a piece entitled "Sunday-School Celebration in Brooklyn: A Dream," from *Voice from the Forge* (1848) by the "Learned Blacksmith" and pacifist, Elihu Burritt. Here it is:

The event and scene of this grand juvenile celebration presented no sterile subject for the pencilling of an excited imagination. The scene which my fancy had painted, moved before my mind's eye throughout the day. I thought I could see the youthful host moving before me by hundreds and thousands, with their peace-speaking banners floating on the breeze; with music on their lips, and in their hearts, and upon their tongues, the benediction which the exulting angels gave to the world at the birth of its Redeemer.

The place of this beautiful spectacle was not barren of thrilling reminiscences. Sixty-three years ago, and almost the very rendezvous of that lovely multitude had been the scene where thousands of mutual foes had rushed into the deadly onset of battle.

There, in view of the spot where a myriad of young and happy beings were to send up their hymns to their country's God, beneath his over-arching heavens, their ancestors had done battle and died.

While my mind was busy throughout the day portraying to itself the spectacle of this youthful multitude, it would involuntarily fill the back ground of the picture with the scenes of that bloody day when Washington marshaled his army for the battle of Brooklyn.

But it was in the deep slumbers of the night that my excited fancy revelled among the incongruous and distorted visions of the actors and events of these two days so important in American history.

That the earth beneath my feet was tremulous with a heavy hollow sound, as of the rumbling of subterranean thunder, was the first incident to my imagination. Then a low distant wailing came swelling and rolling along, until the heavens reverberated, and the earth shook with a cry, as of a world of human beings in agony. Sharp, piercing, unearthly shrieks were heard among the dreadful explosions of the deafening thunder. There was no sun, nor moon, nor stars in the heavens; but clouds of horrid blackness rode along, just above the ground, and like incumbent Etnas, shot forth their tortuous, sulphuric flames; and the faint short cry for mercy, or the gurgling imprecation of the dying, told where the hissing thunderbolt had fallen.

I thought I was standing upon the heights of Brooklyn, with my knees tottering with mortal consternation at the terrific spectacle. Every inanimate object seemed under the influence of a continuous earthquake; half demolished edifices, spireless churches, trees and turrets were all in a state of frightful oscillation, like that of vessels moored by the shore of a tempestuous ocean.

The harbour of New York, which I had so often contemplated with delight, was filled with black, roaring, mountain billows, from whose bloody summits scaly leviathans would rear up their horned heads into the very clouds, and strike together their ponderous jaws, as if in defiance of the thunderbolts. Here and there, tossing about upon the surges, the sulphuric blaze of the ignited clouds revealed broken-ruddered ships, with tattered sails of crape instead of canvass, and with blood trickling down their splintered masts.

My imagination could not sustain this horrid sketch of her pencil; and the scene changed with the magic of a dream.

I thought I tried to evade this diorama of horrors by flight; I thought I ran with the velocity of the winds from the scene, until I had reached the centre of a deep forest in the interior of Long Island. For a moment I thought I was safe; and I sat down by the foot of a tall pine to rest. All at once the roar of a thousand cannons and the shout of battle started me upon my feet. The earth trembled under the tramp of horses; the clash of swords and bayonets rang through the forest; shouts, imprecations, cries, and groans filled the air. I turned to flee. I dashed away again through the wood, when a company of men, with white frocks, rushed across my path; their faces were familiar to me. I looked upon the front-pieces in their hats, and saw inscribed, "The Fourteenth Regiment, Farmington Grenadiers." They were those grey-headed veterans who had told me the story of that disaster a thousand times by my father's fireside. I mingled with them, and we ran with our might through the forest. The swords of our pursuers were almost suspended over our heads; when one of the company, who was running by my side, caught me by the arm, exclaiming with a faint voice, "Take my gun, William," and fell. It was a familiar voice; I stopped to raise him; the hot blood was pouring out of his cloven breast; it was my father! I held up my hand to shield off the

410

descending sword of a giant Hessian; The next moment I was lying across my father's body, and felt the blood welling out of my own bosom. Then a thousand spectre-like images moved and vanished before my eyes; the clang of the trumpet and clash of swords died away with the last sentiment of my existence.

From a short interregnum of oblivion, I was awakened by the merry and melodious chime of a thousand bells, which seemed to me the prelude of the general resurrection. I opened my eyes upon the new scenes in which I was to participate. I was again standing upon the heights of Brooklyn, with a vista before me which seemed to extend into the regions of paradise. The harbour lay smiling before me like a vast immovable flood of translucent silver, with the reflected images of thousands of aerial songsters fluttering away down in its still depths. A tinted mellowed light, as of sunbeams reflected from polished gold, rested upon every edifice of the city. Hundreds of gilded spires ran up into the heavens, entwined with chaplets of flowers, which seemed to have budded and blossomed in the sky. Then all at once the careering birds were still; the bells ceased to sound; when suddenly the enchanting melody of myriads of voices arose from the green fields behind me. I looked around me; it was the grand and closing scene in the drama, the *chef-d'oeuvre* of my imagination. The armies of Howe and Washington were drawn up in two parallel lines *vis-à-vis* to each other, with a space of a few yards between them, both headed by their generals, who sat upon their horses like equestrian statues. Not a motion nor a sign of life could be seen through the whole length of the two lines, which seemed to extend far beyond the scope of the eye. The two hosts stood as upright and immovable as if they were two parallel rows of petrifactions. Their arms no more glittered in the sun, but hung rusted and corroded by their sides. I looked upon Washington, as he sat upon his great white horse, opposite to the scarlet-coated Clinton; the same sublimity of expression, the same dignified suavity, appeared in his noble countenance, but they were rather the sculptured lineaments of a marble statue, than those of a living being. The music, which had directed my eyes to this spectacle, came rolling on in a full tide of melody. I strained my eyes towards the end of the two motionless lines of martial spectres, and discerned the vanguard of a juvenile host, moving down that narrow space, with their fluttering banners floating in the air. On, on they came by hundreds and thousands.

They marched not to the sound of "the piercing fife, or spirit-stirring drum," but to such strains of music as were heard by the Magi of the East, while they followed the Star of Bethlehem. Each youth was dressed in garments of the purest white; each with a Bible bound to

411

his breast, and with a frontlet of pearl bearing the inscription of his name, and that of his school and teacher.

The youthful battalions, as they wheeled by the Father of his country, cast each a flower at his feet, and a sprig of cypress at those of his British foe. When the last rank of juvenile multitude had passed, the spectre armies vanished from my sight.

The sound of the church-going bell of my own native village had interrupted the interesting scenes and incidents of my dream.[17]

This is strictly speaking not a dream of glory but a dream of the end of (military) glory. What gives it power is the vividness of its composite scenes from the American Revolution, and the realization that to be truly impressive the peace movement too must have its army, numbered by hundreds and thousands, with banners floating in the air. A curious sidelight is that though he appears to be drawing upon childhood Connecticut memories, since his father served as a private soldier in the Revolution, his father in fact survived the war. Burritt's inverse dream, his nightmare of glory, is heightened by the moment of invented horror in which a giant Hessian hacks at his father and then aims a fatal blow at him. Silliman's reverie speaks for the slayers, Burritt's for the slain. In both, warfare has provided an extraordinary imaginative stimulus: all the more extraordinary in that neither had ever taken part in a battle. Neither needed to when their society supplied so many literary and pictorial representations of man in his ultimate postures of heroism — or bestiality.

QUAKER, RIFLEMAN, CHEVALIER

Bringing together dreams and actualities, we perceive that the American military ethos in the century between the Revolution and the Civil War reveals a number of recurrent themes. Conventional definitions are however somewhat misleading, and fail to accommodate the nuances of the subject. Thus, there is some validity in the conception of a triple heritage: antimilitarist, antiprofessional or amateur, and professional. The defect of this conception is that it exaggerates the gulf between professional and amateur soldiers, although such a gulf certainly existed and was to become wider in subsequent decades. There is a good deal less validity in the idea of a "Southern" military tradition — though one certainly developed *after* the Civil War — unless the term is employed mainly as a synonym for romantic-gentry attitudes of the Silliman variety.

Perhaps the most satisfactory way of visualizing a complex situation is to restate the triple heritage in the shape of three "model" viewpoints, those of what we may call the Quaker, the Rifleman and the Chevalier. As with other models, these did not often exist in pure, separate form among actual people; but they do embody actual and fairly distinct alternatives.

The *Quaker* position was in general that of Crèvecoeur, Benjamin Franklin and Walt Whitman (and of Elihu Burritt). Of these men, of course, only Whitman had Quaker affiliations, and even he was not an orthodox Friend. The significant feature is that all three were considered Quakerish by others, and were content to be so regarded. Crèvecoeur, though he lived in New York state, presented himself in his *Letters from an American Farmer* as an inhabitant of western Pennsylvania, the Quaker state, and heightened the illusion by using the Quaker "thee" in the book's dialogue. True, the *Letters* disclose that the "American Farmer" is apparently not a Quaker. Still, his references to the Society of Friends are highly sympathetic, above all in the account of the activities of the Quaker botanist John Bartram with their perfect blend of the idyllic and the ascetic. Crèvecoeur's horrified reaction to the upheavals of the Revolutionary War breathes the spirit of Quakerish quietism: he cannot believe violence will be productive of good and longs to be left alone. Franklin of Philadelphia, the City of Brotherly Love, was often described in France as "le bon Quaker" because he seemed to epitomize the Quaker virtues.

Defined in this broad sense, the Quaker represents one enduring aspect of the American outlook. He stands for simplicity, shrewdness, ingenuity, diligence, decency, piety. A good citizen, he is nevertheless indifferent to the state and resists its demands

— especially the demand that he shoulder a musket in its service. All the features associated with war — parades, weapons, display, hierarchies of rank, collective anger — are alien to him. Burritt belongs to the Quaker type. He is a plain man, self-educated, unassuming, tireless, altruistic. He is skilled in the strenuous and sensible trade of the blacksmith, one who knows how to beat swords into plowshares. Much in Whitman too is Quakerish. Writing of war, he pities the defeated as much as he exults with the victorious. In the Civil War, ill at ease with martial themes, he frequents the hospitals:

*Arous'd and angry, I'd thought to beat the alarum, and urge
      relentless war,*
*But soon my fingers fail'd me, my face dropp'd and I resign'd
      myself,*
*To sit by the wounded and soothe them, or silently watch the
      dead.*

War is tragic: to the practical Quaker it is also supremely wasteful. In the words of Franklin: "What vast additions to the Conveniences and Comforts of Living might Mankind have acquired, if the Money spent in Wars had been employed in Works of public utility!"

The Quaker outlook can even be discerned among West Pointers such as Oliver Otis Howard, and more particularly among the gifted graduates who became engineers; for the concern of engineers is to construct not to destroy. To a few of these men the army's rituals were an irrelevance. Herman Haupt (another Philadelphian), one of the engineering geniuses of the Union army, had resigned his commission in 1835, only three months after he left the Academy. He gained a brilliant reputation as a designer of bridges and builder of railways. During the Civil War, working with concentrated energy and intelligence, he managed to restore Virginia's shattered railroad system. Lincoln marveled at an Aquia Creek bridge which Haupt had fashioned out of "beanpoles and cornstalks." Haupt, accepting neither rank nor pay, showed scant respect for senior officers. "Be as patient as possible with the generals," he was warned by the Assistant Secretary of War; "some of them will trouble you more than they do the enemy." After eighteen months, deciding that his task was completed, he insisted on returning to civil life: he now needed to finish building a railroad in Massachusetts.

The *Rifleman*, likewise an individualist, likewise unimpressed by rank and authority, represents a different side of the American military ethos. Easily stirred by appeals to his patriotism or virility, he embodies the volunteer spirit. He is to be found among the Virginians led by George Washington in Braddock's ill-fated army; with the Massachusetts minutemen in 1775; with Andrew Jackson at New Orleans; in regiments raised overnight for the Mexican War, such as the Mississippi Rifles (in which William C. Falkner, then a lieutenant, marched with a company known as the Tippah Volunteers); and again in the innumerable units, North and South, which swarmed to the colors — or more often first swarmed and then designed their own colors — in 1861 —

> *To the drum-taps prompt,*
> *The young men falling in and arming.*

Though sometimes an officer, the Rifleman is more usually in the ranks — Johnny Reb, Billy Yank. He is in our period probably a countryman, not a townsman, and in his most readily identifiable form one of the breed described in D. R. Hundley's *Social Relations in Our Southern States* as a "yeoman":

He always possesses a manly independence of character, and though not so impetuous as the gentry of the South usually are, still, in the midst of the dangers of the battlefield . . . he marches right on to where duty and honor call, and with unblanched cheek meets death face to face.

The favorite weapon of the yeoman is "the deadly rifle — even in his sports — and this he handles with such skill as few possess, even in America":

With his rifle the Yeoman shoots squirrels, ducks, turkeys, deer, bear, buffalo, and whatever else he pleases. . . . This is the kind of school in which were trained the hunting-shirt heroes of King's Mountain, and those unerring riflemen . . . at the memorable battle of New Orleans. . . . So also were trained those brave defenders of Texan independence – Crockett, Travis, and their compeers, who buried themselves beneath the countless heaps of Mexicans slain at the heroic defense of the Alamo.

All in all, Hundley concludes, there is not "a more reliable citizen soldiery" in the world than the "yeomanry of our Southern States."

George Cary Eggleston, though he praised the spirit of his Virginia comrades among the Confederate volunteers of 1861, admits that they had practically no military knowledge and were "not used to control of any sort." This is a further characteristic of the Rifleman and – despite the charming evocation in Eggleston's *Rebel's Recollections* – not always militarily or socially desirable. Here as in other wars there was in fact very little difference between North and South: the Rifleman's mood is perhaps best categorized as "Western." Hundley indeed concedes that the Southern yeoman "much resembles in his speech, religious opinions, household arrangements, indoor sports, and family traditions, the middle class farmers of the Northern States" – though he insists that the Southerner has the edge over his Northern counterpart in political sophistication, marksmanship and other yeoman qualities.[18] At any rate the "manly independence" of the Rifleman makes him a somewhat wayward soldier. Eager to enlist, he is easily bored. He expects his wars to end quickly. In his own eyes, even a short spell of service qualifies him to be known as a "veteran." Courageous in battle, he is sometimes murderous in spells of inactivity, as during the Mexican War. He is swift to discover and voice a grievance, yields no automatic obedience to those in command, and believes firmly in his right to vote his commanders in and out of office as if they were a pack of political candidates – which of course they also sometimes are. Being intolerant of long enlistments, the Rifleman on occasion marches away from the battle, not because he is a coward but because his time is up and he feels he is a civilian again. Resourceful in combat, he is also sometimes resourceful in the base military arts of scrounging, looting and desertion. After the fighting is done the Rifleman, much more of a "joiner" than the Quaker, is fond of reunions. A mixture of the genial and the brutal, the callous and the sentimental, of patriotism and patrioteering, he is the prime type of a nation which is "martial but unmilitary." And as such he is ready to adore those leaders in whom his trust is complete.

Sometimes, though not always, the Rifleman's admired leader is a *Chevalier* in style. Eggleston, for example, refers to J. E. B. Stuart as the "Chevalier of the Lost Cause." On the death of the Confederate general George Pickett, his onetime adversary G. B. McClellan paid a similar compliment. Pickett's "whole history, when told," said McClellan, "will reveal a modern type of the Chevalier Bayard, *sans peur et sans reproche.*" Robert E. Lee has been dubbed the "Bayard of the Confederacy."

The reference is to Pierre du Terrail, Chevalier de Bayard, a French knight who was the hero of several Italian campaigns in the early sixteenth century, and who was celebrated as the knight without fear or blemish, *le chevalier sans peur et sans reproche.* The Chevalier is a mounted figure,* an officer, a gentleman, proud of his family, proud of his calling. He is represented, even to the name, by George Dashiell Bayard of the 1st Cavalry, whose family claimed descent from the original Chevalier. As a child George Bayard was fascinated by his great-grandfather Colonel John Bayard, who had commanded the First Troop of Philadelphia Cavalry in the Revolution. He yearned to become a cavalry officer. His letters as a West Point cadet uphold the Chevalier aspiration almost to the point of absurdity, so imperious are they. "I have not submitted to the drudgery . . . of the last four years, merely for the privilege of chasing Indian thieves, or rotting in some remote . . . post of the interior. Alexander, Caesar and Bonaparte were only soldiers, so far as it respected their ascent to fame and power." If there should be no war

---

* "Bayard" has a second romantic association: it is also the name of the magical bay horse given by Charlemagne to the Four Sons of Aymon.

involving the United States, young Bayard announces that he will "seek some other field after a few years. . . . It may be Asia or Africa; or if nothing else offers" — here a note of anticlimax — "there is the *law*. That profession is allied by nature to the military profession. It is perpetual war on rascality. The bar and the bench are always engaged in that sort of war." A few months later, having graduated from the Academy, Second Lieutenant Bayard utters a prophecy from Fort Leavenworth: "The army within this generation will be called upon to perform great deeds, and in the shadowy mists of the future . . . I see the military, the chief of all the professions. I may not live to see it, but I see it now with my mind's eye."

The Bayards were socially prominent. So were the Kearnys of New York. Stephen Watts Kearny commanded the 1st Dragoons in the 1830's. His nephew Philip as a boy played at mimic campaigns with a set of several thousand lead soldiers, and continued this amusement when he was a student at Columbia. For the rest of his career, which ended with death in the Civil War, Philip Kearny was in and out of the American army, serving in the cavalry or associating himself with French units in North Africa and Italy.[19]

The Chevalier model has more elements of make-believe than the other two. It is naturally represented for the most part inside the regular army, but cannot find an altogether comfortable niche in an organization so small, so dispersed, so often called upon to deprecate or deny those very features which distinguish the Chevalier: dignity, breeding, display. Later this figure was successfully incorporated in American folklore, in the democratized guise of nature's aristocrat, the Cowboy.* In the decades before the Civil War the type even lacks a label by which he could be known. Everyone could have guessed what might be implied by *Quaker* and *Rifleman;* not everyone would have been able to say what was meant by *Chevalier.* This is only to stress that the specifications of the model are more diffuse, more clandestine, because less approved.

* The transition is nicely illustrated in the classic early cowboy novel, Owen Wister's *The Virginian* (1902). Though Wister's novel is set in Wyoming his hero comes from Virginia, which in romantic convention was conceded to be the especial realm of the American Chevalier.

Baudelaire describes the "dandy" of the period — the elegant, haughty man-about-town — as *"Hercule sans emploi,"* Hercules without labors to perform. The American Chevalier may be described in similar terms. He is a romantic hero in a society which likes to read about romantic heroes but can find no regular place for them and is committed to the proposition that they are somewhat un-American. At one extreme they fall under ridicule as dudes, tenderfeet, kid-glove gentry. At the other they are soldiers of fortune, adventurers, filibusters, outlaws. It is their fate to be ignored or laughed at until some later generation or the eye of memory endows them with that golden glow which eluded them in their own lifetime. Here is a picture by one of William Walker's filibusters, written half a century afterward:

In the 50's men looked upon life from a more romantic viewpoint than they do now. There was more sentiment, . . . more writing of love verses to sweethearts; grace and gallantry lent a charm to society . . .; the cavalier, with his plumes and ribbons, had not departed, and the music of the troubadour still tinkled amidst . . . the revelry. Those were the days when the ardor for adventure by land and sea was hot in the breasts of men. . . . Men had not outgrown the customs of their forefathers, and if they resorted to the *code duello* in defense of their honor, and the honor of women, they were moved by sincerity, and surrounded by traditions still too potent to be cast aside. Such were the men who took service under Walker, and were led by him in his desperate struggles to make real a dream that might have dazzled the great Corsican himself.[20]

This is such a medley of standard romantic images (including the allusion to "the great Corsican," Napoleon Bonaparte) that it lacks almost all sense of actuality. A similar queer unreality surrounds the old volunteer companies. Gazing at the sheet-music lithographs and the Huddy and Duval prints of these vanished troops, we are in the presence of an enigma. They are toy soldiers come to life; but it is only a dream life. This is how the sons of the republic, the clerks and attorneys and manufacturers, wish to be, once a week or once a month, and how their wives and girl friends wish them to be: gallants, gentlemen, Chevaliers. The need *is* felt in this American society, and to some extent gratified. George Bayard and Philip Kearny are confronted by the war they

THE DAUGHTER OF THE REGIMENT.

long for — though it kills them both. The filibusters do find themselves in possession of dream kingdoms — though they too nearly
all yield their lives in the attempt. The battlefields of Mexico do
witness sudden flowerings of the improbably gorgeous blossoms
of war. The Chevaliers step out of the pages of romantic literature, endowed for a moment with flesh and blood — and presently step back again into make-believe. They have an odd
abstract centrality in American history.

Quaker, Rifleman, Chevalier: the three styles tend to merge
into one another. The Quaker neither achieves nor quite desires
total detachment from the martial spirit, for he too in his way is a
patriot.* Franklin cannot help being pleased that John Paul

* Alexander McClurg, who reached the rank of colonel in the Civil War, said
that beforehand he hated war. He had been "deeply moved by . . . Charles
Sumner's splendid peace orations." He had "never taken any interest in volunteer
or militia soldiering," feeling contempt for "the showy uniforms and pompous
paradings." Mabel McIlvaine, ed., *Reminiscences of Chicago During the Civil War*
(Chicago, 1914), 100. Samuel G. French, the son of a lapsed Quaker, went to

Jones's flagship is named after his Quakerish creation, *Poor Richard*. Whitman cries hurrah for manifest destiny, a Quaker who admires the Rifleman though he has little enthusiasm for Chevalier gentilities. The Rifleman would sometimes like to be taken for a Chevalier. The latter, in his filibustering persona, is close to the aggressive, plundering Rifleman. Indeed, Charles Sumner pointed this out with Quakerish zeal in his peace address on "The True Grandeur of Nations" in 1845:

The Chevalier Bayard, cynosure of chivalry, . . . battling with the Spaniard, Señor Don Alonso de Soto Mayor, succeeded by a feint in striking him such a blow that the weapon, despite the gorget, penetrated the throat four fingers deep. The wounded Spaniard grappled with his antagonist until they both rolled on the ground, when Bayard, drawing his dagger, and thrusting the point directly into the nostrils of his foe, exclaimed, "Señor Don Alonso, surrender, or you are a dead man!" a speech which appeared superfluous, as the second of the Spaniard cried out, "Señor Bayard, he is dead already; you have conquered." The French knight "would gladly have given a hundred thousand crowns, if he had had them, to have vanquished him alive," says the Chronicle; but now . . . he . . . rose and drew his dead enemy from the field, saying to the second, "Señor Don Diego, have I done enough?" To which the other piteously replied, "Too much, Señor Bayard, for the *honor* of Spain!" When the latter very generously presented him with the corpse, it being his right, by the Law of Honor, to dispose of it as he thought proper: an act highly commended by the chivalrous Brantôme, who thinks it difficult to say which did most *honor* to the faultless knight, — not dragging the dead body by a leg ignominiously from the field, like the carcass of a dog, or condescending to fight while suffering under an ague.

In such a transaction, conferring honor upon the brightest son of chivalry, we learn the real character of an age whose departure has been lamented with such . . . eloquence. Thank God! the age of chivalry is gone; but it cannot be allowed to prolong its fanaticism of honor into our day. This must remain with the lances, swords, and daggers by which it was guarded, or appear, if it insists, only with its inseparable American companions, bowie-knife, pistol, and rifle.[21]

West Point and was converted into Chevalier-dom through marriage. Acquiring a Mississippi plantation, he forgot his New Jersey origins and became a Confederate major general. *Two Wars: An Autobiography of Gen. Samuel G. French* (Nashville, 1901), 132,181.

Quakerish, as Mark Twain is when he pours scorn on warfare and chivalry. But one suspects some of Sumner's scorn derives from a persistent Chevalier streak; we recall that he once sought a West Point nomination. He has discovered that Bayard was capable of the behavior of a frontier brawl; and gentlemen do not brawl.

Putting the matter more favorably, Rifleman and Chevalier in the United States disclosed a certain kinship in their response to heroic individualism. There are, however, basic differences. The Quaker and Rifleman models are avowedly democratic. The Rifleman is usually on foot, usually an enlisted man; he is a skirmisher, a rulebreaker. When he gets on to a horse he is a bummer, a bushwacker. The Chevalier, on the other hand, is a mounted gentleman, the symbol of authority, the conscious heir of a gracious tradition: the tradition of European officers, who being of the gentry do not kill prisoners and do not fraternize with rankers.[22] His code of honor antedates the spirit of nationalistic warfare. Ready to die for his country, he would also like to be able to die for something closer: his regiment perhaps, or his family, or the young woman whose lock of hair he carries.

In folklore the Chevalier has been assigned to the American South. Stuart, Pickett, Lee were all Virginians, and all described as Chevaliers. One reason, we have seen, was that the Chevalier idea is associated with yesteryear. It is a mode defeated by time, gracious and oddly compelling but on the whole an anachronism, more legendary than actual. The Lost Cause belongs in the same romantic limbo; in defeat the South claimed a monopoly of the Chevalier model.

The model was in truth almost as appealing in its very romanticism to the pre–Civil War North, whose gentry culture had a more genuine financial basis than that of the slave states. The crucial difference between the sections lay perhaps not in the greater Southern prevalence of the Chevalier model but in the greater Northern attachment to the Quaker model. Decade by decade the Quakerish mode became less common in the South. By 1860 it could be said that the Quaker model was represented there mainly in the figure of the slave — unarmed, rendered docile and without a voice. The Chevalier was left to speak for the charms of peaceable society: for instance in W. J. Grayson's *Hireling and Slave* (1854). But charms, as Grayson's poem demonstrates, cannot be very incisively rendered; and the Southern Chevalier had other, contrary values to uphold. North and South, the models of Chevalier and Rifleman were virtually interchangeable. It was the third element, the Quaker, that did not have a proper hearing below the Mason and Dixon line.

The American military ethos was composed of three rival yet complementary patterns. American society generally has functioned as an orchestration, even a harmony, of discords. For the nation as a whole the ethos worked surprisingly well. Quaker, Rifleman and Chevalier corresponded to broader divisions of reason, appetite, and sensibility. The first looked to the future, the second to the present, the third to the past. To the extent that it neglected the first, the antebellum white South enjoyed a greater apparent harmony. This was why some Northern soldiers fancied the Southern atmosphere was more congenial to them. But lacking the full, strident buzz of contradiction, the South was to suffer the consequences far into the future.

12

EPILOGUE: BULL RUN AND THE AFTERMATH

Our people remember with gratitude the great captains who, in the late war, led their soldiers to victory to save the Republic from overthrow.

— General James A. Garfield, *North American Review,* 1878

The People who were so grateful in 1865 for military service, now begrudge us every cent of pay and every ounce of bread we eat.

— General William T. Sherman, 11 January 1879

The Civil War virtually ended at Appomattox Court House in April 1865 when Lee surrendered to Grant. The house where they met belonged to one Wilmer McLean. In 1861 he had lived at Manassas Junction, close by the battleground of First Bull Run. McLean remarked that the war began in his back yard and finished in his front yard.[1]

We might expect these four terrible years of conflict to have far wider implications for the United States. There were plenty of signs of a changing attitude while the war was in progress. Young Harvard gentlemen such as Oliver Wendell Holmes, Jr., Charles Russell Lowell, Robert Gould Shaw, Henry Lee Higginson and Charles Francis Adams, Jr., welcomed the summons to action and leadership. America had been ailing; war's curative properties would set things right. Nor was it only those with aristocratic leanings who discerned the dawn of a new dispensation. Ralph Waldo Emerson, hitherto the gentlest and most withdrawn of men, began to exult in the purifying and organizing power of war. In 1863 he even accepted an appointment to the Board of Visitors at West Point. He much admired what he saw at the Academy; professional military training was the best possible basis of a "true aristocracy or 'the power of the Best,' — best scholars, best soldiers, best engineers, best commanders, best men."[2]

At a lower level the response of Charles Edwards Lester is fairly typical. Lester, a prolific and commonplace author, devoted himself to tending the wounded in Washington hospitals and from his experience drew some sketches entitled *The Light and Dark of the Rebellion* (1863). In his introduction he considers why America's early promise has not been sustained. Slavery, the "Dragon of Human Servitude," is one explanation; "greed for gain" is another. Then, "in the midst of our National Belshazzar-Feast, of pride, voluptuousness, and enchantment, the shot at Fort Sumter fell like a bolt of lightning. It struck the hearts of the revellers, and we began to take our eyes from the dust and turn them up to heaven." Later, discussing the lack of a cohesive national sentiment, Lester — as Secretary of State Seward had done in 1861 — recommends a foreign war as a sovereign remedy. To him and to others, including Senator Charles Sumner, with whom he was closely acquainted, war against England seemed the most satisfactory recourse. In this way Americans would recover their old martial heritage and with it their old pride of nationhood.[3]

Men of letters enlisted in the cause more readily than we would guess from the examples of the trio of young "draft-dodgers" — Mark Twain, William Dean Howells, Henry James — who were later to define the literary history of the Gilded Age. Charles Godfrey Leland, best known previously for his comic German dialect poetry, edited the staunchly patriotic *Continental Monthly* in 1862–1863 and became a contributor to the *United States Service Magazine*, a well-produced monthly which started publication in January 1864. In between its articles on military affairs come contributions like Leland's survey of "War-Songs and Their Influence in History," and poems by the Reverend E. A. Washburne such as "The Battle of the Dead Cid":

O my country! God through trial brings the Man as pure, as strong!
O blind giant, shorn and fettered by thy little masters long;
Grinding still for greedy factions, groping dim thro' years of sleep,
Long enow the lazy currents thro' thy drowsy veinlets creep,
Long enow thine iron manhood eaten hangs with selfish rust.
Wakes to-day that hero-spirit, stands erect that hero-dust!

A less turgid piece, in the June 1864 issue of the *Service Magazine*, was "The Probable Influence of the New Military Element on Our Social and National Character," by Charles Astor Bristed. Before the war Bristed, the great-grandson of John Jacob Astor, had studied at Yale and Cambridge and written such volumes as *The Upper Ten Thousand: Sketches of American Society* (1852), *Five Years in an English University* (1852), and *Pieces of a Broken-Down Critic* (1858). With the outbreak of fighting Bristed expressed himself in more forcible accents. The titles of his new works indicate the change: *Now Is the Time to Settle It* (1862), *No Surrender* (1863), *The Cowards' Convention* (1864). In his *Service Magazine* article this fastidious cosmopolite assumes that the "new military element" will be permanent. What is more, he delights in the prospect. Henceforward, thanks to America's awakened martial instincts, his countrymen will take more physical exercise. "Soldiers," he says, "must be men of considerable physical strength or endurance, or both; and, as uniforms are sure to be popular and fashionable, manly qualities will also become so." Second, the "presence of a military element among us" will bring about "a more correct appreciation of some classes of men" who have hitherto not been highly esteemed: namely, those who "prefer shooting and fishing excursions and country rambles, to the confinement of an office or shop." Third and most important will be "the establishment of an orderly spirit and a settled regard for law." Lawlessness formerly permeated the nation. But "men trained in the stern, unyielding discipline of the camp . . . will not be apt hastily to violate the law of the land or excuse its violation in others."[4]

When the war was over something of this mood remained. To thoughtful ex-officers it was an experience from which profound lessons could be drawn. In the eyes of Oliver Wendell Holmes, Jr., and many of his stamp the years of bloodshed were more formative than any college. Discipline, attachment to a cause, comradeship, stoicism, chivalric conduct: these were so valuable that for their sake alone the Civil War would have been worthwhile. The conservatively minded, shocked by the persistent lawlessness of the 1870's and 1880's, wistfully recalled the days when the Union had a million men under arms and the authorities were prompt to clap troublemakers into jail. For a while government service, which they conceived as quasi-military in its scope for firm, centralized, elitist direction, appealed to such competent veterans as Francis A. Walker and John Wesley Powell. For similar reasons they gave enthusiastic support to schemes of civil service reform, which would utilize "the power of the Best."[5]

Certain reformers with larger hopes described their imagined America in language reminiscent of Charles Astor Bristed. A good example is Edward Bellamy's Utopian novel *Looking Backward* (1888). Bellamy's Boston of A.D. 2000, though a most benevolent society, is nevertheless based upon an "Industrial Army" differentiated by military rank and recruited by means of a type of conscription. Plunged back from this neat, obedient society into the competitive, shapeless, unhappy Boston of 1887, Bellamy's hero is comforted by the sight of a military parade. "Here at last," he exclaims, "were order and reason, an exhibition of what intelligent cooperation can accomplish. The people who stood looking on with kindling faces — could it be that the sight had for them no more than but a spectacular interest? Could they fail to see that it was their perfect concert of action, their organization under one control, which made these men the tremendous engine they were, able to vanquish a mob ten times as numerous?"

Bellamy abhorred war. But he respected soldiers because theirs was the one pursuit in which "every sordid standard of merit and achievement" was rejected. The military in the act of joining the colors "throw away the purse": they absent themselves from what C. E. Lester called the nation's "Belshazzar-Feast" of greedy materialism. Bellamy's high regard for the military was reciprocated. A Boston Bellamy Club, founded in September 1888, was composed of retired army officers. From it grew the Nationalist movement, which sought to propagate Bellamy's generous-hearted if unwittingly authoritarian notions.[6]

Other reformers also paid tribute, especially in imaginative literature, to the integrity and dignity of professional soldiers. In Benjamin Rush Davenport's *Uncle Sam's Cabins* (1895), one of the crop of fantasies inspired by Bellamy, America has succumbed to a sort of corrupt feudalism. Davenport's clergyman-hero, wounded in an affray, is safeguarded by a regular army battalion whose commander refuses to hand him over to the wicked authorities ("The colonel regarding Weaving with eyes in which shone the old, gallant, honest fire of the West Point cadet, before age and lack of promotion has dimmed its lustre, continued, 'My honor is at stake in the matter. . . . As much as I value his Excellency's favor, I cannot forget that I am a gentleman as well as a soldier'"). Another novel of the future, *Philip*

EPILOGUE: BULL RUN AND THE AFTERMATH

Dru: Administrator (1912), written by Woodrow Wilson's friend Colonel Edward M. House, envisages a social revolution led by a virtuous despot who is a West Point graduate inspired by lofty patriotic ideals. General Dru, assembling an army in Wisconsin, advances eastward on his grand liberating errand. He destroys the forces of the administration in one sanguinary battle which claims over sixty thousand lives, consoling himself with the thought that those killed on his own side "had died in order that others might live the better. Twice before had the great republic been baptized in blood and each time the result had changed the thought and destiny of man." So soothing is this reflection that Dru, wearied by his exertions, at once falls into "a dreamless, restful sleep."[7] The values of the Military Academy are upheld too in some of the cozier fiction of the post–Civil War decades, for instance in Frederick Whittaker's *The Cadet Button: A Novel of American Army Life* (1878). The only cads in Whittaker's tale of Indian fighting and romantic entanglement are persons who have been commissioned direct from civilian life: the officers educated at the Point prove to be splendid fellows.

The nation's revised view of its army might seem to be summed up in the words of James A. Garfield, war hero and prominent Republican, in an article written for the *North American Review* in 1878, two years before he was elected to the presidency: "A republic, however free, requires the service of a certain number of men whose ambition is higher than mere private gains, whose lives are inseparable from the life of the nation, and whose labors and emoluments depend absolutely upon the honor and prosperity of the Government, and who can advance themselves only by serving their country."[8] Forgotten apparently were the wartime doubts as to West Point loyalty. Remembered certainly were the political advantages of war service: except for Grover Cleveland, every President from Grant to McKinley had been an officer in the Union army.

The appearance is deceptive. In the fever of the Civil War, as in 1917–1918 and in 1941–1945, articulate Americans reacted with a belligerence that was both fierce and short-lived. Few retained such vehemence for long. The desire for a quasi-military

431

elite faded away in face of the triumph of *laissez-faire,* and was not revived until the next fit of excitement engendered in 1898 by the Spanish-American War. Emory Upton's *Military Policy of the United States,* left incomplete at his death by suicide in 1881, was not published until 1904. He had fallen a prey to illness and despair during the "Army's Dark Ages" — the title of the chapter covering the years 1865–1880 in W. A. Ganoe's *History of the United States Army.* Despite Garfield's optimistic assurances, Congress reverted to its old suspicion of the military establishment. William T. Sherman, who followed Grant as general commanding the army in 1869, was so exasperated by Washington intrigue that from 1874 to 1876 he set up headquarters in far-off St. Louis. Complaining of a bill in Congress to reduce the number of army officers, he noted that after every American war there had been the same ruthless axing of personnel. "The People who were so grateful in 1865 for military service," he said bitterly, "now begrudge us every cent of pay and every ounce of bread we eat." Though the reduced army of twenty-five thousand men was highly professional, its very professionalism isolated it the more from the general population. True, West Point's austerely genteel code of "duty, honor, country" was no longer a subject for dispute; but the Academy's educational status stood lower than before the war: there were many more colleges in existence, and two or three which offered engineering courses — once the Academy's special pride — of comparable merit. The standing of the navy in the "Dark Ages" before modernization was ignominious. Captain Alfred Thayer Mahan, who was to win international acclaim for his writings, recollected that in the early days of his career there was not sufficient national interest even to dispute the necessity of the navy's existence, although as late as 1875 "an old-time Jeffersonian Democrat repeated to me with conviction the master's dictum, that the navy was a useless appendage."[9]

Such opinions were in fact not confined to antique political partisans. The reformer Henry George declared in 1883 that "the American Republic has no more need for its burlesque of a navy than a peaceable giant would have for a stuffed club or a tin sword. It is only maintained for the sake of the officers and the naval rings. . . . If war should ever be forced upon us, we could safely rely upon science and invention which are already superseding navies faster than they can be built." He thought the army equally useless and, like the navy, "repugnant to the democratic idea" because of the caste-line between officers and men. The system was "an insult to democracy."[10]

Inside the system, sensitive professionals were dismayed by the nation's renewed hostility or indifference. A captain in the Corps of Engineers tried in 1878 to account for the "unfriendly feeling towards our little army and its nursery, the Academy." One factor was that the army, still mainly Northern in composition, had inevitably been regarded in the South during the Reconstruction period as an alien occupation force. In the North radical sentiment had been inflamed the previous year by the widespread deployment of regular troops to suppress "the organized class rebellions known as labor strikes." North and South, the army attracted further odium by having to act "as a *posse* to suppress illicit distilling, an art but recently free to all." Finally, the army was resented as forming a distinct class: "they seem not to be of the people, nor as many would argue, for the people."

Colonel Kautz, another intelligent soldier and of long experience, maintained in 1876 that despite the terrible cost in life and property the Civil War had "taught us nothing." In the event of another war, "I shall expect to see gallant men marched like sheep to the slaughter, the victims of military ignorance, and every other profession than the military contending for martial honor at the expense of national life and treasure."[11]

As in the prewar doldrums, officers grew querulous and petty. In the closing months of his life poor Emory Upton, who had begun active service at Bull Run under Irvin McDowell, was now once more commanded by McDowell, out in San Francisco; and was irked because his chief insisted that every dollar of expenditure be strictly accounted for. One observer felt that the army was at least partly to blame for its depressed condition. In 1880 a former officer, Duane Greene, produced a resentful analysis of the *Ladies and Officers of the United States Army*. The service was, he charged, full of "patrician prejudice" — heightened by snob-

433

bish wives. It was "a little domain . . ., isolated by its peculiar customs . . .; an aristocracy by selection and the halo of tradition . . . an unexplored region to the mass of the people, and . . . not the Dorado of morality, honor and chivalry that many believe." Officers with a "haughty assumption of superiority" made life miserable for the men in their charge. Greene described the case of an educated young German who had run away from home, come to America, and enlisted in a cavalry troop. The captain in command of the troop victimized him until he was driven to desert.[12]

Perhaps then the distance between Bull Run and Appomattox was not great after all. Seen in this light, the remarkable feature of the Civil War is not that it wrought so much change but that it wrought so little. One begins to wonder whether the conflict — apart from ending slavery and denying the possibility of future attempts at secession — did anything more than confirm Americans in their existing prejudices, and provide them with an additional store of anecdotes, legends and metaphors — ranging from the roseate to the apocalyptic. Otherwise, it can be argued, matters remained more or less as before. Not entirely, of course. The nation's conception of combat was somewhat modified. This war had seen fighting of a scale and duration unprecedented in American history. It was less easy now to believe in dazzling, decisive victories achieved by one man or a handful of men. The techniques of mass warfare were dimly emerging. A theorist endowed with prophetic insight might have perceived — in the huge civilian armies, the dismounting of cavalry, the reliance on trenches, the destructive power of short-range artillery — the shape of things to come half a century hence.

Such lessons were not learned, in Europe or the United States. One reason is that they were enigmatic, pessimistic lessons. War was hell, and likely to become more hellish. The only way to minimize its horror, seemingly, was to emulate the Prussian example and organize society as if war might break out tomorrow. If this was the major lesson of Bull Run and all the other slaughter-grounds stretching on to Appomattox, Americans were perhaps right to immerse themselves instead in civilian concerns. Better Belshazzar's Feast than the garrison state. As in the aftermath of 1918 and 1945, so the reaction to 1865 was hasty demobilization (eight hundred thousand men were released from the Union army in a few months), a frantic picking up of the threads of civilian life, and a gradual retrospective romanticizing of the war's events. Then as later it was necessary to believe that individual courage and skill still counted decisively, that the dead had died valiantly and valuably, and that certain special heroes — deified by praise, humanized through nicknames — such as Stonewall Jackson, Jeb Stuart, Fustest-with-the-Mostest Forrest, Phil Sheridan and Uncle Billy Sherman, had revealed well-nigh magical talents. If the true war did not get into the books this was because many of the participants, in common with soldiers of other wars, no longer knew what the true war had been. Moreover, Americans could justifiably feel that the supreme lesson of the war was in fact optimistic. God might have punished the nation for past errors: he had at length helped America to a victory which had at moments seemed impossible.

Otherwise much in the Civil War was to be forgotten. Involvement in it was intense yet oddly superficial. Afterward, the United States was not transformed by any "new military element." The only major social innovation of a military nature was the establishment of the Grand Army of the Republic. But the annual encampments of the G.A.R., with their blend of nostalgia, politics and lobbying, were firmly in the old American tradition. The regular army seemed essentially the same as before: enlisted men drawn from immigrants, officers mostly from West Point. The militia, until the reforms of 1903 created a genuine National Guard, was as hitherto a welter of individual units with a few ardent or vociferous spokesmen to reiterate grievances and aspirations. The fears of Colonel Kautz were to be borne out in 1898 when, as he foretold, short-service regiments would return from war "with ranks depleted and constitutions broken," not by an enemy but through their inability to take care of themselves.*

In the post-Appomattox world American society was possibly

* "The death rate from disease was higher during a part of the time in the army of 1898 than in the army of 1861." Walter Kempster, M.D., "The Army of 1898 and The Army of 1861 — A Comparison" (paper read December 6, 1899 before the Commandery of . . . Wisconsin, Military Order of the Loyal Legion of the U. S.).

even more civilian in outlook than before. The captains of industry rather than the captains of armies were the nation's modern heroes. Bellamy's "Industrial Army" was more a metaphor than a martial recommendation. Nowhere is this more crisply dramatized than in a short novel, *The Great War Syndicate* (1889), by the humorous writer Frank R. Stockton, which could be construed as an ironical gloss on Garfield's vision of "the service of . . . men whose ambition is higher than mere private gain," or as inspired by Henry George's belief in the efficacy of "science and invention" in winning America's future wars. Stockton imagines such a war, in the quite near future, between the United States and Britain.

The American government, faced with this crisis, is in no condition to launch an invasion of Canada — theoretically the most obvious step — or to protect its coasts against the formidable British navy. Its perplexity is suddenly resolved by the initiative of a group of "great capitalists," men "accustomed to occupying themselves with great enterprises." Forming a syndicate, they offer to "assume the entire control and expense" of the war on a contract basis, with an appropriate schedule of forfeits and bonuses. The quicker they win the war the more money they make. One stipulation is that "the land and naval forces of the United States . . . should be maintained as a defensive force and not brought into action unless any failure on the part of the Syndicate should render such action necessary."

The government accepts the offer, reflecting that "the men who offered to relieve the executive departments of their perilous responsibilities" possess great ability and prodigious resources. The public shares their confidence. The Syndicate's own reasoning is a world away from that of the old-time Chevaliers: "success would be a vast benefit and profit, not only to the business enterprises in which these men were severally engaged, but to the business of the whole country. To save the United States from a dragging war, and to save themselves from the effects of it, were the prompting motives for the formation of the Syndicate." In other words, what is good for the Great War Syndicate is good for the country.

Calling in scientists and engineers, the Syndicate devises two entirely new weapons of war. The first, a "crab," is a monitor-like vessel equipped with a pair of huge underwater claws. The second, a "repeller," is an armor-plated ship mounting a single gun which fires a strange projectile known as the "instantaneous motor." This turns out to be a kind of atomic bomb. In various bloodless engagements the Syndicate's flotilla of crabs paralyzes the enemy's war fleet by ripping away its screws and rudders. The repellers demonstrate their appalling destructive capacity by blowing up remote sections of coastline. Well within the twelve months allowed by contract, the Syndicate persuades the British government that further resistance is futile. Peace is signed. Britain and the United States become allies, agreeing to preserve and share the secret of the instantaneous motor. They begin to disarm, followed by the rest of mankind. In the whole impeccable operation the American army plays no part whatsoever. Nor does the navy, except when one bellicose captain breaks the rules by trying to sail out against the British and is towed helplessly back to port by a crab. The Syndicate's ships are manned by civilians.[13]

From the hindsight of the 1960's, Stockton's story seems almost uncannily prescient except for its cheerfulness. Since then war has indeed become largely a problem of "science and invention," obliterating any clear division between soldier and civilian. We may therefore wonder why *The Great War Syndicate* is not more widely known. Part of the answer is that Stockton, with his whimsical humor and his conventional style, appears to have defined his own place as a minor author — one who does not try for big effects. His little novel amused contemporaries, as he intended. As he also intended, it did not startle them; for his readers recognized it as belonging to a comic genre which depended for effect upon paradox and improbability. It employed the same idiom as those cartoons of the period which pretended to predict the future. The joke lay in reversing familiar, accepted standards: so women were drawn in men's clothes, men in aprons holding babies; and in telling technological tall tales: cities in the sky, housework done by merely pressing buttons. To Stockton and his audience the *War Syndicate* was a joke rather than a parable.

Its impact might have been much greater if the story had been set in Wilhelmine Germany, where the military actually were in high authority and would have taken affront.

In the United States the response was simply mild amusement, in part because the joke was too old and in part because it was seen as only a joke. Within the American military heritage was a habitual assumption that soldiers must always defer to civilians: they always had done. There was also, with no real contradiction, an acceptance that the nation could not fight a war without at least some trained officers and men. Stockton was only teasing. He had written a funny little exercise in exaggeration, more or less in the Quaker tradition: witty enough to have amused Benjamin Franklin, ingenious enough to have pleased, say, Herman Haupt. After all, where would the Syndicate have found its scientific experts, if not in the Corps of Engineers?

CHAPTER NOTES

The sources on which this volume depends are I hope sufficiently indicated in the chapter notes. A great deal exists in printed form: for example, congressional debates, the annual reports of Secretaries of War, *American State Papers: Military Affairs,* a vast quantity of biographies, memoirs and institutional histories. The most important unprinted material is to be found in the National Archives, Washington, D.C., among the ledgers, files and letter-books of the War Department. I am conscious of having done no more than sample these, though enough to be reasonably sure that I was on the right track.

Until recently, American military history has tended to be narrative or antiquarian in approach. Some admirable work (including the narrative volumes of Bruce Catton and Douglas Southall Freeman) has been produced within this tradition. Much of it however was conceived in a narrow spirit. Fresh vitality has been imparted to the study of military affairs by such scholars as William H. Goetzmann, Samuel P. Huntington, Morris Janowitz, Jay Luvaas, Walter Millis, Louis Morton, Allan Nevins, Theodore Ropp, Russell F. Weigley and T. Harry Williams, who have demonstrated that it may be used to shed light upon American society as a whole. Two works of this broad nature, published too late for me to benefit from them, are Walter Millis, ed., *American Military Thought* (New York, 1966), a valuable anthology, and Russell Weigley's comprehensive and dispassionate *History of the United States Army* (New York, 1967). Another book that appeared too late for me to plunder is Stephen E. Ambrose's account of West Point, *Duty, Honor, Country* (Baltimore, 1966).

CHAPTER 1: PROLOGUE: FIRST BULL RUN AND ITS MEANINGS

1. Much of the material in this chapter has been drawn from standard reference works, including the *Dictionary of American Biography;* Joseph Mills Hanson, *Bull Run Remembers* (Manassas, Va., 1953); Robert U. Johnson and Clarence C. Buel, eds., *Battles and Leaders of the Civil War* (4 vols., New York, 1884–1887), especially "Campaign of the First Bull Run" in vol. 1; Mark M. Boatner, III, *Civil War Dictionary* (New York, 1959); Douglas Southall Freeman, *Lee's Lieutenants* (3 vols., New York, 1942–1944), vol. 1, *Manassas to Malvern Hill;*

Ezra Warner, *Generals in Gray* (Baton Rouge, La., 1959) and *Generals in Blue* (Baton Rouge, 1964); and Frank Moore, ed., *Rebellion Record* (11 vols., New York, 1861–1865), a rich miscellany from which most of the newspaper references are taken. A general view of the battle is provided in R. M. Johnston, *Bull Run: Its Strategy and Its Tactics* (Boston, 1913), and in R. H. Beatie, Jr., *Road to Manassas* (New York, 1961), though neither is of great value.

2. On newspapers and correspondents, in addition to F. Moore, see W. H. Russell, *My Diary, North and South* (2 vols., London, 1863); Emmet Crozier, *Yankee Reporters, 1861–1865* (New York, 1956); and Bernard Weisberger, *Reporters for the Union* (Boston, 1953).

3. Whether or not Chatham R. Wheat deserves a whole biography to himself, he gets one in Charles L. Dufour, *Gentle Tiger* (Baton Rouge, La., 1957). George Utassy and others are more tersely described in Ella Lonn, *Foreigners in the Union Army and Navy* (Baton Rouge, 1951). John B. Gordon's early experiences are recounted in his *Reminiscences of the Civil War* (New York, 1903); on clothing, see 26–27. Beauregard is the subject of an admirable biography by T. Harry Williams, *Napoleon in Gray* (Baton Rouge, 1954). Corcoran is referred to again in Chapter 7.

4. Slocum's premonition is described in *The Diary of George Templeton Strong* (4 vols., New York, 1952), III, 179; and Bartow's in Bruce Catton, *The Coming Fury* (London, 1962), 472–473. The Mangum story is from Moore, *Rebellion Record*.

5. The raising and the initiation of a company of the New York 27th are vividly conveyed in H. Seymour Hall, "Personal Experience . . . ," a paper read before the Kansas Commandery of the Military Order of the Loyal Legion of the U.S. on 4 May 1892. The *Richmond Despatch* report is in Moore, II, 49. The Ewell anecdote is from J. B. Gordon, *Reminiscences*, 42–43.

6. The religious qualms of O. O. Howard are revealed in his *Autobiography* (2 vols., New York, 1907), I, 164–165; and those of T. J. Jackson in Lenoir Chambers, *Stonewall Jackson* (2 vols., New York, 1959), I, 476. The poem from the *Boston Herald* is in Moore, II, "Poetry, Rumors, and Incidents," 4.

7. Most of the information in these paragraphs comes from Boatner, *Civil War Dictionary*. On Ruffin's appearance at Bull Run, see Avery Craven, *Edmund Ruffin* (New York, 1932), 230–231.

8. Angus J. Johnston, II, *Virginia Railroads in the Civil War* (Chapel Hill, N.C., 1961), 30–31, 263.

9. On Wadsworth and the McCooks, see L. E. Chittenden, *Personal Reminiscences, 1840–1890* (New York, 1893), 304–309, and *D.A.B.*, XI, 600–604, XIX, 308–309. On Thomasson see *History of the 71st Regiment N.G., N.Y.* (New York, 1919), 185.

10. Logan's dramatic appearance on the battlefield is depicted in his *Volunteer Soldier of America* (Chicago, 1887), 73. The disappointment of Confederate officials, left behind in Richmond while Davis went off to Manassas, is described in William C. Harris, *Leroy Pope Walker: Confederate Secretary of War* (Tuscaloosa, Ala., 1962), 95. The disintegration of the 71st New York is delicately explained in *History of the 71st Regiment*, 183, 192–194.

11. P. S. Michie, *Life and Letters of Emory Upton* (New York, 1885), 54–55; *DAB* XI, 435–436. In the same letter, written four days after the battle, Upton added: "I have a high respect for Mr. Lovejoy, because he fights for his principles and is a brave man." See also Stephen E. Ambrose, *Upton and the Army* (Baton Rouge, 1964). The courage of Washburne and Kellogg is cited in Moore, II, 87. Wade's performance is described in Lloyd Lewis, *It Takes All Kinds* (New York, 1947), 24–25.

12. The arguments of Logan's huge, vehement *The Volunteer Soldier of America* (Chicago, 1887) are more or less repeated in Benjamin F. Butler, *Butler's Book* (Boston, 1892) and in such works by John McA. Palmer as *Three War Statesmen: Washington, Lincoln, Wilson* (Garden City, N.Y., 1930) and *America in Arms* (New Haven, 1941).

13. For example, in Arthur A. Ekirch, Jr., *The Civilian and the Military* (New York, 1956).

14. Michie, *Upton*, 429 (letter of 31 October 1879).

15. Nolan P. Harmon, *The Famous Case of Myra Clark Gaines* (Baton Rouge, 1943), 243; Henry S. Commager, *Theodore Parker* (Boston, 1947), 191–193.

16. Paul M. Angle, ed., *Herndon's Life of Lincoln* (Greenwich, Conn., 1961), 115.

17. Emerson, *Journals*, 10 January 1847, in Bliss Perry, ed., *The Heart of Emerson's Journals* (London, 1927), 221.

CHAPTER 2: THE CONFUSED HERITAGE AND ITS CONTINUANCE

1. For a concise outline of British civil-military experience, see J. S. Omond, *Parliament and the Army, 1642–1904* (Cambridge, 1933), 1–59. A good summary of the Anglo-American military tradition is provided in Theodore Ropp, *War in the Modern World* (Durham, N.C., 1959), ch. 3.

2. Thomas Babington Macaulay, *The History of England from the Accession of James II* (Everyman ed., London, 1906), III, 530, 534–547.

3. C. M. Clode, *Military Forces of the Crown* (London, 1869), I, 223–224; Daniel J. Boorstin, *The Mysterious Science of the Law: An Essay on Blackstone's Commentaries* (repr. Boston, 1958), 3–4.

4. Basil Williams, *The Whig Supremacy, 1714–1760* (Oxford, 1939), 203–211.

5. J. R. Western, *The English Militia in the Eighteenth Century* (London, 1965), is an excellent study. For earlier work, see Col. George J. Hay, *An Epitomized History of the Militia (The "Constitutional Force")* London, c. 1905), a dreary compendium, and Cecil Sebag-Montefiore, *A History of the Volunteer Forces . . . to . . . 1860* (London, 1908).

6. There is an admirable analysis in Daniel J. Boorstin, *The Americans: The Colonial Experience* (New York, 1958), 345–372. See also Howard H. Peckham, *The Colonial Wars, 1689–1762* (Chicago, 1964). For a detailed account of the crisis of 1675–1676, Douglas E. Leach, *Flintlock and Tomahawk: New England in King Philip's War* (1958; repr. New York, 1966), and Bernard Bailyn, ed., *Pamphlets of the American Revolution, 1750–1776,* I (Cambridge, Mass., 1965), 41–44, for a valuable condensed discussion.

7. Clarence E. Carter, "The Office of Commander in Chief: A Phase of Imperial Unity on the Eve of the Revolution," in Richard B. Morris, ed., *The Era of the Revolution* (1939; repr. New York, 1965), 171–172. George Otto Trevelyan, *The American Revolution,* condensed and ed. by Richard B. Morris (New York and London, 1965), 57–74.

8. Merrill Jensen, *The Articles of Confederation: An Interpretation of the Socio-Constitutional History of the American Revolution, 1774–1781* (Madison, Wis., 1940; repr. 1959), 194.

9. G. H. Guttridge, *English Whiggism and the American Revolution* (Berkeley, Cal., 1942, repr. 1963), 104; Douglas Southall Freeman, *George Washington,* V (New York, 1952), 416, 429–437; Louis Smith, *American Democracy and Military Power* (Chicago, 1951), 23–24.

10. *Papers of Alexander Hamilton,* ed. Harold C. Syrett and Jacob E. Cooke (New York 1961—), III, 291–293; VI, 333–335; Orville T. Murphy, "The American Revolutionary Army and the Concept of *Levée en Masse," Military Affairs,* XXIII (Spring 1959), 13–20; Durand Echeverria and Orville T. Murphy, eds., "The American Revolutionary Army: A French Estimate in 1777," *Military Affairs,* XXVII (Spring 1963), 1–7. The author of this account is tentatively identified as a young ex-officer named Louis de Recicourt de Ganot.

11. Harry M. Ward, *The Department of War, 1781–1795* (Pittsburgh, 1962), 57, 75–81. For this and the next few paragraphs see also James R. Jacobs, *The Beginning of the U. S. Army, 1783–1812* (Princeton, N.J., 1947).

12. Quoted in William B. Prendergast, "The Navy and Civil Liberty," *U. S. Naval Institute Proceedings,* LXXIV (October 1948), 1263.

13. Charles P. Whittemore, *A General of the Revolution: John Sullivan of New Hampshire* (New York, 1961), 217; Smith, *American Democracy and Military Power,* 27–28; *Papers of Alexander Hamilton,* V, 169.

14. *Journal of William Maclay,* ed. Edgar S. Maclay (New York, 1890), 226–227.

15. There is an excellent analysis of the issues in James Morton Smith, *Freedom's Fetters: The Alien and Sedition Laws and American Civil Liberties* (Ithaca, N.Y., 1956), 373–382.

16. Jacobs, *Beginning of the U. S. Army,* 131, 192; William A. Ganoe, *History of the United States Army* (New York, 1942), 99–103.

17. Smith, *Freedom's Fetters,* 376n.

18. Harold Sprout and Margaret Sprout, *The Rise of American Naval Power, 1776–1918* (Princeton, N.J., 1942), 55–57; Felix Gilbert, *To the Farewell Address: Ideas of Early American Foreign Policy* (Princeton, N.J., 1961), 19–43.

19. Walter Millis, *Arms and Men: A Study of American Military History* (New York, 1956), 43–53.

20. Representative Troup of Georgia, quoted in John William Ward, *Andrew Jackson: Symbol for an Age* (New York, 1955), 8. Ward's whole analysis of Jacksonian attitudes, military and otherwise, is worth reading.

21. Millis, *Arms and Men,* 80–85; C. Joseph Bernardo and Eugene H. Bacon, *American Military Policy: Its Development Since 1775* (Harrisburg, Pa., 1955), 148–151.

22. [Richard Cobden], *England, Ireland, and America, by A Manchester Manufacturer* (London, 1835), 110–114.

23. Emerson Davis, *The Half Century; or, A History of Changes . . . Between 1800 and 1850* (Boston, 1851), 87. Davis estimates the annual cost of a normal school at $2,000–$2,500.

24. Arthur E. Ekirch, Jr., *The Civilian and the Military* (New York, 1956), 6, 12.

25. Alice Felt Tyler, *Freedom's Ferment* (Minneapolis, 1945; New York, 1962), 397–398.

26. Merle E. Curti, *The American Peace Crusade, 1815–1860* (Durham, N.C., 1929), 6–34; Tyler, 402–404; Arthur A. Ekirch, Jr., *The Idea of Progress in America, 1815–1860* (New York, 1944, 1951), 67; Christina Phelps, *The Anglo-American Peace Movement in the Mid-Nineteenth Century* (New York, 1930), 36–40.

27. Thomas C. Upham, *The Manual of Peace; Exhibiting the Evils and Remedies of War* (Boston, 1842), 152–153; Merle Curti, *The Learned Blacksmith: The Letters and Journals of Elihu Burritt* (New York, 1937).

28. Charles Sumner, *Addresses on War,* ed. Edwin D. Mead (Boston, 1902), 47, 86–92; Abiel Abbot Livermore, *War with Mexico Reviewed* (Boston, 1850), 240–242.

29. Upham, *Manual of Peace*, 208. For a hostile account of Jefferson's "Chinese policy," see J. T. Danvers, *A Picture of a Republican Magistrate of the New School* (New York, 1808), 41–44.

30. Clifford S. Griffin, *Their Brothers' Keepers: Moral Stewardship in the United States, 1800–1865* (New Brunswick, N.J., 1960), 244–245; John Morley, *Life of Richard Cobden* (2 vols., London, 1908), II, 117–118.

CHAPTER 3: THE MARTIAL SPIRIT

1. See Howard H. Peckham, *The Colonial Wars, 1689–1762* (Chicago, 1964).

2. Page Smith, *John Adams* (Garden City, N.Y., 1962), I, 202, 462.

3. Charles Sumner, *Addresses on War,* ed. Edwin D. Mead (Boston, 1902), 10, 94–96; Thomas C. Upham, *The Manual of Peace; Exhibiting the Evils and Remedies of War* (Boston, 1842), 177–178.

4. Upham, *Manual of Peace*, 157–158, 183.

5. George H. Calcott, "History Enters the Schools," *American Quarterly*, XI, no. 4 (1959), 476. Horace Mann, the Massachusetts educator, was one of the contemporaries who complained that children's schoolbooks placed too much emphasis on warfare. Arthur E. Ekirch, Jr., *The Civilian and the Military* (New York, 1956), 79.

6. Charles J. Peterson, *The Military Heroes of the War of 1812*, and *The Military Heroes of the War with Mexico* (2 vols. in 1, Philadelphia, 10th ed., 1852), 91. Peterson, a Philadelphia author, also published books on the Revolutionary War and the U. S. Navy. The reference to Lincoln is in Arthur E. Bestor, David C. Mearns and Jonathan Daniels, *Three Presidents and Their Books* (Urbana, 1963), 71. Among other works of this kind were Thomas Wilson, *The Biography of the Principal American Military and Naval Heroes* (2 vols., New York, 1817–1819); Thomas Wyatt, *Memoirs of the Generals, Commodores, and Other Commanders . . . in the American Army and Navy . . .* (Philadelphia, 1848); Fayette Robinson, *An Account of the Organization of the Army of the United States* (2 vols., Philadelphia, 1848); John Frost, *The Mexican War and Its Warriors* (Philadelphia, 1848); Henry W. Harrison, *The Battle-Fields of the Republic from Lexington to the City of Mexico* (Philadelphia, 1857); Jacob K. Neff, *The Army and Navy of America* (Lancaster, Pa., 1857), an enlarged edition of a work first published in 1845, and Robert Tomes, *Battles of America by Sea and Land* (3 vols., New York, 1859–1861).

7. *The Letters of Herman Melville,* ed. Merrell R. Davis and William H. Gilman (New Haven, 1960), 29; Abiel Abbot Livermore, *War with Mexico Reviewed* (Boston, 1850), 227–229; Lieutenant Colonel C. M. Sleigh, *Pine Forests and Hacmatack Clearings* (London, 1853), 310–313.

8. Brainerd Dyer, *Zachary Taylor* (Baton Rouge, 1946), 267, 280, 293, 303; "Military Presidents," *United States Magazine and Democratic Review*, XXVI (June 1850), 480–498; Albert Somit, "The Military Hero as Presidential Candidate," *Public Opinion Quarterly*, XII (Summer 1948), 192–200; Livermore, *War with Mexico Reviewed*, 206–207.

9. William H. Sumner, *An Inquiry into the Importance of the Militia . . .* (Boston, 1823), 70; Charles Roll, *Colonel Dick Thompson: The Persistent Whig* (Indianapolis, 1948), 22–23; *Army & Navy Chronicle*, X (2 April 1840), 220; Charles Dickens, *Life and Adventures of Martin Chuzzlewit* (London, 1954), 262; *Texas Times* (Galveston), 19 October 1842, quoted in W. Eugene Hollon and Ruth Lapham Butler, eds., *William Bollaert's Texas* (Norman, Okla., 1956), 80–82; and see Arthur K. Moore, *The Frontier Mind: A Cultural Analysis of the Kentucky Frontiersman* (Lexington, Ky., 1957), 122.

10. There is much interesting detail, and some less interesting, in William Couper, *One Hundred Years at V.M.I.* (4 vols., Richmond, Va., 1939). See also Oliver J. Bond, *The Story of the Citadel* (Richmond, Va., 1936).

11. Henry B. Stanton, *Random Recollections* (New York, 1887), 29. Stanton became a prominent abolitionist. A generation later an Alabama boy of fifteen was dazzled by a display of the same type presented by the cadets of La Grange Military Academy at a county fair. "The beautifully fitting uniforms of gray and white, . . . the guns and bayonets glinting in the sunlight, . . . the complicated maneuvers carried out with marvelous precision," made him enroll at La Grange, with the ambition to become a soldier (John A. Wyeth, *With Sabre and Scalpel* [New York, 1914], 160–161).

12. On Partridge, see Grenville M. Dodge and William A. Ellis, *Norwich University, 1819–1911* (3 vols., Montpelier, Vt., 1911), I, 4–21, 65–72, 87, 395–401; and many references, at first highly favorable, in *Letters from John Pintard . . . , 1816–1831* (4 vols., Collections of the New-York Historical Society, LXX–LXXIII, 1940–41). Mount Airy is described in Samuel F. Hotchkin, *Ancient and Modern Germantown, Mount Airy and Chestnut Hill* (Philadelphia, 1889), 367–376, and in Edward W. Hocher, *German-town 1683–1933* (Germantown, 1933), 139–140. There is an article on Mount Pleasant Academy in *Frank Leslie's Illustrated Newspaper*, X (14 July 1860), 120–122. The Highland Academy is mentioned in *Dictionary of Worcester (Massachusetts) and Its Vicinity* (Worcester, 1889), 33–34. On other schools, see S. H. Elliot, *The Attractions of New Haven, Connecticut* (New York, 1869), 84–85, and Rachel M. Hartley, *The History of Hamden, Connecticut, 1786–1959* (Hamden, 1959), 252–255.

13. Wallace E. Davies, *Patriotism on Parade* (Cambridge, Mass., 1955), 1–3; Jacob J. Oswandel, *Notes of the Mexican War* (Philadelphia, 1885), 627.

14. Livermore, *War with Mexico Reviewed*, 279–280.

15. Livermore, 7; *Abraham Lincoln: A Documentary Portrait*, ed. Don E. Fehrenbacher (New York, 1964), 34–43. Some of the references which follow are drawn from the excellent discussion in David B. Davis, *Homicide in American Fiction, 1798–1860: A Study in Social Values* (Ithaca, N.Y., 1957), 237–290. American unrest shocked an otherwise favorably impressed French observer, Michel Chevalier, whose account was first published in 1836. See Chevalier, *Society, Manners, and Politics in the United States*, ed. John William Ward (Garden City, N.Y., 1961), 371–380, and René Rémond, *Les États-Unis devant l'Opinion Française, 1815–1852* (2 vols., Paris, 1962), II, 700–702.

16. George Meade, ed., *Life and Letters of General George Gordon Meade* (2 vols., New York, 1913), I, 109–110.

17. There is a good account of this "personal warfare" in Franklin, *The Militant South*, 33–62. Congress prohibited dueling in the District of Columbia by an act of 1839. The act was sharply criticized by Senator Thomas Hart Benton in his *Thirty Years' View* (2 vols., New York, 1856), II, 148–150, on the ground that it stimulated worse forms of violence. On Jackson's affairs of honor, see John S. Bassett, *The Life of Andrew Jackson* (New York, 1916), I, 61–70, and William N. Chambers, *Old Bullion Benton, Senator from the New West* (Boston, 1956), 50–53; on the Foote-Benton fracas, Chambers, 359–362. Ben Wade's militance is breezily described in Lloyd Lewis, *It Takes All Kinds* (New York, 1947), 13–30. Horace Greeley of the *New York Tribune* was assailed by an Arkansas congressman in 1856; see Glyndon G. Van Deusen, *Horace Greeley, Nineteenth-Century Crusader* (Philadelphia, 1953; New York, 1964), 201–202.

18. David D. Dana, *The Fireman: The Fire Departments of the United States* (Boston, 1858), 59–60.

19. James E. Cutler, *Lynch-Law: An Investigation in the History of Lynching in the United States* (New York, 1905), 90–136; Alan Valentine, *Vigilante Justice* (New York, 1956), 115–171; George R. Stewart, *Committee of Vigilance: Revolution in San Francisco, 1851* (Boston, 1964); A. Russell Buchanan, *David S. Terry of California: Dueling Judge* (San Marino, Cal., 1956), 20–70; Stanton A. Coblentz, *Villains and Vigilantes* (New York, 1957); John W. Caughey, *Their Majesties the Mob* (Chicago, 1960); Lloyd Lewis, *Sherman, Fighting Prophet* (New York, 1932), 91–93. Mary Floyd Williams, *History of the San Francisco Committee of Vigilance of 1851* (Berkeley, 1921), 424–427, agrees with Cutler that lynching was virtually unknown outside the United States. The positive aspects of frontier justice are stressed in Daniel J. Boorstin, *The Americans: The National Experience* (New York, 1965), 72–90. See also Ashbel Woodward, *Life of General Nathaniel Lyon* (Hartford, Conn., 1862), 232.

20. Dana, *The Fireman,* 20–21, 37–40.

21. Dana, 214–221, 334–345; Ray A. Billington, *The Protestant Crusade, 1800–1860* (New York, 1938; repr. Chicago, 1964), 223–230.

22. Clarence H. Forrest, *Official History of the Fire Department of . . . Baltimore* (Baltimore, 1898), 55–79.

23. Herbert Asbury, *The Gangs of New York* (New York, 1927), 107–112; Richard Moody, *The Astor Place Riot* (Bloomington, Ind., 1958). For a splendidly florid militia view of these troubled years, see *Recollections . . . of the Seventh Regiment* (New York, 1868), especially 132–140.

24. *Diary of George Templeton Strong,* ed. Allan Nevins and Milton H. Thomas (4 vols., New York, 1952), II, 412–413.

25. Joseph Rossi, *The Image of America in Mazzini's Writings* (Madison, Wis., 1954), 18–20; Jeremiah A. O'Leary, *My Political Trial and Experiences* (New York, 1919), 4; *Harper's Weekly,* III (29 January 1859), 76; *Military Gazette,* III (15 April 1860), 122.

26. *Richmond Whig,* 22 April 1861, quoted in Frank Moore, ed., *The Rebellion Record* (New York, 1861), I, *Rumors and Incidents,* 56; John P. Little, *History of Richmond* (Richmond, Va., 1933), 230. Dr. Little's work originally appeared in 1851–1852 as a series of articles in the *Southern Literary Messenger.*

27. Edward S. Wallace, *Destiny and Glory* (New York, 1957); Howard R. Floan, *The South in Northern Eyes* (Austin, Tex., 1958); Franklin, *Militant South,* 99–128; Albert Z. Carr, *The World and William Walker* (New York, 1963).

28. Harrison Hayford, ed., *The Somers Mutiny Affair* (Englewood Cliffs, N.J., 1959); *Diary of George Templeton Strong,* I, 194; M. A. De Wolfe Howe, ed., *Home Letters of General Sherman* (New York, 1909), 189.

CHAPTER 4: THE PROFESSIONALS: UNPOPULARITY

1. Alexander M. Delavoye, *Life of Thomas Lord Lynedoch* (London, 1880), 748–750; *Military Sketch-Book: Reminiscences of Seventeen Years in the Service,* by an Officer of the Line (London, 1827), 27.

2. *Personal Memoirs of U. S. Grant* (New York, 1885), I, 44; Richard W. Johnson, *A Soldier's Reminiscences* (Philadelphia, 1886), 35–36; Randolph B. Marcy, *Thirty Years of Army Life on the Border* (London, 1866), 364–365. For a similar experience in 1841, see *The Making of a Soldier: Letters of General R. S. Ewell,* ed. Percy G. Hamlin (Richmond, Va., 1935), 42.

3. Mason Weems, *Life of Washington,* ed. Marcus Cunliffe (Cambridge, Mass., 1962), 136; Parmenas T. Turnley, *Reminiscences* (Chicago, c. 1892), 281.

4. *Speech of Mr. Giddings, of Ohio, Upon the Bill to Supply the Deficiency of Appropriations for the Year Ending June 30, 1848, delivered in the House of Representatives, February 28, 1848.* (Washington, 1848), 9; Benjamin P. Thomas and Harold M. Hyman, *Stanton: The Life and Times of Lincoln's Secretary of War* (New York, 1962), 11.

5. *The Military Academy, at West Point, Unmasked: or, Corruption and Military Despotism Exposed,* by "AMERICANUS" [Alden Partridge], (Washington, 1830), 3, 20. A previous attempt to abolish the Academy, as "aristocratic" in its selections and appointments, was made in 1820 by Representative Newton Cannon of Tennessee; see Arthur A. Ekirch, Jr., *The Civilian and the Military* (New York, 1956), 79. Cannon had served as a colonel in the War of 1812 and was later governor of Tennessee.

6. I am indebted for some of the information in these and in succeeding paragraphs to A. W. Mitchell, "The Jacksonian Attack on West Point" (B. A. thesis, University of Manchester, 1963). A great deal of information is reprinted in *American State Papers: Military Affairs* (7 vols., Washington D.C., 1789–1838), e.g. IV, 603 (report of the 1830 Board of Visitors), VII, 25 (report to House of Representatives on Military Academy, 1837), VIII, 89 (petitions against West Point).

7. Thomas H. Benton, *Thirty Years' View* (2 vols., New York, 1854), I, 466; 26th Congress, 2nd Session, Senate Doc. No. 1, 152. Partridge's memorial is reproduced in 26th Congress, 2nd Session, H. of R. Doc. no. 69, 1.

8. For Hawes, see Register of Debates in Congress (Gales & Seaton), XI (8 December 1834), 755. A similar exchange between Amasa Dana and a fellow congressman took place on 6 March 1844. For Sawyer, see *Speech of Hon. William Sawyer, . . . House of Representatives, . . . May 11, 1846* (Washington, 1846), 5. The Fish document, a substantial piece of work, is 28th Congress, 1st Session, H. of R. Report no. 476, *Military Academy,* May 15, 1844. Representative John Reynolds, a former governor of Illinois, offered a comprehensive indictment of West Point in June 1842: see Benton's *Abridgment of the Debates of Congress* (New York, 1860), XIV, 417–421.

9. The 1838 act is in J. F. Callan, *Military Laws of the United States* (Baltimore, 1858), 337. For details of the Rome, N.Y., military convention see *New York Military Magazine,* I (1841), 329–330, 410.

10. "Address of the Temperance Society of Fort Snelling (Upper Mississippi)," *Army & Navy Chronicle,* II (12 May 1836), 301; Callan, 101, 270, 309, 359, 362, 425–426; William P. Johnston, *Life of Albert Sidney Johnston* (New York, 1879), 242–243.

11. *United Service Journal,* I (7 December 1850), 197; Percival G. Lowe, *Five Years a Dragoon ('49 to '54) and Other Adventures on the Great*

Plains (Kansas City, 1906), 7, 9–10, 25–26, 28; Rodney Glisan, *Journal of Army Life* (San Francisco, 1874), 454.

12. Glisan, *Journal*, 83 (a diary entry from "Fort Arbuckle, Indian Territory, May 12, 1851"); and see Mrs. Teresa Vielé, *Following the Drum* (Philadelphia, 1864), 37. Moonlight's manuscript autobiography is in the Coe Collection of Western Americana at Yale University. See Mary C. Withington, comp., *Western Americana* (New Haven, 1952), item 351, 192–193.

13. On the La Guardias, see Arthur Schlesinger, Jr., *The Age of Roosevelt* (Boston, 1960), III, 126. Some of Paldi's drawings were used to make the first illustrations of the Mexican War; *An Album of American Battle Art, 1775–1918* (Washington, D.C., 1947), 129. A number of Heger's drawings are in the Coe Collection at Yale. Some of these, and others, are reproduced in George P. Hammond, ed., *Campaigns in the West, 1856–1861: The Journals and Letters of Colonel John Van Deusen Du Bois* (Arizona Pioneers Historical Society, Tucson, Ariz., 1949). Another item in the Coe Collection (Withington, *Western Americana*, 443) relates to an artist in the 4th Infantry, Private Gustavus Sohon.

14. Poinsett-Gilpin Papers, Historical Society of Pennsylvania, item 405; *Army & Navy Chronicle*, VIII (21 March 1839), 179. A Polish soldier charged with desertion at a court-martial at Fort King, East Florida, in July 1837, understood so little English that he had to have an interpreter. The court was lenient, on the presumption that he might never have grasped what he was letting himself in for; see National Archives, JAGO, checklist 13, box 66, case 225. On the German musician, see James D. Elderkin, *Biographical Sketches and Anecdotes* (Detroit, 1899), 38.

15. *Army & Navy Chronicle*, I (10 December 1835), 393, and IX (7 November 1839), 302; Elderkin, *Biographical Sketches*, 51; Francis P. Prucha, *Broadax and Bayonet: The Role of the United States Army in the Development of the Northwest, 1815–1860* (Madison, Wis., 1953), 204–206.

16. Glisan, *Journal*, 83, 454; *Army & Navy Chronicle*, I (10 December 1835), 393; Elderkin, 5–6, 49; James Larson, *Sergeant Larson, 4th Cav.* (San Antonio, Tex., 1935), 38.

17. *Army & Navy Chronicle*, I (19 November 1835), 376, and II (19 May 1836), 316; Henry S. Hamilton, *Reminiscences of a Veteran* (Concord, N.H., 1897), 27–38; Laurence Oliphant, *Minnesota and the Far West* (Edinburgh, 1855), 221–222.

18. "Statistics of the Army of the United States," New York *Military Gazette*, II (15 May 1859), 151; other figures taken from National Archives, AGO, item 89, Registers of Enlistments, which give the declared country of birth of each recruit. Since the British army was to a considerable degree Irish in composition, "ex-English" presumably

REFERENCES TO PAGES 120–127

includes many Irish. And see Prucha, *Broadax and Bayonet*, 41–45. The situation was similar in the American navy, regular and merchant. There is some discussion of this in "MAJOR MARCH" [Orlando B. Willcox, USMA, 1847], *Faca: An Army Memoir* (Boston, 1857), 60–61.

19. Dabney H. Maury, *Recollections of a Virginian* (New York, 1894), 61; Johnston, *Life of Albert Sidney Johnston*, 243; *Army & Navy Chronicle*, VI (17 May 1838), 314: a letter whose writer says he has served "as an enlisted soldier for more than twenty years"; *Hints Bearing on the United States Army*, by a late Captain of Infantry [August v. Kautz], (Philadelphia, 1858), 25–26. See also Louis Pelzer, *Marches of the Dragoons in the Mississippi Valley* (Iowa City, 1917), 2–7, and Edgar B. Wesley, *Guarding the Frontier: A Study of Frontier Defense from 1815 to 1825* (Minneapolis, 1935), 123–124, 131–132, 139–142.

20. Elderkin, *Biographical Sketches*, 13–14; Prucha, *Broadax and Bayonet*, 46–51.

21. Letter from 2nd Lt. Joseph S. Gallagher, Bangor, Me., 21 September 1829, enclosed with report from Major General Edmund P. Gaines, National Archives, IGO, checklist no. 1, vol. 2 (Inspection Reports, 1825–1829), 236–237; National Archives, JAGO, box 66, no. 224, General Court-Martial at Fort Miconopy, East Florida, 27 June 1837; box 70, no. 352, G. C. M. at Madison Barracks, October 1838, to try various prisoners.

22. Library of Congress, Jacob Brown MSS, Letter Books, II (20 November 1824), 252–253 (part of a long letter to the Secretary of War, John C. Calhoun, on the problem of desertion). The 1829 punishments and Gaines's protest are in National Archives, IGO, serial 1, vol. 2 (Inspection Reports, 1825–1829), 225–228, 241–242. There is abundant material on these and other matters in Francis P. Prucha, ed., *Army Life on the Western Frontier: Selections from the Official Reports Made Between 1826 and 1845 by Colonel George Croghan* (Norman, Okla. 1958). Regulations on flogging are summarized in W. A. Ganoe, *History of the United States Army* (New York, 1942), 129–130, 173–174, 262; and see Callan, 152, 194, 310. The aim of branding soldiers was, supposedly, to make it impossible for them to reenlist.

23. Library of Congress, John P. Hatch MSS, 29 April 1850.

24. Lenoir Chambers, *Stonewall Jackson* (New York, 1959), I, 49–50; *General George Crook: His Autobiography*, ed. Martin F. Schmitt (Norman, Okla., 1946), xvi.

25. J. S. Bassett, ed., *Correspondence of Andrew Jackson* (7 vols., Washington, D.C., 1926–1935), Library of Congress, Jubal A. Early MSS, vol. I, letters 79 (23 March 1834), 82 (2 June 1934), 90 (3 September 1834); Chambers, *Stonewall Jackson*, I, 66. Daniel H. Calhoun, *Professional Lives in America: Structure and Aspiration, 1750–1850* (Cambridge, Mass., 1965), 16–17, says that Americans "only occasionally

thought of the military as one of the learned professions"; but he suggests that the very "infrequency with which they included it in lists of the professions signalized the extent to which they feared it."

26. Quoted in Forest G. Hill, *Roads, Rails and Waterways: The Army Engineers and Early Transportation* (Norman, Okla., 1957), 205.

27. Benjamin F. Butler, *The Military Profession in the United States* (pamphlet, New York, 1839), 8–10; letter of 16 March 1844, quoted in Joseph H. Parks, *General Edmund Kirby Smith, C.S.A.* (Baton Rouge, 1954), 28; Grant, *Personal Memoirs*, I, 39–40. Ephraim's letter is quoted in Arthur H. Noll, *General Kirby-Smith* (Sewanee, Tenn., 1907), 22.

28. Hill, *Roads, Rails and Waterways*, 92; William H. Goetzmann, *Army Exploration, 1803–1863* (New Haven, 1959), *passim.*

29. For information on the Academy class of 1852, see "Personal Memoirs of Major General D. S. Stanley," *Military Historian and Economist*, I (January 1916), 23 (separate pagination); Library of Congress, Jubal A. Early MSS, vol. I, letter 166 (Fort Cass, Tennessee, 19 November 1838), signature illegible; *Army & Navy Chronicle*, I (5 November 1835), 357.

30. "JUSTITIA," *Letter to the Honorable Mr. Hawes, in Reply to his Strictures on the Graduates of the Military Academy* (pamphlet, New York, 1836), 18; *Army & Navy Chronicle*, III (29 December 1836), 412.

31. *Army & Navy Chronicle*, III (1 September 1836), 138–139; Glisan, *Journal*, 462–463; *Militia Law of the State of Tennessee* (Nashville, 1840), section 30.

32. Poinsett-Gilpin Papers, Historical Society of Pennsylvania, item 223, H. M. Rutledge to Joel R. Poinsett, 8 August 1838.

33. Library of Congress, MSS Division, Dr. Benjamin King papers, letter to King from Dr. L. A. Birdsall, Fort Holmes, E. Florida, 19 July 1841. Birdsall left the army in 1842.

34. National Archives, AGO, checklist entry 313, "Register of Appointment from Civil Life, 1833–1842"; Stephen E. Ambrose, *Upton and the Army* (Baton Rouge, 1964), 14.

35. The quotation from Worth is in Francis H. Smith, *West Point Fifty Years Ago* (New York, 1879), 13. On Scott's quarrels see his *Letter to the Secretary of War; or, Review of the Controversy . . . between Generals Scott and Gaines* (New York, 1827), and Charles W. Elliott, *Winfield Scott: The Soldier and the Man* (New York, 1937), 277 ff.

36. Senate Ex. Doc. no. 34, 203, 239–240, 251–252; J. B. Fry, *Brevets in the Armies of Great Britain and the United States* (New York, 1877), 208–209; Erasmus D. Keyes, *Fifty Years' Observation of Men and Events* (New York, 1884), 8–11, 171–173.

37. Keyes, *Fifty Years' Observation*, 8–9; Elliott, *Winfield Scott*, 423.

38. Library of Congress, E. A. Hitchcock MSS, box 2, 1842–1850; letter of 27 June 1842. The effect of all these matters on the army is well shown in a series of articles by "A SUBALTERN" (Braxton Bragg) in the *Southern Literary Messenger* in 1844–1845. Comparable resentments within the navy were voiced in articles in the same magazine, written by Matthew Fontaine Maury in 1840–1841; and see C. O. Paullin, "Naval Administration under the Naval Commissioners, 1815–1842," *U.S. Naval Institute Proceedings*, XXXIII (1907), 628–629. Within the army, the infantry as a whole felt that it was a poor relation of the other arms of the service; see the testimony of Major Theophilus Holmes, 8th Infantry, in 36th Congress, 2nd Session, Misc. Doc. no. 3, *Report of the Commission . . . of 1860, to examine . . . West Point*, 156.

39. On Davis, see National Archives, JAGO, box 66, case 219, court of inquiry on the conduct of Lt. Col. R. B. Mason. See also Don C. Seitz, *Braxton Bragg* (Columbia, S.C., 1924), 4; George R. Stewart, *John Phoenix, Esq . . . , A Life of Captain George H. Derby, U.S.A.* (New York, 1937), 85–92; Chambers, *Stonewall Jackson*, I, 173–199; Library of Congress, MSS Division, letters of John P. Hatch. Almost every volume of army memoirs yields similar stories: see for example *Reminiscences of Winfield Scott Hancock*, by His Wife (New York, 1887), 21–24.

40. The wide-ranging, erudite and somewhat esoteric interests of Hitchcock are discussed in I. Bernard Cohen, *Ethan Allen Hitchcock, Soldier, Humanitarian, Scholar* (Worcester, Mass., 1952). His army friend W. W. S. Bliss (U.S.M.A. 1833) of New Hampshire was a man of similar stamp.

CHAPTER 5: THE PROFESSIONALS: CONSOLIDATION

1. Russell F. Weigley, *Towards an American Army: Military Thought from Washington to Marshall* (New York, 1962), 1–9; Marcus Cunliffe, *George Washington: Man and Monument* (Boston, 1958).

2. Weigley, *Towards an American Army*, 21.

3. Samuel P. Huntington, *The Soldier and the State: The Theory and Politics of Civil Military Relations* (Cambridge, Mass., 1957), 211 ff.

4. William H. Riker, *Soldiers of the States: The Role of the National Guard in American Democracy* (Washington, D.C., 1957), 39.

5. Marvin A. Kreidberg and Merton G. Henry, *History of Military Mobilization in the United States Army, 1775–1945* (Washington, D.C., 1955), 53–56, citing *American State Papers: Military Affairs*, I, 514–516.

6. Howard White, *Executive Influence in Determining Military Policy in the United States* (University of Illinois Studies in the Social Sciences, XII, Urbana, Ill., 1924), 201–208.

7. J. S. Bassett, ed., *Correspondence of Andrew Jackson* (7 vols., Washington, 1926–1935), III, 190.

8. G. W. Cullum, *Biographical Sketch of Sylvanus Thayer* (New York, 1883), 14.

9. *Memoirs of General Joseph Swift* (Worcester, Mass., 1890), 141–149; Sidney Forman, *West Point* (New York, 1950), 53. Lester A. Webb, *Captain Alden Partridge and the United States Military Academy, 1806–1833* (Northport, Ala., 1965), though an amateurish overstatement, shows that there is a real case for Partridge.

10. *North American Review*, XXXIV (January 1832), 254; *Savannah Republican*, reprinted in *Army and Navy Chronicle and Scientific Repository*, III (8 February 1844), 173–174; *United States Military Academy, West Point: Report of the Agent of the Massachusetts Board of Education* [Birdsey G. Northrop], 1864, 22–23; *American Journal of Education*, XIII (n.s., vol. III, December 1863), 688.

11. *Citizen Soldier*, I (22 July 1840), 1–4; *New York Military Magazine*, I (30 October 1841), 329–330 (6 November 1841), 351; R. Ernest Dupuy, *Where They Have Trod* (New York, 1940), 235–236.

12. 28th Congress, 1st Session, Report no. 476 (15 May 1844), *Military Academy*, 17; *Army & Navy Chronicle*, I (24 December 1835), 413; Joel R. Poinsett Papers, Historical Society of Pennsylvania, Van Antwerp to Van Buren, 20 November 1837 (passed on by Van Buren to Poinsett); T. H. S. Hamersly, *Complete Regular Army Register* (Washington, D.C., 1880), 236 (though note that Van Antwerp was admitted from New York). Only half the cadets admitted between 1840 and 1860 managed to graduate.

13. Cullum, *Biographical Sketch of Thayer*, 14–15. After six months at the Academy, the bookish Leonidas Polk (U.S.M.A. 1827) declared enthusiastically in 1823 that "in point of mathematics and philosophy and the other sciences . . . , this institution is inferior to none in the United States, and I may in justice to ourselves say the *world*." William M. Polk, *Leonidas Polk: Bishop and General* (2 vols., New York, 1915), I, 72.

14. Quoted in Forman, *West Point*, 106.

15. *Life, Letters, and Journals of George Ticknor* (2 vols., Boston, 1876), I, 372–375.

16. Henry A. Murray, *Lands of the Slave and the Free; or, Cuba, the United States, and Canada* (London, 1857), 311; Laurence Oliphant, *Minnesota and the Far West* (London, 1855), 220–221; *Military and Naval Magazine of the United States*, IV (December 1834), 255.

17. Stanley memoirs in *Military Historian and Economist*, I (January 1916), 18–19; Parmenas T. Turnley, *Reminiscences* (Chicago, c. 1892), 28–44. For other unprivileged cadets, see *Army & Navy Chronicle*, V (14 Sep-

tember 1837), 172; and Library of Congress, MSS Division, John P. Hatch letter of 28 October 1845.

18. "Justitia" in *Army & Navy Chronicle*, II (16 and 23 June 1837), 370–373, 386–389; 28th Congress, 1st Session, H. of R. Report No. 476, 15–16. The Board of Visitors for 1841 said: "No matter to what influence a cadet may owe his appointment . . . he is received on perfect equality with his comrades. Name, influence, fortune, family — all alike are merged in one common consideration — individual merit" (27th Congress, 2nd Session, Senate Doc. no. 1, 159). This is emphatically confirmed in other accounts, e.g. [J. B. Kinsman], *Cadet Life at West Point* (Boston, 1862), 88–89. Kinsman also confirms (128–131) the vagueness of such categories as "indigent," and the understanding on the part of cadets that the Academy was anxious to defend itself against charges of privilege and aristocracy.

19. The information documented in this and the next three notes is drawn from a number of works. The most useful include George W. Cullum, *Biographical Register of the Officers and Graduates of the U.S. Military Academy* (2 vols., New York, 1868; supplementary vol., 1879); *Dictionary of American Biography* (*D.A.B.*); Mark M. Boatner, *The Civil War Dictionary* (New York, 1959); Francis B. Heitman, *Historical Register and Dictionary of the United States Army* (2 vols., Washington, D.C., 1903); and Ezra J. Warner, *Generals in Gray* (Baton Rouge, 1959) and *Generals in Blue* (Baton Rouge, 1964). On James Monroe, see Angus Davidson, *Miss Douglas of New York* (London, 1952), 48–53; on Lee, Douglas S. Freeman, *R. E. Lee: A Biography* (New York, 1934), I, 41–42. On Blair, see William E. Smith, *The Francis Preston Blair Family in Politics* (2 vols., New York, 1933), I, 96–97; on Barry, see George I. Oeste, *John Randolph Clay, America's First Career Diplomat* (Philadelphia, 1966), 103, 140. The Harrisons are mentioned in Turnley, *Reminiscences,* 46–50. On Sully, who, incidentally, remained in the army until his death in 1879, see Langdon Sully, "General Sully Reports," *American Heritage*, XVI, no. 1 (December 1964), 52–63. The circumstances of Lucius Walker's appointment are described in Charles Sellers, *James K. Polk, Continentalist, 1843–1846* (Princeton, N.J., 1966), 271.

20. In addition to sources already cited, see J. B. Hood, *Advance and Retreat* (Bloomington, Ind., 1959), 5; *Autobiography of Oliver Otis Howard* (2 vols., New York, 1907), I, 40–41; and — on Lane — Sidney Forman, *West Point* (New York, 1950), 118. There is a mention of the Gwins in Frank Moore, ed., *The Rebellion Record* (New York, 1861), I, 55.

21. There are sketches of Porter and the du Ponts in William Baumer, Jr., *Not All Warriors* (New York, 1941).

22. On the Smith family, see Joseph H. Parks, *General Edmund Kirby Smith, C.S.A.* (Baton Rouge, La., 1954). The Clitzes are described in

Milo M. Quaife, ed., *From the Cannon's Mouth: The Civil War Letters of General Alpheus S. Williams* (Detroit, 1959), 360.

23. See for example *North American Review*, XXXIV (January 1832), 246–261, and LVII (October 1843), 269–292; and *American Quarterly Review*, XI (June 1832), 495–503, and XXII (September 1837), 77–131. In 1830 it printed an analysis of the U.S. navy by Alexander S. Mackenzie. *The Southern Literary Messenger*, founded in 1834, began some articles on the navy, by Matthew F. Maury, in 1841. In 1842–1843 it published Philip St. George Cooke's *Scenes and Adventures in the Army*. The November 1843 issue included a defense of West Point by "F.H.S." (presumably Francis H. Smith). From February 1844 to February 1845 it printed eight articles, "Notes on our Army," by "A SUBALTERN" (Braxton Bragg) together with a reply signed "FAIR PLAY."

24. On Homans and his publications see Frank L. Mott, *History of American Magazines* (4 vols., Cambridge, Mass., 1930–1957), I, 456, and Wilhelmus B. Bryan, *A History of the National Capital* (2 vols., New York, 1916), II, 227–228. And see *Civil, Military and Naval Gazette: devoted to the interests of the Citizen, Soldier and Sailor*, ed. W. F. Davidson (26 September 1850), 21; and *Southern Literary Messenger*, XI (January 1845), 38. A number of other short-lived publications, such as the New York *Military Journal* (November 1845–January 1846) and the Albany, N.Y., *Military Gazette* (January 1858–April 1861) were intended mainly for the militia; some though not all were hostile to the regular army.

25. On Tompkins see *Army & Navy Chronicle*, IX (17 October 1839), 255, and XIII (29 January 1842), 24, and New York *Military Magazine*, I (24 July 1841), 107. Stephen Foster's failure to secure an appointment is noted in Bernard De Voto, *The Year of Decision* (Boston, 1943), 137. On Edward Bellamy, see George M. Fredrickson, *The Inner Civil War: Northern Intellectuals and the Crisis of the Union* (New York, 1965), 225–226. A similar disappointment was suffered in 1881 by a young senator-to-be, Albert J. Beveridge: see Claude G. Bowers, *Beveridge and the Progressive Era* (New York, 1932), 11–12.

26. John M. Schofield, *Forty-Six Years in the Army* (New York, 1897), 10–12; Samuel J. Bayard, *The Life of George Dashiell Bayard* (New York, 1874), 16–18, 58–62. The reports of Board of Visitors are to be found in 21st Congress, 1st Session, H. of R. Ex. Doc. no. 2, 25, 103; 27th Congress, 3rd Session, Senate Ex. Doc. no. 1, 278; and 31st Congress, 1st session, Senate Ex. Doc. no. 1, 243–244.

27. *Addresses delivered in the Chapel at West Point, by the Hon. Ashbel Smith of Texas, and Col. A. W. Doniphan of Missouri, June 16, 1848* (pamphlet, New York, 1848), 21; Alexis de Tocqueville, *Journey to America*, ed. J. P. Mayer (London, 1959), 271; Don C. Seitz, *Braxton*

Bragg (Columbia, S.C., 1924) 544; Benjamin P. Thomas and Harold M. Hyman, *Stanton* (New York, 1962), 64–66.

28. Edward D. Mansfield, *The Utility and Services of the United States Military Academy* (pamphlet, New York, 1847), 32; *Addresses delivered in the Chapel at West Point*, 21; [Josephine Seaton], *William Winston Seaton:* . . . *A Biographical Sketch* (Boston, 1871), 249 (a letter to an English friend, 12 November 1846); Leonard D. White, *The Jacksonians, 1829–1861* (New York, 1954), 210, quoting Hone's diary for 28 September 1847; and see the tributes cited in Edward J. Nichols, *Toward Gettysburg: A Biography of John F. Reynolds* (State College, Pa., 1958), 47, 231.

29. On Poinsett's arrangements for professional travel see *Army & Navy Chronicle*, IX (29 August 1839), 137; XI (26 November 1840), 345–346. Delafield's *Report on the Art of War in Europe* was first printed in 1860 as 36th Congress, 1st Session, Ex. Doc. no. 59; Mordecai's *Military Commission to Europe* as Ex. Doc. no. 60. Among other substantial contributions to military knowledge, likewise printed on a generous scale, were two volumes of statistics on sickness and mortality in the U. S. army for the years 1839–1855 (34th Congress, 1st Session, Senate Ex. Doc. no. 96) and 1855–1860 (36th Congress, 1st Session, Senate Ex. Doc. no. 52).

30. Marcus C. Hammond, *The Duties and Requirements of an American Officer* (oration delivered to the Dialectic Society, U.S.M.A.; New York, 1852), 22; *The Diary of George Templeton Strong*, ed. Allan Nevins and Milton H. Thomas (4 vols., New York, 1952), II, 105, 182, 231.

31. *Centennial of the United States Military Academy* (2 vols., Washington, D.C., 1904), I, 489; E. D. Mansfield, "The United States Military Academy at West Point," *American Journal of Education*, n.s., XXX, no. 5 (March 1863), 46.

CHAPTER 6: THE AMATEURS: APATHY AND THE MILITIA

1. Louis Morton, "The Origins of American Military Policy," *Military Affairs*, XXII (Summer 1958), 75–82; Jack S. Radabaugh, "The Militia of Colonial Massachusetts," *Military Affairs*, XVIII (Spring 1954), 1–18.

2. David Levin, *History as Romantic Art: Bancroft, Prescott, Motley, and Parkman* (Stanford, Cal., 1959), 35.

3. John McA. Palmer, *Three War Statesmen: Washington, Lincoln, Wilson* (Garden City, N.Y., 1930), 76–81. The next few paragraphs are also drawn mainly from Palmer.

4. The Knox plan is given in full in *American State Papers: Military Affairs*, I (Washington, 1832), 6–13. It is reproduced with approving comments in John A. Logan, *The Volunteer Soldier of America* (Chicago, 1887), 126–155.

5. Walter Millis, *Arms and Men: A Study of American Military History* (New York, 1956), 48–49; Jack Franklin Leach, *Conscription in the United States: Historical Background* (Rutland, Vt., 1952), 9–29; Frederick M. Cutler, "The History of Military Conscription with Especial Reference to the United States," *Historical Outlook*, XIV (May 1923), 170–171; Palmer, *Three War Statesmen*, 121–122.

6. John K. Mahon, *The American Militia: Decade of Decision, 1789–1800* (University of Florida Monographs: Social Sciences, no. 6, Gainesville, Fla., Spring 1960), 42–43, 53.

7. *The Diary of George Templeton Strong*, ed. Allan Nevins and Milton H. Thomas (4 vols., New York, 1952), I, 73; Fred L. Israel, "New York's Citizen Soldiers," *New York History*, XLII (April 1961), 154n.

8. John Lambert, *Travels through Lower Canada and the United States of North America* (3 vols., London, 1810), II, 438; B. R. McElderry, Jr.'s, introduction to Augustus Baldwin Longstreet, *Georgia Scenes* (New York, 1957), viii; Jay B. Hubbell, *The South in American Literature* (Durham, N.C., 1954), 669, and 947–948, pointing out that Prince's sketch first appeared in a Georgia newspaper in June 1807; Kenneth S. Lynn, *Mark Twain and Southwestern Humor* (Boston, 1960), 86.

9. Nils Erik Enkvist, *Caricatures of Americans on the English Stage prior to 1870* (Helsinki, 1951), 35.

10. Henry H. Riley, *Puddleford Papers* (New York, 1857), 9, 19, 227, 239.

11. Hugh McCulloch, *Men and Measures of Half a Century* (New York, 1888), 84. For an account of an 1835 drill in Franklin County, Mo., see William G. Bek, "Followers of Duden," *Missouri Historical Review*, XVI (April 1922), 363–365. Conditions in Illinois are described in Isabel Jamison, "Independent Military Companies of Sangamon County in the 30's," *Journal of the Illinois State Historical Society*, III (January 1911), 22–23.

12. "Reply to General Crary," 15 February 1840, *Speeches of Thomas Corwin*, ed. Isaac Strohm (Dayton, Ohio, 1859), 260–262.

13. William H. Riker, *Soldiers of the States: The Role of the National Guard in American Democracy* (Washington, D.C., 1957), 30–31; *Diary of Philip Hone*, ed. Allan Nevins (2 vols., New York, 1928), I, 52–53; speech to the Springfield Scott Club, August 1852, in *Collected Works of Abraham Lincoln*, ed. Roy P. Basler (8 vols., New Brunswick, N.J., 1953), II, 149–150; L. E. Chittenden, *Personal Reminiscences, 1840–1890* (New York, 1893), 47–50. An Iowa burlesque of 1857 is mentioned in Fred A. Shannon, *The Organization and Administration of the Union Army, 1861–1865* (2 vols., Cleveland, Ohio, 1928), I, 28–29.

14. *American State Papers: Military Affairs*, I, 337.

15. *Writings of Thomas Jefferson*, ed. P. L. Ford (12 vols., Washington, D.C., 1896), XI, 436–437.

16. *American State Papers: Military Affairs*, I, 642–643; C. Joseph Bernardo and Eugene H. Bacon, *American Military Policy: Its Development Since 1775* (Harrisburg, Pa., 1955), 147.

17. John K. Mahon, "A Board of Officers Considers the Condition of the Militia in 1826," *Military Affairs*, XV (Summer 1951), 85–94; *American State Papers: Military Affairs*, III, 599–602.

18. Bernardo and Bacon, *American Military Policy*, 158–159.

19. Leach, *Conscription in the United States*, 71–126; William Theobald Wolfe Tone, *Essay on the Necessity of Improving Our National Force* (New York, 1819), 59.

20. See Robert G. Gunderson, *The Log-Cabin Campaign* (Lexington, Ky., 1957), 94–95.

21. *An Inquiry into the Importance of the Militia to a Free Commonwealth: in A Letter from William H. Sumner . . . to John Adams, late President of the United States; with His Answer* (Boston, 1823). Adams's letter, 69–70, is dated 19 May 1823. The Clausewitz reference is in Mahon, "Condition of the Militia in 1826," 92.

22. Radabaugh, "Militia of Colonial Massachusetts," 16.

23. This and other annual messages are in J. D. Richardson, ed., *Messages and Papers of the Presidents* (10 vols., Washington, D.C., 1907). They are conveniently reprinted in Fred L. Israel, ed., *The State of the Union Messages of the Presidents, 1790–1966* (3 vols., New York, 1966), in which the Polk and Pierce citations are in I, 686–687, 733–734, and 888–889. See also Charles Sellers, *James K. Polk, Continentalist, 1843–1846* (Princeton, N.J., 1966), 434–435.

24. Lena London, "The Militia Fine, 1830–1860," *Military Affairs*, XV (Fall 1951), 136–138: a very useful article.

25. The *Citizen Soldier*, 22 July 1840, 6–7 (a short-lived Vermont periodical); Mr. Bigelow of Boston, in Massachusetts House of Representatives, reported in *Army & Navy Chronicle*, I (29 October 1835), 347.

26. *Diary of George Templeton Strong*, I, 113.

27. *Message of . . . the Governor . . . , returning the Bill . . . for Regulating . . . the Militia of This Commonwealth, with His Objections* (Boston, 1833); Daniel Wells, *An Examination of the Message of . . . the Governor* (Cambridge, Boston, 1833). For an instructive comparison see George F. G. Stanley, *Canada's Soldiers, 1604–1954: The Military History of an Unmilitary People* (Toronto, 1954), 209–213. The Canadian solution, in an act of 1855, was to divide the militia into "Active" and "Sedentary" groups. The latter did nothing: the former were paid to train for ten days in each year.

28. *Report of the Adjutant General of the Louisiana Militia* (New Orleans, January 1857), 3–4; John G. Westover, "Evolution of the Missouri Militia, 1804–1919" (unpublished dissertation, U. of Missouri, 1953), 79; Jacob Dolson Cox, *Military Reminiscences of the Civil War* (2 vols., New York, 1900), I, 7–10.

29. "The Militia," *United States Service Magazine*, II (September 1864), 227–228.

30. Riker, *Soldiers of the States*, 22–27; Mahon, "Condition of the Militia in 1826," 86, 89.

31. London, "The Militia Fine," 141–144; *Report of the Adjutant-General of . . . New-Hampshire for the Year Ending June 1, 1868. Part II: Military History of New Hampshire . . . to the Year 1861* (Manchester, N.H., 1868), 377–378.

32. Riley, *Puddleford Papers*, 230.

CHAPTER 7: THE AMATEURS: ENTHUSIASTIC VOLUNTEERS

1. Quoted in the New York *Military Gazette*, II (15 June 1859), 177, which also referred to articles in praise of the American volunteer system in *The Times* of London.

2. Lieutenant Colonel C. M. Sleigh, *Pine Forests and Hacmatack Clearings* (London, 1853), 310–313. Francis Grund said that it was to the independent companies that "English travellers frequently allude, when speaking of the American militia"; quoted in George E. Probst, ed., *The Happy Republic: A Reader in Tocqueville's America* (New York, 1962), 67.

3. Much of the information in these paragraphs is drawn from two useful articles by Frederick P. Todd, "Our National Guard," *Military Affairs*, V (Summer and Fall 1941), 73–86 and 152–170. See also Herbert L. Adams, *Worcester Light Infantry, 1803–1922* (Worcester, Mass., 1924), 23; John H. Niebaum, "The Pittsburgh Blues," *Western Pennsylvania Historical Magazine*, IV (April, July and October 1921), 110–122, 175–185, 259–270, and V (July 1922), 244–250; and Louis F. Ostendorff, *Historical Sketch of the Washington Light Infantry* (pamphlet, Charleston, S.C., 1943), 1–9.

4. *Army & Navy Chronicle*, I (8 October 1835), 327.

5. *Proceedings at the Fiftieth Anniversary of the New England Guards* (Boston, 1863), 42, 52–53, 87–88; James D. Elderkin, *Biographical Sketches and Anecdotes* (Detroit, 1899), 127; *Harper's Weekly*, IV (21 July 1860), 460–461.

6. Charles W. Hall, ed., *Regiments and Armories of Massachusetts* (2 vols., Boston, 1899–1901), I, 121–122, 412 ff.

7. *Adjutant-General's Report for 1920* (Atlanta, Ga., 1921), 169–174; *Philadelphia Sunday Dispatch*, 22 May 1859; David L. Pierson, *History of the Oranges to 1921* (3 vols., New York, 1922), II, 312; *The Militia and Patrol Laws of South Carolina* (Columbus, S.C., 1860), 75–77; Thomas H. Murray, *History of the Ninth Regiment, Connecticut Volunteer Infantry, "The Irish Regiment," 1861–1865* (New Haven, 1903), 12–14. The Meagher Guards were named in honor of the Irish patriot Thomas Francis Meagher, who settled in the United States in 1853. Other units were named after John Mitchel, another Irish patriot who, after being transported by the British to Australia, escaped and came to America in 1853. Meagher fought with the 69th at Bull Run and was slightly wounded. See Michael Cavanagh, *Memoirs of General Thomas Francis Meagher* (Worcester, Mass., 1892), and Robert G. Athearn, *Thomas Francis Meagher: An Irish Revolutionary in America* (Boulder, Colo., 1949).

8. Powell A. Casey, "Early History of the Washington Artillery of New Orleans," *Louisiana Historical Quarterly*, XXIII (April 1940), 471–473; James B. Avirett, *The Memoirs of General Turner Ashby* (Baltimore, 1867), 62; Edward S. Wallace, *General William Jenkins Worth* (Dallas, 1953), 6.

9. New York *Military Gazette*, III (1 March 1860), 67; *Asmonean*, III (22 November 1850), 37, and XVII (5 February 1858), 133; Robert Ernst, *Immigrant Life in New York City, 1825–1863* (New York, 1949), 129; Merle Curti, *Roots of American Loyalty* (New York, 1946), 88. A company of Virginia boys, active c. 1856–1858, is mentioned in John A. Cutchins, *A Famous Command: The Richmond Light Infantry Blues* (Richmond, Va., 1934), 66, and in John S. Wise, *The End of an Era* (Boston, 1899), 59–60.

10. Casey, "Washington Artillery," 472–474; *Boston Daily Advertiser*, quoted in *Army & Navy Chronicle*, V (21 September 1837), 189; Daniel G. Macnamara, *History of the Ninth Regiment, Massachusetts Volunteer Infancy* (Boston, 1899), 1–5; Oscar Handlin, *Boston's Immigrants* (Cambridge, Mass., 1941), 161–162, 196–197; Benjamin F. Butler, *Butler's Book* (Boston, 1892), 125–127; Murray, *Ninth Regiment, Connecticut Volunteer Infantry*, 15–22.

11. Herbert C. Damon, *History of the Milwaukee Light Guard* (Milwaukee, 1875), 10–12, describing the formation of a nativist company in 1855; Henry Whittemore, *History of the Seventy-First Regiment, NGSNY* (New York, 1886), 1–5, 27; George A. Hussey, *History of the Ninth Regiment, NYSM* (New York, 1889), 7–14. New York's Seventh Regiment congratulated itself on making no discrimination on religious grounds: see Emmons Clark, *History of the Seventh Regiment* (2 vols., New York, 1890), I, 397.

12. Cavanagh, *Meagher*, 353–354; *Harper's Weekly*, IV (20 October 1860), 658, an editorial on "Our Irish Soldiers."

13. Paul Angle, *Here I Have Lived: The Story of Lincoln's Springfield, 1821–1865* (New Brunswick, N.J., 1935), 50–51; *Frank Leslie's Illustrated Newspaper*, X (4 August 1860), 161–162. The City Guard, a wealthy company, were particularly active in arranging visits. They entertained, for example, the Baltimore Greys in 1850 and the Ancient and Honorable Artillery of Boston in 1860; see *United Service Journal*, I (22 June 1850), 8, and *Military Gazette*, III (15 February 1860), 52–54.

14. George M. Whipple, *History of the Salem Light Infantry* (Salem, Mass., 1890), 57; Theodore G. Gronert, "The First National Pastime in the Middle West," *Indiana Magazine of History*, XXIX (September 1933), 185–186.

15. Clark, *History of the Seventh Regiment*, I, 286, 428–429; Frederick P. Todd, "The Huddy and Duval Prints: An Adventure in Military Lithography," *Journal of the American Military Institute*, III (Fall 1939), 170; *Adjutant-General's Annual Report for Massachusetts, 1857* (Boston, 1858), 32–33.

16. Charles J. Peterson, *Military Heroes of the Mexican War* (Philadelphia, 1852), 269–274.

17. Angle, *Here I Have Lived*, 50–51; *Dictionary of American Biography* (*D.A.B.*) (New York, 1943), I, 518.

18. J. F. H. Claiborne, *Life of John A. Quitman* (2 vols., New York, 1860), I, 65, 78, 93, 141, 164, 170–171, II, 11, 216–217.

19. *D.A.B.*, X, 271–272; J. W. de Peyster, *Personal and Military History of Philip Kearny* (New York, 1869).

20. *D.A.B.*, VII, 203–204.

21. Milo M. Quaife, ed., *From the Cannon's Mouth: The Civil War Letters of General Alpheus S. Williams* (Detroit, 1959), 6–8.

22. Paul Fatout, *Ambrose Bierce: The Devil's Lexicographer* (Norman, Okla., 1951), 10–11, 33–34; Ambrose Bierce, *In the Midst of Life, and Other Tales*, ed. Marcus Cunliffe (New York, 1961), 250–254.

23. *D.A.B.*, XIX, 375–376; John H. B. Latrobe, *Reminiscences of West Point* (East Saginaw, Mich., 1887).

24. Robert S. Holzman, *Stormy Ben Butler* (New York, 1954), 7–11.

25. Edward K. Gould, *Maj.-Gen. Hiram G. Berry* (Rockland, Me., 1899), 24.

26. *Biographical Memorial of Daniel Butterfield*, ed. Julia L. Butterfield (New York, 1904), 10.

27. Thomas G. Belden and Marva R. Belden, *So Fell the Angels* (Boston, 1956), 42–54.

28. Logan, *Volunteer Soldier of America*, 561; Schofield, *Forty-Six Years in the Army*, 535; John Niven, *Connecticut for the Union: The Role of the State in the Civil War* (New Haven, 1965), 122–123. Terry remained in the regular army after the war.

29. Henry S. Nourse, *The Military Annals of Lancaster, Massachusetts* (Lancaster, 1889), 290, 368.

30. This account is based chiefly on Charles A. Ingraham, *Elmer E. Ellsworth and the Zouaves of '61* (Chicago, 1925). See also "Ellsworth," *Atlantic Monthly*, VIII (July 1861), 119–125, an article attributed to John Hay; "Ellsworth's Zouaves," *Reminiscences of Chicago During the Civil War*, ed. Mabel McIlvaine (Lakeside Classics, Chicago, 1914), 15–40; *Lincoln Lore*, no. 1435 (September 1957); and Ruth P. Randall, *Colonel Elmer Ellsworth* (Boston, 1960).

31. "The Zouaves," in *The Poems and Stories of Fitz-James O'Brien* (Boston, 1881).

32. The eyewitness account by the *Tribune* correspondent, E. H. House, is quoted in Luther E. Robinson, "Ephraim Elmer Ellsworth, First Martyr of the Civil War," *Illinois State Historical Society Transactions, 1923*, 122.

33. *Proceedings of the Military Association of the State of New York, 1860* (Albany, 1861), 10, 17–18, 39–41. The first annual meeting of the Association was held in 1853 or 1854. Reports of the proceedings for 1856, 1857 and 1860 are in the Library of Congress.

34. *Massachusetts Adjutant-General's Report for 1857* (Boston, 1858), 23–26; *Butler's Book*, 127.

35. Issues of these newspapers are held by the New-York Historical Society.

36. Nelson A. Miles, *Serving the Republic* (New York, 1911), 9–10, 17–18.

37. Hugh Jameson, "A Note on the Minute-Men," *Journal of the American Military Institute*, IV (Winter 1940), 258–260.

38. Clark, *History of the Seventh Regiment*, II, 487–489.

CHAPTER 8: PROFESSIONALS AND AMATEURS:
A BALANCED VIEW

1. Irenée de Lacroix, *Military and Political Hints*, tr. Samuel Mackay (Boston, 1808), 118; J. D. Richardson, *Messages and Papers of the Presidents* (11 vols., New York, 1911), I, 486–487; *Memoirs of General Joseph Swift* (Worcester, Mass., 1890), 126; Lester A. Webb, *Partridge and the . . . Military Academy*, 207; article in *Southern Literary Messenger*, X (November 1843), 665–670, by "F.H.S." (presumably Francis H. Smith, superintendent at V.M.I.), recommending a combination as at V.M.I. of *"pay* with *free* cadets . . . The condition of the

gratuitous education should be, that the cadet should be obliged to serve for a term of years after graduation, while it might be left optional with the pay cadet to enter the army or not."

2. Letter by Mahan read out at the Albany *Proceedings of the Military Association of New-York* (pamphlet, New York, 1860), 16.

3. *Memoirs of Swift*, 141–149.

4. Cited in *American Journal of Education*, XIII (n.s., vol. III, December 1863), 686.

5. The cadets' side of the controversy is laid out in three pamphlets published at Newburgh, N.Y., in 1819: *An Exposé of Facts, Concerning Recent Transactions, Relating to the Corps of Cadets of the United States Military Academy;* Thomas Ragland, *Defence before a General Court-Martial, held at West-Point; Memorial to Congress,* from Nathaniel H. Loring, Thomas Ragland, Charles R. Holmes, Charles R. Vining and Wilson M. C. Fairfax.

6. Walter L. Fleming, "Jefferson Davis at West Point," *Louisiana State University Bulletin*, I (new series, No. 3, March 1910), 264–265, repr. from Mississippi Historical Society *Publications*, X; William M. Polk, *Leonidas Polk: Bishop and General* (2 vols., New York, 1915), I, 79–88, 115–116; Francis H. Smith, *West Point Fifty Years Ago* (New York, 1879), 4–7; G. W. Cullum, *Biographical Sketch of Sylvanus Thayer* (New York, 1883), 24; R. N. Dupuy, *Where They Have Trod* (New York, 1940).

7. Samuel P. Huntington, *The Soldier and the State: The Theory and Politics of Civil Military Relations* (New York, 1957), 11–18. The "management of violence" is Harold Lasswell's phrase. Gaetano Mosca, *The Ruling Class* (New York, 1939), 233. The two volumes of his work first appeared in Italian, as *Elementi di scienza politica*, in 1896 and 1923. See also Walter Millis, *Arms and Men: A Study in American Military History* (New York, 1956), 73.

8. Raoul Girardet, *La Société Militaire dans la France Contemporaine, 1815–1939* (Paris, 1953), 55–62; "Promotion of the Rank and File of the Army," *Military and Naval Magazine*, III (1834), 121–124; *Army & Navy Chronicle*, VIII (21 February 1839), 122; *American State Papers: Military Affairs*, VI, 988; *Army & Navy Chronicle*, VI (28 June 1838), 411, 415; and see Guy V. Henry, *Military Record of Civilian Appointments in the U.S. Army* (2 vols., New York, 1870, 1873). In the Library of Congress, Peter Force MSS, vol. 32 includes some letters sent by enlisted men to William Q. Force, editor of the newly revived *Army & Navy Chronicle*. There is for instance a letter of 15 February 1843 from First Sergt. George Hall, 6th Infantry. He writes from Fort Gibson to ask for a subscription, adding: "there is some ten or more non commissioned officers at this post who wish to subscribe to your valuable paper."

9. *Recollections of the United States Army . . . by an American Soldier, Written During a Period in "the Service," since 1830* (Boston, 1845), preface and 46–47, 71; James Hildreth, *Dragoon Campaigns to the Rocky Mountains* (New York, 1836), 44–45. Joseph B. Thoburn, "The Dragoon Campaigns to the Rocky Mountains," *Chronicles of Oklahoma*, VIII (March 1930), 35–41, suggests both books were written by the same man, a wellborn Englishman who had once been an officer in the British army. His theory is fairly plausible, if the gap in publication dates may account for a difference in tone; but the *Recollections* have a nativist flavor that one would not expect in a foreign-born author.

10. Coe Collection, Yale University, letter from Isaac I. Stevens to Hon. D. J. Pearce of 5 June 1848; *Autobiography of Oliver Otis Howard* (2 vols., New York, 1907), I, 94–95. Howard appears to have got his dates slightly wrong. He says the article was published in 1858. But he seems to be referring to a piece entitled "Military Subordination," by "Lieut. O. O. H.," read before the officers at West Point in March 1860 and reprinted in the *Military Gazette*, III (1 May 1860), 137–142. For Polk's comments see *The Diary of James K. Polk*, ed. Milo M. Quaife (4 vols., Chicago, 1910), III, 30–32.

11. *Letter to the Honorable Mr. Hawes, in Reply to His Strictures on the Graduates of the Military Academy, by "JUSTITIA"* (pamphlet, New York, 1836), 29–30.

12. Philip St. George Cooke, *Scenes and Adventures in the Army* (Philadelphia, 1859), 156–167.

13. Letter from an officer reprinted in *Army & Navy Chronicle*, VI (8 March 1838), 151; Library of Congress, Dr. Benjamin King MSS. Letter from King to Surgeon Henderson, Fort Foster, Florida, 13 February 1838; *Correspondence of John Sedgwick, Major-General* (2 vols., n.p., 1902), I, 38–39, 173: letters to his sister, dated Reynosa, Mexico, 23 November 1846 and Chapultepec, 18 March 1848. See also *An Artillery Officer in the Mexican War 1846–7: Letters of Robert Anderson* (New York, 1911), 112.

14. 25th Congress, 1st Session, H. of R. Ex. Doc. no. 46, *Proceedings of the Court of Inquiry in the case of Brevet Brigadier General Wool*, 9 October 1837, 69, 84.

15. Coe Collection, Yale University: "Wool's Campaign," a scrapbook compiled by Elwood Evans. Wool's words are quoted from the *National Intelligencer* of 2 May 1856, and Lane's speech from the same source, 13 May 1856. In 1857 Wool was transferred to the Department of the East. Though Lane criticized him as one "trained to arms according to the tactics of West Point," Wool was not in fact an Academy graduate. Isaac I. Stevens, the governor of Washington Territory, with whom he crossed swords, *was* a West Pointer, who had graduated at the head of his class in 1839.

16. Library of Congress, E. A. Hitchcock MSS, box 2, 1842–1850, letter of 9 January 1842; A. B. Bender, "Military Posts in the Southwest, 1848–1860," *New Mexico Historical Review*, XVI (April 1941), 141–144. Francis P. Prucha, *Broadax and Bayonet* (Madison, Wis., 1953), 64–103, illustrates the difficulties which the army faced and the hostility its actions aroused among civilians. Other instances are given in W. O. Croffut, ed., *Fifty Years in Camp and Field: Diary of Major-General Ethan Allen Hitchcock* (New York, 1909), 115–118, 121–129, 381.

17. National Archives, JAGO, checklist no. 15, box 66, case no. 200.

18. 30th Congress, 1st Session, Senate Ex. Doc. no. 65, 2 August 1848, *Proceedings . . . in the case of Major General Pillow;* Elliott, *Winfield Scott,* 437–438; Otis A. Singletary, *The Mexican War* (Chicago, 1960), 116–127.

19. John G. Barrett, *Sherman's March Through the Carolinas* (Chapel Hill, N.C., 1956), 205; Dabney H. Maury, *Recollections of a Virginian* (New York, 1894), 61.

20. Cooke, *Scenes and Adventures,* 158; Van Antwerp letter in Poinsett-Gilpin papers, Historical Society of Pennsylvania; Mordecai memoirs in *North Carolina Historical Review*, XIII (January 1945), 83, 88; letter signed "Sam Jones" in *Army & Navy Chronicle*, IX (24 October 1839), 265–266. There is an amusingly contemptuous example of regular contempt for the militia in Mrs. John H. Kinzie, *Wau-Bun: The Early Day in the Northwest* (Menasha, Wis., 1930), 357–358.

21. *Speech of the Hon. William Sawyer . . . in the House of Representatives, May 11, 1846* (pamphlet, Washington, D.C., 1846), 7; C. O. Paullin, "Naval Administration, 1842–1861," *U.S. Naval Institute Proceedings*, XXIII (December 1907), 1469–1470; Leonard D. White, *The Jacksonians, 1829–1861* (New York, 1954), 232–240.

22. John J. Lenney, *Caste System in the American Army: A Study of the Corps of Engineers and their West Point System* (New York, 1949), xiii; and Lenney, *Rankers: The Odyssey of the Enlisted Regular Soldier of America and Britain* (New York, 1950).

23. Richard Taylor, *Destruction and Reconstruction* (Edinburgh, 1879), 123; *West Point and the War,* "dedicated by a Western Officer to his Eastern-Fellow-Soldiers" (pamphlet, St. Louis, 1863), 5–6; Jacob D. Cox, *Military Reminiscences* (New York, 1900), I, 183–184; "A Citizen Soldier," *Red-Tape and Pigeon-Hole Generals* (New York, 1864), 170; Milo M. Quaife, ed., *From the Cannon's Mouth: Civil War Letters of General Alpheus W. Williams* (Detroit, 1959), 40–41, a letter of 7 December 1861; Howard, *Autobiography* I, 83–84, 105–106. The conversation with the adjutant general is recorded in *General George Crook: His Autobiography,* ed. Martin F. Schmitt (Norman, Okla., 1946), 84. There is abundant detail in T. Harry Williams, "The Attack Upon West Point during the Civil War," *Mississippi Valley Historical*

Review, XXV (March 1939), 491–504; and see Allan Nevins, *The War for the Union: The Improvised War, 1861–1862* (New York, 1959), 192–193, 228.

24. Cox, *Military Reminiscences*, I, 170–171, 185–186; David Lloyd George, *War Memoirs*, 3416, quoted in F. M. Stern, *The Citizen Army* (New York, 1967), 361.

25. *The Autobiography of Lyman Beecher*, ed. Barbara M. Cross (2 vols., Cambridge, Mass., 1961), I, 194–195.

26. *Aristocracy Exposed: A Candid Appeal to the Citizens of Massachusetts* (pamphlet, n.p., October 1804), 10; and see Stephen G. Kurtz, *The Presidency of John Adams: The Collapse of Federalism, 1795–1800* (Philadelphia, 1957), 330–331.

27. Quotations from Randolph, Quincy and Scott taken from Marcus Cunliffe, "Madison: 1812–1815," in Ernest R. May, ed., *The Ultimate Decision: The President as Commander in Chief* (New York, 1960), 25–53; *Speech of Mr. Washington Barrow, of Tennessee, on the Reference of the President's Annual Message* (Washington, J. S. Gideon, 1848), 24 January 1848. The same suspicions were aired in the Senate, for example by George E. Badger of North Carolina, in a speech on the Ten Regiment Bill on 18 January 1848.

CHAPTER 9: POLITICS AND MILITARY AFFAIRS

1. Russell F. Weigley, *Towards an American Army* (New York, 1962), 53; letter to J. R. Poinsett, February 1839, quoted in Charles W. Elliott, *Winfield Scott: The Soldier and the Man* (New York, 1937), 369; letter to Buchanan in *Memoirs of Lieutenant-General Scott* (2 vols., New York, 1864), II, 609; *McClellan's Own Story* (New York, 1887), 34–35.

2. Samuel J. Bayard, *Life of George Dashiell Bayard* (New York, 1874), 37. The politically minded cadet was presumably James M. Goodell of New York (see T. H. S. Hamersly, *Complete Army Register* [Washington, D.C., 1880], 209), and presumably the nephew of the Free-Soil candidate, John P. Hale of New Hampshire. Parmenas T. Turnley, *Reminiscences* (Chicago, c. 1892), 247–250.

3. Cecil D. Eby, Jr., *A Virginia Yankee in the Civil War: The Diary of David Hunter Strother* (Chapel Hill, N.C., 1961), 277–278; P. S. Michie, *Life and Letters of Upton*, 88–89, 116, 423–424; Stephen E. Ambrose, *Upton and the Army* (Baton Rouge, La., 1964), 26–34.

4. T. P. Abernethy, *D.A.B.*, repr. as "Andrew Jackson" in Edward T. James, ed., *The American Plutarch* (New York, 1964), 181; E. Merton Coulter, *A Short History of Georgia* (Chapel Hill, N.C., 1933), 227–228; Rollins Bingham, "Missouri's Old Militia Law," *Missouri Historical Review*, VIII (July 1914), 213; George F. Howe, *Chester A. Arthur:*

A Quarter-Century of Machine Politics (New York, 1935), 19; Frank Allaben, *John Watts de Peyster* (2 vols., New York, 1908), I, 227–228.

5. Eugene P. Link, *Democratic-Republican Societies, 1790–1800* (New York, 1942), 181–182. Link, however, is unreliable on this point; he confuses the militia with the independent companies and exaggerates the Republicanness of such units.

6. Herbert L. Adams, *Worcester Light Infantry, 1803–1922* (Worcester, Mass., 1924), 20, 36–37, and S. Hathaway, *History of the Worcester Guards and the Worcester City Guards from 1840 to 1896* (Worcester, 1896), 5–7; on the Salem Light Infantry, note by H. W. Williams, Jr., *Military Collector and Historian,* VI, no. 1 (March 1954), 18; John A. Cutchins, *A Famous Command: The Richmond Light Infantry Blues* (Richmond, Va., 1934), 47.

7. "Mexican War Letters of Col. William Bowen Campbell of Tennessee, . . . to Governor David Campbell of Virginia, 1846–1847," *Tennessee Historical Magazine,* I (June 1915), 134–136; letters of 4 June and 3 July 1846.

8. *General George Crook: His Autobiography,* ed. Martin F. Schmitt (Norman, Okla., 1946), xvi; Lorenzo D. Johnson, *Chaplains of the General Government* (New York, 1856), 26; John M. Schofield, *Forty-Six Years in the Army* (New York, 1897), 11–12.

9. Bayard, *Life of George Dashiell Bayard,* 80–81, 90, 129, 170, 205–206.

10. Edward J. Nichols, *Toward Gettysburg: A Biography of General John F. Reynolds* (State College, Pa., 1958), 4, 9–10, 46–52, 59, 70; Don C. Seitz, *Braxton Bragg* (Columbia, S. C., 1924), 7; John McA. Palmer, *Three War Statesmen: Washington, Lincoln, Wilson* (New York, 1930), 191.

11. T. Harry Williams, *P. G. T. Beauregard* (Baton Rouge, La., 1954), 34–45. For instances of Beauregard's maneuvering against Davis with members of the Confederate Congress, see 73–74, 96–97, 111–114, 123–124.

12. Allan Nevins, *The War for the Union,* Vol. I: *The Improvised War, 1861–1862* (New York, 1959), 168, and Dabney H. Maury, *Recollections of a Virginian* (New York, 1894), 68; Russell F. Weigley, *Quartermaster General of the Union Army* (New York, 1959), 75–112.

13. Poinsett's statement, G. O. no. 79, Dept. of War, 21 December 1837, is in *Army & Navy Chronicle,* V (28 December 1837), 416. The discussion on service officers and politics ran in the *Army & Navy Chronicle* from January to May 1836 ("ALCIBIADES," II, 13; "ARISTIDES," II, 108–109; "Olive Branch," II, 139–140; "JUSTICE," II, 315–316); and see Samuel P. Huntington, *The Soldier and the State: The Theory and Politics of Civil Military Relations* (New York, 1957), 207–208 *et passim.,* for good comments on the whole issue.

14. On Monroe and Armstrong see Marcus Cunliffe, "Madison," in May, ed., *The Ultimate Decision* (New York, 1960), 37–40; and see Elliott,

Winfield Scott, 210. Most of the material on Scott in this chapter is drawn from Elliott's admirable biography.

15. Poinsett-Gilpin papers, Historical Society of Pennsylvania, no. 237, 7 June 1839; Elliott, *Winfield Scott,* 395.

16. Elliott, *Winfield Scott,* 432 n. For a brief, clear statement of the range of problems see Otis Singletary, *The Mexican War* (Chicago, 1960), chs. 5 and 6. *The Diary of James K. Polk During his Presidency, 1845 to 1849,* ed. Milo M. Quaife (4 vols., Chicago, 1910), is a fascinating source. The last chapters of Charles Sellers, *James K. Polk, Continentalist* (Princeton, N.J., 1966), are excellent on the early months of the Mexican War as Polk saw them. Also valuable are the biographies of Zachary Taylor by Holman Hamilton and Brainerd Dyer; and a few passages in William N. Chambers, *Old Bullion Benton, Senator from the New West* (Boston, 1956). Polk's executive ability is sympathetically analyzed in Leonard D. White, *The Jacksonians,* 50–66.

17. Polk, *Diary,* II, 227.

18. Polk, *Diary,* II, 408–409.

19. Calhoun was one such observer; see Elliott, *Winfield Scott,* 442n.

20. Polk, *Diary,* II, 384–386; *Tennessee Historical Magazine,* I, 148.

21. Robert Anderson, *An Artillery Officer in the Mexican War* (New York, 1911), 26–27 (letter of 2 February 1847); *Tennessee Historical Magazine,* I, 159–161 (letters of 20 and 28 March 1847).

22. Polk, *Diary,* II, 452, 462, 480; III, 17.

23. Polk, *Diary,* III, 195–196; 20 October 1847.

24. Scott, *Memoirs,* II, 416.

25. Polk, *Diary,* III, 266–67, 282.

26. *Proceedings of the Two Courts of Inquiry in the Case of Major General Pillow,* 30th Congress, 1st Session, Senate Ex. Doc. no. 65. For Hitchcock's letter see 529; for Trist's, 23.

27. Allan Nevins, *The War Becomes Revolution, 1862–1863* (New York, 1960), 46; Otto Eisenschiml, *The Celebrated Case of Fitz John Porter* (Indianapolis, 1950), 16–17.

28. *Correspondence of John Sedgwick* (2 vols., n.p., 1903), II, 161–162. From other dangers he did not escape: Sedgwick was killed at Spotsylvania in May 1864. See Warren G. Hassler, *McClellan: Shield of the Union* (Baton Rouge, La., 1957) for the view that McClellan was shabbily treated, by Lincoln, by Stanton, and by the radical Republicans in Congress.

29. Quoted in William W. Pierson, Jr., "The Committee on the Conduct of the War," *American Historical Review,* XXIII (April 1918), 550–576. For an ampler analysis, from which much of my discussion is drawn,

see T. Harry Williams, "The Committee on the Conduct of the War: An Experiment in Civilian Control," *Journal of the American Military Institute*, III (Fall 1939), 139–156, and *Lincoln and the Radicals* (Madison, Wis., 1941, 1960). A partial vindication is offered in Hans L. Trefousse, "The Joint Committee . . . : A Reassessment," *Civil War History*, X (March 1964), 5–19. See also Louis C. Smith, *American Democracy and Military Power* (Chicago, 1951), 193–206.

30. There is a sympathetic account of Stone's arrest in James G. Blaine, *Twenty Years of Congress* (2 vols., Norwich, Conn., 1884), I, 381–395.

31. Nevins, *War Becomes Revolution*, 43–46; Hassler, *McClellan*, 62.

32. Quoted in Williams, *Lincoln and the Radicals*, 206–207.

33. *The Diary of George Templeton Strong*, ed. Allan Nevins and Milton H. Thomas (4 vols., New York, 1952), III, 501 (14 October 1864); *McClellan's Own Story* (New York, 1887), 151.

34. *Diary of George Templeton Strong*, III, 297, 509. For an analysis of the radicals, see the essays by David Donald and T. Harry Williams in Grady McWhinney, ed., *Grant, Lee, Lincoln and the Radicals: Essays on Civil War Leadership* (Evanston, Ill., 1964; repr. New York, 1966).

35. Charles M. Segal, ed., *Conversations with Lincoln* (New York, 1961), 332; *Letters from Lloyd Lewis Showing Steps in the Research for His Biography of U. S. Grant* (Boston, 1950), 13, 22, 36, 38; Reinhard H. Luthin, *The Real Abraham Lincoln* (Englewood Cliffs, N.J., 1960), 496.

36. William B. Hesseltine, *Lincoln and the War Governors* (New York, 1948), 379–383; *Letters from Lloyd Lewis*, 29–30.

37. Jacob D. Cox, *Military Reminiscences* (2 vols., New York, 1900), I, 170–171, 185–186.

38. There are good general discussions in S. E. Finer, *The Man on Horseback: The Role of the Military in Politics* (London, 1962); Dorothy B. Goebel and Julius Goebel, Jr., *Generals in the White House* (Garden City, N.Y., 1952); and T. Harry Williams, "The Macs and the Ikes: America's Two Military Traditions," *American Mercury*, LXXV (October 1952), 32–39. For an example of "Cromwell talk," see *Inside Lincoln's Cabinet: The Civil War Diaries of Salmon P. Chase*, ed. David Donald (New York, 1954), 95. On Boulangism, see D. W. Brogan, *The French Nation from Napoleon to Pétain* (London, 1957), 180–182.

CHAPTER 10: A SOUTHERN MILITARY TRADITION?

1. Robert D. Meade, "The Military Spirit of the South," *Current History*, XXX (April 1929), 55; James C. Bonner, "The Historical Basis of Southern Military Tradition," *Georgia Review*, IX (Spring 1955), 76.

2. Willard Thorp, ed., *A Southern Reader* (New York, 1955), 287–288.

3. Rollin G. Osterweis, *Romanticism and Nationalism in the Old South* (New Haven, Conn., 1949; repr. Baton Rouge, 1967), 3–4, 42–52.

4. Esther J. Crooks and Ruth W. Crooks, *The Ring Tournament in the United States* (Richmond, Va., 1936), 11, 34, 70, 76, 85.

5. John Hope Franklin, *The Militant South, 1800–1861* (Cambridge, Mass., 1956), 10, 13, 249.

6. Samuel P. Huntington, *The Soldier and the State: The Theory and Politics of Civil Military Relations* (Cambridge, Mass., 1957), 211–221. For a detailed picture of Southernness in the navy see Charles O. Paullin, "Naval Administration, 1842–1861," *U. S. Naval Institute Proceedings*, XXXIII (December 1907), 1435–1477: "During the period 1815–1842, New England continued to be more interested in the national marine than the Southern States, and likewise the Eastern States more than the Western." In the period 1842–1861, however: "In Congress, probably no one man so much determined naval legislation as Stephen R. Mallory, of Florida, who in 1861 became the Secretary of the Navy of the Southern Confederacy. For several years he was chairman of the Senate Committee on Naval Affairs. Of the eleven secretaries . . . [1842–1861], all except three, Henshaw, Bancroft, and Toucey, came from States south of Mason and Dixon's line. The joint service of Henshaw and Bancroft was only two years; and Toucey, Buchanan's naval secretary, was a Southerner in his sympathies."

7. Benjamin P. Thomas, *Abraham Lincoln* (London, 1953), 171.

8. Entry on Tyler in G. W. Cullum, *Biographical Register . . . of the U.S. Military Academy* (2 vols., New York, 1868), I, 226; E. D. Keves, *Fifty Years' Observation* (New York, 1884), 429–430; David Donald, ed., *Inside Lincoln's Cabinet: The Civil War Diaries of Salmon P. Chase* (New York, 1954), 167–168; George P. Hammond, ed., *Journals of Col. John Van Deusen Du Bois* (Tucson, Ariz., 1949), 110–112.

9. D. R. Hundley, *Social Relations in Our Southern States* (New York, 1860), 49–50; Frank Moore, ed., *The Rebellion Record* (New York, 1861), I, 59, 114.

10. Joseph W. Revere, *Keel and Saddle: A Retrospect of Forty Years of Military and Naval Service* (Boston, 1873), 269–270; William Wetmore Story, *The American Question* (pamphlet, London, 1862; reprinted from the *Daily News*), 64; *Correspondence of John Sedgwick* (2 vols., n.p., 1903) I, 80–81; "A Citizen Soldier," *Red-Tape and Pigeon-Hole Generals* (New York, 1864), 186–187.

11. *Home Letters of General Sherman*, ed. M. A. De Wolfe Howe (New York, 1909), 163; P. S. Michie, *Life and Letters of Emory Upton* (New York, 1885), 30. There is a good summary of the Floyd "conspiracy" in James Ford Rhodes, *History of the United States from the Compromise of 1850* (7 vols., New York, 1893–1906), III, 238–241.

12. *A Virginia Yankee . . . : The Diaries of David Hunter Strother,* ed. Cecil D. Eby, Jr. (Chapel Hill, N.C., 1961), 254–255.

13. Cited in Robert A. Lively, *Fiction Fights the Civil War* (Chapel Hill, N.C., 1957), 104.

14. Grace Warren Landrum, "Sir Walter Scott and His Literary Rivals in the Old South," *American Literature,* II (November 1930), 256–276, disputes Scott's dominance by showing that Southerners did not unanimously admire him, and that they did admire such other authors as Burns and Bulwer-Lytton. The article does not follow up an incidental remark that scholars "have based their ideas on publishers' accounts of loads of Scott's novels sent into the South, without comparing sales there with those of other sections." See also Crooks, *The Ring Tournament,* 150–151; *The Autobiography of Lyman Beecher,* ed. Barbara M. Cross (2 vols., Cambridge, Mass., 1961), I, 391; Ola Elizabeth Winslow, "Books for the Lady Reader," in George Boas, ed., *Romanticism in America* (Baltimore, 1940; repr. New York, 1961), 93 (on Catharine Sedgwick); *The Works of Rufus Choate,* ed. Samuel G. Brown (2 vols., Boston, 1862), I, 320–346; G. Harrison Orians, "The Romance Ferment After *Waverley,*" *American Literature* III (January 1932), 408–431; Samuel S. Cox, *A Buckeye Abroad* (New York, 1852), 414–418.

15. George A. Billias, ed., *George Washington's Generals* (New York, 1964).

16. Quoted in Richard Hofstadter, William Miller and Daniel Aaron, *The American Republic* (2 vols., Englewood Cliffs, N.J., 1959), I, 287.

17. Figures taken from Thomas H. S. Hamersly, *Complete Regular Army Register of the United States* (3rd ed., Washington, D.C., 1881), II, 204.

18. H. Wager Halleck, *Elements of Military Art and Science* (3rd ed., New York, 1862), 396–397. The most favorable assessment of Halleck is Kenneth P. Williams, *Lincoln Finds a General* (5 vols., New York, 1949–1959): see, e.g., V, 271–282, from which the Grant and Sherman quotations are taken.

19. See for example Frank E. Vandiver, "The Southerner as Extremist," in Vandiver, ed., *The Idea of the South: Pursuit of a Central Theme* (Chicago, 1964), 43–45.

20. Isabella Lucy Bird, *The Englishwoman in America,* ed. Andrew Hill Clark (Madison, Wis., 1966), 164–165, 387; John S. Wise, *The End of an Era* (Boston, 1899), 110; F. L. Olmsted, *Cotton Kingdom,* cited in Edmund Wilson, *Patriotic Gore* (New York, 1962), 228.

21. John A. Logan, *The Volunteer Soldier of America* (Chicago, 1887), 244–246; Lloyd Lewis, *Sherman: Fighting Prophet* (New York, 1932), 54; Franklin, *Militant South,* 144; R. E. Dupuy, *Compact History of the U. S. Army* (New York, 1956), 122–123.

22. Figures from 28th Congress, 1st Session, H. of R. Report no. 476 (May 15, 1844), Appendix C, 26–27.

23. Cited in Lewis, *Sherman,* 164. Italics added.

24. Ezra J. Warner, *Generals in Gray: Lives of the Confederate Commanders* (Baton Rouge, La., 1959), xxii–xxiv.

25. Eric L. McKitrick, "Party Politics and the Union and Confederate War Efforts," in William N. Chambers, ed., *The American Party Systems* (New York, 1967), 117–151.

26. Wise, *End of an Era,* 175–176.

27. W. Birkbeck Wood and James E. Edmonds, *The Civil War in the United States* (London, 1937, repr. 1958), 318–319; Theodore Ropp, *War in the Modern World* (Durham, N.C., 1959), 159. Doubts on the ability of Albert S. Johnston are voiced in T. Harry Williams, *Beauregard* (Baton Rouge, La., 1954), 116, 139.

28. *Letters from Lloyd Lewis Showing Steps in the Research for His Biography of U. S. Grant* (Boston, 1950), 49–50.

29. T. Harry Williams, "The Attack Upon West Point During the Civil War," *Mississippi Valley Historical Review,* XXV (March 1939), 491–504; Major J. G. Barnard, *Letter to the Editors of the National Intelligencer* (pamphlet, New York, 1862), 14–15; Edward C. Marshall, *Are the West Point Graduates Loyal?* (pamphlet, New York, 1862). Marshall's answer to the question was yes.

30. Thomas J. Pressly, *Americans Interpret Their Civil War* (Princeton, N.J., 1954), 83*n;* Edgar S. Dudley, "Was 'Secession' Taught at West Point?" *Century,* LXXVIII (August 1909), 629–635 (Dudley shows that the legend was false. The book in question, Rawle's *View of the Constitution,* was only used for one year, and was not an official text); Logan, *Volunteer Soldier,* 335–338.

31. *The Diary of George Templeton Strong,* ed. Allan Nevins and Milton H. Thomas (4 vols., New York, 1952), II, 425. Some of these aspects are analyzed in Charles G. Sellers, ed., *The Southerner as American* (New York, 1960), W. R. Taylor, *Cavalier and Yankee: The Old South and American National Character* (New York, 1961) and George M. Frederickson, *The Inner Civil War: Northern Intellectuals and the Crisis of the Union* (New York, 1965); and see David H. Strother, *A Virginia Yankee* (Chapel Hill, N.C., 1961), 190, for his response to a jeremiad by the Unitarian clergyman Henry W. Bellows.

32. Roy P. Basler, ed., *Collected Works of Abraham Lincoln* (8 vols., New Brunswick, N.J., 1953–1955), VI, 500.

33. Richard P. Weinert, "The Confederate Regular Army," *Military Affairs,* XXVI (Fall 1962), 97–107. One of the first officers commissioned in this ghost army was Lieutenant David Todd, the brother of Mrs. Abraham Lincoln.

34. *General George Crook: His Autobiography* (Norman, Okla., 1946), 83–84.

35. *Personal Memoirs of U. S. Grant* (New York, 1885), 282–283; John M. Schofield, *Forty-Six Years in the Army* (New York, 1897), 514–516; Michie, *Life and Letters of Emory Upton*, 441–442; *McClellan's Own Story* (New York, 1887), 97; Marvin A. Kreidberg and Merton G. Henry, *History of Military Mobilization in the U.S.A. 1775–1945* (Washington, D. C., 1955), 97, 116; *Autobiography of Oliver Otis Howard* (2 vols., New York, 1907), I, 105–106; R. W. Johnson, *A Soldier's Reminiscences* (Philadelphia, 1866), 171–173.

36. A. R. Tyrner-Tyrnauer, *Lincoln and the Emperors* (London, 1962), 31–32.

37. Fredrickson, *Inner Civil War*, 161–165; "Personal Memoirs of Major-General D. S. Stanley," *Military Historian and Economist*, I (January 1916), 18–19.

38. *9th Annual Report of the Massachusetts Peace Society* (Boston, 1825), 6. James F. Rhodes, *A History of the United States from the Compromise of 1850* (7 vols., New York, 1893–1906), I, 361–362, compares the Southern planter's outlook with that of an army officer.

39. David Bertelson, *The Lazy South* (New York, 1967), 245; Taylor, *Cavalier and Yankee*, 95–141. Northern gentry styles are explored in Douglas T. Miller, *Jacksonian Aristocracy: Class and Democracy in New York, 1830–1860* (New York, 1967), 155–189.

40. C. Vann Woodward, *Tom Watson: Agrarian Rebel* (New York, 1938; repr. 1963), 13; Williams, *Beauregard*, 109–110; Ruth Painter Randall, *Colonel Elmer Ellsworth* (Boston, 1960), 234. For a description of a flag presentation in Galena, Illinois, in 1861 see Augustus L. Chetlain, *Recollections of Seventy Years* (Galena, 1899), 72–73.

CHAPTER 11: THE AMERICAN MILITARY ETHOS

1. Samuel J. Bayard, *The Life of George Dashiell Bayard* (New York, 1874), 162–163. Berkeley, a member of Parliament, had met Bayard in 1859 when he came to the United States to shoot buffalo.

2. Morris Schaff, *The Spirit of Old West Point* (Boston, 1908), 2.

3. D. W. Brogan, *The French Nation from Napoleon to Pétain* (London, 1957), 139–140. For an excellent detailed investigation see Raoul Girardet, *La Société Militaire dans la France Contemporaine, 1815–1939* (Paris, 1953). There has been a dearth of sophisticated work on the nineteenth-century British army. Some material may be gleaned from Marcus Cunliffe, "The British Army as a Social Institution, 1815–1854" (Oxford B. Litt. thesis, 1947).

4. G. S. Hillard, *Life and Campaigns of George B. McClellan* (Philadelphia, 1864) 35–37, 70–77; David Donald, *Lincoln Reconsidered: Essays on the Civil War Era* (New York, 1956), 87–90. There are abundant details of de Peyster's military travels and writings in Frank Allaben, *John Watts de Peyster* (2 vols., New York, 1908).

5. Ruth Miller Elson, "American Schoolbooks and 'Culture' in the Nineteenth Century," *Mississippi Valley Historical Review*, XLVI (December 1959), 417–420; E. D. Mansfield, *Utility and Services of the U. S. Military Academy* (New York, 1847), 37–39.

6. The debate on soldiers and statesmen took place in the Graham Society of Washington College, Lexington, Va., in 1855: W. G. Bean, *Stonewall's Man: Sandie Pendleton* (Chapel Hill, N.C., 1959), 9, and letter to the author of 11 August 1965 from Mr. John Hughes of Washington and Lee University. On the historians, see W. Charvat and M. Kraus, *Prescott: Representative Selections* (New York, 1943), cx.

7. Eli Thayer, *A History of the Kansas Crusade, Its Friends and Its Foes* (New York, 1889), 40–41.

8. P. S. Michie, *Life and Letters of Emory Upton* (New York, 1885), 18. Other examples of the Northern penitential mood are given in Fredrickson, *The Inner Civil War: Northern Intellectuals and the Crisis of the Union* (New York, 1965). It may be detected also in Lincoln's second inaugural address of March 1865.

9. Mansfield, *Utility . . . of the U. S. Military Academy*, 21–26.

10. John W. Ward, *Andrew Jackson: Symbol for an Age* (New York, 1955), plates V and VI; J. F. H. Claiborne, *Life and Correspondence of John A. Quitman* (2 vols., New York, 1860), I, 181; Carl Bode, *The Anatomy of American Popular Culture, 1840–1861* (Berkeley, Cal., 1959), 54–55, 246–249, 260.

11. *Pen and Sword: The Life and Journals of Randal W. McGavock*, ed. Herschel Gower and Jack Allen (Nashville, Tenn., 1959), 224; Benjamin Silliman, *A Visit to Europe in 1851* (2 vols., New York, 1856), II, 358; Lenoir Chambers, *Jackson* (2 vols., New York, 1959), I, 265; and John A. Owens, *Sword and Pen; or, Ventures and Adventures of Willard Glazier, . . . in War and Literature* (Philadelphia, 1889), 59.

12. J. W. de Peyster, *Philip Kearny*, 45; Stephen E. Ambrose, *Upton and the Army* (Baton Rouge, La., 1964), 5.

13. Emerson's essay on Napoleon exists in innumerable editions of *Representative Men;* Lincoln's address is available in most selections of his writings. See Edmund Wilson, *Patriotic Gore* (New York, 1962), 108; Seymour M. Lipset, *The First New Nation* (New York, 1963), 1–2, 203, 213.

14. For late nineteenth-century expressions of this, see Ernest Samuels, *Henry Adams: The Major Phase* (Cambridge, Mass., 1964), 180–182.

15. Ruth Painter Randall, *Colonel Elmer Ellsworth* (Boston, 1960), 151–152, 167.

16. Augustus E. Silliman, *A Gallop among American Scenery: or, Sketches of American Scenes and of Military Adventure* (New York, 1843), 141–143, 199–200. Some of the sketches originally appeared in the *New York American*.

17. Elihu Burritt, *Voice from the Forge* (London, c. 1848), 94–98; Merle Curti, *The Learned Blacksmith* (New York, 1937), 1–2.

18. D. R. Hundley, *Social Relations in Our Southern States* (New York, 1860), 199–203; George Cary Eggleston, *A Rebel's Recollections*, ed. David Donald (Bloomington, Ind., 1959), 70–71.

19. Samuel J. Bayard, *Life of George Dashiell Bayard* (New York, 1874), 91, 93–94, 108–109; J. W. de Peyster, *Personal and Military History of Philip Kearny* (New York, 1869), 44–46.

20. James Carson Jamison, *With Walker in Nicaragua* (1909), quoted in Edward S. Wallace, *Destiny and Glory* (New York, 1956), 149. There are perceptive comments in Albert Z. Carr, *The World and William Walker* (New York, 1963): see for example 272–274.

21. Charles Sumner, *Addresses on War* (Boston, 1902), 66–67.

22. There is a good account of eighteenth-century European armies in Walter Dorn, *Competition for Empire, 1740–1763* (New York, 1940), ch. 3, quoted in Gordon B. Turner, ed., *A History of Military Affairs in Western Society Since the Eighteenth Century* (New York, 1952), 3.

CHAPTER 12: EPILOGUE: BULL RUN AND THE AFTERMATH

1. Earl S. Miers, *The Great Rebellion* (New York, 1961), 251.

2. George M. Fredrickson, *The Inner Civil War: Northern Intellectuals and the Crisis of the Union* (New York, 1965), 166–180. Though I do not agree with all of Mr. Fredrickson's conclusions I have learned much from his excellent book.

3. [Charles Edwards Lester], *Light and Dark of the Rebellion* (Philadelphia, 1863), 9–10, 264–272; *D.A.B.*, XI, 189–190. Compare Cadet George Bayard's reaction to a diplomatic contretemps between Britain and the U.S. in 1855: "An English war for Americans is esteemed preferable to a war with any other country. England's hate for us is heartily reciprocated. Nothing but dollars and cents keep us at peace so long. As it was with Carthage and Rome, one or the other . . . will have to succumb; and of course it will be Great Britain." Samuel J. Bayard, *The Life of George Dashnell Bayard* (New York, 1874), 73.

4. The Washburne poem, one of several by him displaying more ardor than talent, is in *United States Service Magazine*, I (1864), 295–296; the

Bristed article in the same volume, 594–602. On Bristed see *D.A.B.*, III, 53–54.

5. Fredrickson, *Inner Civil War*, 201–211.

6. Edward Bellamy, *Looking Backward: 2000–1887* (New York, 1960), 212–213; Glenn Negley and J. Max Patrick, *The Quest for Utopia* (New York, 1952), 77–78.

7. Benjamin Rush Davenport, *Uncle Sam's Cabins: A Story of American Life Looking Forward a Century* (New York, 1895), 208; [Edward M. House], *Philip Dru: Administrator* (New York, 1912), 140; Christopher Lasch, *The New Radicalism in America, 1889–1963* (London, 1966), 230–234.

8. Cited in Herman D. Reeve, comp., *The Staff Departments of the U.S. Army* (Washington, D.C., 1900), 187.

9. M. A. DeWolfe Howe, ed., *Home Letters of General Sherman* (New York, 1909), 388–389 (letter of 11 January 1879); A. T. Mahan, *From Sail to Steam: Recollections of a Naval Life* (London, 1907), 8.

10. Henry George, *Social Problems* (London, 1884), 226–227.

11. Captain J. M. Trowbridge, "National Defense and Military Education," *Western Review of Science and Industry*, II (June 1878), 141–150; *Federal Aid in Domestic Disturbances, 1787–1903* (57th Congress, 2nd Session, Senate Doc. no. 209, Washington, D.C., 1903), 107–205; remarks by Colonel August v. Kautz in Reeve, *Staff Departments*, 188–189.

12. Stephen E. Ambrose, *Upton and the Army* (Baton Rouge, La., 1964), 146; Duane M. Greene, *Ladies and Officers of the United States Army; or, American Aristocracy. A Sketch of the Social Life and Character of the Army* (Chicago, 1880), 3, 103–106.

13. Frank R. Stockton, *The Great War Syndicate* (London, 1889), 13–15; Marcus Cunliffe, "The American Military Tradition," in H. C. Allen and C. P. Hill, eds., *British Essays in American History* (London, 1957), 207–209.

ACKNOWLEDGMENTS

This book has been a long time in the making. I was enabled to get it under way thanks to an American Studies fellowship from the Commonwealth Fund and a grant for research in the History of American Military Policy from the Social Science Research Council. Some of the ideas in the book were brought further forward through things I learned in 1957–1958 as a fellow at the Center for Advanced Study in the Behavioral Sciences, Palo Alto, California. I was given the opportunity to try out preliminary portions in lectures and seminars at the American Embassy in London, Harvard University, Mount Holyoke College, Ohio State University, the University of Sussex, the University of Wyoming, and the 1967 NASA conference in Helsinki, Finland. I have benefited from periods of leave provided by the University of Manchester and the University of Sussex.

I owe a great deal to various collections of material, including those in the Library of Congress, the U.S. Military Academy, the Widener Library, the New York Public Library, the New-York Historical Society, and the Ministry of Defence Library in London. I am grateful to the Library of Congress and the National Archives, Washington, D.C., the Historical Society of Pennsylvania, and the Coe Collection of Western Americana, Yale University, for permission to quote manuscript material. The New-York Historical Society was unfailingly helpful in turning up pictorial material, some of which is reproduced in this volume. For permission to make use of much other material for illustrations, I wish to offer special thanks to Mrs. Anne S. K. Brown of Providence, Rhode Island, whose magnificent collection has now been presented to Brown University.

Through correspondence, conversation, hospitality and other courtesies I have been helped by many individuals, not all of

ACKNOWLEDGMENTS

whom may recollect the occasion or approve of the result. An incomplete list of those on whom I have battened includes Donald Bigelow, Henry S. Commager, Wallace E. Davies, Robert Walker Davis, C. E. Dornbusch, Sidney Forman, William T. R. Fox, J. L. Garland, Walter Gellhorn, Edmund A. Gibson, Victor Gondos, Jr., Rear Admiral John D. Hayes, Michael Howard, Jay B. Hubbell, James Ripley Jacobs, Morris Janowitz, Maldwyn Jones, William L. Kohlmann, T. A. Larson, John K. Mahon, Louis Morton, Colonel W. J. Morton, Lieutenant Colonel Allan B. Nash, Kenneth Powers, Francis Paul Prucha, S.J., Frederick L. Rath, Jr., Edward Shils, Allen Tate, William R. Taylor, Colonel Frederick P. Todd, and Edmund Wilson.

In addition to my wife's many indirect contributions she has designed the jacket of the present edition.

Marcus Cunliffe

INDEX

Abbott, J. S. C., *History of Napoleon Buonaparte*, 400
Adams, Brooks, 402
Adams, Charles Francis, Jr., response to war, 427
Adams, John: disbands army in 1800, 51; on war, 66; on militia, 200
Adams, John Quincy: annoyed by Scott-Gaines feud, 136; on militia, 195; annoyance with Brown, 303
Adams, Samuel, 39
Adventures of Roderick Random (Smollett), 37
Alabama, 6th, uniform, 7
Albert Edward, Prince of Wales, 6, 160, 229
Alexander, E. P., 4
American Classical and Military Lyceum, 78
American Husbandman, quoted, 54
American Journal of Education, 154
American Literary, Scientific and Military Academy (Norwich University), 76-77
American Military Biography (Blanchard), 69
American Peace Society, 59, 61
American Quarterly Review, 166, 355
Ancient and Honorable Artillery Company of 1638, 217
Anderson, Capt. Robert, on political maneuverings of Mexican War, 311
Anderson, Richard H., 165
Anderson, Willoughby, dismissal from and reinstatement to West Point, 262
Annapolis. *See* United States Naval Academy
Antimilitarist sentiment, 22. *See also* Pacifism
Argument Showing, that a Standing Army, with Consent of Parliament, Is Not Inconsistent with a Free Government (Defoe), 34
Arms, right to bear, 38, 44
Armstrong, Frank Crawford, 14
Army & Navy Chronicle, 166, 167, 333, 341, 354; on military titles, 74; on promotion, 131; on dismissal of West Point cadets, 155-156; on Scott, 248n.; on *Complete Treatise on Field Fortification*, 180; on politics and the military, 300-302, 334

Army, British: militia as foundation, 32; compared with American (1830-1835), 55; living conditions in, 112-113; weaknesses, 389
Army, Confederate: system of rank, 370n.; dissatisfaction with rank, 378n.
Army, French, as model for American army, 389-390
Army Mastered, or Great Brittain's Joy, The, 39
Army Register, 369
Army, standing: origins, 31-37; Macaulay on, 33; Swift on, 34; popular resentment, 36, 37-38; colonial grievances against, 39-41; congressional control of, 43-45; arguments for and against, 45-50; term unclear, 49-50; sentiment in favor of, 147; as political issue, 284
Army, Union, strength at Bull Run, 17
Army, U.S.: regulars *vs.* volunteers, 19-20, 125, 147-151, 268-274, 276; training, 23; British and American compared (1830-1835), 55; colonial view of regulars, 38; civilian contempt & hostility toward, 102-110; pay, 112, 131-132; reasons for enlistment, 112-120; immigrants in, 114-116, 119-120; recreation in, 116-117; effect of public opinion on soldiers, 117; desertion, 118, 119, 120, 123, 125, punishments for, 123-124; discontents of enlisted men, 120-126, 264-276; drunkenness in, 121-122; officers' grievances, 126-134, 138-141; construction of canals and railroads, 130; promotion in, 131, 133, 135, 265-266, 342; commissions to civilians, 134; officers' quarrels, 135-142; professionalism, 149-151; controlled by executive, 150; influence of West Point, 151, 169; study of European Military establishments, 174; insubordinate officers, 271-272; criticism of, 276-281; and fear of military expansionism, 283, 283n.; patronage, 285-286; and politics, 289-292, 295-304, 332-333; importance of rank, 302; staff duties ill defined, 318-319; conditions at outset of Civil War, 319; rigged voting, 329; military tradition in South, 337-342; Southerners politi-

cally favored, 367–368; number of officers in command from North and South, 367–370; conditions summarized, 387–389; international historical background, 389–392; as outlet for romanticism, 399–412; arrogance of officers, 433–434; postwar attitudes toward, 433–434; demobilization, 435; death rate from disease, 435n.

Arnold, Benedict, 17

Arnold, Richard, 164

Arsenal, the (military academy), 76

Arthur, Chester A., given political appointments, 293

Articles of Confederation, 41

Ashworth, Charles, circumstances of enlistment, 118

Asmonean Guard, 226

Astor, Mrs. John Jacob, Jr., 382

Astor Place Riot (1849), 93

Atlantic Monthly, 247

Aztec Club, 81

Baker, E. D., military career, 237

Balloon, observation, 4

Baltimore, riots, 92–93

Banks, Nathaniel P., 18, 281, 291, 323, 327, 331

Barnard, Henry, on Partridge, 154

Barnard, John G., 163; on defections to the South, 374

Bartow, Francis, 19; premonition of death, 10

Barry, John W., 163

Barry, William F., confusion at Bull Run, 11–12, 14

Barry, William T., 163

"Battle of the Dead Cid, The" (Washburne), 428

Baxter Blues, 89

Bayard, George D., 169, 387; on lack of politics at West Point, 290; on value of political influence, 296–297; idealistic aspirations, 417–418

Bayard, John, 417

Bayard, de, Pierre du Terrail, Seigneur, 417; described by Sumner, 421–422

Bayard, Samuel J., 169n., 296

Beauregard, Pierre Gustave Toutant, 3, 4, 7, 14n., 19, 130; closes Bull Run battle zone to civilians, 9; as candidate for mayor of New Orleans, 23; opposes Know-Nothing party, 88–89; use of political influence, 298–299

Beauregard (Williams), 382

Benton, Jesse, 84

Bee, New London, 49

Beecher, Henry Ward, 86

Beecher, Lyman, on threat of military despotism, 283

Beecher's Bibles, 86

Beene, Jesse, 108

Bellamy, Edward, 168; *Looking Backward,* 430

Belmont, August, 84

Ben Hur (Wallace), 239

Benton, Thomas Hart, 84, 85, 273–274; on West Point, 107–108; influence with Polk, 308–310

Berkeley, Grantley F., on shortcomings of American army, 387–388

Bernard, Simon, 259n.

Bickley, George Washington Lafayette, 95–96

Bierce, Ambrose: *Can Such Things Be?,* 239; *Tales of Soldiers and Civilians,* 239

Bierce, Lucius Verus, 239

Bigelow, Charles H., 367

Bill of Rights, 33, 45

Billeting, 39, 44, 45; unpopularity in England, 35

Billy Budd (Melville), 97

Biographical Register of . . . the U. S. Military Academy (Cullum), 361

Bird, Isabella Lucy, on militia, 356

Birney, William, 16

Black Hawk volunteers, described, 275

Black Joke Fire Company, 89

Black Joke Volunteers, 89

Blackstone, William, *Commentaries on the Laws of England,* 35, 380

Blair, Francis P., 163

Blair, Montgomery, 163

Blanchard, Amos, *American Military Biography,* 69

Blenker, Louis, 19

Bliss, W. W. S., 166

Bonham, Milledge, 19

Bonner, James C., on South as contributor to military and presidency, 338

Boone, Daniel, 75

Boston, riot of 1837, described, 90–91

Boston Advertiser, 379

Boston Herald, poem on Bull Run, 13

Boston Massacre, 39

Boston Riots of 1897, 90–91

Boston Whig, on civil unrest, 83

Boudinot, Elias, militia bill, 183–184

Bourke, Private, quoted, 122

Bragg, Braxton, 143, 171, 276–277; and Gates, 141; resigns commission, 298; post-army career, 366; on Confederate dissatisfaction with rank, 378n.

INDEX

Bragg, Thomas, 78
Breckinridge, John C., 164
Bridgeport Farmer, 228
Briggs, George N., 107
Bristed, Charles Astor: on benefits of awakened martial instincts, 428–429; "The Probable Influence of the New Military Element on Our Social and National Character," 428; *The Upper Ten Thousand: Sketches of American Society,* 428; *Five Years in an English University,* 428; *Pieces of a Broken-Down Critic,* 428; *Now is the Time to Settle It,* 429; *No Surrender,* 429; *The Cowards' Convention,* 429
Brogan, Denis, on French enlistment terms, 390
Brooks, Preston, assaults Sumner, 84
Brown, Jacob, 136, 163, 303; on desertion, 123; in War of 1812, 302–303
Brown, Jacob (the younger), 163
Brown, N. S., visit to Waterloo, 400
Brownson, Orestes, 78
Brumby, Arnoldus V., 367
Buckner, Simon Bolivar, 143
Buchanan, James, 163, 202; on United States Zouave Cadets, 246; political appointments, 297–298; considered complaisant and treacherous, 345
Buell, Don Carlos, 327, 332
Buford, Abraham, 143
Bull Run, first battle of, 3–4, 7; early retreat, 7–8; pre-battle atmosphere, 8–9; civilian visitors to battlefield, 9, 13; untrained state of troops, 10–11; effect of diverse uniforms, 11–12; political aspects, 18–19; antipathy between regulars and volunteers, 19; panic caused by Griffin's battery, 19; West Point officers at, 19
Bull's Run, The Battle of, 17 (illus.)
Burke, Aedanus, 41–42
Burnside, Ambrose, 3, 143, 324, 329
Burr, Aaron, duel with Hamilton, 84
Burritt, Elihu ("the Learned Blacksmith"), 22, 60, 98; *Voice from the Forge,* 409–412; Quaker outlook, 413
Butler, Benjamin F., 18, 20, 168, 291, 327; oration to West Point Dialectic Society, 127–128; refuses to disband immigrant companies, 227–228; military aspirations, 239; on annual encampments, 251; criticism of West Point, 281; as military commander, 331, 332
Butler, William O.: volunteer commission, 308; supersedes Scott, 314

Butterfield, Daniel, military career, 240
Byron, George Gordon, 6th Baron, 402

Cadet Button, The: A Novel of American Army Life (Whittaker), 431
Cadwalader, George, 236
Cadwalader, John, 236
Cadwalader, Thomas, 236
Calhoun, John C., 149, 157, 164, 303; scheme for "expansible" army, 54; attempts consolidation of regulars, 201–202
Calhoun, Patrick, 164
Cameron, Simon, 85, 373
Campbell, W. B.: on Taylor and his army, 311; enthusiasm for Taylor, 311–312
Can Such Things Be? (Bierce), 239
Canning, George, 160
Carolina Regulators, 85
Cass, George W., 163
Cass, Lewis, 70, 163, 180
Chandler, Zachariah, 85, 321–322; on West Point, 374
Channing, William Ellery, 59
Charles O'Malley (Lever), 409
Charleston Mercury, on Southern army, 344
Chase, Salmon P., 327, 343
Chase, Judge Samuel, 49
Chatham Artillery Company, 217
Chevalier, as viewpoint of military ethos, 417–423
Choate, Rufus, admiration for Scott, 348
Cilley, Jonathan, 84
Cincinnati, Society of the, 41, 81
Citadel, the (military academy), 76, 352
Citizen-Soldier, 154
City Guards (Lowell, Mass.), 222
Civil, Military and Naval Gazette, 167
Civil War (American): communications, 319; army conditions at outset, 319
Civil War (English), 31
Clare, John, on soldiers in peace, 125
Clay, Henry, 84, 198
Clay, Colonel, 403, 406 (illus.)
Clemens, Samuel L. *See* Mark Twain
Clitz, Henry B., 165
Clitz, John, 165
Cobden, Richard, 55
Cold Water Army, 98
Collegiate and Commercial Institute, 79
Collins, John, 36
Columbian Guards, 227

485

INDEX

INDEX

Gardner, Henry, on disbanding immigrant volunteer companies, 227
Garfield, James A., 436; on army, 431
Garibaldi, Giuseppe, offered command in Union army, 379
Garrison, William Lloyd, founds New England Non-Resistance Society, 62
Gates, Colonel, and Bragg, 141
Gates, Horatio, 42
Gazette of the United States, on militia, 185
Geary, John White, military career, 238
George III, King of England, 40
George, Henry, 436; on army and navy, 432–433
Georgia Military Institute, 76
Georgia Review, on South as contributor to military and presidency, 338
Georgia Scenes (Longstreet), 187, 358
Gibbon, Edward, *The Decline and Fall of the Roman Empire,* 37
Gibson, Thomas W., 262
Giddings, Joshua R., on disbanding army, 104–105
Gifford, C. H., *History of the Wars Occasioned by the French Revolution,* 187
Gist, William Henry ("States Rights"), 15
Glisan, Rodney, 115–116; on reasons for enlistment, 114, 117
Gordon, John B., 7
Governor's Foot Guard, 217
Grand Army of the Republic, established, 435
Grant, Ephraim, on army as profession, 130
Grant, Ulysses S., 102, 129–130, 143, 342; lack of political influence, 298; incurs displeasure of Committee on the Conduct of the War, 324; as presidential candidate, 328; distaste for political intrigue, 329; praises Halleck, 354; on Union misuse of manpower, 378; opinion of Union Army, 379; on Jackson, 383n.
Graves, William, 84
Grayson, W. J., *Hireling and Slave,* 351; 95, 423
Great Conspiracy, The (Logan), 375
Great Riots of New York, The (Headley), 90
Great War Syndicate, The (Stockton), 436–438
Greeley, Horace, 171
Greene, Duane, *Ladies and Officers of the United States Army,* 433–434

Greene, Nathanael, 42
Griffin, Charles, 14
Griffin, William H., 367
Griffin's battery, 19
Grimké sisters, 67
Groton Artillery, uniform, 222
Gwin, William M., 164

Half Century, The, on West Point, 56,
Halleck, Henry Wager, 164, 171; *Elements of Military Art and Science,* 61, 180; *Report on the Means of National Defence,* 353–354
Hamilton, Alexander, 41–42, 164, 257; on standing army, 45–49; service in Revolution, 66; shot by Burr, 84; and reorganization of militia, 180–181
Hamilton, Henry, circumstancs of enlistment, 118–119
Hamilton, Schuyler, 164
Hamm, John, 108
Hammond, Edward Payson, 98
Hammond, Marcus C., on popularity of army, 175
Hampton, Wade, 18, 50, 274–275, 327
Hardin, Benjamin, 109
Hardee, William J., 340, 368
Hardy, Thomas, *The Trumpet Major,* 187
Harney, William Selby, arrested by Scott, 310–311
Harper's Monthly, 400
Harper's Weekly, on Putman Phalanx, 220; on Irish soldiers, 229–230
Harrison, William H., 70, 71 (illus.), 195, 198, 304, 337; satirized by Corwin, 190
Harrison, Montgomery Pike, 164
Harry Lorrequer (Lever), 409
Hartranft, John, 21
Harvey, William H. ("Coin"), fear of military expansionism, 283n.
Hatch, John P., 142; letter to mother, 143–144
Haupt, Herman, 367; Quaker outlook, 414–415
Havelocks, 5
Hawes, Albert Gallatin, 107; on abolishing West Point, 109
Hay, John, on Ellsworth, 244–245, 247
Headley, Joel T., 69; *The Great Riots of New York,* 90, 93; *Napoleon and His Marshals,* 90, 400; *Washington and his Generals,* 90
Hébert, Louis, 367
Hébert, Paul, 367
Heger, Joseph, 115

488

INDEX

Heintzelman, S. P., 3, 323
Henry, Patrick, on Congressional control of militia, 44
Herbert, Alfred, 367
Higginson, Francis Lee, 384n.
Higginson, Henry Lee, response to war, 427
Highland Military Academy, 78
Hildreth, James, *Dragoon Campaigns to the Rocky Mountains*, 114, 266
Hill, D. H., 142
Hireling and Slave (Grayson), 95, 423
History of England (Macaulay), on standing army, 33
History of Napoleon Buonaparte (Abbott), 400
History of the Navy (Cooper), 395
History of the United Netherlands (Motley), 396
History of the United States Army (Ganoe), 432
History of the Wars Occasioned by the French Revolution (Gifford), 187
Hitchcock, Ethan Allen, 271; on army life, 140; on liberty of the press, 273; on Pillow, 315; quoted, 326n.
Hlasko's Academy, 79
Holmes, Oliver Wendell, Jr., 384n.; response to war, 427; postwar mood, 429–430
Holt, Charles, 49
Homans, Benjamin, 166
Hone, Philip, on "Invincible Fantasticals," 190–191
Hood, John B., 158n., 164
Hooker, Joseph, 141, 143, 317, 324, 328; appointed commander of Army of the Potomac, 328; political leanings, 329–330
Horace (Corneille), 58
Hosmer, James K., *The Thinking Bayonet*, 346
"Hounds," 87
House, Edward M., 74; *Philip Dru: Administrator*, 430–431
Houston, Sam, 84
Howard, Oliver Otis, 3, 15, 164, 281; on fighting on the Sabbath, 12–13; on class distinction in army, 267; on Seminole campaign, 279–280; on status of regulars *vs.* volunteers, 280; chosen to command Army of the Tennessee, 334; Quaker outlook, 414
Howells, William Dean, response to war, 428
Hundley, Daniel R., *Social Relations in Our Southern States*, 343, 415–416

Hunter, David, 19; opinion of Jefferson Davis, 291–292; raid on Shenandoah Valley, 346
Huntington, Samuel P., 149; on professionalization of army, 264; *The Soldier and the State*, 340; on Southern military tradition, 340–341

Idylls of the King (Tennyson), 402
Illustrated London News, on American volunteers, 215
Importance of the Militia to a Free Commonwealth, The, (Sumner), 199–200
Indians, dispossessed and exterminated, 270–272
"Invincible Fantasticals," 190–191
Ivanhoe (Scott), 348
Iverson, Alfred, 167

Jackson, Andrew, 52, 70, 73, 138; involved in duel, 84; on remaining in the army, 127; praise and support of West Point, 151; as presidential candidate, 275–276; and Scott, 136; in War of 1812, 302–303; rendered in Napoleonic poses, 399
Jackson, Thomas J., 143, 337, 352; acquires nickname "Stonewall," 3; on fighting on Sunday, 13; as head of V.M.I., 76; appointment to West Point, 126; quarrel with French, 141–142; on classification of militia, 196–197; on leaving army, 362; post-army career, 366; postwar image, 382; Grant on, 383n.; on Napoleon's defeat, 400
James II, King of England, 32–33
James, Henry, response to war, 428
Jefferson, Thomas: antimilitary prejudices, 40; on naval force, 43; and Barbary pirates, 51; on militia, 193, 194
Jefferson Military College, 78
Jesup, Thomas S., 136, 138
Johnson, Cave, 107
Johnson, Richard W., 102
Johnston, Albert Sidney: on army pay, 112; on enlisted men, 120; quoted, 290–291
Johnston, Joseph E., 3, 4, 14n., 19, 337; post-army career, 367
Jomini, Baron Henri, 392
Julian, George W., radical sentiment, 321

Kautz, August V., on futility of war, 433

489

INDEX

London Peace Society, 58
Longfellow, Henry Wadsworth, "Excelsior," 402
Longstreet, Augustus Baldwin, *Georgia Scenes*, 187, 358
Longstreet, James, 3
Looking Backward (Bellamy), 430
Loring, Charles G., 220
Loring, Colonel, 142
Lossing, Benson, J., 69
Louisiana, 7th, uniform, 5
Louisiana Tigers, uniform, 5, 7
Lovejoy, Elijah P., 16, 86
Lovejoy, Owen, 16, 21
Lowe, Percival, on reasons for enlistment, 113–114
Lowell, Charles Russell, 383–384; response to war, 427
Lowell, James Russell, 59
Lynch law, 85–87

Macaulay, Thomas Babington, 1st Baron Macaulay, 34; *History of England*, on standing army, 33
Mackenzie, Alexander Slidell, 96–97
Mackenzie, William Lyon, 239
Maclay, William, opinion of military, 48–49
Macomb, Alexander, 136; court inquiry into liberty of the press, 272–273; in War of 1812, 302–303
Macready, W. C., 93
Madison, James, 45, 54, 152; war message of 1812, 17; on militia, 193–195; on military academies, 257, 258; military patronage, 285
Magruder, "Prince" John, 140
Mahan, Alfred Thayer, on U. S. Navy, 432
Mahan, Denis Hart, 155, 157, 340, 341; sent to study in Europe, 174; *Complete Treatise on Field Fortification*, 179; on West Point, 258; avoidance of politics, 289
Manassas Railroad, 4, 16
Mangum, Willie P., 10
Mann, Abigail, 107
Mann, Horace, 170
Mansfield, E. D., on military ideals, 393; on Napoleon, 399
Mansfield, Jared, 153
Manual of Peace (Upham), 59–60
Marble, Manton, 326
Marcy, Randolph B., 102
Marcy, William, 307; and Scott, 308

Mark Twain, 422; *Life on the Mississippi*, 339; *A Connecticut Yankee in King Arthur's Court*, 401; response to war, 428
Martindale, John H., 367
Mason, James, 165
Massachusetts Peace Society, 58; report on slave system, 380
Massachusetts Volunteer Militia, 222–223
Mathews, Charles, on militia musters, 188
Maury, Dabney, 120, 275
Maury, Matthew Fontaine, 341
McCall, George A., on liberty of the press, 273
McClellan, George B., 120, 142, 210, 275, 320 (illus.), 329, 330, 342; as presidential candidate, 73; appointed to investigate Crimean War, 130; sent to study in Europe, 174; ignorance of politics, 290; Democratic leanings suspected, 322–323; antagonism toward Stanton, 325; opinion of Union army, 379; report on Crimean War, 391–392; on Pickett, 417
McClung, Alexander, 85
McClurg, Alexander, 420n.
McCook, Alexander, 18
McCook, Charles, 18
McCook, Daniel, 18
McCulloch, Hugh, on backwoods drill, 189
McDowell, Irvin, 19, 323, 328; at Bull Run, 4, 9, 14n., 163; stinginess, 433
McKitrick, Eric, 371
McLane, Louis, 163–164
McLane, Robert M., 163
McLaws, Lafayette, distaste for politicians, 292n.
McLean, Wilmer, on Civil War, 427
McLeod, Hugh, 367
McLernand, John A., 291
McRee, William, 259n.
Meade, George Gordon, 78, 327; criticized by Committee on the Conduct of the War, 324; as presidential candidate, 328
Meade, Robert D., 349; on part of South in Civil War, 337
Meagher, Thomas Francis, 94
Mechanic Light Infantry, 295
Mechanic Phalanx, uniform, 222
Meigs, Montgomery C., 130; use of political influence, 300
Melville, Herman: on Mexican War, 69–70; *Billy Budd*, 97

491

INDEX

INDEX

New York Pioneer, 89

New York regiments: 7th, 222, 356; New York 8th, 7, 8; 27th Volunteers, 11; 39th (Garibaldi Guard), uniform, 5; 69th, uniform, 5–6; 71st, 19; 79th (Highlanders), 5 (illus.), uniform, 6; Zouaves (Fire Zouaves), 5, 20, 248

New York Sun, 315

New York Times, 9, 321

New York Tribune, 247, 321

New York World, 21, 326

Nicolay, John G., 244

Niles' Register, on civil unrest, 83

Ninety-day regiments, 7–8

No Surrender (Bristed), 429

North: opinion of South, 94–96, 349–351, 375; preponderance of military commanders in Revolutionary War, 349–350; volunteer companies and military periodicals, 356; population, 361; quality of soldiers, 372–373

North American Review, 166, 355, 431; on Partridge, 153–154

North Carolina Military Institute, 142

Now Is the Time to Settle It (Bristed), 429

O'Brien, Fitz-James, poem on Zouaves, 245

Ohio, 2nd, uniform, 5

Oliphant, Laurence, on immigrant soldier, 119

Olmsted, F. L., 356–357

On Public Absurdities in England (Swift), 34

Osterweis, Rollin G., *Romanticism and Nationalism in the Old South,* 339

Otis, James, 41

Pacifism, 22, 56–62, 66–67

Pakenham, Sir Edward Michael, 53

Paldi, Ange, 115

Paldi, Ange Charles, 115

Palfrey, Francis, 220

Palfrey, John Gorham, 383

Parker, Theodore, views on war, 24

Parkman, Francis, 384, 396, 397; deplores Northern life, 379; view of South, 380; on military instincts, 395

Partisan Leader, The: A Tale of the Future (Tucker), 346

Partridge, Alden ("AMERICANUS"), 257, 352; career as head of various military academies, 76–80; on public education, 108; evaluated by West Point chroniclers, 151–152; compared with

Thayer, 152–153; reaction to dismissal from West Point, 153; plans for additional military academies, 258; hostility to West Point, 259–260; *The Military Academy, at West Point, Unmasked,* 106, 153

Patriotic Gore (Wilson), 401

Patterson, Robert, 308

Peace movement. *See* Pacifism

Peace societies. *See* Pacifism

Pennsylvania, 4th, 7

Peterloo Massacre, 200

Peterson, Charles Jacobs, 69, 395

Petition of Right (1628), 31

Phelan, John D., 108

Philadelphia, riot (1844), 91–92, 93, 236n.

Philadelphia City Cavalry, 217

Philip Dru: Administrator (House), 430–431

Phillips, Wendell, 392

Phoenix Brigade, 96

Phoenix Society, 94

Pickett, George, 374n., 417

Pieces of a Broken-Down Critic (Bristed), 428

Pierce, Franklin, 202, 298–299, 304; on army, 204

Pike, Zebulon Montgomery, 69

Pillow, Gideon, 273; in Mexican War, 308; dispute with Scott, 313–316

Pirate's Own Book, 96

Pittsburgh Blues, 217

"Plan for the General Arrangement of the Militia of the United States" (Knox), 182–184

Poe, Edgar Allan, 167; army career, 113

Poinsett, Joel R., 115, 149, 304; sent to study in Europe, 174; plan for organizing militia, 197, 202; on army politics, 300

Polk, James K., 139, 164; war policy, 17; response to Mexican War, 150; praises volunteers, 203–204; on commissions for enlisted men, 267; military appointments, 273–274; military patronage, 285–286; problems at onset of Mexican War, 305–307; and Scott, 307–308; influenced by Benton, 308–310; on arrest of Harney, 310–311; reaction to Scott's and Taylor's victories, 312–313; replaces Scott, 314; on Pillow, 316

Polk, Leonidas, 143; complaints against Thayer, 261

Polk, Marshall T., 164

493

INDEX

Poore, Ben Perley, on annual encampments, 250–251

Pope, John, 271–272, 323, 328

Porter, David Dixon, 166

Porter, Fitz-John, 165–166, 290, 319, 321, 332; popular hostility toward, 323

Porter, Horace, 165

Porter, Peter B., 163

Powell, John Wesley, 429

Prescott, William H., 396–397; on war, 395

Presidency, military chiefs as candidates for, 70–73, 333

Press, court inquiry into liberty of, 272–273

Prince, Oliver Hillhouse, 187

"Probable Influence of the New Military Element on Our Social and National Character, The" (Bristed), 428

Progress of the United States in Population and Wealth in Fifty Years (Tucker), 56

Puddleford Papers, The (Riley), 188–189

Putnam Phalanx, 220

Quaker viewpoint in military ethos, 413–415, 420–423

Quarantine Station, Staten Island, destruction of, 93–94

Quinby, Isaac F., 142

Quincy, Josiah, 59; on Madison, 285

Quitman, John A., 298; military career, 237; volunteer commission, 308; on battlefield at Waterloo, 399–400

Raccoon Roughs, uniform, 7

Raleigh Banner, on Southern army, 344

Randolph, John, 84; on Madison, 285

Rathbun, George, 107

Raymond, Henry, at Bull Run, 9

Rebel's Recollections (Eggleston), 416

Recollections of the United States Army, 114, 265–266

Rector, Wharton, 134

Regulators, Society of, 87

Renick, Robert M., 367

Republican Fusiliers, 294

Revolutionary War, military attitudes, 17

Reynolds, John F., on Political influence, 297–298; as presidential candidate, 328

Richmond Dispatch, on confusion at Bull Run, 12

Richmond Light Infantry Blues, 217

Richmond Whig, on reign of terror in New York, 94–95

"Rifleman," viewpoint of military ethos, 415–417, 420–423

Riker, William H., on regulars *vs.* militia, 149

Riley, Henry H., *The Puddleford Papers; or, Humors of the West,* 188–189; on decline of military glory, 212

Ringgold, Major, 403, 406 (illus.)

Ring Tournament in the United States, The (Crooks), 339, 347–348

Riots, 90–94

Rip Rap Club, 92

Rise of the Dutch Republic (Motley), 396

Roach Guards, gang, 90

Romanticism, 405, army as outlet for, 399–412

Romanticism and Nationalism in the Old South (Osterweis), 339

Root, Elihu, quoted, 52

Ropp, Theodore, on educational level and quality of soldier, 372

Rosecrans, William S., 143, 328

Rosser, Thomas Lafayette, 14

Ruffin, Edmund, 15

Ruling Class, The (Mosca), 264–265

Rush, Benjamin, pacifist sentiments, 57

Russell, William H., 79

Russell, William Howard ("Bull Run"), 4, 16

Rutledge, H. M., on merits of army *vs.* civilian life, 132–133

Ryan, Jack, offers drink to Taylor, 121–122

Salignac, Colonel, 252

Salignac Drill Club, 357–358

Salvation Army, 98

Savannah Republican, on Partridge, 154

Sawyer, William, 107, 109; on West Point, 161; on unnecessary appointments to navy, 277

Schaff, Morris, on officers, 388

Schenck, Robert C., 18, 19, 296, 378; on nominations to West Point, 127

Schofield, John M., 169; on Terry, 241; on value of political influence, 296; on Union misuse of manpower, 378

Schurz, Carl, 291

Scott, J. W., 108

Scott, John, 36

Scott, Sir Walter, 402; popularity of novels, 348; *Ivanhoe,* 348; *Kenilworth,* 348

INDEX

Scott, Winfield ("Old Fuss and Feathers"), 173, 248n., 337; as presidential candidate, 73; feud with Gaines, 135–136; disputes with Jackson, Macomb and Jesup, 136; antagonism toward Davis, 136–137, 318; Keyes on, 137–138; on himself, 139; on Hitchcock, 140; claims back pay, 277; on unfair patronage, 285; avoidance of politics, 289–290; in War of 1812, 302–303; political temptation, 303–304; and Polk, 307–308; and Marcy, 308; arrests Harney, 310–311; dispute with Pillow, 313–316; and Worth, 314; superseded by Butler, 314

Scott Legion, 81

Seaton, William Winston, on West Point, 173

Sedgwick, Cathrine Maria, on *Kenilworth*, 348

Sedgwick, John, on regulars *vs.* volunteers, 269–270; on superior Southern army, 344

Seminole campaigns (1833–1842), 133–134

"Sentiments on a Peace Establishment" (Washington) 180–181

Seward, Augustus H., 164

Seward, William H., 164

Seymour, Horatio, 78

Shaw, Robert Gould, response to war, 427

Shays's Rebellion, 42–53

Sherman, John, 343

Sherman, William Tecumseh, 11, 14, 16, 98, 143, 164, 342, 345; at Bull Run, 3, 4; head of Louisiana Military Academy, 76; tries to restore order in San Francisco, 88; use of political influence, 298; distaste for political intrigue, 329; chooses Howard to command Army of the Tennessee, 334; praises Halleck 354; exasperated by Washington intrigue, 432

Sheridan, Philip, 131, 379

Shields, James, 25

Siege of Monterey, The (Falkner), 405

Sigel, Franz, 331

Silliman, Augustus, *A Gallop among American Scenery*, 405–409

Silliman, Benjamin, visit to Waterloo, 400

Simms, William Gilmore, *Woodcraft*, 86–87

Slaves, escaped, treatment of by army, 326

Slidell, John, 298

Slocum, Henry, opinion of Hampton, 274–275

Slocum, John, 9–10

Smith, Edmund Kirby, 3; on army as profession, 129

Smith, Ephraim Kirby, 165

Smith, Francis H., on Thayer, 261; at West Point, 262

Smith, Francis O. J., 107; on public education, 108

Smith, Gustavus W., 143

Smith, Joseph, 86

Smith, Joseph Lee Kirby, 130n., 165

Smollett, Tobias, *Adventures of Roderick Random*, 37

Smyth, William, 108

Social Relations in Our Southern States (Hundley), 343, 415–416

Soldier and the State, The (Huntington), 340

Solemn Review of the Custom of War (Worcester), 58–59

Somers, alleged mutiny, 96, 97

South, opinion of North during Civil War, 94–96; military tradition in, 337–342; opinion of Southern forces, 349–351; population, 361; quality of soldiers, 372–373; cavalier concept in, 380; desire for glory, 402

Southern Literary Messenger, 166, 167, 276–277, 341, 354–355

Southern Reader, A (Thorp), 338–339, 349

Spafford, Carrie, 242, 247

Spanish Heroine, The (Falkner), 405

Spencer, Herbert, 402

Spencer, John C., 97, 140

Spencer, Philip, 96–97

Sprague, William, at Bull Run, 11; military career, 240

Spring Election Riots (New York), 93

Standing army. *See* Army, standing

Stanley, D. S., on types of West Point cadets, 160; on plantation life, 380

Stanton, Edwin M., 171, 318; political interference in military problems, 291; Upton on, 292; arrests Stone, 322; antagonism toward McClellan, 325

Stark brothers, 17

Stephens, Alexander H., on political influence of South, 367–368

Steuben, Friedrich Wilhelm Ludolf Gerhard Augustin, Baron von, 50; *A Letter on the Subject of an Established Militia,* 182

495

INDEX

liferation of immigrant companies, 223–224, 225 (illus.); social and ethnic diversity, 223–230; in funeral procession of General Worth, 224–226; children's companies, 226; Jewish companies, 226–227; reaction against immigrant companies, 227–230; social aspects, 230–235; military efficiency, 235–241; function as police, 236; evaluated, 247–254; military associations and conventions, 249–250; annual encampments, 250–252; political partisanship among, 294–295; commissions, 308; more prominent in North, 356–357; as expression of romanticism, 404

Volunteer Soldier of America, The (Logan), 21, 360–361, 375

Wade, Benjamin F., 21, 321–322, 343
Wade, George, on barracks, 35
Wade Hampton's Legion, 16
Wadsworth, James S., 18, 323; as military commander, 331–332
Wadsworth, Jeremiah, 184
Walker, Francis, 429
Walker, William, 402; filibustering raids, 95, 419, 420
Wallace, Lew, *Ben Hur*, 239, military career, 239
War: American orientation toward, 65–70; political overtones in American history of, 317–318; techniques of mass warfare, 434
War Correspondents, first American use, 4
War of 1812, 52–53; threats of secession, 17
"War-Songs and Their Influence in History" (Leland), 428
Warner, Ezra J., analysis of *Army Register*, 368–369
Warren, Gouverneur Kemble, 164
Warren, Mrs. Mercy, on younger generation's desire for nobility, 41
Warren Light Guard, uniform, 223
Washington Artillery (Washington Light Guards), uniform, 223
Washington Federalist, 350
Washington and his Generals (Headley), 90
Washington, George, 38, 67 (illus.), 70, 337, 393; on dependence on militia, 20; proposed as king, 41; on policy of political non-involvement, 55; in favor of standing army, 148–149; "Sentiments on a Peace Establishment," 180–181; quoted, 229

Washburne, Rev. E. A., "The Battle of the Dead Cid," 428
Washburne, Elihu, 21
Washington Light Infantry, 217, 218
Watson Light Guards, uniform, 223
Wayland, Francis, 61
Wayne, Anthony, 50
Wayne, Henry C., 164
Wayne, James M., 164
Webb, Alexander Stewart, 164
Webb, James Watson, 164
Webster, Lucien B., 130, 165
Webster, Noah, 41
Weed, Thurlow, 306
Weems, Mason, *Life of Washington*, 102
Welles, Gideon, 78
Wells, Daniel, 209
West Point. *See* United States Military Academy
West Point Dialectic Society, 128
Weston Boarding School, 79 (illus.)
Wheat, Chatham Roberdeau, 4, 5, 7, 95
Whistler, James McNeill, as West Point cadet, 167
Whiting, Charles J., 367
Whitman, Walt, 421; *Leaves of Grass*, 394–395, 405; Quaker outlook, 413–414
Whittaker, Frederick, *The Cadet Button: A Novel of American Army Life*, 431
Wide-Awakes, 96
Wild, Edward A., 15–16
Wilkinson, James, 302
William III, King of England, 32–33
Williams, Alpheus S.: military career, 238–239; criticism of army, 279; criticism of West Point, 281
Williams, Henry P., 107
Williams, T. Harry, 333
Wilson, Edmund, *Patriotic Gore*, on Lincoln's role, 401
Wilson, Thomas, 395
Wirt, William, 157
Wisconsin, 2nd, uniform, 7
Wise, Henry A., 327
Wise, John S., 356; on West Point officers, 371
Withers, James M., 367
Wood, Fernando, 93
Wood, W. B., 372
Woodcraft (Simms), 86–87
Wool, John E., on dispossessing Indian tribes, 270–271

498